Paul and the Meaning of Scripture

Paul and the Meaning of Scripture

A Philosophical-Hermeneutic Approach to Paul's Use of the Old Testament in Romans

MATTHEW L. HALSTED

PICKWICK *Publications* • Eugene, Oregon

PAUL AND THE MEANING OF SCRIPTURE
A Philosophical-Hermeneutic Approach to Paul's Use of the Old Testament in Romans

Pickwick Publications
An Imprint of Wipf and Stock Publishers
199 W. 8th Ave., Suite 3
Eugene, OR 97401

www.wipfandstock.com

PAPERBACK ISBN: 978-1-6667-0769-4
HARDCOVER ISBN: 978-1-6667-0770-0
EBOOK ISBN: 978-1-6667-0771-7

Cataloguing-in-Publication data:

Names: Halsted, Matthew L., author.

Title: Paul and the meaning of scripture : a philosophical-hermeneutic approach to Paul's use of the Old Testament in Romans / Matthew L. Halsted.

Description: Eugene, OR: Pickwick Publications, 2022 | Includes bibliographical references and index.

Identifiers: ISBN 978-1-6667-0769-4 (paperback) | ISBN 978-1-6667-0770-0 (hardcover) | ISBN 978-1-6667-0771-7 (ebook)

Subjects: LCSH: Bible. Romans—Criticism, interpretation, etc. | Bible. Romans—Relation to the Old Testament. | Bible. Old Testament—Quotations in the New Testament. | Bible. Old Testament—Relation to Romans.

Classification: BS2665.52 H357 2022 (paperback) | BS2665.52 (ebook)

08/22/22

Dedicated to Tosha, my beautiful wife.

Contents

Preface

The Bible will never mean something it never meant. So goes a popular mantra, at least. For those of us who grew up learning how to interpret the Bible within the context of American evangelicalism, such statements are well known. In fact, in some narrow sectors of that movement, the mantra functions as a sort of creed, the affirmation of which is necessary to ensure hermeneutic faithfulness. As a creed, it serves as a rallying cry and identity marker—indeed, as a litmus test—for those who wish to be faithful to the Bible's message and meaning. The concern is that if the Bible is ever allowed to mean something it never meant, then all claims about the Bible's trust-worthiness are null and nonsense.

What is interesting, though, is that St. Paul seems to have never received the memo.

A cursory reading of Paul's letters, for example, reveals that he inter-prets Old Testament texts in rather fanciful ways, frequently going beyond their original context. For him, the Bible often *does* mean something it never meant. To those who have sworn an oath to the mantra above, Paul's readings might appear odd, disjointed, and perhaps even shocking. Truly, Paul is a remarkably creative interpreter, someone who seems to bend all the important hermeneutical rules and methods—rules and methods, mind you, that are taught in not a few seminaries and divinity schools. It has often been said that Paul would never pass a modern introduc-tory course in hermeneutics. What an understatement! The real question, though, is not whether he would pass our modern tests but whether we moderns would pass his.

And yet, for all his creativity, Paul is far from an interpretive quack. Just because he does not think "the Bible will never mean something it never meant" does not imply that he believes "the Bible can mean just any-thing I want it to mean." Indeed, a close examination of Paul's quotations reveals, I think, a careful rhythm and guided cadence that stems from a deep respect for Scripture. For all the innovations his interpretations enjoy, Paul, like every skilled artist, nonetheless operates within the framing boundaries of a canvas. If his readings are imaginative, they are still punctuated with discipline and marked with sensibility.

A careful look at Paul's use of Scripture will reveal an underlying hermeneutic logic at work—one that affords him both interpretive freedom and, at the same time, judicious restraint. As I hope to show, Paul's interpretive posture is one that can be characterized as being open to the voice of Scripture as a partner in dialogue, thus allowing the text to be wholly other. And yet, one cannot speak of Paul's interpretive posture without also acknowledging the person toward whom his entire being was postured, namely, toward Christ Jesus. Indeed, there is a certain ontological and existential aspect that is operative at the hermeneutic level, for as interpreters, we exist within the constraints of finitude. Being historically situated within time and place, we are formed and shaped by our traditions and experiences such that we are what we are because of them. Paul is no exception to the rule. His experience of Christ on the Damascus Road arguably demonstrates this fact. That experience set him on a new and surprising trajectory; not all at once, of course, but slowly and gradually—yet no less decisively. As a matter of fact, his experience on that road changed the course of his life forever. The experience also changed the course of his *hermeneutics* forever.

That question of hermeneutics is, indeed, the question that cries out for attention: What is the nature of Paul's hermeneutic? What characterizes his interpretive posture toward the Old Testament? What components made up his hermeneutic? These questions obviously draw us into larger conversations about hermeneutic theory: How do we understand anything at all—whether events, speeches, plays, movies, jokes, songs, and even texts like the Bible? Like an antique clock with a complex set of interlocking gears, wheels, and cogs, there is a host of parts inherent to every act of interpretation. This is true whether one interprets the Bible, Bradbury, Lewis, or a love note. Every text, originating from within a certain time and place, comes to its interpreter having been immersed in a particular set of assumptions and traditions and questions—some of which can be quite foreign to latter interpreters. And yet, in order to find meaning in them, *we* must do something with them—in the *here* and *now*.

That task becomes rather tricky when we consider ancient texts. The reason is because readers cannot help but bring to texts modern assumptions, some of which are very different when compared to the underlying assumptions of a text that belongs to a bygone era. Every interpreter is quite naturally immersed into his or her own contemporary culture's tradition and history. These traditions have a profound effect upon how interpreters approach texts. They exert a powerful influence over how he or she makes sense of them, applies them, and finds meaning in them. Indeed, the *world* of the interpreter and the *world* of the text to be interpreted are both—not least, again, in the case of ancient texts—far different from the other.

This does not mean, however, that interpreters are hopelessly bound to their own tradition, unable to escape its jealous grasp such that understanding becomes impossible. Quite the contrary. Traditions, because they give shape to the reality of a person's being, actually make it possible to interpret anything at all. Each and every interpreter inherits from their tradition a set of pre-understandings. These pre-understandings serve as a pathway into the text, for they allow the interpreter to have an initial understanding of what it is they are about to read. This is true even when the interpreter's pre-understandings are limited or mistaken.

Consider the following example. When a person sits down to read *Moby Dick* for the first time, he or she may come to that classic text already knowing something about it—even if all they know is that it features a whale. As meager as this initial understanding might be, it still serves as a launching point for the reader to learn more. Even if a person began reading *Moby Dick* with initial misconceptions and wrong assumptions, these pre-understandings still allow the reader to approach the story itself in the act of reading. Even if a person knows next to nothing about *Moby Dick*, he or she still approaches the story perhaps knowing a little something about oceans, ships, and adventures.

As the reader moves from page to page, learning about each character, these basic initial assumptions and pre-understandings are either altered, revised, or confirmed as the story progresses. In this manner, the reader engages in the process of understanding. Pre-understandings, then, provide the *possibility* for meaning, serving as a frame of reference, as it were, so that the story can be understood in all its fullness. In this way, pre-understandings, far from impeding interpretation, serve to make it possible in the first place.

What this means is that readers are not blank slates, for one does not come to texts without pre-established assumptions and pre-conceived notions. Texts do not present meaning to readers as if they were passive bystanders. On the contrary, readers are *active* participants in the act of reading. As some have pointed out, a "pure reading" of texts is simply a myth.[1] No reader finds meaning in a text until he or she approaches the text in a meaningful way, that is, in a way that meaningfully expects something

1. Starling, *Hermeneutics as Apprenticeship*, 1.

from the text. Thus, readers do not read meaning out of texts without, at the same time, also reading something into them.

These insights are, of course, not new. Ever since the Enlightenment's project, beginning with Descartes' infamous *cogito* argument, there has been a plethora of interaction with, and reaction to, the idea that people can know things purely and objectively. Indeed, reaction to the Enlightenment's ideals has revealed that the acts of *knowing* and *understanding* are far more than a scientific, objective endeavor. Interpreters are not, as it were, mindless robots that merely receive textual data and then spit out a carbon copy of that data and call *that* "the meaning of the text." To the contrary, interpreters are human beings—a species packed with emotions, biases, hopes, fears, desires, loves, hates, questions, and answers. These are some of *the postures of interpretation*. And none of them lay dormant in the act of reading; they are always operative, active, dynamic—always on the move. They make up our essential constitution as interpreters, subsequently giving shape to our readings.

These postures of interpretation are what they are because we are human *being*. That is to say, we exist in a particular time and in a specific place. We live in communities and neighborhoods, cultures and sub-cultures, nations and people groups—all of which are shaped by us and serve, in turn, to shape us as a people. Each culture passes on a set of traditions, assumptions, biases, and prejudgments that exert a tremendous amount of influence over its members, guiding and directing the way they interpret things like the Bible. With a nod to St. Paul himself, I often tell people that there is no one who is unbiased, for all are human and fall short of the glory of a god-like objective interpretation.

The reality of these observations came to a head when I began researching Paul's use of the Old Testament. During my time as a MTh student, I explored the relationship between Paul's concept of glory and his use of righteousness language in Romans. During the course of things, I inevitably realized how Paul's understanding of righteousness was deeply rooted in Old Testament texts and stories (an understatement, if there ever was one!). What became interesting was how Paul employed Old Testament texts with a considerable amount of freedom and fresh creativity. To establish his own arguments, Paul would often offer revisionary readings of the Old Testament in order to support his arguments and advance a particular vision for the churches he served.

After transferring from MTh to PhD, I began writing my doctoral thesis on what I think is one of the more creative uses of Scripture in Romans, namely, the use of Hosea in Rom 9:25–26. Here Paul quotes Hos 2:25 and 2:1 (LXX) to argue that God has called gentiles into his new covenant family.

He introduces the quotations by describing members of the new covenant, saying they are "vessels of mercy" (v. 23) and that they are "called" (v. 24a).[2] These people are "not only of the Jews but also of the Gentiles," which, Paul believes, was foretold "in Hosea" (vv. 24b-25). He then quotes two passages from the prophet: "I will call the Not-My-People, 'My People,' and the Not-Loved, 'Loved.' And it will be in the place where it was said to them, 'You are not my people,' there they will be called sons of the living God" (vv. 25–26). With these Hosea quotations, Paul makes his case for *gentile* inclusion.

A brief glance at the original context of Hosea, however, reveals that the original meaning of the prophecy is at odds with the new meaning that Paul has given it. Paul, astonishingly, has taken what was originally intended as a prediction of Jewish re-inclusion and has applied it to gentiles. Is Paul taking the Hosea oracle out of its original context? Is he ignoring the original meaning altogether? Is he twisting the text's meaning to suit his own fancies? As I began reflecting on these and other questions, I came to discover that Paul was not merely restating the prophecy in a sort of cut-and-paste approach. The apostle was no literalist. But I also came to see that Paul was not completely re-inventing Hosea's prophecy either. He was no textual relativist. Paul's innovative vision and his deep respect for Scripture ran too deep for any of these extremes. And so, the question remained: How can we make sense of Paul's interpretation?

I knew that a hermeneutic needed to be put forward that could make sense of what I was observing. The hermeneutic that I had been familiar with (i.e., the historical-grammatical method) was woefully inadequate to account for Paul's use of Hosea and, for that matter, his other uses of the Old Testament that I had observed. A better approach was needed, one that was both (a) stable enough to account for how Paul argues *from* Scripture and (b) flexible enough to account for how Paul is creative *with* Scripture.

My *Doktorvater*, Dr. Thorsten Moritz, was instrumental in pressing me to think hermeneutically. As a native German, Thorsten would often nudge me to consider the influential continental philosophers of the past—F. D. E. Schleiermacher, Martin Heidegger, and Hans-Georg Gadamer, to name a few. In the course of things, I found the insights of that last philosopher to be particularly appealing. Gadamer's musings on hermeneutics offered what seemed to me a conceivable paradigm by which I could discern the intricacies of Paul's interpretive maneuvers. Indeed, Gadamer's reflections offered a *stability* and *flexibility* that was required to account for Paul's use of the Old Testament.

2. Unless otherwise indicated, all translations from original sources are my own. For the GNT, LXX, and MT, I use the NA28, GS, BHS, respectively (unless noted otherwise).

As I worked through Paul's reading of Scripture through Gadamerian eyes, what I discovered was how the apostle could appeal to Scripture for his arguments and, at the same time, read into Scripture his christological assumptions. I found that Gadamer's concepts of pre-judgment (Vorurteil) and application (Anwendung), as well as his definition of understanding as a "fusion of horizons" (Horizontverschmelzung), offered a suitable framework by which Paul's readings of the Jewish texts could be analyzed and even clarified.[3] Prominent scholars have done well to bring Gadamer's insights into the realm of biblical studies.[4] That being so, I felt there was room for more work to be done, specifically with respect to biblical-intertextual studies.

In this book, I offer a study on Paul's use of Scripture in Romans through Gadamerian eyes. Romans is one of Paul's most important letters, and it interacts frequently with the Old Testament. Moreover, throughout Romans, Paul quotes and employs a range of Old Testament texts, concepts, and stories in creative and innovative ways. In my estimation, then, employing Romans as a test site for Gadamer's hermeneutic is worthwhile.

My conclusion, perhaps controversial, is that Paul's use of Scripture ought to be described as *dialogical re-authoring*. This description, as I will show, accounts for how Paul argues *from* Scripture even as he creatively reads *into* Scripture his convictions about what God has done through Christ. Gadamer's hermeneutic offers a paradigm by which we can understand how Paul engaged scriptural texts—without requiring us to fall into the snare of frenzied relativism or retreat toward a naïve quest for hermeneutic objectivity.

In the end, Paul's own mantra is straightforward: *The Bible will always mean something new, fresh, and surprising—like it always meant to.*

---

3. See, respectively, Gadamer, *TM*, 268–85, 306–36, 305.

4. One thinks of scholars like Ulrich Luz (e.g., his *Matthew in History* and his Hermeneia commentary on Matthew).

Acknowledgments

This book represents a significant revision and expansion of my PhD thesis, which was defended on January 2018 at London School of Theology in the United Kingdom. It would not have been possible to complete this book without the support and encouragement of many people—all of whom I owe an incredible amount of gratitude. I would first like to thank Thorsten Moritz, my *Doktorvater*. His supervision throughout my research has been constructive and encouraging. I am indebted to a host of other scholars, mentors, and colleagues who provided guidance, feedback, constructive criticism, and encouragement as I completed my PhD. Among them, my second supervisor and director of studies, Graham Twelftree; my examiners: Kent Brower, Calvin Samuel; my transfer and upgrade committee: Steve Walton, Jean-Marc Heimerdinger, Conrad Gempf, and Mark Beaumont. In the course of my research, I was privileged to have had brief conversations with the well-known Gadamer scholar, the late Richard Palmer. I will always remember his helpful and kind spirit.

I am grateful to the faculty, staff, and students at Eternity Bible College, where I am privileged to teach. I am appreciative to President Heath Thomas of Oklahoma Baptist University, who, while Dean of Hobbs College, invited me to share my research in a faculty seminar. I am grateful to the entire theology and ministry faculty for not just their gracious feedback, but also their friendship.

Many thanks are due to Joe McGee, Andrew Hollingsworth, and Chandler Warren for their ongoing willingness to dialogue with me about Paul and Gadamer's philosophical hermeneutics. Along the way, they have offered invaluable critiques and constant encouragement. I am most thankful, though, for their friendship through the years. They are iron. I am grateful to First Baptist Church, Sonora; First Baptist Church, McLoud; and New Life Bible Church, Norman. Each of these congregations have been a great source of encouragement and blessing to me. I am forever grateful to my parents, in-laws, siblings, and grandparents for their constant support as I completed my research.

Most of all, my wife, Tosha, has been my joy, my love, and my anchor. It would be impossible to count how many times she has pulled double duty while I was secluded in my office writing this book. The long hours, late nights, early mornings, routine trips to libraries—all of these and more have required sacrifice on her part. Without her support and encouragement, this book would not have been possible. Words cannot express how much I cherish her. My four children—Isaac, Gracie, Hannah, and Simon—have kept my feet on the ground. Their faith, their giggles, and their imaginations remind me daily about what it means to be a true follower of Jesus. I want to be like them when I grow up.

My research for this book began when I first registered for MTh studies—some eleven years ago. Looking back at various key moments, I can see how God's guiding hand was quite active along the journey—nudging me this way and that to help me grow and develop as a student of Scripture. Undeniably, I still have a long way to go and much more to learn. But for whatever insights my research has to offer, my prayer is simple: May the Holy Spirit use this book to bring the Father glory, fostering unity in the church catholic under the name of our Lord Jesus Christ.

MLH

Abbreviations

AB	Anchor Bible
ACCBS	A Compendium of Contemporary Biblical Scholarship
AARTTS	American Academy of Religion Texts and Translation Series
BBR	*Bulletin for Biblical Research*
BECNT	Baker Exegetical Commentary on the New Testament
BHS	Elliger, K and W. Rudolph, eds. *Biblia Hebraica Stuttgartensia*, 5th ed. Stuttgart: Deutsche Bibelgesellschaft, 1997.
BHT	Beiträge zur historischen Theologie
BJHP	*British Journal for the History of Philosophy*
BNTC	Black's New Testament Commentaries
BSac	*Bibliotheca sacra*
BTB	*Biblical Theology Bulletin*
BZNW	Beihefte zur Zeitschrift für die neutestamentliche Wissenschaft
CBQ	*Catholic Biblical Quarterly*
CCP	*Contemporary Continental Philosophy*
CEP	Continental European Philosophy
COQG	Wright, N. T. Christian Origins and the Question of God. 4 vols. Minneapolis: Fortress, 1992–2013.
CRBS	*Currents in Research: Biblical Studies*
CRINT	Compendia Rerum Iudaicarum ad Novum Testamentum
CQS	Companion to the Qumran Scrolls

DCCT   *A Dictionary of Cultural and Critical Theory*. Edited by Michael Payne and Jessica Rae Barbera. 2nd ed. Oxford: Wiley-Blackwell, 2010.

DOTP   *Dictionary of the Old Testament Prophets*. Edited by T. Desmond Alexander and David W. Baker. Downers Grove, IL: InterVarsity, 2003.

DSD   *Dead Sea Discoveries*

EA   *Encyclopedia of Aesthetics*. Edited by Michael Kelly. Oxford: Oxford University Press, 1998.

EP   *Encyclopedia of Phenomenology*. Edited by Lester Embree et al. Contributions to Phenomenology 18. Boston: Kluwer, 1997.

FH   *Fides et Historia*

FPIJP   *Forum Philosophicum: International Journal for Philosophy*

GNT   Greek New Testament

GW   Hans-Georg Gadamer. *Gesammelte Werke*. 10 vols. Tübingen: Mohr Siebeck, 1985–2010.

GQ   *German Quarterly*

GS   *Göttingen Septuagint: Vetus Testamentum Graecum*. 24 vols. Auctoritate Academiae Scientiarum Gottingensis Editum. Göttingen: Vandenhoeck & Ruprecht, 1931–2006.

HBT   *Horizons in Biblical Theology*

Hermeneia   Hermeneia: A Critical and Historical Commentary on the Bible

HZNT   Handbuch zum Neuen Testament

HUT   Hermeneutische Untersuchungen zur Theologie

IBC   Interpretation: A Bible Commentary for Teaching and Preaching

ICC   The International Critical Commentary on the Holy Scriptures of the Old and New Testaments.

Int   *Interpretation*

IJPS   *International Journal of Philosophical Studies*

IPJP   *Indo-Pacific Journal of Phenomenology*

JBL   *Journal of Biblical Literature*

JBQ   *Jewish Bible Quarterly*

JETS   *Journal of the Evangelical Theological Society*

JPSTC	Jewish Publication Society Torah Commentary
JSNT	*Journal for the Study of the New Testament*
JSOT	*Journal for the Study of the Old Testament*
JSOTSup	Journal for the Study of the Old Testament Supplement Series
JSNTSup	Journal for the Study of the New Testament Supplement Series
JSSSup	Journal of Semitic Studies Supplement
JTI	*Journal of Theological Interpretation*
JTS	*Journal of Theological Studies*
L&N	*Greek-English Lexicon of the New Testament: Based on Semantic Domains*. Edited by Johannes P. Louw and Eugene Albert Nida. 2 vols. New York: United Bible Societies, 1996.
LNTS	Library of New Testament Studies
LXX	Septuagint
MNTC	Moffatt New Testament Commentary
MT	Masoretic Text
NA[28]	Nestle-Aland, *Novum Testamentum Graece*. 28th ed.
NAC	New American Commentary
Neot	*Neotestamentica*
NIB	The New Interpreter's Bible
NICNT	The New International Commentary on the New Testament
NICOT	The New International Commentary on the Old Testament
NIGTC	The New International Greek Testament Commentary
NovTSup	Supplements to Novum Testamentum
NRSV	New Revised Standard Version
NSBT	New Studies in Biblical Theology
NTA	Neutestamentliche Abhandlungen
NTS	*New Testament Studies*
NUSPEP	Northwestern University Studies in Phenomenology and Existential Philosophy
OCP	*The Oxford Companion to Philosophy*. Edited by Ted Honderich. 2nd ed. Oxford: Oxford University Press, 2005.
PBM	Paternoster Biblical Monographs

PFG	N. T. Wright. *Paul and the Faithfulness of God.* COQG 4. Minneapolis: Fortress, 2013.
PH	Hans-Georg Gadamer. *Philosophical Hermeneutics.* Translated and edited by David E. Linge. Berkeley: University of California Press, 1976.
PL	*Philosophy and Literature*
PNTC	The Pillar New Testament Commentary
RP	*Research in Phenomenology*
RQ	*Restoration Quarterly*
SAHS	Scripture and Hermeneutics Series
SCJ	*Stone-Campbell Journal*
SCT	Studies in Continental Thought
SDSSRL	Studies in the Dead Sea Scrolls and Related Literature
SJP	*Southern Journal of Philosophy*
SNTSMS	Society for New Testament Studies Monograph Series
SP	*Studia Phaenomenologica*
SPEP	Studies in Phenomenology and Existential Philosophy
ST	Scriptural Traces: Critical Perspectives on the Reception and Influence of the Bible
STI	Studies in Theological Interpretation
TBl	*Theologische Blätter*
TCPC	The Church and Postmodern Culture
TDNT	*Theological Dictionary of the New Testament.* Edited by Gerhard Kittel and Gerhard Friedrich. Translated by Geoffrey W. Bromiley. 10 vols. Grand Rapids: Eerdmans, 1964–76.
TECC	Theological Explorations for the Church Catholic
THP	Topics in Historical Philosophy
TM	Hans-Georg Gadamer. *Truth and Method.* Translated by Joel Weinsheimer and Donald G. Marshall. 2nd rev. ed. New York: Continuum, 2004.
TNCI	The New Critical Idiom
TNTC	Tyndale New Testament Commentaries
TZ	*Theologische Zeitschrift*

VTSup	Supplements to Vetus Testamentum
WBC	Word Biblical Commentary
WM	Hans-Georg Gadamer. *Wahrheit und Methode: Grundzüge einer philosophischen Hermeneutik.* 7th ed. GW 1. Tübingen: Mohr Siebeck, 2010.
WTJ	*Westminster Theological Journal*
WPS	Wadsworth Philosophers Series
YSH	Yale Studies in Hermeneutics
ZAW	*Zeitschrift für die Alttestamentliche Wissenschaft*
ZNW	*Zeitschrift für die Neutestamentliche Wissenschaft und die Kunde der* älteren Kirche

PART 1

Introduction

Chapter 1

The Riddle of Paul's Use of Scripture

History does not belong to us; we belong to it.

HANS-GEORG GADAMER[1]

INTRODUCTION

When you read Paul, you encounter a person shaped and molded by Scripture. The Jewish texts and stories, along with the traditions that flowed from them, were integral to his formation as both a diaspora Jew and, later, as an apostle of Christ. Paul often appeals, for example, to Old Testament texts as a foundation for his apostolic mission. He believed that his "gospel" was rooted in, and based upon, the "holy Scriptures" (Rom 1:1–2).[2] He understood well the role the Torah and Prophets played in bearing witness to the gospel, to faith, to the Messiah (Rom 3:21). And yet, Paul's relationship to Scripture cannot be described as unilateral—a monological, one-way street such that his "reading" of the scriptural texts consisted of nothing more than the etching of information upon him like chalk on a *tabula rasa*. It is true that the whole of Paul's theology—i.e., his views about God, God's people, and God's salvation—all of it flows *from* Scripture. And yet, one

---

1. Gadamer, *TM*, 278.
2. See also Rom 3:21–22; 10:5–13.

must come to terms with the fact that Paul's *understanding* of Scripture was what it was due to the *preunderstandings* he brought to the text.[3]

This is an important point to make given that, in many instances, Paul's interpretations of the texts he quotes are rather revisionary, often going beyond the quotation's original context. One example of this is the use of two verses from Hosea in Rom 9:25–26. These quotations in particular serve well as an initial case study into Paul's use of Scripture—not least because it is representative of the creative pattern of interpretation one often sees in Romans. Although a more substantive analysis of this text is postponed for chapter 6, in what follows, I wish to draw attention to three important things about Paul's use of Hosea: (1) The creative use of the text itself (*How does Paul alter the grammar and syntax? What substitutions and omissions does Paul make with respect to vocabulary?*); (2) the fresh and revisionary meaning Paul mines from the quotations (*How does the meaning Paul claims to find stack up against Hosea's original meaning?*); and (3) the interpretive components in play (*What hermeneutical concepts and categories have some scholars employed to make sense of the quotations?*).

The quotations from Hosea are interesting on a number of levels, both of which are reproduced below, along with the Göttingen text for comparison.

Rom 9:25b καλέσω τὸν οὐ λαόν μου λαόν μου καὶ τὴν οὐκ ἠγαπημένην ἠγαπημένην	Hos 2:25b LXX καὶ ἐλεήσω τὴν Οὐκ ἠλεημένην καὶ ἐρῶ τῷ Οὐ λαῷ μου Λαός μου εἶ σύ
I will call the Not-My-People "My People," and the Not-Loved "Loved."	And I will have mercy on the "Not Mercied," and I will say to Not-My-People, "You are my people."

3. There is a large body of literature that addresses Paul's use of the Old Testament, among them see: Bates, *Hermeneutics*; Wagner, *Heralds*; Moyise, *Paul and Scripture*; Watson, *Paul and the Hermeneutics of Faith*; Starling, *Not My People*; Stanley, *Paul and the Language of Scripture*; Stanley, *Arguing with Scripture*; Lim, *Holy Scripture*; Hays, *Echoes* (cf. Bates, "Beyond Hays's Echoes of Scripture."); Fuß, *"Dies ist die Zeit"*; Koch, *Schrift*; Porter and Stanley, *As It Is Written*. For an overview of intertextuality and some of the issues relevant for this study, see Bartholomew, *Hermeneutics*, 121–26; Thiselton, *New Horizons*, 38–42, 495–99 (esp. 497). The term "intertextuality" was put forward by Julia Kristeva to describe how texts were not "self-contained" but rather exist as a "transformation of other texts" (Heath, "Intertextuality," 348). See Kristeva, *Desire in Language*, 64–91, esp. 66 (see also the editor's entry "intertextuality" on 15); Kristeva, *Revolution in Poetic Language*, 57–61, esp. 59–60. See also Allen, *Intertextuality*, 8–58. For a critique of Kristeva and intertextuality, see Irwin, "Against Intertextuality." In terms of *biblical* intertextuality, Bartholomew (*Hermeneutics*, 125–26) is correct to highlight N. T. Wright's storied approach. See Wright, *New Testament and the People of God*. See also the volume edited by Oropeza and Moyise, *Exploring Intertextuality*.

Rom 9:26 καὶ ἔσται ἐν τῷ τόπῳ οὗ ἐρρέθη αὐτοῖς· οὐ λαός μου ὑμεῖς, ἐκεῖ κληθήσονται υἱοὶ θεοῦ ζῶντος.	Hos 2:1cd LXX καὶ ἔσται ἐν τῷ τόπῳ, οὗ ἐρρέθη αὐτοῖς Οὐ λαός μου ὑμεῖς, κληθήσονται καὶ αὐτοὶ υἱοὶ θεοῦ ζῶντος.
And it will be in the place where it was said to them, "You are not my people," there they will be called sons of the living God.	And it will be in the place where it was said to them, "You are not my people," they will also be called sons of the living God.

Several observations can be made. One immediately notices, for example, how freely Paul manipulates the first quotation (Hos 2:25). Christopher Stanley remarks that it "has been so thoroughly adapted to suit its present application that few of its original words remain intact."[4] Stanley is correct that Paul's reworking of the text is quite significant. Paul flips the original text on its head, substituting one word for another for the purpose of emphasizing certain key points he wants to make.[5] To be sure, Paul is not concerned here with merely *copying* the text word-for-word, and neither does he seem to think such copying would be a requirement for a faithful interpretation of it.

This is an important observation, as it highlights a core element of Paul's interpretive posture that, as I will show in the pages that follow, he routinely employs throughout Romans itself. In this vein, Steve Moyise is correct to ask whether or not one can say (and if so, how) Paul *respects* the Old Testament texts he quotes.[6] There are, indeed, many things to note about this question regarding the way Paul alters the *wording* of Hosea's prophecy. We will have occasion to do so in a later chapter. At present, however, there is a second, and much more important, observation to consider—namely, the way Paul alters the *meaning* of Hosea's prophecy.

In the context of Rom 9:24–29, it is clear Paul employs the prophecy to argue for the full inclusion of Gentiles into the covenant. The problem, however, is that nothing in Hosea's original context suggests such an idea. Historically, Hosea was forecasting the return of rebellious Israel, not the Gentiles.[7] Richard Hays describes this as a "revisionary interpretation,"

4. Stanley, *Paul and the Language of Scripture*, 109.

5. For details regarding both quotations, see Stanley, *Paul and the Language of Scripture*, 109–13; Wagner, *Heralds*, 79–81; Moyise, "Hosea as a Test Case," 46–47; Hays, *Echoes*, 66.

6. See Moyise, "Hosea as a Test Case," esp. 39–40.

7. Hays, *Echoes*, 66.

saying Paul "deconstructs the oracle" by means of a "hermeneutical coup."[8] These are strong words, to be sure. And yet, they seem to accurately describe the situation.

Scholars have differed on how to make sense of Paul's interpretation. I offer a tour of some of these proposals below. This survey is but a sample of the scholarly discussion and is by no means intended to be exhaustive in scope. I simply intend for them to highlight what I consider to be the main issues regarding Paul's interpretive practices. This will set the stage for subsequent, more thorough, discussions that occur later.[9] Moreover, I offer Paul's Hosea quotations as more than an isolated instance of Paul's creative approach to Scripture. They are, as I said above, representative of a larger pattern of revisionary interpretation seen throughout Romans as a whole. Paul's use of Hosea, then, is no mere snippet but rather an illustration of how Paul routinely rereads various Old Testament motifs, texts, and stories.

PAUL'S USE OF HOSEA: WHAT'S GOING ON?

Though I am cautious to avoid banal generalities, it is helpful to classify the various opinions in the following four ways: (1) Contextual/Original; (2) Non-Contextual/Eschatological; (3) Typological/Principle; and (4) Presuppositional/Christological.[10] Admittedly, these categories are not sufficiently precise, as some scholars reviewed below could very well be placed within two (or more) of them. That said, these are still quite helpful to reveal what is distinctive and emphatic in each respective view.

1. Contextual/Original

This view can be described as "contextual/original" because its adherents appeal to the original context for clarity into Paul's seemingly revisionist interpretation. The reason Paul can quote Hosea the way that he does is because Hosea himself originally intended to include Gentiles in the covenant, along with Jews. David Starling observes that only a "small number of

8. Hays, *Echoes*, 66–67. Hays is not employing these descriptions in a negative sense, and it is important to locate these comments within his larger discussion (see 66–68).

9. See chapter 6.

10. Cf. the classification in Starling, *Not My People*, 118–27, which, though different, served as an inspiration for the categories that follow.

commentators" have held this view.[11] He mentions John Calvin, Theodore Ferdinand Karl Laetsch, and Thomas Edward McComiskey.[12]

McComiskey, for example, argues that Hosea's appeal to the Abrahamic covenant ("And the number of the sons of Israel will be as the sand of the sea, of which can be neither measured nor counted" [Hos 2:1]) serves to reveal the prophet's "theology of hope."[13] He says, "This affirmation that God will increase the numbers of his people beyond counting not only assures God's loyalty to his promise and to his people, but it envisions the inclusion of countless numbers of Gentiles in the promise as well."[14] This, he goes on to argue, is the basis for which Paul can later apply the prophecy to the Gentiles.[15]

Calvin held to a similar position. At the beginning of his comments, he notes how the calling of non-Jews had been forecasted by Hosea. In this vein, he says, Paul's application to the Gentiles fails to be a novelty.[16] In the same breath, he admits that "there is some difficulty in the application of this testimony; for no one can deny but that the prophet in that passage speaks of the Israelites."[17] Describing Paul's application of Hosea as a "knot" that needs to be untied, he evaluates one popular opinion at the time regarding this quotation. This idea, says Calvin, is that "What may seem to be an hinderance to the Gentiles to become partakers of salvation did also exist as to the Jewish nation: as then God did formerly receive into favour the Jews, whom he had cast away and exterminated, so also now he exercises the same kindness towards the Gentiles."[18] We might call this the *principilizing thesis*, which states that because God can renew Israel as the *Not-My-People*, he can in principle do the same for another kind of *Not-My-People*, namely, the Gentiles.[19]

Calvin, while sympathetic to this approach, dismisses it in the end. He goes on to ask if "it would not be a more suitable view to regard the consolation given by the prophet, as intended, not only for the Jews, but

11. Starling, *Not My People*, 118.

12. Starling, *Not My People*, 118n39.

13. McComiskey, "Hosea," 29. He says Hos 2:1 "recalls the imagery of the words God spoke to Abraham" in Gen 22:17 (29).

14. McComiskey, "Hosea," 29. See also 48.

15. McComiskey, "Hosea," 29.

16. Calvin, *Romans*, 371.

17. Calvin, *Romans*, 371.

18. Calvin, *Romans*, 371–72.

19. Calvin does not use these terms. Dunn argues for this thesis too. See below.

also for the Gentiles."[20] For Calvin, the best answer is to posit that Hosea had always intended the inclusion of the Jews *along with the Gentiles*. His reasoning is that the Old Testament prophets often did this sort of thing anyway. Routinely, he says, they would announce judgment and wrath on Israel for the purpose of pointing them "to the kingdom of Christ, which was to be propagated through the whole world." Calvin says that this would, in effect, cause the Jews to be "reduced to a common class, and put on a level with the Gentiles. The difference being taken away, God's mercy is now indiscriminately extended to all the Gentiles."[21]

With respect to McComiskey and Calvin, a few responses are in order. On the former, I agree with Starling that it is hard to substantiate McComiskey's view on the mere basis of Hosea's reference to the Abrahamic promise.[22] The original context does not suggest Hosea is interested in discussing the inclusion of the Gentiles with respect to the Abrahamic promise. McComiskey seems to reach his conclusions based upon a theological deduction. The evidence does not suggest, however, that Hosea was thinking along these lines. What *could* be the case, though, is that Paul was himself making these sorts of connections. More will be said about this in subsequent chapters.

With respect to Calvin, there exists some ambiguity.[23] In my estimation, while Calvin's proposal is consistent with Hosea's horizon of understanding, it seems to go beyond Hosea's immediate concerns. He is correct, though, to bring christology to bear upon the issue. I am not convinced, however, that Hosea had the sort of christological insights Calvin thinks he did—enough, at least, that he (Hosea) could have intended Gentile inclusion. There is little evidence to suggest otherwise.[24] That said, I do think *Paul* read Hosea's oracle with christology in view (see chapter 6 below). Furthermore, if Hosea had originally intended for the oracle to speak of Gentile inclusion, one would have expected him to have said so. As it stands, Hosea seems to have only wayward Israel in view. The main problem with Calvin's

---

20. Calvin, *Romans*, 372.

21. Calvin, *Romans*, 372.

22. Starling, *Not My People*, 119. He says, "there is hardly sufficient evidence within Hosea to support a reading of Hos. 1:10 (LXX and MT 2:1) as an explicit reference to the salvation of Gentiles."

23. Throughout his comments, Calvin does give the impression that he is not certain about his views. Starling is correct to observe that Calvin offers his view "somewhat tentatively" (Starling, *Not My People*, 119).

24. Hosea does mention a future Davidic king who will unite Israel in 3:5, but this hardly sustains the notion that Hosea thereby intended to include Gentiles as being part of the group to be united.

thesis, then, is not that he posits christology as a necessary prejudgment such that the Gentiles could be included, but rather that he thinks Hosea originally shared this prejudgment.

2. Non-Contextual/Eschatological

Ernst Käsemann believes Paul was not reflecting on the original sense.[25] His view is that the provoking nature of the quotations has an eschatological emphasis, saying, "Der Reihenfolge in 24 chiastisch entgegengestellt, sind die Heidenchristien die Empfänger der Verheißung, welche sie aus dem Chaos herausgeholt und zu Geliebten, also zu Kindern und zum eschatologischen Gottesvolk gemacht hat."[26] For Käsemann, the original meaning has been ignored because it has been superseded.[27]

Other scholars can be quite blunt about the matter. For example, C. H. Dodd describes Paul's choice of using Hosea in Rom 9 as "ill-chosen." He says,

> It is rather strange that Paul has not observed that this prophecy referred to Israel, rejected for its sins, but destined to be restored: strange because it would have fitted so admirably the doctrine of the restoration of Israel which he is to expound in chapter xi. But, if the particular prophecy is ill-chosen, it is certainly true that the prophets did declare the calling of the Gentiles.[28]

Both Käsemann and Dodd are similar in that they both believed Paul disregarded the original sense of the prophecy. And yet, there are noticeable differences between the two. On the one hand, Käsemann views the quotation as being "eschatologically-focused oracles,"[29] while Dodd dismissed the legitimacy of Paul's use of the quotation altogether.[30] The assumption behind Dodd's view is that Paul is a less-than-careful reader of Scripture. Such

25. Käsemann, *Römer*, 264. He says, "Wie üblich versteht der Apostel die Sprüche als eschatologisch ausgerichtete Orakel, ohne über ihren ursprünglichen Sinn zu reflektieren."

26. Käsemann, *Römer*, 264.

27. Käsemann's views are better understood when one takes into account his thoughts on the preceding argument in Rom 9. See Käsemann, *Romans*, 260–72.

28. Dodd, *Romans*, 172. Though his conclusion is that Paul still sees the oracle as possibly still referring to Israel remains a stretch, see Starling, *Not My People*, 119–20, for a helpful critique of the view that Paul is not talking about Gentiles at all, but rather Jews, in vv. 25–26.

29. Käsemann, *Römer*, 264.

30. Dodd, *Romans*, 172.

an idea is difficult to substantiate, however. To show how, let us consider Dodd's view in more depth. He states that the preceding argument in Rom 9 laid the groundwork for what is to come in vv. 25–26. Paul, he argues, has defended God's right to choose who can be in the covenant as being his own sovereign right, which "[constituted] a new 'Israel' of Jews and Gentiles."[31] Dodd adds by saying that this "constituting . . . is in accordance with what the prophets said regarding God's designs."[32] Specifically, he says that the inclusion of Gentiles into this new people was "established" by the Hosea oracle.[33] When Dodd declares that Gentile inclusion was "established" by the Hosea prophecy, he should not be understood as meaning it was *satisfactorily* proved by the oracle (recall he thinks the oracle was "ill-chosen"). This must be seen, rather, as a reference to the way the oracle functioned rhetorically within Paul's argument, that is, the *implied author* of Romans understood it as being established. Thus, what compelled Dodd to understand the Hosea quotation as "ill-chosen" was his recognition of how the oracle functioned rhetorically.

It is possible that Paul might not have noticed his own blunder nor anticipated objections from his Jewish contemporaries—objections like Dodd's. But this seems unlikely. First, Dodd's argument assumes that Paul was ignorant (or at least forgetful) of other prophetic texts that spoke more explicitly of Gentiles—such texts of which even Dodd claims to be aware.[34] Second, out of all the Jewish texts Paul could have chosen, Hosea's oracle seems to have been *purposefully* placed where it was. This claim is supported by the fact of its rhetorical place and function, namely, its specific position to persuade the reader that Gentiles were now included (something Dodd also recognized about the implied author). Third, when Dodd says the Hosea oracle would have been utilized better by Paul in Rom 11, the glaring fact that it is *not* used there only strengthens the point that its position nearby in Rom 9 is deliberate.[35] The absence of any hint that Paul anticipated objections is also interesting. Of course, that such an objection would have registered for Paul in the first place assumes that he was committed to similar hermeneutical assumptions that prevail among modern interpreters. The absence is nonetheless telling as Paul is quite capable of foreseeing rejoinders, anticipating objections, and then offering pre-emptive responses.[36]

---

31. Dodd, *Romans*, 172.

32. Dodd, *Romans*, 172.

33. Dodd, *Romans*, 172.

34. Dodd, *Romans*, 172.

35. Dodd, *Romans*, 172.

36. E.g., see Rom 2:1–4, 17–24; 3:1, 27–31; 4:1; 6:1, 15; 7:7, 13; 9:6, 14, 19; 11:1, 7, 11.

Given how integral the oracle is to Paul's argument, as well as the fact he never anticipates any objection to it, it is perhaps more likely to posit that something else is at play hermeneutically. Instead of imposing upon Paul modern hermeneutical criteria (and thus concluding that he was misapplying texts), it might prove beneficial to explore other hermeneutical elements possibly at play in his use of the Jewish texts.[37]

Käsemann's eschatological view appears helpful since it provides an alternative way of dealing with some of the problems of context—that is, the problem of Paul's placing the Hosea text within his own context, thus giving it different meaning. Although it is reasonable to bring an eschatological perspective to the discussion, a further hermeneutic account is needed. While there should be no question that Paul's use of Hosea has taken on a fresh and new eschatological meaning, further elucidation is required to show how he did so without ignoring the horizon of the Hosea text itself (after all, the oracle is quoted as a contribution to Paul's argument; see below).

Käsemann, like other scholars, does well to describe *what* Paul is doing, but offering a philosophical-hermeneutic approach will fill the gaps mentioned above. In this way, consistent with Käsemann, Paul's eschatological approach can be preserved and highlighted but, perhaps *beyond* Käsemann, a total overcoming of the original horizon of the oracle is not necessary.[38] A thorough critique of his overall thought is beyond the scope of this study. Yet, one wonders if the particular problem with Käsemann's approach to the intertextual situation is not due to his other hermeneutical commitments which, as has been pointed out, remains problematic since it does not account for a deeper Jewish narrative that runs throughout Paul's thought.[39] In full acknowledgement of Käsemann's insights, it is important to integrate what is friendly to his efforts with a more clarified account of Paul's narrative approach, not least to the application of the Hosea oracle

37. See the critique of Longenecker and Gardener in Hays, *Echoes*, 180–81. Moyise ("Does Paul Respect the Context?," 98) is correct to warn of anachronism when evaluating Paul's creative use of texts under modern criteria.

38. For all the noteworthy things about Käsemann's work—not least his commentary on Romans—I am hesitant to adopt the entirety of his apocalyptic framework. At times, Käsemann appears to emphasize a radical newness of Paul's thought at the expense, arguably, of the underlying narrative features that are, in my view at least, present within the Pauline writings themselves. For example, Käsemann, *Romans*, 273, beginning his comments on vv. 24–29, says, "The promise which has been given to Israel and the goal of God's saving counsel which is perceptible at present diverge. Hence Paul has to show that the divine promise is neither calculable nor a human privilege. Salvation history is not a process of continuous development. It is the history of the word which constantly goes forth afresh and accomplishes election and rejection. In this way the Jewish belief in election is transcended."

39. See, e.g., Wright, "New Tübingen School," esp. 64, 67.

itself.[40] This allows one to move, arguably, beyond talk of Paul's disregard for the oracle's horizon in favor of Paul's, but rather to reframe the phenomenon into the more helpful concept of *Horizontverschmelzung*.[41]

This leads to the following questions. How does one make sense of an eschatological emphasis in Rom 9:25–26 *textually* and *conceptually*? Textually, how does one account for the way the text functions rhetorically in the argument? Paul utilizes it, after all, with the assumption that it will contribute to his argument. Should this rhetorical feature not be allowed to have full force? More importantly: *Can* it have full force in a way that also allows for Paul's revisionary reading? Conceptually, given the historical context and agenda of Hosea, at what point can Paul alter, or at the very least add to, the oracle from being an exclusive one about the return of rebellious Israel of Hosea's time and upon the Gentiles of his time? Does Paul on some level bring his own paradigm to the text of Scripture, imposing upon it the details he sees fit? If so, what hermeneutic can adequately account for this?[42] One wonders, moreover, if the choice between these two differing horizons are indeed mutually exclusive *or* if the relationship between the two is much more intuitive and closer than one might think. In the end, Käsemann's way forward does not ultimately absolve Paul from the charge of misguided exegesis nor does it answer (with full clarity) the question about the relationship between the horizons of the original oracle and its latter interpreter.[43]

3. Typological/Principle

James Dunn takes exception with Dodd, saying he "misses the point" because "Hosea's allegorical case study and the promise to the Northern Kingdom of Israel enshrine a principle (that those once rejected can be taken back again)."[44] That is, what God promised to do for Israel can be applied to the Gentiles. He adds that while this "principle . . . can be referred to rejected

---

40. With respect to the so-called "apocalyptic" and "salvation-historical" debate, see Bird, *Anomalous Jew*, 114. He notes those scholars who have sought to account for an "apocalyptic" reading of Paul all the while still being sensitive to the "storied nature of Paul's theology" (see also 114–23). This remains the general spirit behind the present work. See also Wright, *Paul and His Recent Interpreters*, 135–218.

41. See chapter 3 below.

42. See Starling's comments below concerning Tanner's work.

43. At the very least, our study provides conceptual and textual clarity to what is otherwise overlooked in Käsemann's comments.

44. Dunn, *Romans 9–16*, 571. See also Starling, *Not My People*, 123–24, concerning the various terminological descriptions.

Ishmael, Esau, and Pharaoh," it can just "as much [be applied] to hardened Israel," which Dunn believes might have been part of Paul's intention anyway.[45]

The point emphasized by Dunn is that, on the one hand, while the Hosea prophecy pointed to a return of Israel in its original context, Paul merely used it as a "principle" for the inclusion of the Gentiles, and since Paul might have had in mind physical Israel anyway, Paul's use of this text is not at odds with its original context.[46] By going this route, one might argue that at least some of the hermeneutical tension has been eased on Paul's use of the prophet.

But at what cost? By seeing a principle at play, Dunn offers a route around the problem of opposing agendas (Hosea's on the one hand, Paul's on the other). The problem, however, is that this does not give due weight to the rhetorical nature of the quotations. This would mean Paul's argument rests upon the assumption that, just because God *can* in principle do something that he *is* therefore doing it. While this has the appearance of a viable solution, it is too weak. Analogical arguments can only go so far, after all. It is unlikely, then, that Paul would have argued in this, or in any similar, manner given how much is at stake for him in the context.[47]

Another noteworthy treatment comes from David Starling. Starling understands the "narrative and salvation-historical dimensions" as giving legitimacy to the thesis of a typological relationship between God's past redemptive work for Israel and in the present work of Christ.[48] His typological approach is not reduced to "illustrative tropes," for it recognizes that Paul's "correspondences . . . between Israel's history and the gospel of Christ are understood as correspondences between the actions of the one God, whose ways (even when they are surprising) are grounded in a consistency of character and purpose within the one grand narrative."[49]

---

45. Dunn, *Romans 9–16*, 571. Dunn reaches this conclusion because the Hosea quotations occur after the discussion in 9:6–23. Cf. Barrett, *Romans*, 178; Starling, *Not My People*, 164.

46. Cf. Seifrid, "Romans," 648–49.

47. In the second edition to his commentary, Moo (*Romans* [2nd ed], 632–33) appears more open to the analogical thesis than he was in the first edition. Nonetheless, Moo thinks Paul employs Hosea as part of a "larger biblical-theological picture." This is due to Hosea's apparent echo to the Abrahamic promise (see 632n302). Moo thinks Paul, being familiar with the context of Hosea, would naturally have understood this to encompass a worldwide family that included Gentiles. Cf. Moo, *Romans* (1st ed), 613. Because of the popularity of Moo's Romans commentary, I will often reference his first edition along with his recently-published second edition. For the same reasons, I will do this for Schreiner's commentary, too.

48. Starling, *Not My People*, 123n62.

49. Starling, *Not My People*, 123–24n62.

Moreover, Starling claims to find warrant for a typological reading because of how, in the verses leading up to the Hosea quotation (i.e., vv. 6–23), "the dominant mode of argumentation is by analogy and example," not least in regard to scriptural references.[50] Paul's aim in 9:25–26, then, was to refer back to the Hosea oracle as an analogical reality for what God was doing in the first century.[51] Thus, the typological appropriation of the Hosea texts in vv. 25–26 finds collusion with other instances of correspondence between Israel's story and other motifs in the whole of Romans itself.[52] According to Starling's view, Paul has not "forgotten" or "overlooked" the oracle's original context and would possibly still affirm its "continuing relevance to the Israel of his day."[53]

Starling's observations are especially insightful. His overall narrative approach is commendable, not least his keen eye for typological construals that relate the story of Israel with other themes in Romans itself. Nonetheless, there are still questions which need answered and gaps to be filled.[54] For example, consider Starling's rebuttal to Terence Donaldson's understanding of Rom 9:25–26 (and texts like them). Donaldson states that "the texts establish what Paul wants them to establish only if one shares his convictions at the outset."[55] Starling thinks Donaldson's claim here rests upon the assumption that scriptural texts "must either do all the work or none of the work in establishing the point to be proved."[56] In contrast, Starling believes that original texts and the assumptions from their latter interpreter are more intimately related such that while the former "would scarcely have suggested the inclusion of Gentiles apart from the 'mystery' revealed to Paul," they would still "provide partial, retrospective confirmation of that revelation in the way that they describe the dealings of God with Israel."[57]

This is surely correct. In this vein, a hermeneutic that is capable of shedding light on *how* exactly this happens would serve to clarify the issue. Though it is not Starling's intention to address specific

---

50. Starling, *Not My People*, 125. Starling (125) goes so far as to argue that "it is far from certain that Paul is framing the Isaiah texts simply and univocally as prophetic predictions fulfilled in Paul's own time."

51. Starling, *Not My People*, 126.

52. Starling, *Not My People*, 163–64. Specifically, Starling notes how Paul depicts typological correspondence between the story of Israel and that of Adam, the church, the Gentiles, individual Jews and believers, and even himself (163). See his larger discussion on 139–62.

53. Starling, *Not My People*, 120 (see also 164).

54. See above.

55. Donaldson, *Paul and the Gentiles*, 101, quoted in Starling, *Not My People*, 122n54.

56. Starling, *Not My People*, 122n54.

57. Starling, *Not My People*, 122n54.

philosophical-hermeneutical issues, when he does touch on matters related to them, there remains room, I think, for more precision and lucidity. For example, Starling rightly acknowledges the positive role Paul's convictions played in enabling his interpretation of Hosea. He is, however, overly cautious in granting too much hermeneutical weight to Paul's reception of the "mystery" and to his christological convictions, as this will result in nothing but a "circular argument."[58] In this regard, Starling pushes against two groups of scholars. There are (1) those who think Paul's christological convictions entirely "supplanted" the original meaning of Hosea *and* (2) those who think these convictions offered a means of "expansion" of that original meaning in order to accommodate the inclusion of Gentiles along with the Jews.[59] Starling cites Ernst Käsemann[60] as an example of the first group and J. Paul Tanner[61] as an example of the second.

But Starling's caution about circularity is not altogether clear and, perhaps if clarified, it could serve to advance his own arguments.[62] He is specifically uneasy with views (such as Käsemann's and Tanner's) that give primacy to Paul's christological/eschatological horizon on the grounds that it cannot, at the same time, account for how Paul argues *from* Scripture in those verses.[63] Starling is right to acknowledge that Paul quotes Hosea in the context of an argument and, because of this, he wants to preserve the idea that Paul "intends his Scripture citations to make some material contribution to the force of the argument."[64] I agree with this, but why must the fact that Paul *argues from Scripture* be a necessary denial of the thesis that *Paul's reading of Hosea only works if his assumptions are first shared*? Conceivably, Paul's christological, pre-judged reading of Hosea can be at the same time his argument *from* Hosea. To be sure, both must be held in tension, as Starling seems to agree.[65] In this regard, I think a philosophical-hermeneutical approach can address the issue sufficiently. It does away with the temptation to dismiss the

---

58. Starling, *Not My People*, 121–22.

59. Starling, *Not My People*, 121.

60. Starling, *Not My People*, 121n49. He also references Hays (*Echoes*, 67), saying he "flirts with this approach, without actually embracing it" (Starling, *Not My People*, 121n49).

61. Starling, *Not My People*, 121n50. For my review of Tanner's position, see below.

62. Although, compare with what he says elsewhere. See e.g., Starling, *Hermeneutics as Apprenticeship*, 1–21.

63. Starling, *Not My People*, 122.

64. Starling, *Not My People*, 122.

65. See again Starling, *Not My People*, 122n54, and his discussion about the "(fallaciously) excluded middle."

hermeneutic priority of Paul's christology (as Starling appears to do) *all the while* avoiding the pitfalls of which Starling is so understandably cautious.[66]

4. Presuppositional/Christological

In an important essay, J. Paul Tanner offers crucial observations about Paul's use of Hosea.[67] He argues that it was Paul's "New Covenant awareness"—manifested in various New Covenant "events"—which "set the stage for [his] fresh understanding" of the Hosea oracle.[68] Tanner acknowledges the New Covenant "was not overtly promised" to the Gentiles in Hosea.[69] Nevertheless, their inclusion was a "direct fulfillment" since they "participated in the New Covenant."[70] He readily admits that "Nothing in the context of these passages makes reference to Gentiles, nor did Hosea imply that the fulfillment of the promises would be with Gentiles."[71] He notes the hermeneutical dilemma when he recognizes that Paul used Hosea in order to "prove" that Gentiles were now included in the covenant.[72] The essence of Tanner's argument is that Paul never rejected the original meaning of Hosea but simply sought "*to affirm a fulfillment also with Gentiles.*"[73]

Tanner also takes exception with the idea that Paul used the Hosea prophecy to convey a principle.[74] His ultimate solution to the hermeneutical

66. Again, Starling should not be faulted for not bringing philosophical hermeneutics to bear upon his project, as that was not his aim. Perhaps in more ways than one, then, my study could offer a philosophical underpinning for his.

67. Tanner, "New Covenant."

68. Tanner, "New Covenant," 106; see esp. 103–10. Tanner speaks of "events" such as the revelation Paul received concerning Gentile inclusion, Jesus' announcement of the New Covenant at the Last Supper, and the coming of the Spirit—not least upon Gentiles. Cf. Moyise, *Paul and Scripture*, 78, 85.

69. Tanner, "New Covenant," 109.

70. Tanner, "New Covenant," 102, 108.

71. Tanner, "New Covenant," 100.

72. Tanner, "New Covenant," 98. Tanner says (101) that "Hosea 1:10 and 2:23 clearly refer to Israel. And yet in Romans 9:25–26 Paul quoted those verses and applied them to Gentile believers of the church."

73. Tanner, "New Covenant," 101.

74. Tanner, "New Covenant," 109–10. Tanner says, "Paul's treatment of the Hosea passages must not be seen as a mere utilization for purposes of analogy or application of principle. The inclusion of the Gentiles was a legitimate phase of fulfillment for the Hosea passages, as 1 Peter 2:4–10 confirms. Believing Gentiles had now become 'the people of God,' full and equal participants in the New Covenant. The unfolding events of the New Testament (coupled with the Holy Spirit's revelation of the mystery of the church) allowed the Hosea passages to be seen in their fullest perspective" (109–10). Cf. Dunn, *Romans 9–16*, 571.

conundrum is to say that the apostles—not least Paul—had gained a "New Covenant awareness" which would have helped shed light upon passages like Hosea.[75] Tanner's idea of an apostolic "New Covenant awareness" was made possible due to certain experiences and events, such as what was experienced at Pentecost—namely, that it was not only believing Jews who were receiving the Spirit, but also the uncircumcised, believing Gentiles.[76] Thus,

> The apostolic understanding that Gentiles were participants in the New Covenant helped the apostles see that the promise in Hosea of *status change* pertained not only to Jews in the New Covenant but to *all* who participated in the New Covenant—and hence also to Gentiles. If the New Covenant passages like Jeremiah 31:31–34 included Gentiles (though seemingly promised only to Israel), then the same hermeneutic applied to the Hosea promises. Gentiles would be included in the fulfillment of the New Covenant, even though it was not overtly promised to them. What Hosea was clear about was that the fulfillment would come with those participating in the New Covenant. The passing of time clarified that the Gentiles also would participate in the New Covenant and hence in the promises given through Hosea![77]

Tanner's insights are commendable as they account for Paul's new horizon of understanding. However, his overall solution to the dilemma opens other questions. First, one is left wondering how Paul's "New Covenant awareness," inspired by certain "events," can rightly be said to serve as the interpretive tool for Paul's use of Hosea when in fact this seems contrary to the rhetorical place and function of the Hosea quotation itself.[78] Tanner rightly emphasizes the fact that Paul had certain experiences that helped him come to see that Gentiles were now included into covenant blessings and that also illuminated certain Old Testament texts.[79] Though such a move is necessary, there is more to the interpretive situation than just this,

---

75. Tanner, "New Covenant," 106.

76. Tanner, "New Covenant," 103–6. Cf. Wright, *PFG*, 758–60.

77. Tanner, "New Covenant," 108–9.

78. Tanner, "New Covenant," 104–6, 110. Cf. Starling, *Not My People*, 121–22n50, who likewise notices the weakness of this and similar positions.

79. Tanner, "New Covenant," 104–6, 110. Tanner states (105): "following the Day of Pentecost it was undoubtedly apparent to the apostles that the New Covenant promised in Jeremiah and Ezekiel was underway, and at least these aspects of the New Covenant were now being realized by the 'believing remnant' of Israel (which at the beginning is all that they expected the church to be). The events of Acts 10–11 would have significantly escalated their understanding, and those who witnessed this stood amazed at what was happening."

as the place and function of the quotations suggest. Paul does not merely set forth the idea of "New Covenant awareness" in order to shed light upon the prophecy in Hosea, but rather the opposite: The Hosea prophecy functions as a proof *for* New Covenant awareness.[80]

But this is not necessarily fatal for Tanner's position—if the hermeneutic tension is handled properly. As I mentioned in my critique of Starling's view above, proposals like Tanner's ought not be dismissed on the mere grounds that Paul was employing Hosea in the context of an argument. Under the proper framework, there is a way to conceive of how Paul's assumptions (his "New Covenant awareness") can engage in a back-and-forth, dialogical relationship with Scripture such that *both* his reading into the text *and* his arguments from the text can be accounted for sufficiently. The philosophical-hermeneutic approach I propose below allows for this.

Moreover, if one were to proceed with Tanner's view, a further inquiry into the formative nature that hermeneutic *experiences* have over interpreters would need to be clarified.[81] How, for example, can Paul's apostolic experiences play a role in his interpretation of Old Testament texts such as Hosea? To answer this (and to validate suggestions like Tanner's), a proposal would need to be put forward that is capable of recognizing the hermeneutic value of ontological experiences for explaining hermeneutic phenomenon. There needs to be explanation, in other words, about Paul's *being in the world* and how that serves to construct his interpretive horizons as an apostle, and from there, the role his prejudgments play in reading texts like Hosea. This would necessarily entail, I think, a thorough explanation for how Paul's *christological* prejudgments impact his reading of the Old Testament.

Doug Moo raises an interesting point in this regard. Commenting on Paul's use of Hosea, he says that "God's final revelation in Christ gives to him [Paul] a new hermeneutical key by which to interpret and apply the OT."[82] If that is the case, then Paul's christology—on some level, at least—is integral to understanding Paul's interpretative practices. And so deep questions emerge: What sort of association exists between Paul's assumptions and the Old Testament texts he interprets? How can Paul's *present* christological assumptions be the axis around which Paul's reading of *past* texts turn? More

---

80. See again the discussion in Starling, *Not My People*, 122.

81. The reader is encouraged to keep this in mind when Gadamer's use of *Erfahrung*, experience, is discussed below.

82. Moo, *Romans* (2nd ed), 633n303. In context, this quote is employed to distinguish his view from that of Hays (*Echoes*, 67; cf. Starling, *Not My People*, 121n49). In conjunction with christology, Moo thinks Paul was also attentive to the underlying biblical-theological themes in Hosea, such as the mention of the Abrahamic promise (632–33).

generally speaking, what is the nature of the relationship between past and present, between an original text and its subsequent reading?

THE RIDDLE

Though the survey above was brief and far from exhaustive, it was sufficient to introduce readers to the riddle that is Paul's interpretation of the Old Testament. In the views examined, each scholar sought ways to account for Paul's use of Hosea. But certain sacrifices had to be made to do so. Take Calvin, for example. In acknowledging Paul's Gentile-oriented use of the oracle, he was compelled to expand Hosea's original horizon of understanding in order to better comport with Paul's. Käsemann simply has Paul disregarding the original meaning altogether, thus effectively erasing Hosea's horizon to make way for Paul's. Dodd, in recognizing the tension between *both* the oracle's original meaning *and* Paul's subsequent use of it, felt compelled to delegitimize the latter. In this way, he fails to entertain any possibility for fusion between the two horizons (Paul's and Hosea's). In so doing, he obscures the structure of Paul's horizon of understanding—effectively depriving it of being able to produce anything hermeneutically significant with respect to Hosea. Dodd may very well be correct in this regard, but one should be hesitant to adopt his conclusion until all other possible avenues that could bring fusion are exhausted. In this vein, Starling's view is similar. It was largely ambiguous with respect to *how* Paul's hermeneutic assumptions related to the narrative of Scripture (and vice versa). Tanner's view lacked clarity in this regard as well. Thus, we see the real hermeneutical issues emerge: How can the horizons of both text and interpreter sufficiently relate? How can these horizons remain distinct in all their otherness and yet, at the same time, attain genuine fusion so that understanding can result? Moreover, if such a hermeneutic could be found, would it cohere with what one actually sees elsewhere in Paul's exegesis of Scripture (not least in Romans)?

This book proposes a hermeneutic that, arguably, meets these criteria. It offers a sufficient account for how historically distanced texts (such as Hosea's) can meaningfully speak into an interpreter's present situation (such as Paul's). It also reveals how Paul's situation influences the meaning(fulness) of the Old Testament texts he quotes.

To accomplish these things, an important question will be addressed: How can one manage—or better, *how can one account for*—the subject-object tension that exists between texts and their interpreters? I am convinced that one hurdle to understanding Paul's use of the Old Testament is the failure to question certain assumptions that have been bequeathed to us by modernity. It goes without saying, but Paul was not an interpreter who was influenced by Enlightenment assumptions. It would seem odd, then, to critique him under the influence of the same. Instead, one needs a hermeneutic that is free from the constraints of certain Enlightenment ideals.

Furthermore, such a hermeneutic will help in navigating the issue of historical distance—the contextual-time gap that exists between the text and interpreter. Consider once again Paul's use of Hosea. The problem is really about different agendas—differences which are nestled in the cradle of differing situations and times. On the one hand, Hosea speaks of Israel's re-inclusion—an issue of profound relevance for those living in, and experiencing the harsh realities of, Hosea's time. On the other hand, Paul quotes Hosea to speak of Gentile inclusion—an issue of critical relevance for those living in, and experiencing the tricky realities of, a Jew-Gentile church in Paul's time. Thus, the agendas are different because their situations are different; their *experiences* are different. But can these agendas merge? Or perhaps a better question ought to be asked: What hermeneutical components were at work that served to bring *fusion* between the original text of Hosea and Paul's later use of it—not by overcoming the tension of historical distance (and hence differing agendas)—but by accounting for the tension itself? Concomitant questions will need to be answered, too: Can Paul's use of Hosea be seen strictly as *copying* the text (i.e., restating it), *re-authoring* the text (i.e., revising it), or something else altogether?[83]

We need a way to answer all these questions because the quotations from Hosea are not isolated instances of Paul's creative interpretation. To the contrary, they are representative of Paul's larger project of re-appraising and re-configuring key Jewish texts, motifs, and stories in Romans. In this epistle, Paul routinely—and almost casually—draws out new and fresh meaning from old concepts, creatively interpreting and recontextualizing them around his Christian assumptions. And to make matters daunting for modern interpreters, he often hangs much theological and ecclesiastical weight upon his interpretations. To answer these questions, and to address these issues, I propose that the philosophical-hermeneutics of Hans-Georg Gadamer be brought to bear upon the matter. Conceivably, it offers the right conceptual framework, affording modern interpreters precise and detailed clarity into Paul's otherwise enigmatic use of Scripture. In fact, my thesis is

---

83. I am indebted to my *Doktorvater*, Thorsten Moritz, who, early in my PhD research, brought to my attention the concept of *re-authoring* as a possible category for consideration. As the reader will see in the chapters that follow, I tweak this concept by qualifying it as "*dialogical* re-authoring" in order to fully capture two fundamental elements in Gadamer's conception of interpretation—namely, *dialogue* and *newness*. See below.

that Gadamer's hermeneutic offers a philosophical account for Paul's interpretation of the Old Testament.

In the pages that follow, I will walk through Paul's letter to the Romans, noting the ways in which Paul handles his Old Testament quotations, giving them fresh meaning—all the while not doing violence to their original context. Before we can see how this works, however, we need to become familiar with Gadamer's hermeneutic theory, which is the subject of the next two chapters.

PART 2

Philosophical Hermeneutics

Chapter 2

The Anticipation of
Philosophical Hermeneutics

The understanding and the interpretation of texts is not merely a
concern of science, but obviously belongs to human experience of
the world in general.

HANS-GEORG GADAMER[1]

WHY PHILOSOPHICAL HERMENEUTICS?

The core of my methodology in assessing Paul's use of Scripture is philosophical hermeneutics as conceived by its founder, Hans-Georg Gadamer.
At its core, philosophical hermeneutics seeks to bring clarity to the process of understanding. Contrary to popular conceptions of hermeneutics,
Gadamer's theory is less concerned with developing a system consisting
of rules, flow charts, and directions for interpreting texts. Instead, philosophical hermeneutics seeks to uncover the ins and outs of the experience of
understanding. "My real concern," says Gadamer, "was and is philosophic:
not what we do or what we ought to do, but what happens to us over and

---

1. Gadamer, *TM*, xx.

above our wanting and doing."[2] In other words, "The task of philosophical hermeneutics . . . is ontological rather than methodological."[3]

At first glance, it would appear problematic to take a non-methodological theory such as Gadamer's and employ it as a methodology. This problem, however, is superficial. Gadamer's hermeneutics neither negates nor contradicts method *per se*. It seeks, rather, to get beneath the question of method and into the more fundamental question of the interpreter's being. Thus, this way of engaging hermeneutical questions is by starting not with guidelines, rules, or methods, but by addressing the more pertinent question of one's place in the world.[4] Therefore, my use of Gadamer's theory functions more like a tool by which I can "clarify" the "miracle of understanding" than it does a methodology *per se*.[5]

Philosophical hermeneutics proves useful for a study on biblical literature (especially regarding issues that concern the New Testament's use of the Old). This point is underscored by J. B. Torrance, who, in his foreword to Anthony Thiselton's *The Two Horizons*, observed that "One of the central concerns in contemporary theology and biblical studies has been the interest in linguistics and hermeneutics."[6] He continues,

> It is impossible to do genuine scientific biblical study today without raising questions of hermeneutics—the science of interpretation—and we cannot raise the question of interpretation without raising questions about the nature of knowledge, the use of language, and the scientific and ontological presuppositions operative in the mind of the exegete.[7]

Thiselton, moreover, addresses those who would express concern for the intermingling of philosophy with biblical studies.[8] He states rightly that "concepts drawn from philosophy" can serve to "facilitate the description and critical appraisal of the hermeneutical task."[9]

Indeed, one of the great benefits that philosophy affords the interpreter is that it provides helpful categories which allow otherwise enigmatic hermeneutical phenomena to be spoken of more coherently. In fact, "certain

---

2. Gadamer, *TM*, xxv–xxvi.

3. Linge, "Editor's Introduction," xi.

4. More will be said below.

5. Gadamer, *TM*, 292.

6. Torrance, "Foreword," xi.

7. Torrance, "Foreword," xi. Cf. Bartholomew, *Hermeneutics*, 329.

8. Thiselton, *Two Horizons*, 3–4. See also Bartholomew, *Hermeneutics*, 282–84.

9. Thiselton, *Two Horizons*, 4. See also Olhausen, "Role of Hermeneutics," 112, who defines hermeneutics "as the philosophy of understanding."

perspectives and conceptual schemes which have been drawn from philosophy may serve in certain circumstances to illuminate the text of the New Testament itself."[10] It is beneficial to use philosophical categories, particularly the philosophical hermeneutics of Gadamer, for an intertextual study such as this because the *situational* assumptions of both the original writers (e.g., of the Old Testament) and their subsequent reader (i.e., Paul) can be sufficiently addressed.

Rightly, Flemming Lebech says that "one of the key concepts" of Gadamer's entire hermeneutical project was the "finitude of human life and understanding," meaning each person is bound to his or her own place within "culture, history, and tradition."[11] Indeed, it is precisely the issue of Paul's and Hosea's differing life-situations—resulting in their differing understandings of, and agendas for, the oracle itself—that epitomize the task at hand. The benefit, specifically, of using Gadamer's hermeneutical theory therefore is that it "does not consider this to be an epistemological problem."[12] Thus Lebech says,

> While every individual subject is fundamentally conditioned through their cultural and historical background, Gadamer rejects entirely the presupposition of absolute, objective knowledge. *On the other hand, he considers such embeddedness to be a necessary condition for judging, acting, and understanding. In the absence of pre-understanding, one would be unable to engage appropriately in concrete situations, or adequately comprehend subject matter.* One's embeddedness creates a horizon beyond which one cannot see. *However it simultaneously provides the means by which one may critically examine one's pre-understanding, expanding its horizons and broadening one's knowledge of the matter at hand.*[13]

If the idea that one's "embeddedness" within "culture, history, and tradition" can be substantiated as a plausible component from which knowledge and understanding is achieved, then it is clearly beneficial to employ such concepts in the study of Paul's use of Scripture. Given this, one would be obligated not only to address the question of his quotations in terms of merely grammar, syntax, and lexical arrangements, but also expound upon the underlying features implicit within Paul's text itself—features such as

10. Thiselton, *Two Horizons*, 40. Thiselton refers to theological categories, though the point about the benefit of philosophy is clear (cf. pp. 47, 415–27).

11. Lebech, "Concept of the Subject," 222.

12. Lebech, "Concept of the Subject," 222.

13. Lebech, "Concept of the Subject," 222; emphasis added. Cf. Wright, *PFG*, 67.

Paul's own "tradition" (in the way Gadamer means it), as well as his pre-understandings. Philosophical hermeneutics provides a clear way forward by giving the modern reader the opportunity to look not just at the explicit features which entailed Paul's use of Scripture, but rather into the more fruitful area of Paul's thought-world, i.e., his "embeddedness" within his own socio-theological "culture, history, and tradition."[14] Enquiry into these and related areas could shed light on the riddles regarding Paul's interpretive activity.

Philosophical hermeneutics offers a system of evaluation that can account for not just the text being interpreted but also the interpreter of the text. This is important, of course, because the focus of hermeneutics concerns the question of meaning and understanding claimed by the interpreter with respect to his or her encounter with a text. This fact alone demands that all hermeneutic analyses enquire into how the text *and* interpreter can come together meaningfully. Thiselton's observation on this matter is relevant. He says, "From the standpoint of hermeneutics, traditional approaches to language usually carry with them an inbuilt limitation, namely that they concentrate attention on the language of the ancient text, and do not attempt to bring about a fusion of horizons between the world of the text and that of the interpreter."[15] Should not the hermeneutical process account for the world of the interpreter as well? If so, then it remains evident that an examination into just the "world of the text," while necessary, remains far from sufficient.[16] Any description of what it means to understand, therefore, will need to take into consideration both *the thing understood* and *the one who understands*—the *very* issue which concerns the *Old Testament*

---

14. Lebech, "Concept of the Subject," 222. Cf. Wright, *PFG*, 24–27. Watson, *Paul and the Hermeneutics of Faith*, 3–4, recognizes the role of "presuppositions and commitments" when interpreting texts, though with some caution: "We cannot assess the contrasting readings of Habakkuk 2:4 by Paul and the Qumran pesherist without some sense of what this text might mean within Habakkuk and the Book of the Twelve as a whole, quite apart from what its early readers do with it. It is true that the differences between such readings expose the crucial part played by the presuppositions and commitments that individual readers bring to a text. Yet it is wrong to imagine that the text itself is no more than a blank screen onto which readers project their various concerns: it is normally possible to show that the text itself is implicated in the readings it occasions. To interpret is always to interact with a text, and it is also to be *constrained* by the text." The benefit of utilizing Gadamer's hermeneutic is that, as we shall see, both the horizon of the interpreter and the text is respected and held in tension. On the notion of contextual "respect," see again Moyise, "Does Paul Respect the Context?," 97–114, who observes that term "respect" can be ambiguous.

15. Thiselton, *Two Horizons*, 117. See also his discussion on Sawyer et al. on 117–24, esp. 120.

16. Thiselton, *Two Horizons*, 117.

and *Paul's* later reading of it, respectively. As we will see, this is precisely the benefit of using Gadamer's theory, specifically his concepts of *prejudice*, *horizon*, and *tradition*.

As every first-year seminary student knows, "context" is the key to understanding a text. And my own project, with its philosophical-hermeneutical approach, is able to adopt a thoroughly broad contextual awareness. In this vein, philosophical hermeneutics is well-suited for the task because it is by definition *descriptive*, addressing ontological questions rather than methodological ones.[17] As already said, this is especially useful since my goal is to describe how fusion between historically-distanced texts—that is, between the texts of the Old Testament and Paul's use of them—can be attained. And this is precisely the issue that needs to be addressed, namely, the question of *historical distance*.

One may be tempted to think that historical distance is a liability to overcome. Many hermeneutical strategies seek to do this very thing. We often speak, for example, of *getting into the mind of the author* so that we can understand what exactly he or she was meaning. The assumptions are, of course, that the meaning of the text is found in the author's mind *and* that it is possible to enter into it. This problem is all the more pronounced when we are dealing with ancient authors, such as those of the Old Testament. The temptation is to get into the mind of the author because there—and not in the cacophony of voices that have littered the long-distanced stream of history—lies meaning. As will be seen, Gadamer sees things differently, and for good reason. Such a construal, moreover, does not account for what one actually sees in Paul's interpretations of the Old Testament—not least in Romans. If Paul has anything to say about the matter, it is that the original authors of the texts he cites are not the dictators of meaning. This is not to say, of course, that Paul disregards altogether the original horizon of the text he is interpreting. Far from it, as we will see.

Part of the problem is that we are tempted to think in this either/or dichotomy: *Either* Paul unilaterally reads his own assumptions into the text *or* the text unilaterally imposes its own assumptions on Paul. Such thinking, captive as it is to certain Enlightenment assumptions, fails to capture the artistry of Paul's interpretive approach. Certain influences of the Enlightenment—not least upon much of modern American evangelicalism—still linger such that they force thinkers to bifurcate between this either/or paradigm. Gadamer's hermeneutic, which calls into question some of the Enlightenment's most central tenets, is thus beneficial in this regard. The reason is obvious: *Paul himself interpreted Scripture apart from modernity's*

---

17. See again p. 26 above.

influence and assumptions. Paul does not, in other words, share the modern commentator's own Enlightenment presuppositions—ones which, to be sure, inform his or her own *modern* critique of Paul's *pre*-modern hermeneutic. In this vein, a Gadamerian approach has the unique advantage of bringing insight to the question at hand. But before I can outline Gadamer's theory, it is important to first situate him within his own scholarly context.

GADAMER'S INFLUENCE AND CONTEXT

Hans-Georg Gadamer has been called a "most important theoretician,"[18] and E. D. Hirsch Jr., a well-known detractor of Gadamer's ideas, called his *Truth and Method* "the most substantial treatise on hermeneutic theory that has come from Germany in this century."[19] Likewise, Bartholomew says it is "*the* central text in hermeneutical theory."[20] Malpas and Zabala consider Gadamer, along with Heidegger, as one of the "two key figures in the development of modern hermeneutics."[21] And according to scholars who hail from a variety of backgrounds, many of Gadamer's ideas are ripe for use in biblical scholarship.[22] I think this is especially so with respect to a study of the New Testament's use of the Old.

18. Lapointe, "Hermeneutics Today," 111.

19. Hirsch, *Validity*, 245. Thiselton (*Two Horizons*, 25) describes Hirsch as "one of his severest critics." For a concise, introductory overview of Gadamer's thought, see Teigas, "Gadamer," 292–96. For a stimulating intellectual biography, see Grondin, *Hans-Georg Gadamer*.

20. Bartholomew, *Hermeneutics*, 282.

21. Malpas and Zabala, "Introduction," xi. They continue, saying, "while Heidegger's *Being and Time* is certainly a key text in the history of hermeneutics in the twentieth century, it was the publication of Gadamer's *Truth and Method* in 1960 that was the watershed event in the development of philosophical hermeneutics, and that established the hermeneutical as a distinctive mode of philosophical inquiry and engagement. While hermeneutics did not begin with Gadamer, it was Gadamer who first articulated a conception of hermeneutics in its universality, and who enabled the expansion of hermeneutics into the wider framework of contemporary philosophical debate. The implications and significance of the hermeneutical approach—its *consequences* for philosophy—can thus be viewed as largely deriving from the ideas laid out in *Truth and Method* and their elaboration, including the responses to them, over the last half-century" (xi–xii).

22. Gadamer's relevance for biblical scholarship has not gone unnoticed. See e.g., the positive remarks by Dunn ("Biblical Hermeneutics and Historical Responsibility," 85) regarding Gadamer's work on *Wirkungsgeschichte*, calling it "integral to responsible hermeneutics." See also Luz, *Matthew 1–7*, 61–66; Luz, *Matthew in History*, esp. 1–38 (cf. Bockmuehl, *Seeing the Word*, 161–88, on Wirkungsgeschichte); Evans, *Reception History*. Also, Thiselton (*Two Horizons*, 17) notes that Palmer "claims to find a precedent" for a Gadamerian account of hermeneutics in Luke 24:25–27. Cf. Meek, "Hans-Georg Gadamer."

By bringing his philosophical hermeneutics into dialogue with established exegetical practices, one's understanding of Paul's construal of Old Testament texts should be enhanced significantly. His philosophical hermeneutics grants the modern interpreter categories which help describe what may first appear as an interpretive dilemma and render it into something more coherent. Indeed, Gadamer's theory offers "an integrity to the whole discipline of biblical studies."[23] It is conceivable, then, that this is especially true for a project such as my own, namely, one that seeks to bring clarity to, and offer an account of, Paul's use of the Old Testament. After all, the value of Gadamer's hermeneutic is that it is not normative but descriptive, an account of what happens in the act of interpreting.[24]

To better understand Gadamer's hermeneutic, a survey of his scholarly setting is necessary. Gadamer routinely builds upon previous thought, finding both common agreement, as well as disagreement, with those scholars who came before him.[25] The best place to begin is with the father of hermeneutics, namely, Friedrich Schleiermacher.

F. D. E. Schleiermacher

Friedrich Daniel Ernst Schleiermacher operated within the sphere of so-called "romantic hermeneutics."[26] Merold Westphal notes several key characteristics of this school of thought. First, there is the notion of "deregionalization."[27] Schleiermacher sought to draw hermeneutics away from being pigeon-holed into just any one discipline. He envisioned hermeneutics as a broad enterprise such that he sought to find what was "*common to* rather than *distinctive of* the various disciplines."[28] Hence, it was

23. Evans, *Reception History*, 2.

24. See Gadamer, *TM*, 512–13.

25. Palmer, *Hermeneutics*, 166.

26. Westphal, *Whose Community?*, 27. See also McLean, *Biblical Interpretation*, 35; Smith, "Living Religion," 138–39, says that most of those thinkers who would be considered central to "Early Romanticism" (e.g., Schleiermacher) sought to utilize "religion" and its "conceptions" that would serve to "bridge piety and Enlightenment rationality, science and faith." Cf. Thiselton, *Hermeneutics*, 150, who cautions those who want to group Schleiermacher completely in with romanticism. On the contrary, Thiselton argues that Schleiermacher had "strong reservations about 'pure' Romanticism," saying his "Romanticism was strong but not decisive."

27. Westphal, *Whose Community?*, 28; McLean, *Biblical Interpretation*, 37. The term itself, as Westphal (28) acknowledges, comes from Paul Ricoeur.

28. Westphal, *Whose Community?*, 28.

"nondisciplinary."[29] His hermeneutic was to be a *hermeneutica generalis*: a theory of the conditions of possibility for understanding as such."[30] This proved revolutionary.[31] Schleiermacher's project would be to deregionalize hermeneutics in such a way that the question would no longer be, "How shall we understand the biblical text?" but rather, "How do we understand any text at all?"[32] Schleiermacher states that "Da Kunst zu reden und zu verstehen einander gegenüberstehen, reden aber nur die äußere Seite des Denkens ist so ist die Hermeneutik im Zusammenhange mit der Kunst zu denken und also philosophisch."[33]

Second, the concept of a hermeneutical circle was characteristic of Romanticism.[34] Schleiermacher himself calls this a "principle" that is "incontestable."[35] He says,

> daß wie freilich das Ganze aus dem Einzelnen verstanden wird, so doch auch das Einzelne nur aus dem Ganzen verstanden werden könne, ist von solchem Umfang für diese Kunst und so unbestreitbar, daß schon die ersten Operationen nicht ohne Anwendung desselben zu Stande gebracht werden können, ja, daß eine große Menge hermeneutischer Regeln mehr oder weniger auf ihm beruhen.[36]

Understanding, then, does not happen outside the circle, for one must understand the parts before one can understand the whole and vice versa. The interpreter cannot understand a whole sentence until he or she has first taken into account each word of the sentence; yet, the words themselves cannot be properly understood until the entire sentence has been grasped.[37] Thus, "the part and the whole interact to make sense."[38] This necessitates, therefore, the idea of "provisional and preliminary understanding."[39] Un-

29. Palmer, *Hermeneutics*, 40. See also 94.

30. Gjesdal, "Hermeneutics and Philology," 136. See also Gadamer, "Classical and Philosophical Hermeneutics," 50.

31. However, Gjesdal ("Hermeneutics and Philology," 136n9) takes exception with Schleiermacher's claim that he was the first to develop a universal hermeneutics.

32. Palmer, *Hermeneutics*, 86.

33. Schleiermacher, *Hermeneutik*, 80; Schleiermacher, *Hermeneutics*, 97.

34. Westphal, *Whose Community?*, 28; McLean, *Biblical Interpretation*, 43–44.

35. Schleiermacher, *Hermeneutics*, 196.

36. Schleiermacher, *Hermeneutik*, 141–42; Schleiermacher, *Hermeneutics*, 196.

37. Palmer, *Hermeneutics*, 87.

38. Owen, "Hermeneutic Phenomenology," 5–6.

39. Thiselton, *Hermeneutics*, 155. See specifically Schleiermacher, *Hermeneutics*, 198; Thiselton, *Two Horizons*, 103–7.

derstanding must be seen, therefore, as circular, since it is "a basically refer-ential operation."[40] But the hermeneutical circle is not debilitating. In fact, because of the circle itself, understanding remains possible since it provides the means by which revision, and hence "knowledge," can be achieved.

> The relation between whole and part is circular in that each is interpreted in light of the other; interpretation is a reciprocal in-teraction in which neither variable is independent of the other. The interpretation of the parts is guided by and revised in light of the whole, but my view of the whole is guided by and revised in light of my own reading of the parts.[41]

For Schleiermacher, the hermeneutical circle was all the more intrigu-ing, as there were two circles in play: (1) a grammatical-linguistic circle and (2) a psychological circle.[42] For him, these circles both "form a hermeneuti-cally circular whole."[43] In his view, one ought to focus on the philological features of a text (i.e., the grammatical details), for as we have seen above, sentences make little sense if we ignore the individual words (and *vice versa*). But he also sees the need to understand, along with the grammatical side, the *psychology* of the text—or more appropriately, the psychology of the author of the text.[44] He says, "Gewiß aber wird auch die grammatische Seite nicht kön-nen der divinatorischen Methode entrathen."[45] But Schleiermacher is quick to point out that the opposite is true as well, namely, that this "psychologi-cal aspect" ("psychologischen Seite") must be informed by the grammatical,

---

40. Palmer, *Hermeneutics*, 87.

41. Westphal, *Whose Community?*, 29.

42. Westphal, *Whose Community?*, 28; Thiselton, *Hermeneutics*, 156–57; McLean, *Biblical Interpretation*, 39–43. See also Bartholomew, *Hermeneutics*, 307.

43. Westphal, *Whose Community?*, 29. See also Palmer, *Hermeneutics*, 86; This-elton, *Hermeneutics*, 157; Bartholomew, *Hermeneutics*, 307. Cf. McLean, *Biblical Interpretation*, 41.

44. Westphal, *Whose Community?*, 29. See Schleiermacher, *Hermeneutics*, 150–51. Westphal (*Whose Community?*, 29) provides the helpful illustration of reading *Gulliver's Travels*. Whereas one navigates the textual parts in light of the textual whole (and vice versa), there is also the necessity of working through the socio-historical situation of the author, so as to come to see this as "political satire in the guise of kiddy lit." Westphal observes: "Now the parts begin to make more sense but *only to the degree that I know something about the author and his sociopolitical context.* This move from the purely tex-tual to the biographical-historical indicates that the two major circles described by Schlei-ermacher together form a hermeneutically circular whole. We interpret the text in light of the person, though much of what we know about the person we learn only from the text."

45. Schleiermacher, *Hermeneutik*, 138; Schleiermacher, *Hermeneutics*, 192 (see also 150–51). On what is meant by "divinatory" and how it relates to "psychological" inter-pretation, see Thiselton, *Hermeneutics*, 156–57.

specifically in terms of a "comparative operation" ("comparativen Verfahrens") by which words are located and understood in terms of other words.[46] This leads to another characteristic of romantic hermeneutics: *psychologism.*

Psychologism, thirdly, is in search of the author's "inner psychic life,"[47] from which language itself springs forth.[48] Romanticism's project operated from the assumption that meaning lay not on the surface of the text (i.e., the grammatical, lexical), but rather "beyond the text itself [and] in the inner motivations of its original, historical author."[49] Indeed, this was Schleiermacher's "tendency," namely, "to make the real focus of interpretation the author's thoughts and experience that lie behind the text rather than in the text itself."[50] Gadamer calls "psychological interpretation" Schleiermacher's "most distinctive contribution.[51]

46. Schleiermacher, *Hermeneutics*, 192; Schleiermacher, *Hermeneutik*, 138–39. His argument is detailed at this point; e.g., see Schleiermacher, *Hermeneutics*, 190–95; Schleiermacher, *Hermeneutik*, 137–41. See also Bartholomew, *Hermeneutics*, 307–8.

47. See Thiselton, *Hermeneutics*, 157, concerning the relation between Schleiermacher's concepts "psychological" and "divinatory." See also the helpful discussion on how these concepts relate from within the interpretive process as well, including how this gives shape to the hermeneutical circle, in Thiselton, *New Horizons*, 221–25. Cf. Frank, "Text and Its Style," 23–26; Gjesdal, "Hermeneutics and Philology," 142–43; McLean, *Biblical Interpretation*, 42.

48. Westphal, *Whose Community?*, 29. Westphal notes that this is why this specific hermeneutical approach has been called "romantic," since it "shares this expressivism with the wider cultural traditions called romanticism." Cf. Palmer (*Hermeneutics*, 89), who cautions us not to equate "psychologism" with "psychoanalysis." The former is just another way of saying that "understanding is an art of reconstructing the thinking of another person. In other words, the objective is not to assign motives or causes for the author's feelings (psychoanalysis) but to reconstruct the thought itself of another person through interpretation of his utterance." See also Thiselton, *Two Horizons*, 106.

49. McLean, *Biblical Interpretation*, 43.

50. Bartholomew, *Hermeneutics*, 307. It should be noted, however, that there is a dispute as to how much emphasis the psychological aspects really had for Schleiermacher. In the translator's introduction to Kimmerle's edition of Schleiermacher's *Hermeneutics*, James Duke discusses this issue and comments on Lücke's influential "one-side picture" of Schleiermacher's hermeneutics which had as its focus the psychologistic aspect, namely his latter thought (10). Duke comments that Kimmerle's edition, by including more of Schleiermacher's earlier writings, sought to introduce a more well-rounded portrayal, thus smoothing out the so-called latter psychological emphasis with that of the earlier grammatical and linguistic ones (10). Space does not permit a full treatment on the details of this debate, though it suffices to say at present that it is perhaps the case that one should not fail to see, as Duke encourages, that the psychological aspects occur even in the earlier Schleiermacher and the grammatical ones in the latter, thus lending to our view that Kimmerle's case is, seemingly, overstated (11). (See the entire discussion in Schleiermacher, *Hermeneutics*, 9–12.)

51. Gadamer, "Hermeneutics as a Theoretical and Practical Task," 259.

Moreover, psychologistic hermeneutics aims to "reverse the process of writing, to work back from the outer expression to the inner experience, to reconstruct, re-create, refeel, re-experience, relive that inner experience."[52] Schleiermacher says, "Eine Hauptsache beim Interpretiren ist daß man im Stande sein muß aus seiner eignen Gesinnung herauszugehen in die des Schriftstellers."[53] Thus:

> the interpreter must put himself both objectively and subjec-
> tively in the position of the author. On the objective side, this
> requires knowing the language as the author knew it. But this is
> a more specific task than putting oneself in the position of the
> original readers, for they, too, had to identify with the author.
> On the subjective side this requires knowing the inner and outer
> aspects of the author's life (Auf der subject[tive]n in der Ken-
> ntniß seines inneren und äußeren Lebens).[54]

The reason for his commitment to psychologism was because he had come to see a division between thought and expression.[55] Psychologism sought to move the interpreter outside of his or her own realm and into the realm of the author, entering the latter's psyche. Thus,

> For Schleiermacher, understanding as an art is the reexperienc-
> ing of the mental process of the text's author. It is the reverse
> of composition, for it starts with the fixed and finished expres-
> sion and goes back to the mental life from which it arose. The
> speaker or author constructed a sentence; the hearer penetrates
> into the structures of the sentence and the thought.[56]

Another characteristic of romanticism was, fourthly, *objectivism*.[57] Westphal notes that Schleiermacher sought after objectivity, though in what one might call a nuanced manner; that is, for Schleiermacher, the goal of objectivity would be mediated by means of a subjective process.[58]

---

52. Westphal, *Whose Community?*, 29–30. See also McLean, *Biblical Interpreta-tion*, 42; Hoy, *Critical Circle*, 11.

53. Schleiermacher, *Hermeneutik*, 32; Schleiermacher, *Hermeneutics*, 42.

54. Schleiermacher, *Hermeneutics*, 113; Schleiermacher, *Hermeneutik*, 88. The "task," as Schleiermacher famously put it, is "die Rede zuerst eben so gut und dann besser zu verstehen als ihr Urheber" (Schleiermacher, *Hermeneutik*, 87; Schleierm-acher, *Hermeneutics*, 112).

55. Palmer, *Hermeneutics*, 92–93. Cf. Thiselton, *Two Horizons*, 105–6.

56. Palmer, *Hermeneutics*, 86. Cf. the critique in Thiselton, *Hermeneutics*, 154.

57. Westphal, *Whose Community?*, 31.

58. Westphal, *Whose Community?*, 32–33. Westphal comments that Dilthey, too, wanted to raise the *Geisteswissenschaften* to the same level of supremacy as that of the

On this, Westphal carefully observes how Schleiermacher's "divinatory method," contrary to what one might think, ought to be understood not so much as *the* method for Schleiermacher, but rather as the end result of method.[59]

> This result, which is always provisional and subject to revision, is the result of painstaking, methodical labor in which the interpreter (1) works back and forth from smaller parts to a larger whole within the grammatical-linguistic circle, (2) does the same within the psychological-historical circle, and (3) works back and forth with the circle formed by these two in relation to each other.[60]

It is true that the driving emphasis in Schleiermacher's interpretive theory lay in the subjective aspects.[61] Westphal says that, for Schleiermacher, the end result of methodical work—namely, "divination" or "intuition"—is "always provisional and subject to revision."[62] In essence, at this level nothing is certain, but everything is always up for re-evaluation, and of course revision and re-evaluation is possible because one is in constant movement between the whole and the parts. This process entails what Schleiermacher called "uncertainties."[63] At this stage, understanding is on its way to being achieved because false assumptions are being eliminated. The goal, to be sure, is objectivity. Westphal offers a helpful illustration:

> Just as the intuitions of racial bias are mediated by socialization into a world that is itself mediated by a variety of historical and psychological developments, so too are hermeneutical intuitions mediated by scholarly work under the guidance of a method. The former mediation is by means of a particular and contingent social formation, while the latter is supposed to filter out precisely such subjective factors.[64]

---

natural sciences (31). In order to do this, Dilthey thought, the *Geisteswissenschaften* needed to avoid destructive relativism, and because of this, his solution to this would be to propose a method (31–32). This, he thought, would help objectify the human sciences. See below.

59. Westphal, *Whose Community?*, 32.

60. Westphal, *Whose Community?*, 32–33.

61. So Bartholomew, *Hermeneutics*, 307–8.

62. Westphal, *Whose Community?*, 32; Schleiermacher says, "jedes erste Auffassen nur ein vorläufiges und unvollkommnes ist" (Schleiermacher, *Hermeneutik*, 146; *Hermeneutics*, 200).

63. Schleiermacher, *Hermeneutics*, 198.

64. Westphal, *Whose Community?*, 33.

In light of Westphal's observations, then, it is important to point out that, for Schleiermacher, methodical work results in subjective intuition that, at times, will need to be refined by more methodical work.[65] Thus, even though the goal is objectivity, for Schleiermacher, it is only by means of an entirely circular-subjective process that seeks to be chastened, one might say, by method.[66] "The ideal is to start subjectively but end objectively."[67] One must come to appreciate how Schleiermacher wrestled with the fact of subjectivity in interpretation all the while employing methodical work so as to avoid "the specter of relativism."[68]

Wilhelm Dilthey

Though considered to be Schleiermacher's successor, Dilthey's own contributions to hermeneutical theory remain significant (not least in regard to Gadamer's scholarly context).[69] Thiselton notes three big contributions: (1) He broadened the scope of hermeneutics so as to include the social sciences; (2) he placed hermeneutical emphasis on the notion of historicality; and (3) he underscored the importance of interpretive sympathy on behalf of the interpreter, which would be important for getting outside one's self and into the other.[70] The idea of *historicality* was central to Dilthey. In fact, "historical consciousness" was the very heartbeat of his interpretive theory.[71] Dilthey's hermeneutic began to take shape when he "began to see in hermeneutics the foundation for the *Geisteswissenschaften*—that is, all the humanities and social sciences, all those disciplines which interpret expressions of man's inner life, whether the expressions be gestures, historical actions, codified law, art works, or literature."[72] In order to do this, according to Dilthey,

65. See again Westphal, *Whose Community?*, 32–33.

66. See again Westphal, *Whose Community?*, 32–33. That said, one should not understand Schleiermacher's hermeneutics in the traditional sense, i.e., a "mechanical process," but rather as an "art" (Thiselton, *Two Horizons*, 301).

67. Westphal, *Whose Community?*, 33.

68. Westphal, *Whose Community?*, 33. See also 34.

69. Thiselton, *Hermeneutics*, 163.

70. Thiselton, *Hermeneutics*, 163. See also Owen, "Hermeneutic Phenomenology," 6. One can easily see Dilthey's indebtedness to Schleiermacher, especially on this last point. For an interesting discussion on Dilthey's idea of "sympathy" in relation to an Augustinian-influenced Christian epistemology, see Plantinga, "Commitment and Historical Understanding," 29–36.

71. Crowell, "Early Decades," 673.

72. Palmer, *Hermeneutics*, 98. See also Crowell, "Early Decades," 63; Gadamer, "Hermeneutics as a Theoretical and Practical Task," 259–60.

certain methods would need to be devised.[73] However, the natural sciences, properly defined, could not be transposed into the realm of the *Geisteswissenschaften*.[74] That being said, Dilthey understood that hermeneutics, the foundation for the *Geisteswissenschaften*, could be scientific, though in a way different from the natural sciences. The difference lay in the dissimilarities between the propositions that both the natural sciences and the human sciences make, respectively. Thiselton comments that

> Dilthey had great ambition. He recognized that Bacon had done much to found the natural sciences. But what Bacon had done for physical sciences, and what Kant and Hegel had done for philosophy, he hoped to do for the "human sciences." "Science" is simply a coherent complex of propositions, whose propositions are well grounded. But propositions about human life, he insisted, are distinctive over against propositions about the natural world. Human self-consciousness includes a moral, historical, and spiritual dimension that must be recognized.[75]

Thus, the point of inquiry on which both the natural sciences and the human sciences were focused was different: the natural sciences studied objects that could be seen, touched, tasted, but the human sciences inquired into the *Geist*.[76] Thus,

> Dilthey reasons that since the humanities' object of study is different—the human "spirit"—its goal must also be different. The real goal is "understanding," not scientific "explanation." Thus, Dilthey made the important distinction between "explanation" (*Erklärung*) and "understanding" (*Verstehung*) as two *contrasting* approaches to the acquisition of knowledge . . . while the

73. Palmer, *Hermeneutics*, 98. His aim was to discover how "objectively valid knowledge in the human sciences [was] possible" (Crowell, "Early Decades," 674).

74. Palmer, *Hermeneutics*, 98.

75. Thiselton, *Hermeneutics*, 162. On this, it is worth quoting at length Nelson, "Impure Phenomenology," 28, who says, "The natural sciences are oriented toward achieving a mathematically modeled explanatory construction of nature. As such, they are separate from and indirectly related to the nexus of historical life that is the basis of their practice and enactment. The difference between the natural and human sciences consists therefore in how they justify their respective claims. Epistemology emerges from this context with the issue of clarifying and differentiating the multiple modes of justification and validity in the various sciences. Epistemology is the systematic and historical description and analysis of conceptual knowledge, specifically how it occurs in the sciences. Dilthey's transformation of epistemology occurred through situating scientific and conceptual knowledge (*Erkenntnis*) in contextual understanding." See also Palmer, *Hermeneutics*, 103–6; Nelson, "Impure Phenomenology," 29, esp. 33–34.

76. McLean, *Biblical Interpretation*, 68–69.

natural sciences are concerned with the explanation of *general laws* and ascribing *causal* effects in the world, the goal of the "sciences of the human spirit" (Geisteswissenschaften) is concerned with understanding.[77]

Crowell points out that "Dilthey . . . turned first to the concept of consciousness and then to the concept of life as the basis for grasping historical reality."[78] Dilthey discusses the "context of life," specifically how "Die Geisteswissenschaften sind so fundiert in diesem Zusammenhang von Leben, Ausdruck und Verstehen."[79] He continues by saying, "Eine Wissenschaft gehört nur dann den Geisteswissenschaften an, wenn ihr Gegenstand uns durch das Verhalten zugänglich wird, das im Zusammenhang von Leben, Ausdruck und Verstehen fundiert ist."[80] Dilthey's answer, more properly, was *"lived experience."*[81]

Though the details of Dilthey's thought need not be elaborated, a few aspects of his concept of lived experiences need to be pointed out. After all, Dilthey's *lived experiences* have direct bearing on his emphasis upon historicality, that is, the two went hand-in-hand.[82] Expounding on Dilthey's use of "lived experience" (*Erlebnis*), Palmer observes that the implication of such use is none other than *historicality*, saying, *"Experience is intrinsically temporal* (and this means *historical* in the deepest sense of the word), *and therefore understanding of experience must also be in commensurately temporal* (historical) *categories of thought."*[83] Therefore, Dilthey found historical

77. McLean, *Biblical Interpretation*, 69.

78. Crowell, "Early Decades," 673.

79. Dilthey, *Schriften*, 86–87.

80. Dilthey, *Schriften*, 87.

81. Thiselton, *Hermeneutics*, 162. See also Palmer, *Hermeneutics*, 106–15, esp. 107–11 on the etymology of *Erlebnis* and the concept of "lived experiences." McLean (*Biblical Interpretation*, 74–75) states that Dilthey's conception of "lived experience" was due in part to his being influenced by Husserl's phenomenology.

82. Palmer, *Hermeneutics*, 100–111, 116–18.

83. Palmer, *Hermeneutics*, 111. Palmer adds (111): "Dilthey has, then, with the insistence on the temporality of experience asserted the foundation of all subsequent efforts to affirm the "historicality" of human being-in-the-world. Historicality does not mean being focused on the past, or some kind of tradition-mindedness that enslaves one to dead ideas; historicality (*Geschichtlichkeit*) is essentially the affirmation of the temporality of human experience as we have just described it. It means we understand the present really only in the horizon of past and future; this is not a matter of conscious effort but is built into the structure of experience itself. But to bring this historicality to light does have hermeneutical consequences, for the nonhistoricality of interpretation can no longer be assumed and leave us satisfied with analysis that remains firmly in scientific categories fundamentally alien to the historicality of human experience. It makes brutally plain that experience is not to be understood in scientific categories. The

consciousness, fleshed out in *lived experience,* as a place for the foundation of the *Geisteswissenschaften.*[84] Thus, there exists commonality between both Gadamer and Dilthey on the issue of *historical situatedness.*[85] In his effort to develop an expansive hermeneutic, Dilthey understood the importance of paying attention to both the interpreter's historical situation, as well as that of the object being interpreted.[86] He says, "Der Mensch erkennt sich nur in der Geschichte, nie durch Introspektion."[87] And so, "Gadamer applaud[ed] Dilthey's efforts to move away from introspection and self-consciousness to seeing humankind as historically situated within the flow of human life."[88]

Martin Heidegger

There was perhaps no greater influence upon Gadamer's philosophy than Heidegger.[89] While a complete account is unnecessary, it is helpful to keep in mind the key areas of influence.[90] In many ways, Heidegger remained the rightful heir to post-Schleiermacher scholarship, though not without having his own distinctions.[91] Heidegger gleaned from his study of the ancient Greeks, from whom he came to understand his notion of "Being" in both "[primordial] and in temporal terms."[92] In this way, by utilizing the phenomenological work of Husserl, Heidegger was able to offer a hermeneutic

---

task is clear: to work out the 'historical' categories appropriate to the character of lived experience." See also Crowell, "Early Decades," 674.

84. Nelson, "Impure Phenomenology," 27.

85. It should be noted, too, that within Dilthey's hermeneutic of *lived experiences* is the recognition of the hermeneutical circle. This, of course, is significant to understanding Gadamer, for, as we shall see, the hermeneutical circle entails the concept of *Vorurteil,* which is central to Gadamer's hermeneutic. See Palmer, *Hermeneutics,* 118–21.

86. Thiselton, *Hermeneutics,* 162.

87. Dilthey, *Schriften,* 279.

88. Thiselton, *Hermeneutics,* 163.

89. For an overview of Heidegger's influence upon Gadamer, see Thiselton, *Hermeneutics,* 206–11. See also McLean, *Biblical Interpretation,* 175. Palmer ("Heideggerian Elements," 121) says Gadamer "was impressed by the hermeneutical possibilities of the ontology of Dasein in *Being and Time* (1927)." See also Dostal, "Hans-Georg Gadamer," esp. 258.

90. For insight into Gadamer's interactions with Heidegger's thought, see Gadamer, *Heideggers Wege*; Gadamer, *Heidegger's Ways.*

91. See Palmer, *Hermeneutics,* 130, who gives a general placement of Heidegger's thought among Schleiermacher's and Dilthey's.

92. Thiselton, *Hermeneutics,* 208; See also Volpi, "Phenomenology as Possibility," esp. 132–34. Cf. Gadamer, *Heideggers Wege,* 26–28; Gadamer, *Heidegger's Ways,* 25–27.

that was neither romantic nor philological, but rather ontological.[93] "The thing to which philosophy had to find its way back and which was the origin of all meaning, was, for Heidegger, not transcendental consciousness [*à la* Husserl] but life in its originality."[94] István Fehér states further that Heidegger's project could not have been what it was (i.e., his emphasis upon historicity) "without Dilthey's influence."[95] This is not to say that Heidegger agreed with the totality of Dilthey's notion of historicality, for even though "Heidegger appreciated very much indeed Dilthey's attempt to approach historical life," his project fell short since he sought to "attain possibly objective historical knowledge," taking "history to the rank of science."[96] This method, of course, proved contrary to Heidegger's ontological emphasis.[97] What he sought to do was merge the ontological with the phenomenological, or as Richard Palmer put it: "Ontology must become phenomenology."[98] That is, "Being" was to be critiqued and delineated "by an analysis of how appearing occurs."[99] This was an important hermeneutical project.[100]

Because his central idea was ontology, it is easy to see how Heidegger's definition of understanding came to be what it was. What is understanding according to Heidegger? Palmer offers an excellent comparison between the English word "understanding" and how Heidegger conceived of it quite differently. He notes that in English, "understanding" often implies a type of sympathy, where one can be said to relate to the thoughts and mind of the other: "We speak of an 'understanding look' and suggest by this more than mere objective knowledge; it is something like participation in the thing understood."[101] In distinction to this, and to that of Schleiermacher's and Dilthey's definition,[102] for Heidegger, understanding had less to do with at-

93. Palmer, *Hermeneutics*, 124–27, 130; For an overview of Heidegger's critique of Husserl's phenomology, see Fehér, "Religion," 104–15.

94. Fehér, "Religion," 110. (See also Palmer, *Hermeneutics*, 125.)

95. Fehér, "Religion," 110–11.

96. Fehér, "Religion," 120–21.

97. On some facets of Heidegger's "critique" of both Husserl and Dilthey, see Gadamer, *Heideggers Wege*, 50–52; Gadamer, *Heidegger's Ways*, 55–57.

98. Palmer, *Hermeneutics*, 129.

99. Palmer, *Hermeneutics*, 129.

100. Heidegger, *Being and Time*, 61–62. On the "significance" of such a method, see Palmer, *Hermeneutics*, 128–30.

101. Palmer, *Hermeneutics*, 130.

102. Palmer, *Hermeneutics*, 131. Palmer (131) reminds us that Schleiermacher's definition was more *psychologistic* and Dilthey's more centered upon *life*. On Heidegger's scholarly background and its relationship to his criticism of psychologism, see Fehér, "Religion," 102–3.

taining or gaining something (e.g., sympathy) and more to do with *Being*, or as Palmer aptly puts it:

> Understanding is conceived not as something to be possessed but rather as a mode or constituent element of being-in-the-world. It is not an entity in the world but rather the structure in being which makes possible the actual exercise of understanding on an empirical level. Understanding is the basis for *all* interpretation; it is co-original with one's existing and is present in every act of interpretation.[103]

Heidegger's emphasis on *Being* ultimately brings one to the breakdown of any subject-object distinction.[104] That is, Heidegger's emphasis is not upon the notion of the subject dominating the object in question (in the sense of wanting to understand it). Rather, the way to understanding is via *embeddedness* in the world.[105] "Everything, in Heidegger's view, is seen and understood from within a particular horizon. Meaning is that *from* which something is understandable as the thing it is."[106] Heidegger's idea of *Da-sein* conveys the idea that a person is "'thrown into [his/her] own world (*Welt*)."[107] That is, "Da-sein always finds itself *already* in a certain social, cultural, linguistic historical, and religious environment, which is *not of its own choosing*."[108] And so Heidegger says, "*In-Sein ist demnach der formale existenziale Ausdruck des Seins des Daseins, das die wesenhafte Verfassung des In-der-Welt-seins hat*."[109] Da-sein implies both "time" and "place," with "Da" meaning a place or situation and "sein" as pointing to one's temporal existence.[110] With his concept

---

103. Palmer, *Hermeneutics*, 131. Thiselton (*Two Horizons*, 165), says that, for Heidegger, "Meaning is not something which we 'stick' onto some naked object which is present-at-hand. It is not a property attached to objects, but is grounded in human life and attitudes."

104. Palmer, *Hermeneutics*, 135–37. Cf. Gadamer, *Heideggers Wege*, 160–61; Gadamer, *Heidegger's Ways*, 191–92.

105. Palmer, *Hermeneutics*, 135. See also 132–34.

106. Thiselton, *Two Horizons*, 149.

107. McLean, *Biblical Interpretation*, 104. See Heidegger, *Being and Time*, 172–79; 219–24. See also Thiselton, *Two Horizons*, 148, on "Dasein."

108. McLean, *Biblical Interpretation*, 104. On the concept of "world," as well as how it is always presupposed, see the introductory section in Heidegger, *Being and Time*, 91–95. See also Palmer, *Hermeneutics*, 132–34.

109. Heidegger, *Sein und Zeit*, 73; *Being and Time*, 80.

110. McLean, *Biblical Interpretation*, 103. Cf. Gadamer, *Heideggers Wege*, 105; *Heidegger's Ways*, 124. See also Mohanty, "Dasein," 177.

of *Da-sein*, Heidegger doesn't have to concern himself with the traditional subject-object schema.[111] Craig Bartholomew comments,

> Heidegger's philosophy is strongly ontological, and his episte-mology is rooted in his ontology of *Dasein*. *Sein* can only be investigated if one begins with *Dasein*, which does not have a viewpoint outside history. In this sense "the phenomenology of *Dasein* is a hermeneutic." This approach allowed Heidegger to rethink the subject-object relationship in knowing along histor-ical lines, and it is here that his most significant hermeneutical contribution lies. "Worldhood" refers to that whole in which the human person finds himself or herself immersed. It is ontologi-cal and a priori, given along with Dasein and prior to all con-ceptualizing. To conceive of objects as merely "present-at-hand" involves secondary conceptualization. The primary relationship of humans to objects is a "ready-to-hand." This contrasts with the Cartesian scientific orientation, which makes secondary conceptualization primary.[112]

Because *Being* and understanding are taken together as "co-original," Heidegger sees understanding as being something that takes place "prior to the subject-object dichotomy."[113] He says, "Erkennen ist ein im In-der-Welt-sein fundierter Modus des Daseins. Daher verlangt das In-der-Welt-sein als Grundverfassung eine *vorgängige* Interpretation."[114] Thus Gadamer can say, "Heidegger's temporal analytics of Dasein has, I think, shown convincingly that understanding is not just one of the various possible behaviors of the subject but the mode of being of Dasein itself."[115]

One resulting influence upon Gadamer was Heidegger's thought con-cerning the hermeneutical circle, which, he argued, was inherent to under-standing.[116] The circle was not a "vicious" one, but rather an "expression of the existential *fore-structure* [*Vor-Struktur*] of Dasein itself," for "in the circle is hidden a positive possibility of the most primordial type of knowing."[117] In this way, understanding itself is always "provisional, historical, and

111. McLean, *Biblical Interpretation*, 104. See Heidegger, *Being and Time*, 86–87.

112. Bartholomew, *Hermeneutics*, 309, citing Heidegger, *Being and Time*, 62.

113. Palmer, *Hermeneutics*, 136. See also Thiselton, *Two Horizons*, 148, 187–94.

114. Heidegger, *Sein und Zeit*, 84; *Being and Time*, 90.

115. Gadamer, *TM*, xxvii.

116. Thiselton, *Hermeneutics*, 208–9.

117. Heidegger, *Being and Time*, 195; Heidegger, *Sein und Zeit*, 203. For what he says more fully about the circle, see Heidegger, *Being and Time*, 194–95; Heidegger, *Sein und Zeit*, 202–4.

temporal, resting on pre-understanding unavoidably."[118] Heidegger describes pre-understanding as "fore-structure," which is a type of "interpretive framework that we employ when we interpret events in daily life as meaningful. By implication, our experience of the world as meaningful is rooted in an ontological structure with Da-sein, which 'exists' before the act of interpretation, which is why Heidegger terms it a *fore*-structure."[119] Thus, for Heidegger understanding is not presuppositionless: "Die Auslegung von Etwas als Etwas wird wesenhaft durch Vorhabe, Vorsicht und Vorgriff fundiert. Auslegung ist nie ein voraussetzungloses Erfassen eines Vorgegebenen."[120] And again, "Alle Auslegung bewegt sich ferner in der gekennzeichneten Vor-Struktur. Alle Auslegung, die Verständnis beistellen soll, muß schon das Auszulegende verstanden haben."[121] Thus Palmer can conclude:

> The hope of interpreting "without prejudice and presupposition" ultimately flies in the face of the way understanding operates. . . . It is naive to assume that what is "really there" is "self-evident." The very definition of what is presumed to be self-evident rests on a body of unnoticed presuppositions, which are present in every interpretive construction by the "objective" and "presuppositionless" interpreter. This body of already given and granted

---

118. Thiselton, *Hermeneutics*, 209; See also Palmer, *Hermeneutics*, 136. On the notion of provisionality in Heidegger's thought, see Vedder, "Provisionality of Thinking in Heidegger," 643–60.

119. McLean, *Biblical Interpretation*, 113. McLean (113) notes that within Heidegger's concept of fore-structure there is a threefold division, which are all correlated to one another: "[1] 'fore-having' (*Vorhabe*), [2] 'fore-sight' (*Vorsicht*), and [3] 'fore-conception' (*Vorgriff*)." Moreover, McLean says (114) that Heidegger understands "all interpretation [to be] guided by this tripartite fore-structure." This structure is as follows: (1) *Fore-having* has to do with a type of pre-understanding that must be in place before any object can be understood. For example, "a hammer is connected to the totality of construction tools and equipment, such as saws, screwdrivers, measuring tapes, nails, and screws" (114). This is what McLean calls a "broader referential context" (114). (2) *Fore-sight* concerns prior need. That is to say, before a hammer is needed (and hence valuable for use), I will have had already in place a specific need for which the hammer will prove useful. "For example, prior to a hammer being meaningful to me as ready-at-hand, I have the need to repair or build something, or I am able to anticipate such a need in my future" (114). (3) *Fore-conception* describes the process of bringing one's *fore-having* and *fore-sight* together. That is, "fore-conception allows you to make a connection between the tool and the project" (114). See Heidegger, *Being and Time*, 191–92. See also Thiselton, *Two Horizons*, 165–66; and Bartholomew, *Hermeneutics*, 309.

120. Heidegger, *Sein und Zeit*, 200. See the translation note in Heidegger, *Being and Time*, 192n1.

121. Heidegger, *Sein und Zeit*, 202; *Being and Time*, 194. See also Palmer, *Hermeneutics*, 135–36.

presuppositions is what Heidegger uncovers in his analysis of understanding.[122]

Some of these ontological features of hermeneutics will remain prominent for Gadamer, though with deviation and nuance.[123] Concepts like *historicality*—specifically, one's own tradition and *Wirkungsgeschichtliches Bewusstsein*—will occupy central place for him as well.[124] Moreover, the idea of prejudgment (*Vorurteil*) will take the place of the Cartesian view that unmediated individual reflection is an adequate means to understanding.

SUMMARY

It was necessary to consider Gadamer's influences to establish his scholarly context. For example, Schleiermacher's program of *deregionalization* reverberates in Gadamer's own conception of hermeneutics, which centers around understanding as such. Second, reference to the *hermeneutical circle* will be made, as Gadamer seeks to show that there is no starting point to understanding that is neither neutral nor free of prejudice (*Vorurteil*). Third, the idea of *historicality* will be brought to light, as Gadamer revives the central place of tradition and *Wirkungsgeschichte* in hermeneutics. Fourth, Gadamer's philosophy is most basically not methodological, but rather *ontological*, though in a way distinct from that of Heidegger's. Thus, the stage is now set to outline Gadamer's theory so that it can be employed in our analysis of Paul's use of Scripture in Romans.

---

122. Palmer, *Hermeneutics*, 136. See also 137.

123. For example, see Thiselton, *Two Horizons*, 201–2. Thiselton (101) points out that Heidegger's philosophy is too "individualistic." He says that this "contrasts unfavorably with Gadamer's starting-point in life and tradition." And elsewhere, he writes (293) "that although [Gadamer] shared some of Heidegger's perspectives, [his] approach is not identical with Heidegger's, and he is also more systematic and less elusive than the later thought of Heidegger."

124. See Bartholomew, *Hermeneutics*, 309–10.

Chapter 3

The Arrival of Philosophical Hermeneutics

Understanding is always the fusion of these horizons supposedly existing by themselves.

Hans-Georg Gadamer[1]

INTRODUCTION

Gadamer's thought is both complex and intertwined.[2] The ensuing outline follows his own sequence of thought, as given in his magnum opus, *Truth and Method*.[3]

1. Gadamer, *TM*, 305.
2. Palmer, *Hermeneutics*, 166.
3. Cf. Thiselton, *Hermeneutics*, 211–24, who does this as well. Due to space constraints, it is regretful that more explicit attention could not be given to Gadamer's exposition on language which occurs in the third section of *Truth and Method*. This is not to say that his ideas on language remain insignificant or inconsequential but that the "distinctive" qualities of the first two sections of *Truth and Method* have been recognized, not least in regard to influence (Thiselton, *Hermeneutics*, 222), and will therefore be afforded primary attention. Concerning how language factors into Gadamer's overall theory, see Weinsheimer, "Meaningless Hermeneutics?," 162, and the surrounding discussion. See also Johnson, *On Gadamer*, 39–53.

TRUTH BEYOND METHOD

Gadamer begins *Truth and Method* by saying that his aim is to address "the problem of hermeneutics."[4] That "problem" transcends the issue of methodology:

> Even from its historical beginnings, the problem of hermeneutics goes beyond the limits of the concept of method as set by modern science. The understanding and interpretation of texts is not merely a concern of science, but obviously belongs to human experience of the world [menschlichen Welterfahrung] in general. The hermeneutic phenomenon is basically not a problem of method at all.[5]

Thus, Gadamer sees hermeneutics as existing beyond the realm of science and in the realm of world-*experience*, *Welterfahrung*. The concept of "experience" (*Erfahrung*) will prove important to his overall trajectory in his explanation of "tradition" (see below).[6] Before the concept of tradition is explained, his aim will be to establish the primacy of experience, that is, the experience of truth. Gadamer wants to "seek [out] the experience of truth that transcends the domain of the scientific method wherever that experience is to be found, and to inquire into its legitimacy."[7] Therefore, his intention is not just to expound upon experience for its own sake, but rather those experiences of truth that lie outside, and indeed *beyond* the limits of, scientific methodological capabilities. On this, Gadamer says "the human sciences are connected to modes of experience that lie outside science: with the experiences of philosophy, of art, and of history itself. These are all modes of experience in which a truth is communicated that cannot be verified by the methodological means proper to science."[8]

First, he turns to aesthetic experience. Gadamer discusses how the "experience [*Erfahrung*] of art" cannot be supplanted by the rigid scrutiny of scientific methodology.[9] Science is deeply restricted in what it can do. Science simply cannot discover truth from a methodological approach to art like the *experience* of art can.[10] Because of this fact, Gadamer offers his own

---

4. Gadamer, *TM*, xx.

5. Gadamer, *TM*, xx; Gadamer, *WM*, 1.

6. For a helpful overview on the way Gadamer uses *Erfahrung* in comparison to *Erlebnis*, see the translators' preface in Gadamer, *TM*, xiii–xiv.

7. Gadamer, *TM*, xxi.

8. Gadamer, *TM*, xxi.

9. Gadamer, *TM*, xxi; Gadamer, *WM*, 2.

10. Gadamer, *TM*, xxi–xxii.

analysis of the aesthetic experience and from there seeks to pull aesthetic experience into the realm of each and every hermeneutical event.[11] What this means, then, is that, with affinity to Schleiermacher's program of deregion-alization, Gadamer, too, wants to conceptualize hermeneutics as the "*menschlichen Welterfahrung insgesamt.*"[12] Gadamer wishes to take the notions of tradition and art as the proper starting place so as to offer a description of the "hermeneutical phenomenon in its full extent."[13] After all, "in [the human sciences] our historical tradition in all its forms is certainly made the *object* of investigation, but at the same time *truth comes to speech in it.*"[14]

Not wanting to exile the question of understanding and interpretation to the province of scientific methodology, Gadamer moves his enquiries beyond that sphere.[15] There should be therefore no confusion about Gadamer's intentions concerning his investigations. He is not out to propose a method, saying that "The hermeneutics developed here is not, therefore, a methodology of the human sciences, but an attempt to understand what the humans sciences truly are, beyond their methodological self-consciousness, and what connects them with the totality of our experience of world."[16] Elsewhere he states, "My real concern was and is philosophic: not what we do or what we ought to do, but what happens to us over and above our wanting and doing."[17] Although he was not intent on developing a "method," neither was he attempting to discard "methodical work."[18] He does not seek to "confine or limit modern science" as much as he wants to address the very question that goes to "precede it and make it possible."[19] Gadamer wants to ask something more fundamental. His question, primarily, is: "how is

---

11. Gadamer, *TM*, xxii, xxvii.

12. Gadamer, *WM*, 1. See also Westphal, *Whose Community?*, 69.

13. Gadamer, *TM*, xxii.

14. Gadamer, *TM*, xxii.

15. See again Gadamer, *TM*, xx–xxi.

16. Gadamer, *TM*, xxii.

17. Gadamer, *TM*, xxv–xxvi. In the preface to the Second Edition (xxv), Gadamer expounds more on his intentions: "I did not intend to produce a manual for guiding understanding in the manner of the earlier hermeneutics. I did not wish to elaborate a system of rules to describe, let alone direct, the methodical procedure of the human sciences. Nor was it my aim to investigate the theoretical foundation of work in these fields in order to put my findings to practical ends." Cf. Palmer, "Heideggerian Elements," 122. Thiselton (*Two Horizons*, 293) calls it ironic that Gadamer would include the word "method" in the title of his work on hermeneutics. Hirsch, *Validity*, 245, also calls it "somewhat ironic." On this, cf. Weinsheimer, *Gadamer's Hermeneutics*, xi–xii.

18. Gadamer, *TM*, xxvi.

19. Gadamer, *TM*, xxvi.

understanding possible?"[20] Through his analysis of the experience of a work of art, a whole new "realm" begins to emerge, which itself "transcends" scientific methodology in its pursuit of truth.[21] The central point of Gadamer's work is the attention he gives to the interpreter's historical situation.[22] He speaks of how "history does not belong to us; we belong to it."[23] What has served to shape one's understanding has been one's tradition, i.e., things like "family, society, and the state in which we live."[24] Before developing these ideas, he first examines aesthetic consciousness, attempting to establish the idea that one's experience of art is a means by which truth can be attained— and that apart from method. Anticipating this analysis, Gadamer offers preliminary observations that will lend to his aesthetic critique, which will in turn tie into his theses of experience and tradition (mentioned above).

The Problem of Method and *Bildung* as Solution

The first section in *Truth and Method* is entitled "The Problem of Method." Here, he begins by observing that "The logical self-reflection that accompanied the development of the human sciences [Geisteswissenschaften] in the nineteenth century is wholly governed by the model of the natural sciences [Naturwissenschaften]."[25] The problem is that the *Naturwissenschaften* have been the model by which the *Geisteswissenschaften* have been studied. Gadamer faults Mill for giving preferred status to the methodology of natural sciences.[26] Droysen, too, is criticized for wanting a scientific approach to the human sciences in the spirit of Kant.[27] Gadamer even takes issue with Dilthey. The latter, it is remembered, pursued a methodology which took its cues from the natural sciences, though he did, admittedly, attempt to grant independence to the human sciences.[28] But attempts and intentions

20. Gadamer, *TM*, xxvii; cf. Risser, "Gadamer's Hidden Doctrine," 5.

21. Thiselton, *Two Horizons*, 294.

22. Cf. Hirsch, *Validity*, 245–46. Hirsch does not see the novelty of Gadamer's hermeneutic theory as being his assessment of the historical situation, but rather "his mode of presentation," specifically as he "introduces new concepts and gives old words new meanings" (245). Hirsch lists things like *Vorurteil, Horizontverschmelzung, Wirkungsgeschichte*, and art as *Spiel* (245–46), all of which are covered below.

23. Gadamer, *TM*, 278. See also Luz, *Matthew in History*, 25.

24. Gadamer, *TM*, 278.

25. Gadamer, *TM*, 3; Gadamer, *WM*, 9.

26. Gadamer, *TM*, 3; Gadamer, *WM*, 9.

27. Gadamer, *TM*, 5–6.

28. Gadamer, *TM*, 6–7.

are not that beneficial if results are not produced, and Gadamer was quick to recognize this in Dilthey. But if science did not please Gadamer's criteria, what was his own alternative? At this point, Gadamer recognized the profound influence of Herder's notion of *Bildung*, which embodies the "*concept of self-formation, education, or cultivation.*"[29]

Bildung was an important idea for Gadamer because he saw in it the very principle from which the *Geisteswissenschaften* could be based. What science could not do for the human sciences, *Bildung* could.[30] Thus, *Bildung* became part of the solution to the problem of method. *Bildung*, broadly, entails the idea of one encountering the "other," that is, "keeping oneself open to what is other—to other, more universal points of view."[31] Specifically, *Bildung* concerns the idea of formation, namely, that the thing that forms oneself is not lost, but rather "absorbed" into it.[32] Thus, the "other" has been "preserved," and because of this very fact, *Bildung* itself ought to be seen as a "genuine historical idea."[33] This connection with historicality proves to be an important link in Gadamer's conception of understanding. Gadamer views *Bildung* as chained to the idea of "a universal and common sense."[34] Like every other "sense," *Bildung* implies openness to its surroundings.[35] Again, one must not forget that his concept of *Bildung* remains the alternative to the scientific method in being the model for the *Geisteswissenschaften*. Thus, his idea of *Bildung* as "universal and common sense,"[36] and fundamentally as a "genuine historical idea,"[37] is his way of saying that

29. Gadamer, *TM*, 8.

30. See Thiselton, *Hermeneutics*, 212, who remarks, "What is the role of 'method,' Gadamer asks, for the *Geisteswissenschaften*, or humanities, literature, and social science? It is all very well, perhaps, for the sciences, as Droysen, Mill, or even Dilthey conceived of 'science.' The humanities, or Geisteswissenschaften, however are based on *Bildung*, or formative culture."

31. Gadamer, *TM*, 15.

32. Gadamer, *TM*, 10.

33. Gadamer, *TM*, 10.

34. Gadamer, *TM*, 15–16.

35. Gadamer, *TM*, 16. This is what I take Gadamer to mean when he uses the example of sight, saying, "Thus the cultivated consciousness has in fact more the character of a sense. For every sense—e.g., the sense of sight—is already universal in that it embraces its sphere, remains open to a particular field, and grasps the distinctions within what is opened to it in this way. In that such distinctions are confined to one particular sphere at a time, whereas cultivated consciousness [gebildete Bewußtsein] is active in all directions, such consciousness surpasses all of the natural sciences. It is a *universal sense*" (Gadamer, *TM*, 16; Gadamer, *WM*, 23).

36. Gadamer, *TM*, 16.

37. Gadamer, *TM*, 10.

truth, as attained in the *Geisteswissenschaften*, is found in a way other than scientific methodology. In other words, truth can be discovered via historical cultivation and formation, by *Bildung*.[38]

The idea of historicality that Gadamer says is in inherent to the concept of *Bildung* will be further established when he proceeds to investigate the "*humanistische Tradition*" ("*humanistic tradition*"), which will lead him to the idea of the *sensus communis*, and from there, his critique of aesthetic consciousness.[39]

Sensus Communis

Gadamer begins his discussion about the Roman concept of the *sensus communis* with Vico.[40] Gadamer is quick to recognize that Vico is working from a "humanistic tradition that stems from antiquity."[41] He traces this tradition back to the ancient Greeks—to the disputes between the primacy of "philosophy" over and against "rhetoric" (and vice versa).[42] A point of major contention between the Greeks was "the contrast between the scholar and the wise man on whom the scholar depends."[43] He adds that this is "a contrast that is drawn for the first time in the Cynics' conception of Socrates—and its content is based on the distinction between the ideas of sophia and phronesis."[44] The former is concerned more with the theoretical aspect of knowledge, whereas the latter concerns itself with practical knowledge.[45] Gadamer notes that this same conception had been carried down to the time of the latter Roman period, where ideas were aimed more toward "the practical ideal of phronesis than to the theoretical ideal of sophia."[46] What remained helpful in Vico, says Gadamer, is that his conception of the *sensus communis* is focused away from the theoretical and more toward the practical, or more precisely, not on the "abstract" but on the "concrete" aspects of human existence.[47]

---

38. See again Gadamer, *TM*, 16, where he speaks of how "the nature of Bildung suggests an extensive historical context."

39. Gadamer, *WM*, 23–24; Gadamer, *TM*, 16–17.

40. Gadamer, *TM*, 17.

41. Gadamer, *TM*, 18.

42. Gadamer, *TM*, 18.

43. Gadamer, *TM*, 18.

44. Gadamer, *TM*, 18.

45. See Dostal, "Hans-Georg Gadamer," 259.

46. Gadamer, *TM*, 18.

47. Gadamer, *TM*, 19–21. See also Thiselton, *Two Horizons*, 294–95.

One can appreciate Gadamer's focus upon Vico's insights when his (Gadamer's) overall aims and intentions are remembered—namely, finding a legitimate alternative to the scientific approach for the *Geisteswissenschaften*. Vico provides Gadamer with the *sensus communis*, which "obviously does not mean only that general faculty in all men but the sense that founds community."[48] Of course, "community" is the point of study in the *Geisteswissenschaften*. Gadamer remarks that

> There is something immediately evident about grounding philological and historical studies and the ways the human sciences work on this concept of the sensus communis. For their object, the moral and historical existence of humanity, as it takes shape in our words and deeds, is itself decisively determined by the sensus communis. Thus a conclusion based on universals, a reasoned proof, is not sufficient, because what is decisive is the circumstances.[49]

By highlighting the primacy of "circumstances" (*Umstände*) as opposed to "universals" (*Allgemeinen*), the connection with the ancient Greek distinction between *sophia* and *phronesis*, the theoretical and the practical, becomes clear.[50] Thus the significance of "circumstances" and *phronesis* (practical knowledge) remains central. Gadamer will suggest that this is so because humans are situated within tradition, being historically-effected by it.[51] Gadamer is concerned with Vico to show that, contrary to popular

---

48. Gadamer, *TM*, 19.

49. Gadamer, *TM*, 20.

50. Gadamer, *TM*, 20; Gadamer, *WM*, 28. Cf. Kant, *Judgment*, 92–93.

51. On the connection between tradition (specifically in regard to the classics) and *phronesis*, see Atkinson, "Gadamer's Hermeneutics," 285–306, esp. 286–87. Atkinson's essay offers a balanced approach to the question and role of "tradition" in Gadamer's hermeneutic. Specifically, she argues against those who say that tradition played a mere passive role and that it leaves no room for any substantive critique (see esp. 289–92). Additionally, Atkinson takes exception with those who see Gadamer's tradition-centered hermeneutic as a form of "Aristotelian elitism," where those who blindly go along with society's traditions are deemed as "good" and those who do not follow tradition as "bad." Atkinson asks if this is what Gadamer is doing with his concept of "tradition." She says, "My short answer to this [question] is, no. Rather, Gadamer is merely defending Aristotle's claims regarding the nature of moral deliberation and *phronesis*. More specifically, he is proceeding from the premise that one must already be good or, at least, have been brought up with some concern for the good in order to become good. In other words, if someone is nurtured in an environment where no sense of right and wrong is inculcated or cultivated, then he cannot be expected to demonstrate any interest in ethical issues, nor is it likely that he will ask or even understand moral questions" (287). Atkinson goes on to say that the classical theorists remain central to Gadamer because of their insight into the fact that "tradition" plays an integral role in

opinion of the time, the *Geisteswissenschaften* need only to look within to find its own basis, for "the sense of the community mediates its own positive knowledge."[52] The *Geisteswissenschaften* do not need to be "measured by a standard foreign to it—namely the methodical thinking of modern science."[53] Simply put, the *Geisteswissenschaften* have their own built-in way of knowing. What Gadamer is hinting at is the notion that one's "knowing" and one's "understanding" are heavily facilitated by the *sensus communis*.[54] That being established, Gadamer moves toward a discussion of aesthetic consciousness, which will allow him to further establish the primacy of historicality, and from there, tradition. But first, a few further preliminary items need to be addressed.

"Judgment" and "Taste" as a Means to Truth beyond Method

Gadamer's discussions on "judgment" (*Urteilskraft*) and "taste" (*Geschmack*)[55] are necessary because they will provide the basis for his important appraisal of aesthetic consciousness (below). Gadamer says that "judgment" is similar to the *sensus communis* discussed above.[56] It is quite synonymous with the concept of common sense.[57] He notes that, historically speaking, the concept of "judgment" was deemed to be a "basic intellectual virtue," and that this idea was in line with English thinkers who believed "judgment" (moral and aesthetic) was not at all based upon "reason" but was more similar to the concept of "sentiment (or taste)."[58] Thus, the concept of judgment "cannot be taught in the abstract but only practiced from case to case, and is therefore more an ability like the senses. It is something that cannot be learned, because

---

the formation of virtue, because, for them, "one must be good in order to become good . . . [and it is true that] traditions may be political, religious, cultural, historical or some intersection or network of these various strains but no human person exists in a moral or value-free vacuum" (287–88).

52. Gadamer, *TM*, 20–21.

53. Gadamer, *TM*, 21.

54. Gadamer, *TM*, 25. See also his helpful discussion on Oetinger on 25–27, which is integral.

55. Gadamer, *TM*, 27–31, 31–37, respectively; Gadamer, *WM*, 36–40, 40–47, respectively.

56. Gadamer, *TM*, 27.

57. Gadamer, *TM*, 27. Thiselton (*Two Horizons*, 295) observes that "in the earlier German philosophical tradition, what was known in the English and French traditions as 'common sense' appeared in an altered form as 'power of judgment' (*Urteilskraft*)."

58. Gadamer, *TM*, 27.

no demonstration from concepts can guide the application of rules."[59] (Of course, this changed with Kant, who saw little need to let things like sentiment linger around discussions concerning these judgments—hence, perhaps, the outcome of his famous duty-based ethics.)[60]

Next, Gadamer addresses the concept of *taste*. "Taste is defined precisely by the fact that it is offended by what is tasteless and thus avoids it, like anything else that threatens injury."[61] Simply, taste is similar to "sense."[62] It is like a "sense," Gadamer says, because it is not governed by "reasons," for when "taste registers a negative reaction to something, it is not able to say why."[63] Gadamer acknowledges the communal element of taste, saying that it "operates in a community," though quickly adding that it "is not subservient to it."[64] The reason is because a person can exercise "judgment."[65] Interestingly, Gadamer concludes that taste and judgment are ways of knowing.[66] The way in which this happens "cannot be demonstrated," Gadamer says, because one simply "must have a sense for it."[67] Whatever taste and judgment may be specifically addressing in some "concrete" situation, it is doing so in view of a universal whole, though not by a method of "rules" *per se*.[68]

To illustrate, Gadamer considers moral judgments. Even when a person makes moral judgments, he says, one does not merely apply universal truths to specific situations in the sense of cutting and pasting them to some specific moral dilemma. In his view, rather, it is more like what happens in "jurisprudence, where the supplementary function of 'hermeneutics' consists of concretizing the law."[69] That is, laws, which have been codified (i.e., into a universal or whole) only exist in order to be applied (i.e., into a concrete circumstance or part). Thus,

> At issue is always something more than the correct application
> of general principles. Our knowledge of law and morality too is

59. Gadamer, *TM*, 27–28.

60. Gadamer, *TM*, 29; See also Thiselton, *Two Horizons*, 295–96; cf. Kant, *Judgment*, 169–73.

61. Gadamer, *TM*, 33.

62. Gadamer, *TM*, 32.

63. Gadamer, *TM*, 32.

64. Gadamer, *TM*, 33.

65. Gadamer, *TM*, 33. For the entire discussion, see 33–34. See also Kant, *Judgment*, 94.

66. Gadamer, *TM*, 33–34.

67. Gadamer, *TM*, 34.

68. Gadamer, *TM*, 34.

69. Gadamer, *TM*, 34. See also Gadamer, "Classical and Philosophical Hermeneutics," 59–60.

THE ARRIVAL OF PHILOSOPHICAL HERMENEUTICS   55

always supplemented by the individual case, even productively
determined by it. The judge not only applies the law in concreto,
but contributes through his very judgment to developing the
law ("judge-made law").[70]

The relationship between universal laws and its concrete application is
said to be such that the latter is active in "co-determining, supplementing,
and correcting" those universals.[71] What is important here is to remember
that Gadamer is subverting Kant's idea that aesthetic judgments are outside
the realm of knowledge of truth.[72] For Gadamer, concepts like taste are important, for "all moral decisions require taste."[73] Because "taste" functions
within a community setting, both critiquing and affirming it, the concretizing of universal morals to specific situations require special judgments.
But these judgments are not theoretical. On the contrary, by virtue of the
act of application (i.e., "concretization") itself, this is not grounded in pure,
abstract reason. It is not grounded in logic but in the *sensus communis*, that
is, common understanding. And this, ultimately, is an aesthetic process. Gadamer decries Kant, who taught that the aesthetic was not to be considered
a player in his own ethics.[74] All of this, Gadamer states, was detrimental to
the human sciences in general, since aesthetics (judgment and taste) was
"the element in which philological and historical studies lived," and it followed that, once Kant discarded the aesthetic component from the human
sciences, the only method available to it was that of the natural sciences.[75]

For Gadamer, one must remember that the concepts of "judgment"
and "taste" were utilized for more than just an evaluation of how communities (and individuals within them) function. His aims are higher: Matters
of "taste," "judgment," and matters of "universal laws" and "concretizing of
the law," inherent within the living, functioning relationship between individuals and communities are, at the end of the day, hermeneutical. Indeed,
for Gadamer, *all of life* is hermeneutical. His discussions on judgment and
taste, not least his exposition on *Bildung* and the *sensus communis*, bring the
reader to that point. Before this is completely developed, however, the question at hand needs to be answered: Contrary to Kant, can truth be found in

70. Gadamer, *TM*, 34.

71. Gadamer, *TM*, 35.

72. See the discussion in Gadamer, *TM*, 34–37.

73. Gadamer, *TM*, 35. Gadamer continues (35) by saying, though this is true that
taste is "required," this is not to say "that this most individual balancing of decision is the
only thing that governs [moral decisions], but [rather] it is an indispensable element."

74. Gadamer, *TM*, 36.

75. Gadamer, *TM*, 36–37. See Grondin, *Introduction to Philosophical Hermeneutics*,
109–10.

the aesthetic component? Gadamer asks, "Must we not also acknowledge that the work of art possess truth?"[76]

Kant's understanding of "taste" is such that he won't allow it "any *significance as knowledge*."[77] Gadamer goes on to say that Kant "reduces sensus communis to a subjective principle. In taste nothing is known of the objects judged to be beautiful, but it is stated only that there is a feeling of pleasure connected with them a priori in the subjective consciousness."[78]

The Concept of *Erlebnis*

Since Kant's "main concern" was to ground aesthetics upon the "subjective a priori . . . feeling of life" (as opposed to, as Gadamer put it, "[raising] the question of truth in the sphere of art"), in Gadamer's eyes, the Kantian program of *Lebensgefühl* ("feeling of life") demanded a response.[79] Here, Gadamer expounds upon the concept *Erlebnis* ("experience"). He traces the word etymologically, looking first at the older word *Erleben*.[80] *Erleben* implies the "immediacy" of one's experience, i.e., "to be still alive when something happens."[81] This type of knowing has nothing to do with logical conclusions or inferences, but rather one's own direct experience.[82] Next, he observes a second meaning, this time behind another cognate of the word *Erlebnis*, namely, *das Erlebte*. This refers to the "permanent content of what is experienced."[83] Thus, this word deals not with the immediacy of one's experience, but rather the "lasting result" of the experience itself.[84] Gadamer says that both meanings—the "immediacy" *and* "lasting result"— provide the foundation for *Erlebnis*. But why is this word important, and what does it have to do with understanding truth in art?

Gadamer remarks that *Erlebnis* first began to appear in biographical literature.[85] Within this genre, writers would use the word in such a way

---

76. Gadamer, *TM*, 37.

77. Gadamer, *TM*, 38.

78. Gadamer, *TM*, 38. See Kant, *Judgment*, 92–93, 188–96. See also Gadamer, *TM*, 38, 47–52.

79. Gadamer, *TM*, 52; Gadamer, *WM*, 65.

80. Gadamer, *TM*, 53.

81. Gadamer, *TM*, 53.

82. Gadamer, *TM*, 53.

83. Gadamer, *TM*, 53.

84. Gadamer, *TM*, 53.

85. Gadamer, *TM*, 53.

that both meanings (given above) would be understood.[86] Experience, then, was something that spoke of both the immediacy of experience and the "lasting importance" (*bleibende Bedeutung*) of "its being experienced" (*sein Erlebtsein*).[87] Gadamer traces the use of the word, as well as influences upon it, from Dilthey to Rousseau to Schleiermacher, Schilling, and Hegel.[88] He notes that, for Dilthey, *Erlebnis* is primarily "epistemological," in that it is the "basis for all knowledge of the objective."[89] The fact "that life (Leben) manifests itself in experience (Erlebnis) means simply that life is the ultimate foundation."[90]

Aesthetic Consciousness and Gadamer's Critique

But there remained a problem. The problem for Gadamer was that "abstraction remains part of aesthetic consciousness."[91] "What we call a work of art and experience (erleben) aesthetically depends on a process of abstraction."[92] Gadamer laments the fact that, in order to come to see a work of art as a "pure work of art," the process itself has pushed aside everything that has grounded the work of art itself (e.g., he mentions "its original context of life, and the religious or secular function that gave it significance").[93] He credits this to the fact that, for so long, the methodology of the natural sciences has been the mechanism by which the human sciences had been analyzed, which led "to discrediting all the possibilities of knowing that lie outside" scientific methodology.[94] Art had been divorced from "its original context of life."[95] Gadamer says further,

> aesthetic differentiation is an abstraction that selects only on the basis of aesthetic quality as such. It is performed in the self-consciousness of "aesthetic experiences." Aesthetic experience (Erlebnis) is directed towards what is supposed to be the work proper—what it ignores are the extra-aesthetic elements

86. Gadamer, *TM*, 53.

87. Gadamer, *TM*, 53; Gadamer, *WM*, 67.

88. Gadamer, *TM*, 53–55.

89. Gadamer, *TM*, 57; Thiselton, *Hermeneutics*, 213.

90. Gadamer, *TM*, 57.

91. Thiselton, *Hermeneutics*, 213.

92. Gadamer, *TM*, 74.

93. Gadamer, *TM*, 74.

94. Gadamer, *TM*, 73. He also faults Schiller (73) for leading to what he has coined the problem of "aesthetic differentiation."

95. Gadamer, *TM*, 74.

that cling to it, such as purpose, function, the significance of its content. These elements may be significant enough inasmuch as they situate the work in its world and thus determine the whole meaningfulness that it originally possessed. But as art the work must be distinguished from all that. It practically defines aesthetic consciousness to say that it differentiates what is aesthetically intended from everything that is outside the aesthetic sphere. It abstracts from all the conditions of a work's accessibility. Thus this is a specifically aesthetic kind of differentiation. It distinguishes the aesthetic quality of a work from all the elements of content that induce us to take up a moral or religious stance towards it, and presents it solely by itself in its aesthetic being.[96]

Thus, aesthetic consciousness works toward abstracting art from its context, aiming for the bare form, the pure form, of the art itself.

But Gadamer sees this as nonsensical: "Abstracting down to the 'purely aesthetic' obviously eliminates it."[97] The reason is that to observe and "recognize" something (say, a picture) is at the same time to "read" it.[98] "In fact, that is what ultimately makes a picture."[99] Gadamer will even claim this for listening to music, saying, "Even in listening to absolute music we must 'understand' it."[100] After all, "only when we understand it, when it is 'clear' to us, does it exist as an artistic creation for us."[101] All proposals, therefore, to see, read, or observe art in its *pure* form—as aesthetic consciousness under the authority of the natural sciences seems to have dictated—is, at the end of the day, an Enlightenment fiction. "Pure seeing and pure hearing are dogmatic abstractions that artificially reduce phenomenon. Perception always includes meaning."[102] What, then, is the answer to the aesthetic problem, which scientific methodology has brought upon the human sciences? "In order to do justice to art, aesthetics must go beyond itself and surrender the 'purity' of the aesthetic."[103] But how does one accomplish this? It was mentioned above that to perceive a work of art is at the same time to understand it (this was the heart of Gadamer's critique of the so-called "aesthetic

---

96. Gadamer, *TM*, 74. See "Aesthetic differentiation" in Lawn and Keane, *Gadamer Dictionary*, 9; Weinsheimer, "Gadamer and Aesthetics," 265.

97. Gadamer, *TM*, 77. See also Thiselton, *Two Horizons*, 296.

98. Gadamer, *TM*, 79.

99. Gadamer, *TM*, 79.

100. Gadamer, *TM*, 79.

101. Gadamer, *TM*, 79.

102. Gadamer, *TM*, 80.

103. Gadamer, *TM*, 80.

differentiation").[104] What Gadamer is working toward is the concept of *co-creation*, that is, a work of art (say, music or literature) is not to be reduced to bareness, for the very essence of art suggests that there is something to be actively perceived. Before Gadamer can elaborate further on the details, he needs first to address a pressing issue lurking in the background about the nature of interpretation with respect to works of art.

In reply to Paul Valéry's position that works of art are "not . . . completable" (and therefore "endlessly interpretable"[105]), Gadamer proceeds to ask, "If it is true that a work of art is not, in itself, completable, what is the criterion for appropriate reception and understanding?"[106] Does the meaning behind a work of art lie in the *genius* of the observer? Gadamer answers this in the negative:

> A creative process randomly and arbitrarily broken off cannot imply anything obligatory. From this it follows that it must be left to the recipient to make something of the work. One way of understanding a work, then, is no legitimate than another. There is no criterion of appropriate reaction. Not only does the artist himself possess none—the aesthetics of genius would agree here; every encounter with the work has the rank and rights of a new production. This seems to me an untenable hermeneutic nihilism . . . genius in understanding is, in fact, of no more help than genius in creation.[107]

---

104. Gadamer, *TM*, 79.

105. Weinsheimer, *Gadamer's Hermeneutics*, 96.

106. Gadamer, *TM*, 82. This is in the context of discussing Kant's concept of artistic "genius" and how this allowed for "inexhaustible . . . interpretation" (81), as well as how this became problematically unaccounted for when Kant's idea of genius was pushed aside and hence needs to be solved (see Gadamer, *TM*, 80–82). For background on this, see Weinsheimer, *Gadamer's Hermeneutics*, 94–100; see n107 below.

107. Gadamer, *TM*, 82. Weinsheimer, *Gadamer's Hermeneutics*, 95–96, says, "For Kant, genius differentiates the artist from the craftsman in that the products of the artist are complete in themselves, not by reference to a purpose; thus they are inexhaustibly interpretable because their interpretation does not stop when they have fulfilled some purpose. But whereas the use of the concept of genius declined as a credible way of explaining the distinctive character of the artist and the completeness of the artwork, the inexhaustibility of interpretation remained as a problem to be explained—by Gadamer as well as his predecessors. Valéry suggests that art is endlessly interpretable because, if it serves no purpose by means of which its completion can be determined, is itself essentially incomplete. It is as if Valéry conceives all works of literature as fragments, which require the reader to finish them. If the reader can in fact complete a poem, however, that implies he is in possession of precisely the power, the authority, and indeed the genius that the author lacked. But it seems clear that if we want to deny genius to the author, it will not do to transfer it to the reader."

If aesthetics cannot be based upon a criterion of genius—either that of the creator or interpreter—then what about the criterion of *Erlebnis*, which was discussed above? Gadamer dismisses that as well. To say that some "work of art is only an empty form, a mere nodal point in the possible variety of aesthetic experiences (Erlebnisse), and [that] the aesthetic object exists in these experiences alone" results in "absolute discontinuity."[108] He says,

> Following Lukács' ideas, Oskar Becker has stated outright that "in terms of time the work exists only in a moment (i.e., now); it is 'now' this work and now it is this work no longer!" Actually, that is logical. Basing aesthetics on experience [Erlebnis] leads to an absolute series of points, which annihilates the unity of the work of art, the identity of the artist with himself, and the identity of the person understanding or enjoying the work of art.[109]

Erlebnis, therefore, cannot be the foundation for the aesthetic experience. But if not genius or experience (*Erlebnis*), then what? What remains a suitable answer to the aesthetic problem? Considering the above observation that the aesthetic problem itself had to do with aesthetic consciousness and differentiation, and further that this was the result of the domineering of scientific methodology, is it possible that the overarching problem (as Gadamer himself believed) is none other than the false idea that truth can only come via scientific methodology? If it is true that scientific methodology is the only route to truth, then, at least preliminarily, Gadamer has shown that its conclusion of aesthetic differentiation (see above) has rendered troubling results. That said, Gadamer leads one to initially conclude that truth can, and in fact *does*, transcend methodology. But how so? It will be observed below how Gadamer turned not to scientific methodology for the answer, but to the concept of historicality.

Preliminary Discussion on Historicality and Tradition

Gadamer insists on the primacy of historicality.[110] "The pantheon of art is not a timeless present that presents itself to a pure aesthetic consciousness, but the act of a mind and spirit that has collected and gathered itself

108. Gadamer, *TM*, 82.

109. Gadamer, *TM*, 82 (Gadamer, *WM*, 101), citing Oskar Becker, "Die Hinfälligkeit des Schönen und die Abenteuerlichkeit des Künstler."

110. On "historicality" and "historicity" (not least in relation to "historicism"), see Lawn and Keane, *Gadamer Dictionary*, 80–82. See also Grondin, *Philosophical Hermeneutics*, 106–15.

historically."[111] What he means by being "collected and gathered" in a historical fashion is self-understanding. He says that having an "experience of the aesthetic" is a "mode of self-understanding."[112] Moreover, despite his scathing critique of aesthetic experience (*Erlebnis*), Gadamer's goal was not to dismiss experience *per se* and its role in the process of understanding. Rather, his aim was to bring out the fact that *Erlebnis*, as normally conceived, reduced self-understanding, indeed experience itself, to the precarious point of discontinuity (see above). Gadamer wanted to move beyond this. His question was, "how can one do justice to the truth of aesthetic experience (Erfahrung) and [still] overcome the radical subjectivization of the aesthetic that began with Kant's *Critique of Aesthetic Judgment*"?[113] In short, Gadamer wanted to acknowledge the prime role of experience (i.e., *Erfahrung*) in the process of understanding, but not fall into the trap of relegating the process itself to the level of subjectivism.[114] Art, he thinks, has more to do with truth, knowledge, and understanding than previously thought.[115] In fact, the end to which Gadamer is working is to bring validation to the idea that truth can come from the "experience of art itself."[116]

111. Gadamer, *TM*, 83.

112. Gadamer, *TM*, 83. Gadamer continues: "Self-understanding always occurs through understanding something other than the self, and includes the unity and integrity of the other. Since we meet the artwork in the world and encounter a world in the individual artwork, the work of art is not some alien universe into which we are magically transported for a time. Rather, we learn to understand ourselves in and through it, and this means that we sublate (aufheben) the discontinuity and atomism of isolated experiences in the continuity of our own existence. For this reason, we must adopt a standpoint in relation to art and the beautiful that does not pretend to immediacy but corresponds to the historical nature of the human condition. The appeal to immediacy, to the instantaneous flash of genius, to the significance of 'experiences' (Erlebnisse), cannot withstand the claim of human existence to continuity and unity of self-understanding. The binding quality of the experience (Erfahrung) of art must not be disintegrated by aesthetic consciousness" (83–84). See again the discussion above on the concepts of *Erlebnis* and aesthetic consciousness.

113. Gadamer, *TM*, 84.

114. It should be noted that, with respect to my investigation into Paul's use of the Old Testament, Gadamer's notion of historicality allows attention to be given to the past without precluding an emphasis upon newness. That is, Paul's reconstrual of the Old Testament is not an exercise of detachment from his Jewish heritage. Therefore, a focus on continuity with Old Testament Jewish motifs in Paul's thought is as crucial as a focus on what is new in Paul's interpretations.

115. See the important discussion in Gadamer, *TM*, 84, after he asks, "Is there to be no knowledge in art?" Cf. Palmer, "Heideggerian Elements," 126–27.

116. Gadamer, *TM*, 84. Thus, Bartholomew, *Hermeneutics*, 310, can say, "Gadamer argues that experience and not abstraction is the key to understanding art."

Reflections on Play

This leads to Gadamer's "concept of play."[117] Here he seeks to illustrate "the mode of being of the work of art itself."[118] What this means is that art, exhibited in Gadamer's conception of "play," is not to be seen in reference to some subject approaching the object (say, art); that is, an ultimate subject-object distinction ought not to be seen.[119] Of course, a distinction can be made in the sense that "play" and the "behavior of the player" can be detected.[120] However, these penultimate distinctions are not what define the essence of play itself. Never mind the player's cognitive inclinations, says Gadamer.[121] What matters most is not *what*, or *how*, or *why* the player is purposing and aiming to do with the game (e.g., for "recreation"[122]) but rather the built-in "seriousness" the game provides itself.[123] Thus, what really happens is not that the player is being distinguished from the game via the player's own purposes in playing the game, but that the "play fulfills its own purpose only if the player loses himself in play."[124] Therefore, when one looks to unpack the concept of play, one needs to look beyond the cognitive happenings within the player.[125] From this, it is easy to see where Gadamer is headed. Remembering the above discussion on the "genius of the creator" (as well as that of the reader), one is better positioned to see how Gadamer comes to find it implausible to ground the experience of art merely upon the subject's own feelings toward it. Again, he is using the concept of play to illustrate this fact.[126]

---

117. Gadamer, *TM*, 102; See also Eberhard, *Middle Voice*, 65, who says, "Gadamer's notion of play is indebted to the Heideggerian critique of modernity's subjectivism and of the concept of scientific objectivity. It is a continuation of Heidegger's thought but in a more accessible and concrete form. It helps bring to the fore the inadequacy of the dichotomy between subject and object." See also Dostal, "Hans-Georg Gadamer," 258–59; Wright, "Gadamer," 263–64.

118. Gadamer, *TM*, 102.

119. Gadamer, *TM*, 102–3; cf. Eberhard, *Middle Voice*, 63–64; Valgenti, "Tradition of Tradition," 71.

120. Gadamer, *TM*, 102.

121. Specifically, he discusses the "seriousness" the player lacks in the act of playing a game since, presumably, "play" is for relaxation (Gadamer, *TM*, 102–3).

122. Aristotle, *Politics*, VIII.1337b.39, quoted in Gadamer, *TM*, 102.

123. Gadamer, *TM*, 102. Cf. Gadamer, *Relevance of the Beautiful*, 123–30, esp. 130.

124. Gadamer, *TM*, 103.

125. Gadamer, *TM*, 103. See Thiselton, *Two Horizons*, 297; cf. Eberhard, *Middle Voice*, 69–71.

126. Gadamer says, "When we speak of play in reference to the experience of art, this means neither the orientation nor even the state of mind of the creator or of those

What mattered most to Gadamer is that, when it comes to art, it is not an aesthetic consciousness which entails the disastrous result of aesthetic differentiation, but rather "the experience (Erfahrung) of art and thus the question of the mode of being of the work of art that must be the object of our examination."[127] And so,

> Gadamer uses *Spiel* to counter the modern emphasis of subjec-
> tivity in general and aesthetic consciousness in particular. He
> moves against Kant's legacy and the subjectivation of art. Art
> is not the object of the so-called aesthetic consciousness; this
> consciousness is more than it thinks it is because art involves it
> in its play.[128]

On the one hand, Gadamer remained largely critical of experience (*Erlebnis*), wanting to dismiss it altogether as a proper ground for aesthet-ics in general.[129] Yet, on the other hand, he says that the "object of our ex-amination" is to be "the experience (Erfahrung) of art."[130] The confusion can be eliminated when one understands the differences between both *Erlebnis* and *Erfahrung*, despite the appearances of similarity in its English rendering, as both are translated as "experience." The former, of which Gadamer remained largely "critical," deals with experience in the sense of "immediacy," such that *Erlebnis* was associated with the critique of aesthetic consciousness and differentiation.[131] The latter, *Erfahrung*, is different. That is, "*Erlebnis* is something you have, and thus is connected with a subject and with the subjectivization of aesthetics. *Erfahrung* is something you undergo, so that subjectivity is overcome and drawn into an 'event' (*Ge-schehen*) of meaning."[132] With this, Gadamer mounts his case for concepts

enjoying the work of art, nor the freedom of a subjectivity engaged in play, but the mode of being of the work of art itself. In analyzing aesthetic consciousness we recog-nized that conceiving aesthetic consciousness as something that confronts an object does not do justice to the real situation. This is why the concept of play is important in my exposition" (Gadamer, *TM*, 102). See also Gadamer, *Relevance of the Beautiful*, 28.

127. Gadamer, *TM*, 103. Gadamer further says (103), "The 'subject' of the experi-ence of art, that which remains and endures, is not the subjectivity of the person who experiences it but the work itself. This is the point at which the mode of being of play becomes significant. For play has its own essence, independent of the consciousness of those who play. Play—indeed, play proper—also exists when the thematic horizon is not limited by any being-for-itself of subjectivity, and where there are no subjects who are behaving 'playfully.'"

128. Eberhard, *Middle Voice*, 66; see also Palmer, "Heideggerian Elements," 127.

129. See above.

130. Gadamer, *TM*, 103.

131. Weinsheimer and Marshall, "Translator's Preface," xiii. See above.

132. Weinsheimer and Marshall, "Translators' Preface," xiii. See also Thiselton, *Two*

like *historically-effected consciousness* and *tradition* as the basis for which the process of understanding might be grounded.[133] But first, what does the concept of play have to do with art?

Further Reflections on Play: Presentation

Gadamer takes the concept of play, as he has conceived it, and applies it to art.[134] First, Gadamer says that the "mode of being" of play is "self-presentation."[135] The idea of presentation serves as that which is common (a type of link) between play and art. "Gadamer shows from the examples of music and drama that the work of art consists of the performance itself."[136] For example, he talks about a "religious act" and a "drama" in the context of his discussion on play, where the former is a "genuine representation [*Darstellung*] for the community" and the latter is "a kind of playing that, by its nature, calls for an audience."[137] As a result, there exists a special unity and bond between the play and the audience, between the "religious rite" and the believer, such that the performance itself and the person's experience of it are essential for the acquisition of truth and meaning.[138]

Horizons, 297–98; Eberhard, *Middle Voice*, 127–28; Wright, "Gadamer," 262.

133. Though her comments are in regard to moral understanding specifically, see Atkinson, "Gadamer's Hermeneutics," 288, who offers invaluable insight into the differences between Gadamer's approach to understanding (via tradition and prejudgments) as opposed to those who operate under the sway of Modernism. These insights are important for what follows.

134. Thiselton, *Hermeneutics*, 213.

135. Gadamer, *TM*, 108; He says, "Das Spiel ist wirklich darauf beschränkt, sich darzustellen. Seine Seinsweise ist also Selbstdarstellung" (Gadamer, *WM*, 113). For his detailed exposition of the concepts of presentation and imitation, what they are not and what they are, see Gadamer, *TM*, 110–14, esp. 113.

136. Thiselton, *Two Horizons*, 298.

137. Gadamer, *TM*, 109; Gadamer, *WM*, 114. See also Weinsheimer, "Gadamer and Aesthetics," 265.

138. Gadamer, *TM*, 115. See also what he says about the "festival" in Gadamer, "Über Die Festlichkeit Des Theaters," 171 (Gadamer, *Relevance of the Beautiful*, 59): "Ja, Begehung ist die Seinsweise des Festes." Thiselton, *Two Horizons*, 298, says, "A drama exists only when it is played. Music is experienced not simply in reading the composer's score privately, but in the actual event of the concert. Moreover, each performance is an event in its own right. It is not merely a 'copy' of what went on in the consciousness of the composer. Indeed, we might say: it is not 'merely' an interpretation; it is a creative event in its own right." See also Eberhard, *Middle Voice*, 71, who says, "*Darstellung* is the culmination of play. Representation is central because it is the way of being of play. The actual purposes of the game is not the content of game, that which the rules specify. This is only *Scheinzweck*, 'illusory purpose.' . . . The presentation of play is most acute in theater play. When *Spiel* becomes *Schauspiel* play does not leak, so to speak, because of

Thus, Gadamer comes against the idea of aesthetic differentiation, which he considers wrong precisely on the grounds that one cannot describe an experience of a work of art in terms of the work's supposed *true form*, or bare arrangement.[139] And so, "truth is not to be reduced to a mere matter of concepts, but relates to experiences in broader terms."[140] The means by which one comes to understand art is in the experience of it—and this happens in its own presentation, which, again, is its mode of being.[141] Thus, Thiselton rightly comments that, for Gadamer, one cannot divorce the play or the art from its being presented.[142] Gadamer says, "A drama really exists only when it is played, and ultimately music must resound."[143] Gadamer, therefore, wants to advocate a type of *"aesthetic non-differentiation."*[144] This detail is important to Gadamer, for if one's experience of art is more than just an experience of it in its bare arrangement, and is therefore an experience principally in its presentation, then the role of the interpreter cannot be seen as insignificant. The point here is that all experiences of the real world are not to be understood in Cartesian terms—that is, by means of autonomous individuality—but rather by understanding that the person, far from being an autonomous subject, is in constant dialogue with the reality itself and, in fact, has been shaped by it.[145]

---

the openness toward the spectators. On the contrary, the spectators are part of the play's space or volume and fulfill the way of being of play."

139. See again Gadamer, *TM*, 115.

140. Thiselton, *Two Horizons*, 298.

141. See also Valgenti, "Tradition of Tradition," 71.

142. Thiselton, *Hermeneutics*, 213. See also Gadamer (*TM*, 125), who says, "The fact that aesthetic being depends on being presented, then, does not imply some deficiency, some lack of autonomous meaning. Rather, it belongs to its very essence. The spectator is an essential element in the kind of play we call aesthetic." To illustrate this last claim, Gadamer expounds upon Aristotle's *Poetics* in order to discuss the concept of tragedy, for it is "there the spectator's frame of mind figures expressly in the definition of tragedy's essential nature." Gadamer goes on to describe the *"effect (Wirkung)"* that the tragedy has upon the reader, which he argues displays the fact that "the spectator belongs essentially to the playing of the play" (126). On this discussion, see 125–30. More will be said on how this works into our present concerns in the discussion on *Wirkungsgeschichte* below.

143. Gadamer, *TM*, 115. Here he states explicitly (115) that his "thesis, then, is that the being of art cannot be defined as an object of an aesthetic consciousness because, on the contrary, the aesthetic attitude is more than it knows itself. It is a part of the *event of being that occurs in presentation*, and belongs essentially to play as play."

144. Gadamer, *TM*, 116. Cf. Gadamer, *Relevance of the Beautiful*, 143–44.

145. Thiselton, *Hermeneutics*, 214; see also Eberhard, *Middle Voice*, 66; Luz, *Matthew in History*, 13–14. More will be said with *Wirkungsgeschichte* below.

Palmer notes the significance of the concept of play, pointing out a few accomplishments of Gadamer's exposition of it. He says that the work of art itself is no longer to be seen as "static," but rather a "dynamic thing."[146] That is, the experience of a work of art cannot be divorced from the work of art. The experience of the Mona Lisa, for example, is not reduced to an object of unintelligible jots and strokes. Much like a play or drama, its presentation belongs to its essence.[147] The essence of the picture is its being presented, being seen and understood. Its essence is to draw the viewer into a form of play. It is in this sense that Palmer sees a work of art as "dynamic." Thus, Palmer understands Gadamer as moving beyond the traditional hermeneutical distinction between subject and object, calling the distinction full of "inadequacy," saying, "It is precisely the experience of art which shows that the work of art is no mere object that stands over against a self-sufficient subject. The work of art has its authentic being in the fact that, in becoming experience, it transforms the experiencer; the work of art works."[148]

But how does the above discussion work into his overall project? It was noted above that art, like plays and dramas, is presentational. Its essence is performative, in that it is operative through the experience itself. The experience of art in terms of aesthetic differentiation—in what has been described as bare arrangement—ought to be, according to Gadamer, discarded. What counts is not that one experiences a work of art in terms of seeing it as it is in its basic form, but rather in the experience of being caught up in it.[149] That is, one's experience of it is such that the interpreter (e.g., audience) is an integral part to which the essential nature of the work of art itself (i.e., its presentation) is aiming. It is recalled that Gadamer, like Schleiermacher, saw hermeneutics as being a deregionalized discipline, in that it concerned all of life, not just philology, for example.[150] Hence, a line of continuity can be traced from Gadamer's discussions on the aesthetic experience, art, and play to that of the historicality of understanding in general. Palmer's way of describing Gadamer's idea of historicality is helpful:

> Gadamer's hermeneutics and his critique of historical consciousness assert that the past is not like a pile of facts which can

146. Palmer, *Hermeneutics*, 174.

147. See Gadamer, *TM*, 126. On the ontology of picture (in comparison to the performance arts such as dramas), see Gadamer, *TM*, 130–38.

148. Palmer, *Hermeneutics*, 174.

149. See again the discussion on *Erlebnis* and *Erfahrung* above.

150. See again chapter 2 above. Cf. McLean, *Biblical Interpretation*, 176–77. McLean says (177) that Gadamer "argued that the humanities and the natural sciences are *both* a subspecies of a universal practice of hermeneutics."

be made an object of consciousness, but rather is a stream in which we move and participate, in every act of understanding. Tradition, then, is not over against us but something in which we stand and through which we exist; for the most part it is so transparent a medium that it is invisible to us—as invisible as water to a fish.[151]

It is important to avoid confusion on the connection between Gadamer's discussion on the aesthetic and aesthetic consciousness and his concepts of historicality and tradition. What does historicality have to do with aesthetic consciousness? Palmer is quite correct in connecting the two with one another.[152] He laments that some evaluate works of art (specifically literary works of art) under the influence of aesthetic differentiation—that is, in the *bareness* of the work itself (i.e., the "formal aspects"), denying the temporal place and historicality of the same.[153] "To discuss the meaning of the work for the present day would seem to have no justifiable place in their philosophy of a literary work; indeed the tension between the past and present is often swallowed up in the timeless ahistoricality of formal analyses of poetry."[154] The point, therefore, is that, since aesthetic consciousness and experience cannot be reduced down to a mere evaluation of a work of art's bareness, but in its presentation, then according to Gadamer, this necessitates a hermeneutical doctrine of historicality. The work of art, although being rooted in the past, is constantly being experienced in the present. Hence, one can see the resulting effect this has on the nature of interpretation. Thus,

> Gadamer insists that in the case of a work of art its actual being cannot be detached from its representation (*Darstellung*). Hence the *reality* of something written or presented in the past is not recaptured by mere subjective recollection. Gadamer explicitly cites the Lutheran emphasis on preaching or the Catholic view of the mass as examples in which reality is disclosed *afresh*. Interpretation is not a mechanical reproduction of the past in the present, but a creative event in its own right.[155]

151. Palmer, *Hermeneutics*, 176–77. See also Luz, *Matthew in History*, 25.

152. Palmer, *Hermeneutics*, 162–80. Palmer discusses the issue of aesthetics on 162–76, then he immediately segues into a discussion on Gadamer's critical concept of historicality.

153. Palmer, *Hermeneutics*, 175–76.

154. Palmer, *Hermeneutics*, 175–76.

155. Thiselton, *Two Horizons*, 298–99. Cf. Valgenti, "Tradition of Tradition," 71, who says, "The work of art is an exemplar of tradition because any artistic creation is at once an appropriation of a history of artistic effects and the handing-over of a new work to the ongoing history of art." Thus, there is a conceptual link between Gadamer's

For Gadamer, contemporaneity (*Gleichzeitigkeit*) is central to interpretive activity.[156] Gadamer's project, therefore, is concerned with how the pastness of a work of art (e.g., literature) is opened up into the present experience of the same.[157] His hermeneutic, again, is not concerned with *what* methodology needs to be developed to make this dialogue happen; rather he is concerned more with developing an account as to *how* this happens with each and every encounter with a work of art—whether that be a picture, drama, or literature.[158]

The above discussion on aesthetics must be bridged to what follows, namely, to the problem of historical distance and from there, textual considerations. Thus, it is helpful to note that for Gadamer, art is to be seen as an exemplar for the question of hermeneutics because "art is never simply past but is able to overcome temporal distance by virtue of its own meaningful presence," and "even though it is no mere object of historical consciousness, understanding art always includes historical mediation."[159] Indeed, historical mediation is key to the phenomenon of understanding, and it remains integral to Gadamerian hermeneutics.

---

discussion of aesthetics and his upcoming one on tradition (see below).

156. Gadamer (*WM*, 132–33; *TM*, 123–24) says, "Jedenfalls kommt dem Sein des Kunstwerks 'Gleichzeitigkeit' zu. Sie macht das Wesen des 'Dabeiseins' aus . . . In diesem Sinne kommt Gleichzeitigkeit besonders der kultischen Handlung, auch der Verkündigung in der Predigt, zu. Der Sinn des Dabeiseins ist hier die echte Teilhabe am Heilsgeschehen selbst. Niemand kann zweifeln, daß die ästhetische Unterscheidung, etwa der 'schönen' Zeremonie oder der 'guten' Predigt, angesichts des an uns ergehenden Anspruchs fehl am Platze ist. Nun behaupte ich, daß für die Erfahrung der Kunst im Grunde das gleiche gilt."

157. Palmer, *Hermeneutics*, 176. Gadamer sees "the festival" and its "enactment" as paradigmatic of this hermeneutical project, saying, "Ja, Begehung ist die Seinsweise des Festes, und in aller Begehung ist Zeit zum nunc stans einer erhebenden Gegenwart geworden. Erinnerung und Gegenwart sind darin eins" (Gadamer, "Über Die Festlichkeit Des Theaters," 171; Gadamer, *Relevance of the Beautiful*, 59). See also Gadamer, "Hermeneutics as a Theoretical and Practical Task," 253.

158. See Gadamer, *TM*, 512.

159. Gadamer, *TM*, 158. At this point, Gadamer compares the two approaches of Schleiermacher and Hegel. Schleiermacher was preoccupied with reconstruction; that is, he thought hermeneutics ought to be concerned with reconstructing the original place in which the object under consideration once stood, its "original occasion and circumstances" (Gadamer, *TM*, 158–59). Gadamer calls this "nonsensical" (159). Instead of reconstructing the past "nodal point [which originally existed] in the artist's mind" (159), Gadamer opts for a more Hegelian conception of hermeneutics (160–61). Hegel, he says, understood that "the essential nature of the historical spirit consists not in the restoration of the past but in *thoughtful mediation with contemporary life.* . . . In this way his idea of hermeneutics is fundamentally superior to Schleiermacher's" (161).

Tradition, Temporal Distance, and Historicality

Gadamer credits Heidegger (*contra* the Romantics and Schleiermacher) for bringing a "decisive impetus" to hermeneutic theory.[160] Schleiermacher and the romanticism of which he was part were both committed to psychologism (see above). Because of Heidegger, Gadamer argues, the task of hermeneutics cannot be reduced to the reconstruction of the author's mind.[161] That is to say, "the meaning of a text goes beyond its author."[162] Gadamer is hesitant to pick up on the same language used by others who say that the task is always to understand a text better than the author; on the contrary, he says, "Understanding is not, in fact, understanding better, either in the sense of superior knowledge of the subject because of clearer ideas or in the sense of fundamental superiority of conscious over unconscious production. It is enough to say that we understand in a *different* way, *if we understand at all*."[163] This happens due to the fact of temporal distance, that is, the time-difference of the original location of the text and its later interpreter. This temporal distance should not be seen as problematic, "not something that must be overcome."[164] On the contrary, the temporal distance between, for example, the text in its originality and its later interpreter, actually proves to be the foundation for interpretation in general.[165] Gadamer calls it a "positive and productive condition enabling understanding."[166] But how could something as seemingly problematic as temporal distance be a positive thing? One reason is because temporal distance itself is "filled with the continuity of custom and tradition, in the light of which everything handed down presents itself to us."[167] This is a significant feature of Gadamer's hermeneutic.[168] One notices Heidegger's influence. In the previous

160. Gadamer, *TM*, 296.

161. Gadamer, *TM*, 296.

162. Gadamer, *TM*, 296. Cf. an objection to this in Hirsch, *Validity*, 249. Cf. Gadamer, *TM*, 328; Vessey, "Gadamer and the Fusion of Horizons," 533; Atkinson, "Gadamer's Hermeneutics," 298–99. See also Hirsch, *Validity*, 1–23, esp. 14–19. Cf. Porter, "Biblical Hermeneutics and Theological Responsibility," 35–36.

163. Gadamer, *TM*, 296. Against this, see Hirsch, *Validity*, 252–54. Cf. Schleiermacher, *Hermeneutics*, 112.

164. Gadamer, *TM*, 297. Gadamer says (297) that the desire to "overcome" the temporal distance was nothing more than "the naïve assumption of historicism, namely that we must transpose ourselves into the spirit of the age, think with its ideas and thoughts, not with our own, and thus advance toward historical objectivity."

165. Gadamer, *TM*, 297.

166. Gadamer, *TM*, 297.

167. Gadamer, *TM*, 297.

168. Significant as tradition may be to Gadamer's hermeneutic, it is not without

chapter, where Heidegger was discussed, it was said that, integral to his own thought, was the idea that understanding was not about a subject approaching, critiquing, or possessing anything. The situation was more intuitive. Therefore,

> Understanding is conceived not as something to be possessed but rather as a mode or constituent element of being-in-the-world. It is not an entity in the world but rather the structure in being which makes possible the actual exercise of understanding on an empirical level. Understanding is the basis for *all* interpretation; it is co-original with one's existing and is present in every act of interpretation.[169]

It becomes easy to see how Gadamer's project of ontological hermeneutics would remain indebted to Heidegger, for tradition and historicality, in the case of Gadamer, remain central.[170] Emphatically, he states that "history does not belong to us; we belong to it."[171] Thus we are historical beings, having been enveloped, even formed, by our traditions.[172] This remains hermeneutically significant, for,

> Every age has to understand transmitted text in its own way, for the text belongs to the whole tradition whose content interests the age and in which it seeks to understand itself. The real meaning of a text, as it speaks to the interpreter, does not depend on the contingencies of the author and his original audience. It certainly is not identical with them, for it is always co-determined also by the historical situation of the interpreter and hence by the totality of the objective course of history.[173]

---

detractors. See Atkinson, "Gadamer's Hermeneutics," 285–86. Atkinson notes that there have been two main objections to Gadamer's hermeneutical theory. It is interesting to note that, at least according to her, these objections are somewhat ironic, since "they seem to contradict one another" (285). That is to say, she says some critics (Caputo and Warnke) see Gadamer as giving unwarranted authority to tradition, and hence being too conservative. On the opposite end of the spectrum, she notes (286) that others (e.g., Hirsch) deem Gadamer too relativisitic, and hence too liberal (though she herself does not use the word).

169. Palmer, *Hermeneutics*, 131.

170. See Valgenti, "Tradition of Tradition," 71. Valgenti says, "Gadamer's recovery of prejudice, authority, and tradition takes up, and in so doing transforms, the critical legacy handed down from Heidegger's analysis of historicality." He goes on to say (71) that Gadamer has contributed to this legacy with his introduction to it the concept of play. Cf. Hirsch, *Validity*, 256–57. See also Hoy, *Critical Circle*, 43–44.

171. Gadamer, *TM*, 278.

172. So Eberhard, *Middle Voice*, 149. Cf. Atkinson, "Gadamer's Hermeneutics," 302.

173. Gadamer, *TM*, 296. For opposing views on textual meaning being "identical"

By giving prime place to tradition, Gadamer sought to travel a route different than psychologism, which maintained that what ultimately mattered was the author's state of mind in its originality (*à la* Schleiermacher). On the contrary, the hermeneutical process for Gadamer was not about the mental states of the author, but rather the co-determined development of both the text *and* the interpreter's historicality. It is in this vein, moreover, that, by giving prime place to tradition, Gadamer counters enlightenment dogma in that he "refuses to set reason in opposition to tradition."[174] Thiselton remarks that

> Gadamer rejects the Enlightenment outlook which suspects all tradition and authority merely because it is tradition and authority. The acceptance of authority, he argues, is not necessarily blind or irrational obedience. It may be based on the thoroughly rational insight that as an individual of a particular historical generation I have my own built-in limitations, and may stand in need of learning from a source which has a better understanding of something than I do.[175]

Gadamer mentions other positive facets that temporal distance brings to light.[176] When one is removed from the historical situation from which an object originated and discovers that he or she is found to be situated in a *subsequent* historical situation, then the essence of the object can be more clearly discerned.[177] This is easier to see when one compares their observation of a piece of art that is contemporaneous with them. Gadamer says that we come to these familiar artworks "with unverifiable prejudices [Vorurteile], presuppositions that have too great an influence over us for us to know about them; these can give contemporary creations an extra resonance that does not correspond to their true content and significance."[178] Of course, it is relatively clear what Gadamer means. Temporal distance removes the interpreter from the object in such a way that, far from being unhelpful, serves to accomplish the hermeneutical task. "Only when all their relations to the present time have faded away can their real nature appear, so that the understanding of what is said in them can claim to be

---

to the author and his/her first audience as well as the co-determined nature of meaning, see Hirsch, *Validity*, 251–52, 253–54, respectively.

174. Bartholomew, *Hermeneutics*, 310.

175. Thiselton, *Two Horizons*, 305. See Gadamer, *TM*, 278–85; Gadamer, "Rhetorik," 123–24. See also Palmer, *Hermeneutics*, 183.

176. Gadamer, *TM*, 297–99.

177. See Palmer, *Hermeneutics*, 184–85; Palmer, "Heideggerian Elements," 122.

178. Gadamer, *TM*, 297; Gadamer, *WM*, 302–3.

authoritative and universal."[179] The point Gadamer makes is not that temporal distance allows one to read the text in such a way that he or she can know it as a purely historical text;[180] his point, rather, is that temporal distance actually allows something to be done *to* the interpreter such that, if it were not there, one could not come to understand the text at all. Moreover, Gadamer understands temporal distance as a sort of "filtering process," which can weed out the unhelpful prejudices mentioned above.[181] "Often temporal distance can solve question of critique in hermeneutics, namely how to distinguish the true prejudices [Vorurteile], by which we *understand*, from the *false* ones, by which we *misunderstand*."[182] But how is this the case? How does temporal distance, packed with historicity and tradition, go about this filtering process?

For Gadamer, when the interpreter "encounters" some "traditionary text," there is "provocation."[183] The interpreter's prejudices—whether helpful or unhelpful—meet *the other*, that is, the text. "In fact [the interpreter's] own prejudice is properly brought into play by being put at risk. Only by being given full play is it able to experience the other's claim to truth and make it possible for him to have full play himself."[184] Temporal distance provides

179. Gadamer, *TM*, 297; Gadamer, *WM*, 302–3. See also Palmer, *Hermeneutics*, 185.

180. Gadamer, *TM*, 297, admits, "It is true that what a thing has to say, its intrinsic content, first appears only after it is divorced from the fleeting circumstances that gave rise to it." But one must remember that Gadamer maintained that there is more to temporal distance than just this. After all, Gadamer is not content with offering yet another version of "historical consciousness," such that the interpreter seeks to know the thing in itself. One must not forget how Gadamer labored against the idea of (aesthetic) differentiation and how *that* discussion applies to this one. Gadamer (297) found the "implicit presupposition of [the] historical method" problematic because it operates from the wrong footing which claims "the permanent significance of something can first be known objectively only when it belongs to a closed context—in other words, when it is dead enough to have only historical interest." This is aesthetic differentiation all over again, only in the guise of historical studies. Contrary to this, Gadamer believes there is more to what temporal distance *does* than saying it simply means "the extinction of our interest in the object" (298). More will be said below.

181. Gadamer, *TM*, 298. See also Thiselton, *Two Horizons*, 306.

182. Gadamer, *TM*, 298; Gadamer, *WM*, 304. Gadamer (*TM*, 298) prefaces this with: "Not only are fresh sources of error constantly excluded, so that all kinds of things are filtered out that obscure the true meaning; but new sources of understanding are continually emerging that reveal unsuspected elements of meaning. . . . And along with the negative side of the filtering process brought about by temporal distance there is also the positive side, namely the value it has for understanding. It not only lets local and limited prejudices die away, but allows those that bring about genuine understanding to emerge clearly as such." See also Grondin, *Philosophical Hermeneutics*, 113.

183. Gadamer, *TM*, 298.

184. Gadamer, *TM*, 299.

the space in which provocation is possible, since the gap between the text and the interpreter is profound. But what brings about this profundity?

The answer is one's own historical situation. Gadamer says this was precisely the problem with previous thinking on the subject. The problem was such that historical studies focused exclusively on the object and failed to consider the historicity of the modern interpreter. Gadamer's conception of the hermeneutical task, however, is that the subject-object schema gives way to a harmony between both. This was what historical scholars failed to see.[185] The fact is that the interpreter's historicity and the effect of tradition play a highly significant facilitating role in the interpretive process. "We are *wirkungsgeschichtliches Bewusstsein*. . . . My consciousness is not a transparent, self-grounding vehicle that puts me in immediate contact with its 'object' but is rather a grounded opacity (or at best a translucency) that enables a richly mediate contact with its 'object.'"[186] Thus tradition is not a passive item we can choose to ignore, but rather an active and formative part which we cannot.[187] When a reader reads a text, he or she is engaging it, not objectively and freely seeing it in its pure form. Rather, the reader is engaging the text via the efficacious media called tradition:

> By *historically effected*, [Gadamer] means that human consciousness is always shaped by history, culture, tradition, and language, in such a way that every act of interpretation is always "effected" by these factors. Our sense of belonging to a history, culture, tradition, and language always *effects* our horizon of

185. See Gadamer's discussion about "the naivete of so-called historicism" (*TM*, 299). Note especially: "Real historical thinking must take account of its own historicity. Only then will it cease to chase the phantom of a historical object that is the object of progressive research, and learn to view the object as the counterpart of itself and hence understand both. The true historical object is not an object at all, but the unity of the one and the other, a relationship that constitutes both the reality of history and the reality of historical understanding" (299).

186. Westphal, *Whose Community?*, 74. See also Valgenti, "Tradition of Tradition," 72. Valgenti notes how Gadamer differs with Heidegger on this point, saying, "Gadamer's notion of the historically effected consciousness (*wirkungsgeschichtliches Bewußtsein*) marks a turn away from the 'existential' thread in hermeneutics and toward 'historical effect' as a structural possibility for human understanding, an 'a priori' that bridges the differential gap when horizons are fused." According to Palmer ("Heideggerian Elements," 123), Gadamer did not like the word "*Bewußtsein*" because "the term suggested that Gadamer was falling back into thinking about the human subject within a world of objects." According to Palmer, the use of the word was too problematic for Heidegger, and Gadamer himself conceded, acknowledging that he simply "could not find a better term" to use. See also Wright, "Gadamer," 263.

187. McLean, *Biblical Interpretation*, 182. See also Thiselton, *Two Horizons*, 307. Cf. Hirsch, *Validity*, 250.

meaning, how we think, what questions we ask, how we relate to
the past, and what we hope for in the future.[188]

Thus Atkinson can say, "Neither the Romantic ideal of interpretation as divination nor the Enlightenment's faith in the apriority of reason is acceptable
to Gadamer or to anyone who acknowledges that human beings are historically situated."[189] But how does this *wirkungsgeschichtliches Bewusstsein* play
out in the process of interpretation itself?

Vorurteil

For Gadamer, "there is no presuppositionless interpretation."[190] The interpreter's own prejudgments must be brought to light, for they "must inevitably come to the text with 'anticipatory ideas.'"[191] Heidegger's idea of the
fore-structure of understanding is to be recalled at this point. Gadamer
takes this idea and sees in the concept an integral part of the hermeneutical
process. The Cartesian notion that one can assess or interpret things in a
presuppositionless manner, knowing the thing itself in an unmediated and
direct way, is a myth.[192] The human situation itself—being embedded within
tradition, culture, and a social environment—entails this fact.[193] Therefore,

188. McLean, *Biblical Interpretation*, 180–81. McLean (182) explains further Gadamer's ideas of historically-effected consciousness and tradition, saying, "According
to Gadamer, one's historically effected consciousness is also formed by the religious
and intellectual tradition in which one finds oneself. By 'tradition' Gadamer means
the ongoing 'effective history' (*Wirkungsgeschichte*) of the past upon the present."
McLean also notes that this idea of tradition, i.e., its "happening," has significance for
biblical interpretation (see 183). See also the discussion in Gadamer, *Heideggers Wege*,
52 (*Heidegger's Ways*, 58). Cf. Eberhard, *Middle Voice*, 90–91, 94, 144–45; Grondin,
Philosophical Hermeneutics, 113–15; Luz, *Matthew 1–7*, 61–66; Luz, *Matthew in History*, 1–38, esp. 23–38. See also Evans, *Reception History*, 7–8, 14–16, on the translation
of *wirkungsgeschichtliches Bewusstsein* as well as avoiding the temptation to view it as
functioning either in only "passive" or "active" ways.

189. Atkinson, "Gadamer's Hermeneutics," 290.

190. Thiselton, *Two Horizons*, 304.

191. Thiselton, *Two Horizons*, 305.

192. Recall the discussion on aesthetic differentiation above.

193. The relationship between tradition and prejudice for Gadamer cannot be
overemphasized. Palmer, *Hermeneutics*, 183, is clear on this when he writes: "If there
can be no presuppositionless understanding, if, in other words, what we call 'reason'
is a philosophical construction and no final court of appeal, then we must reexam-
ine our relationship to our heritage. . . . Tradition furnishes the stream of conceptions
within which we stand, and we must be prepared to distinguish between fruitful presuppositions and those that imprison and prevent us from thinking and seeing. . . .
Ultimately, Gadamer asserts, the consequences of recognizing that there can be no

the idea of prejudice (*Vorurteil*) remains a central feature within Gadamer's hermeneutic.

It is true that one of the duties of a text is to encounter and adjust, if needed, the interpreter's own prejudgments; the text must be able "to speak what is new," and when it does, it can serve to "revise" the prejudgments that the interpreter brings to the reading.[194] But the interpretive process is not a one-sided monologue, where the text is given primacy over the interpreter and his or her prejudgments; rather, it is a dialogue of question and answer—between the text *and* the interpreter.[195] In understanding a text, then, the fore-structure of the process itself is important to the overall hermeneutical task.[196]

For Gadamer, then, *Vorurteile* should not be seen as adverse. Rather, contrary to the Enlightenment's demands, Gadamer wants to give "positive value" to the concept of prejudice.[197] This is in distinction to the Enlightenment, which taught that supreme authority was to be handed over to reason itself, and as a result, remained critical toward the idea of prejudice, as if it were something to be abandoned.[198] Though prejudice, in the sense of racial or gender prejudice, is by definition both negative and harmful, it seems that Enlightenment thinkers may have overstated their case. Gadamer says that it was only after the Enlightenment that prejudice began to be taken negatively.[199] Thiselton writes,

> In German legal terminology the term signifies a provisional
> legal verdict before the final verdict is reached. It was only the

---

presuppositionless understanding are that we reject Enlightenment interpretation of reason, and both authority and tradition win back a status they have not enjoyed since before the Enlightenment." Cf. Hirsch, *Validity*, 250–61.

194. Thiselton, *Two Horizons*, 304.

195. Gadamer discusses the "hermeneutical priority of the question" when he speaks about the interpreter's experiences with things in general, "We cannot have experiences without having questions. Recognizing that an object is different, and not as we first thought, obviously presupposes the question whether it was this or that" (Gadamer, *TM*, 356). He says further (360) that "the negativity of experience implies a question. In fact we have experiences when we are shocked by things that do not accord with our expectations." Specifically, the question-and-answer schema as dialogue is relevant for hermeneutics precisely because it characterizes the task of hermeneutics itself. In fact, he says (363) when the interpreter encounters an "historical text," the text itself "puts a question to the interpreter." Cf. Gadamer, *Relevance of the Beautiful*, 106; see also Gadamer, "Classical and Philosophical Hermeneutics," 70; McLean, *Biblical Interpretation*, 185–88.

196. See again the discussion on Heidegger above.

197. Gadamer, *TM*, 279.

198. Gadamer, *TM*, 279. This is precisely Gadamer's trouble with Descartes (see 280).

199. Gadamer, *TM*, 273.

rationalism of the Enlightenment, with its maxim, borrowed from Descartes, that nothing could be accepted which might in any way be doubted, that established the purely negative aspect of the term as the decisive one. Gadamer, by contrast, insists that prejudgments are more far-reaching and fundamental for hermeneutics than conscious cognitive acts.[200]

Thus, "Gadamer . . . reverses much of the sting of Enlightenment rationalism and idealism in his call for prejudice to be appropriated positively as part of the hermeneutic process,"[201] as he argues that there are such things as "legitimate prejudices."[202] Prejudices are in fact necessary for knowing anything at all: "Far from arguing that we must leave our prejudices behind, Gadamer claims that our prejudices are indispensable, for, without them, we cannot interpret anything."[203] Gadamer says,

> In fact, the historicity of our existence entails that prejudices [Vorurteile], in the literal sense of the word, constitute the initial directedness of our whole ability to experience. Prejudices are biases of our openness to the world. They are simply conditions whereby we experience something—whereby what we encounter says something to us.[204]

Thus, as a "contrast to Enlightenment attitudes, Gadamer sees all interpretation as always guided by its own prejudice."[205] On this, Gadamer took his cues from Heidegger's concept of the fore-structure of understanding.

> In the face of the sciences' emphasis on the acquisition of objective, universally valid knowledge, Gadamer developed an alternate model that emphasized the importance of appreciating one's own phenomenological *fore*-understanding (or preunderstanding), which both precedes interpretation and makes interpretation possible.[206]

Since prejudices enable understanding, one cannot ignore one's own prejudices.[207] They are the result of one's embeddedness within their own

200. Thiselton, *Two Horizons*, 305. See also Gadamer, *TM*, 273.

201. Bartholomew, *Hermeneutics*, 325.

202. Gadamer, *TM*, 278. See also Gadamer, *PH*, 9.

203. McLean, *Biblical Interpretation*, 184. See also Gadamer, "Classical and Philosophical Hermeneutics," 62.

204. Gadamer, *PH*, 9; Gadamer, "Die Universalität," 106.

205. Bartholomew, *Hermeneutics*, 310.

206. McLean, *Biblical Interpretation*, 177. Cf. Grondin, *Philosophical Hermeneutics*, 111.

207. See McLean, *Biblical Interpretation*, 184. For a critique of Gadamer's concept of

world.[208] Thus, prejudices are significant to interpretation simply because they are a very *real* and *effective* presence. They are part of the interpreter, due to his or her situatedness within tradition.[209] In fact, he says, "It is not so much our judgments [Urteile] as it is our prejudices [Vorurteile] that constitute our being."[210] Therefore, one cannot know anything about the world without them. For Gadamer, in fact, "understanding takes place as an event within a tradition."[211] This is so true, says Gadamer, that not even Enlightenment thinkers are immune to the presence of prejudice: "And there is one prejudice of the Enlightenment that defines its essence: the fundamental prejudice of the Enlightenment is the prejudice against prejudice itself."[212] That being the case, the interpreter—indeed, every interpreter—must be mindful of his or her own bias.[213] This is necessary, he states, "so the text can present itself in all its otherness," which is integral to the hermeneutical task, since it is a dialogue.[214] Thus, it would be a misconstrual of Gadamer's theory to posit that prejudices hinder the text from speaking; on the contrary, prejudices are (indeed, ought to be) taken into account *so that* the text can truly speak.[215] Since it is the case that "all understanding inevitably involves some prejudice,"[216] it must be accounted for in *any* description or theory of understanding—whether that be in regard to a theatrical play, a musical score, or even how an ancient text like the Old Testament can be meaningful for Paul.

Horizontverschmelzung

Integral to Gadamer's hermeneutic is the concept of "horizon."[217] Moreover, he defines understanding itself as the "fusion of . . . horizons"

Vorurteil, see Hirsch, *Validity*, 258–64. Cf. Atkinson, "Gadamer's Hermeneutics," 289.

208. Thiselton, *Two Horizons*, 305. Cf. Hirsch, *Validity*, 260–61.

209. Thiselton, *Two Horizons*, 306. Thiselton remarks (306): "Tradition does not stand over against thinking as an object of thought, but is the horizon within which we do our thinking." See again Palmer, *Hermeneutics*, 176–77; Evans, *Reception History*, 239.

210. Gadamer, *PH*, 9; Gadamer, "Die Universalität," 106.

211. Bartholomew, *Hermeneutics*, 310.

212. Gadamer, *TM*, 272–73.

213. Gadamer, *TM*, 271. So McLean, *Biblical Interpretation*, 184, who says that for Gadamer, "the goal of hermeneutics is not to eliminate prejudices but rather to bring them fully to the level of consciousness." See also Luz, *Matthew in History*, 28–30, esp. 30.

214. Gadamer, *TM*, 271–72.

215. See the careful delineation in Grondin, *Philosophical Hermeneutics*, 112.

216. Gadamer, *TM*, 272.

217. Gadamer, *TM*, 301.

(*Horizontverschmelzung*).[218] The idea is that every person operates from a specific "vantage point," which Gadamer labels a "horizon."[219] He grounds his idea of horizons upon the concept of "situation"—defined as that which "represents a standpoint that limits the possibility of vision."[220] Thus, when understanding is discussed in Gadamerian terms, it is described as the fusion of horizons—of both the text and its reader.[221] His concept of *Horizontverschmelzung* is linked, moreover, to his exploration of *Vorurteil*. "Gadamer . . . employed the term horizon itself to explain the role of one's preunderstanding in all interpretation."[222] In fact, "hermeneutics aims at prejudgments that will foster a fusion of the past with the present, thus facilitating the miracle of understanding, the sharing of a common meaning by temporally distant consciousnesses."[223] If *Vorurteile* are a necessary component in the process of understanding, then a definition of understanding itself will need to account for it. This is the heart of Gadamer's thesis.

It is important, again, to note that it is not only the interpreter who has a horizon, but also the text.[224] Thus,

> [the horizons of the text] constitute the virtual "unsaid" of every text. As such, the founding sense-event of a biblical text does not reside solely in its semantic content, in its words, phrases, and sentences: its "sense" is also structured by these phenomenological horizons, within which the texts have been suspended. Therefore, whenever we translate, read, or interpret a biblical

218. Gadamer, *TM*, 305. Eberhard, *Middle Voice*, 78–79, discusses the "ambiguity" in Gadamer's term *Horizontverschmelzung*. He says (79), "*Horizont* is singular, yet *Verschmelzung* denotes a melting into one another of more than one element." The fact that these two words are combined the way they are is important, Eberhard argues, because of the "apparent hesitation in Gadamer's description of the event of this fusion. [That is,] Gadamer appears to oscillate between accounts where there seems to be only one horizon and accounts where he assumes more than one" (79). Eberhard states that the ambiguity in the combination of the singular *Horizont* with the word *Verschmelzung* is not a "weakness" but it is, rather, "a way of saying that there is one and many horizon(s) at the same time" (79). See also Wright, "Gadamer," 263.

219. Gadamer, *TM*, 301. "The horizon is the range of vision that includes everything that can be seen from a particular vantage point" (301). See also Kögler, "Horizon," 400.

220. Gadamer, *TM*, 301. On the subtle differences between "horizon" and "situation," see Eberhard, *Middle Voice*, 91–92. See also Vessey, "Gadamer and the Fusion of Horizons," 530.

221. Gadamer, "Classical and Philosophical Hermeneutics," 62.

222. McLean, *Biblical Interpretation*, 177; Vessey, "Gadamer and the Fusion of Horizons," 530–31, touches on the link between horizon and preunderstanding. Cf. Thiselton, *Two Horizons*, 307; Eberhard, *Middle Voice*, 85.

223. Bartholomew, *Hermeneutics*, 311.

224. McLean, *Biblical Interpretation*, 191.

text, we always encounter as implied its phenomenological horizons, which are often, of course, strikingly different from our own contemporary horizons of meaning.[225]

While maintaining that there exists the "otherness" of each of these horizons—of the text *and* interpreter—understanding nonetheless occurs when a fusion takes place between the two.[226] For Gadamer, this does not mean that each horizon loses itself in the other and that "otherness" is lost; rather, both are respected and affirmed.[227] Moreover, understanding, which is the fusion of horizons, occurs not when "tension" between the two horizons is overcome (something Gadamer calls "naive assimilation"), but in the act of "bringing it out."[228] The idea here is that of a conversation.[229] Hence, each dialogue partner, in seeking to understand the viewpoint (i.e., "horizon") of the other, does not negate or disregard his or her own horizon in the process.[230]

The goal, simply put, is not for the reader to assimilate his or herself into the horizon (i.e., context, viewpoint, etc.) of the text itself. Again, the "otherness" of the reader *and* the text are to be respected.[231] "In simple terms, the *fusion* of horizons creates the possibility for the interpreter to see her phenomenological horizon and the phenomenological horizon of the text *at one and the same time*."[232] Citing Gadamer, Valgenti comments on the more general nature of the fusion of horizons, that is, its conceptual connection

---

225. McLean, *Biblical Interpretation*, 191. A true contextual awareness will account for this fact.

226. Gadamer, *TM*, 305. Contra Hirsch, *Validity*, 254–55, who sees the concept of *Horizontverschmelzung* as problematic, calling it an "inner contradiction," as it attempts "to fuse together the past and the present while still acknowledging their incompatible separateness." See also Hoy, *Critical Circle*, 14.

227. Gadamer, *TM*, 304. See Eberhard, *Middle Voice*, 87. Eberhard says, "Fusion of horizon(s) is not the subject's putting him or herself at a distance by catapulting him or herself into another horizon while attempting to leave him or herself behind. It is a process that situates him or her within itself. Fusion of horizon(s) is not engulfing and leveling but encompassing and involving." See also Weinsheimer, "Meaningless Hermeneutics?," 159–60.

228. Gadamer, *TM*, 305. See also Thiselton, *Two Horizons*, 307–8.

229. For the relevance this idea has for intertextual issues, see Watson, *Paul and the Hermeneutics of Faith*, 20–21.

230. See the discussion in Gadamer, *TM*, 302–4. See also McLean, *Biblical Interpretation*, 192; Vessey, "Gadamer and the Fusion of Horizons," 535.

231. On what *Horizontverschmelzung* is not, see Evans, *Reception History*, 240.

232. McLean, *Biblical Interpretation*, 192. Cf. Hirsch's critique (*Validity*, 252–54). See also the counterargument to Hirsch in Vessey, "Gadamer and the Fusion of Horizons," 525–36, esp. 526–32.

with tradition and interpreter: "Through 'the interplay of the movement of tradition and the movement of the interpreter,' the problematic gap between the object of a tradition and its audience becomes the site for his famed 'fusion of horizons.'"[233] Thus, everything comes full circle. Gadamer led up to the primacy of tradition through an extensive study of how truth is beyond methodology, which became clear with a treatment on the aesthetic. That, too, was made possible by examples of play and presentation. This, clearly, is how concepts like tradition, horizons, and prejudgments help make up Gadamer's notion of *Horizontverschmelzung*, which happens *on location*—that is, where, as Valgenti has said, "the object of a tradition and its audience" meet.[234]

Anwendung

For Gadamer, application, *Anwendung*, is not something which follows interpretation; on the contrary, it is part of it.[235] That is, one should see "not only understanding and interpretation, but also application as comprising one unified process."[236] Bringing Gadamer's thought into broad scope, Eberhard comments on the link between the discussion on play and application: "Just as play culminates in *Darstellung* as play's involving way of being, so fusion of horizon(s) culminates in *Anwendung* as the involving way of being of understanding history."[237] Helpfully, Gadamer illustrates the primacy of application in the interpretation from both legal and theological examples.

> In both legal and theological hermeneutics there is an essential tension between the fixed text—the law or the gospel—on the one hand and, on the other, the sense arrived at by applying it the concrete moment of interpretation, either in judgment or in preaching. A law does not exist in order to be understood historically, but to be concretized in its legal validity by being interpreted. Similarly, the gospel does not exist in order to be understood as a merely historical document, but to be taken in such a way that it exercises its saving effect. This implies that the text, whether law or gospel, if it is to be understood

233. Valgenti, "Tradition of Tradition," 72, citing Gadamer, *Truth and Method*.

234. Valgenti, "Tradition of Tradition," 72.

235. Gadamer, *TM*, 306. See also Gadamer, "Classical and Philosophical Hermeneutics," 59.

236. Gadamer, *TM*, 307. See also Eberhard, *Middle Voice*, 89–90; Grondin, *Philosophical Hermeneutics*, 115.

237. Eberhard, *Middle Voice*, 89. See also Hoy, *Critical Circle*, 53–54.

properly—i.e., according to the claim it makes—must be understood at every moment, in every concrete situation, in a new
and different way. Understanding here is always application
(Verstehen ist hier immer schon Anwenden).[238]

Gadamer's discussion on the essential role application plays in the
hermeneutical process is detailed.[239] He laments the fact that application
has been relegated outside the bounds of interpretive activity, saying, "The
edifying application of Scripture in Christian preaching, for example, now
seemed very different from the historical and theological understanding of
it."[240] It is easy to see why he says this, given his detailed analysis of historical consciousness and tradition. When it comes to interpretation, says
Gadamer, the goal is not to take the text, for example, and simply "repeat"
what it says and call *that* understanding.[241] On the contrary, the interpreter
is to "express what is said [or written] in the way that seems most appropriate to him."[242] For Gadamer, understanding is situational, that is, from the
standpoint of the particular questions that exist in one's place and time.[243]
Hermeneutics, then, is dialogical (see above). As Georgia Warnke observes,
"For Gadamer . . . all understanding is situated, not only in the sense that
we always understand *from* a particular perspective, but also in the sense
that we always understand *for* a particular situation."[244] This was the point
Gadamer brought in his examples from both theological and legal hermeneutics (see above).

Furthermore, for Gadamer, "what is truly common to all forms of
hermeneutics" is that "the meaning to be understood is concretized and
fully realized only in interpretation, but the interpretive activity considers
itself wholly bound by the meaning of the text. Neither jurist nor theologian regards the work of application as making free with the text."[245] One
cannot twist the text to his or her own fancy.[246] Thus, radical subjectivism

238. Gadamer, *TM*, 307–8; Gadamer, *WM*, 314. See also Thiselton, *Two Horizons*,
308; Dostal, "Hans-Georg Gadamer," 259.

239. Gadamer, *TM*, 321–36.

240. Gadamer, *TM*, 306.

241. Gadamer, *TM*, 307. See Luz, *Matthew in History*, 19.

242. Gadamer, *TM*, 307. Cf. the differences between Heidegger and Gadamer on
application in Atkinson, "Gadamer's Hermeneutics," 294. See also Grondin, "Gadamer's
Basic Understanding," 42–44.

243. Grondin, *Philosophical Hermeneutics*, 116.

244. Warnke, "Literature," 90; emphasis added. See also Luz, *Matthew in History*, 26.

245. Gadamer, *TM*, 328. See also Gadamer, *PH*, 208–11.

246. See again Grondin, *Philosophical Hermeneutics*, 112.

is *not* within Gadamer's purview.[247] Yet, this does not mean application to specific situations is any less part of the hermeneutical process either. Rather, it is central to it. "Understanding is not a theoretical activity, in which man scrutinizes the material before him as passive object. Indeed, in both legal and theological hermeneutics, Gadamer points out, the interpreter aims not at dominating the text, but at submitting to the will of the law or to the will of God."[248] And meaning—not least for biblical texts—proceeds beyond the horizon of the author.[249]

Gadamer illustrates this with the example of an order. "To understand the order means to apply it to the specific situation to which it pertains."[250] Simply repeating the order word-for-word is not what it means to understand, though repeating it back to the one who gave the order might prove beneficial for purposes of clarity.[251] How is repetition not understanding? Because "real meaning" is found only when the order is "carried out and concretized."[252] Gadamer thinks the order's meaning is realized when the situation to which it concerns is comprehended *and* in the actual obedience of the person carrying it out—both of which necessarily involves a level of

247. See Evans, *Reception History*, 230–33, and his comments on Gadamer's dialectical approach to understanding (and hence not objective or subjective). See again Grondin, "Gadamer's Basic Understanding," 42–44. See also Weinsheimer, "Meaningless Hermeneutics?," 159–60.

248. Thiselton, *Two Horizons*, 308.

249. See e.g., Gadamer, *PH*, 210, who says, "If by the meaning of a text we understand the *mens auctoris*, that is, the 'actual' horizon of understanding of the original Christian writers, then we do the New Testament authors a false honor. Their honor should lie precisely in the fact that they proclaim something surpasses their own horizon of understanding—even if they are named John or Paul. This assertion in no way entails an uncontrollable theory of inspiration or pneumatic exegesis. Such things would dissipate the gain in knowledge that we derive from New Testament scholarship. In fact, however, it is not a question of a theory of inspiration. That becomes clear if we consider the hermeneutical situation of theology together with that of jurisprudence, with the human studies and with the experience of art, as I have done in my efforts toward a philosophical hermeneutic. Nowhere does understanding mean the mere recovery of what the author 'meant,' whether he was the creator of a work of art, the doer of a deed, the writer of a law book, or anything else. The *mens auctoris* does not limit the horizon of understanding in which the interpreter has to move, indeed in which he is necessarily moved, if, instead of merely repeating, he really wants to understand."

250. Gadamer, *TM*, 329.

251. Gadamer, *TM*, 329.

252. Gadamer, *TM*, 329. Cf. Hirsch, *Validity*, 251–52.

creativity on behalf of the order's recipient.[253] Thus, application is not just an ancillary part of hermeneutics, but rather central to it.[254]

The implications of this will prove significant for an evaluation of all interpretive acts, not least Paul's. How might Gadamer's concept of *application* shed light upon Paul's use of Scripture? Since Gadamer's insistence that application plays a vital role in the complexity of the "hermeneutical process," it is conceivable Paul's interpretation of, say, texts like Hosea in Rom 9:25–26 can be described along these same lines—namely, as an act of fusing application and interpretation into a single hermeneutical event.[255] Having already noted the importance of considering the rhetorical place and function of the Hosea quotations in Rom 9:25–26, how does this fact cohere with Gadamer's thesis that application remains fundamental to interpretation itself? The striking thing about Paul's use of Hosea is that it, too, is being applied as (and in) a rhetorical event, namely, as an argument for the new covenant's full inclusion of the Gentiles.[256] In more ways than one, in fact, I think these insights can shed light not only on Paul's use of Hosea specifically, but also on Paul's use of the Old Testament generally.

SUMMARY AND FURTHER QUESTIONS

Part Two explored Gadamer's influence and scholarly context. Philosophers such as Schleiermacher, Dilthey, and Heidegger were thus surveyed. Gadamer's similarities and dissimilarities with each respective thinker have been noted. It was observed how Gadamer's hermeneutic sought to challenge the natural science's methodological approach, especially in regard to

253. See Gadamer, *TM*, 330: "The criterion of understanding is clearly not in the order's actual words, nor in the mind of the person giving the order, but solely in the understanding of the situation and in the responsible behavior of the person who obeys. Even when an order is written down so one can be sure it will be correctly understood and executed, no one assumes that it makes everything explicit. The comic situation in which orders are carried out literally but not according to their meaning is well known. Thus there is no doubt that the recipient of an order must perform a definite creative act in understanding its meaning." See also Gadamer, "Hermeneutics as a Theoretical and Practical Task," 256–57.

254. Cf. Gadamer, *Relevance of the Beautiful*, 148–49.

255. Gadamer, *TM*, 307. Cf. Watson, *Paul and the Hermeneutics of Faith*, 4.

256. In the introduction to Gadamer's 1978 essay *Hermeneutik als theoretische und praktische Aufgabe*, Palmer says, "Like rhetoric, Gadamer's hermeneutics thinks in terms of reception, of application" (Gadamer, "Hermeneutics as a Theoretical and Practical Task," 247). In the same article, Gadamer says, "What kind of an art hermeneutics is, then, we can learn from rhetoric" (251). See also Watson, *Paul and the Hermeneutics of Faith*, 20.

how it had been adopted and utilized by thinkers within the human sciences. Gadamer's argument was that hermeneutics did not need to adopt scientific methodology as the exclusive means to discovering truth and meaning. Rather, truth could be attained apart from a scientific approach. He argued for this by way of his critique of aesthetic consciousness, particularly aesthetic differentiation and abstraction. Using this critique as a springboard, Gadamer could dispel the myth that methodology was the only viable means to truth. Furthermore, Gadamer argued that rationalism, which had begun under Descartes with his commitment to unmediated knowledge of truth, ought to be discarded in favor of something more real to the human situation. The human situation, he argued, was one of *embeddedness* and *being thrown* into certain unique traditions—whether cultural or religious, or a mixture of both. Thus, Gadamer sought to recast the human situation in terms of historicality. Furthermore, tradition for Gadamer was efficacious; it impacts the way one interprets, not just texts, but all of life.

Through his reflections on play, Gadamer was able to illustrate the concept of presentation as the primary mode of being of art. A drama exists in being performed, a song in being sung, and a text in being read—each in individual, concrete moments and situations, however unlike the original situation in which they were founded. Moreover, one of the perceived problems of hermeneutics, namely, historical/temporal distance, turns out to be for him an enabling feature of interpretation itself. Because of his concepts of tradition and *Wirkungsgeschichtliches*, Gadamer argued that every interpreter brings with him or her prejudices, *Vorurteile*. These prejudgments, far from being inherently bad or debilitating, pave the way to understanding. The interpreter's situation, their *horizon*, is formed by these prejudgments and, when the interpreter interprets, say, a text, he or she is confronted by the prejudgments and traditions, which form the horizon, of the text. Thus, the opportunity for dialogue is possible. Understanding happens when a fusion of horizons takes place—a fusion between the horizons of the text and its interpreter.

Having laid out Gadamer's hermeneutic, with discussions on those concepts conducive to the hermeneutical task itself—among them items such as *Erfahrung, Spiel, Darstellung, Vorurteil, Horizontverschmelzung,* and *Anwendung*—I will allow my deliberations to come to bear upon the present matter, namely, Paul's use of the Old Testament in Romans. Specifically, Gadamer's ideas about prejudgments and application can be used to understand Paul's more problematic and revisionary interpretations. Thus, I will inquire into what factors shaped Paul's pre-understandings that may not immediately be explicitly evident from his text. Indeed, taking into account Paul's own prejudices—whatever they might have been—will go a long way in my project.[257] If Gadamer is right on the fundamental nature that *Vorurteile* play in the interpretive event, then an examination of Paul's prior-commitments will be indispensable to the task at hand.

If the task of "hermeneutics aims at prejudgments that will foster a fusion of the past with the present,"[258] how can this Gadamerian concept of understanding offer insight into how Paul's horizon and the horizon of the scriptural text came together? Specifically, how can Paul's quotations, and reconstrual, of Old Testament concepts, texts, and stories gain clarity in light of their different contexts? While maintaining the otherness of both the Old Testament texts and Paul, as well as their respective agendas, what are the key hermeneutical fore-structures of understanding that help show genuine fusion between the two? If application is interwoven into the entire hermeneutical process, and not relegated outside of it, how might this influence the way one understands Paul's use of the Old Testament? For example, could it be the case that, in light of the rhetorical role many of Paul's quotations play within his arguments, his use of those texts were what they were by virtue of their application (in the Gadamerian sense), that is, by their application within a new concrete situation—a situation *different* than what existed within the horizon of the quoted texts' original context? And if Gadamer is correct in seeing application as central to hermeneutics, and as a result, as a fresh creative act in the present of a past text, then could it be the case that Paul's use of the Old Testament is not as problematic as it first seems to be? On these last two questions, the answer is a resounding *yes*.

257. That this is valuable, cf. Evans, *Reception History*, 74, who analyzes Murray's and Swartley's interpretations in light of their prejudgments. Here, I do so with respect to Paul's interpretation of the Old Testament in Romans.

258. Bartholomew, *Hermeneutics*, 311.

PART 3

Paul and the Meaning of Scripture

Chapter 4

Old Concepts, New Meaning (Romans 1–3)

The text, whether law or gospel, if it is to be understood properly—i.e., according to the claim it makes—must be understood at
every moment, in every concrete situation, in a new and different
way. Understanding here is always application.

HANS-GEORG GADAMER[1]

INTRODUCTION

In this and the following chapters, I want to bring attention to the way Paul
employs the Old Testament in his letter to the Romans. Routinely, Paul will
reinforce the arguments he is making with either explicit scriptural quotations or by means of echoes and allusions to the same.[2] Specifically, these
texts are employed by Paul to support his particular understanding about
key concepts, motifs, and stories that were so important to the Jewish way of

---

1. Gadamer, *TM*, 307–8.

2. With respect to "echoes" and "allusions," see the insights of Hays, *Echoes*, a classic
work on this issue.

life. Remarkably, Paul reimagines each of these, granting them fresh meaning and new life for his first-century audience.

My investigations will be structured by dividing Romans into four parts. In this chapter, I will look at Rom 1–3, where I isolate three concepts so important for Paul, namely, *faith, Torah,* and *righteousness.*[3] These concepts serve as the face of Paul's scriptural interpretations and are therefore ripe for analysis. What will become evident is that Paul takes these concepts—embedded as they were in the larger story and texts of Israel—and brings them into dialogue with his own horizon of understanding. As we will see, Paul's own christological horizon structures these concepts into an exciting (and for his opponents, controversial) new matrix.[4]

FAITH

The word "faith" is a murky one. Ever since Luther's Reformation, "faith" (often associated with the New Testament) and "works" (often associated with Old Testament law) are commonly presented in some circles as inherently opposed to one another. While it is true that Paul sets *faith* and *works* into antithesis, he does not do so in the way popularly conceived. For Paul, having *faith* concerns more than acquiring a certain inner state of the heart that is devoid of *works.*[5] To the contrary, Paul clings to the Jewish notion of faith as coterminus with the reality of obedience.

All of this becomes clear in Rom 1, where Paul links faith, πίστις, with obedience—a very Jewish thing to do. And yet, he does something else, something quite creative at the same time. He refracts *faith-works* such that

---

3. I do not, of course, intend by "isolate" to convey the idea that these concepts cannot be found elsewhere in Romans. It is not the case, for example, that Paul only talks about faith, Torah, and righteousness in chs. 1–3, only to move on to unrelated topics in chs. 4–8. Faulty thinking such as this has already been soundly critiqued (e.g., Wright, *Paul and His Recent Interpreters*, 204–15; see esp. 209 and 215, where he cautions against the temptation to "isolate" Rom 1–4 from 5–8). That said, because the structure of Romans progresses logically, there is a general sense that certain concepts and topics receive emphatic attention (e.g., "justification" language in chs. 1–4). Thus, I will structure my discussion in step for the most part with what many scholars see as logical sections (chs. 1–4, 5–8, 9–11, 12–16), though with a caveat, namely, that I treat chapter 4 with chs. 5–8 and not 1–3. As the reader will see in the discussion below, I routinely connect the dots, so to speak, between the sections, thus revealing Romans to be a coherent expression of Paul's thought.

4. See Wright, *PFG*, 827. On Paul's use of the law, cf. the study in Rosner, *Paul and the Law* (esp. 111–205).

5. On faith and works, see the helpful study in Bates, *Salvation by Allegiance Alone.* On the early reception of Paul regarding "works of the law," see the excellent analysis in Thomas, *Paul's "Works of the Law."*

it accords with his most fundamental prejudgment, namely, his christological convictions. In order to do both of these things, Paul will have to quote various Old Testament texts to make his case. He will need to make quotations from these texts to show that his christological vision is in continuity with his Jewish tradition, though as we will see, there also exists for Paul an important element of discontinuity.

Romans 1:5—"The Obedience of Faith"

To begin, let us consider Paul's opening lines, namely, Rom 1:1–7, where he discloses his credentials concerning his apostolic role in advancing the "gospel of God" (v. 1).[6] Regarding this Gospel, Paul states that both "grace and apostleship" were given to him "to bring about the obedience of faith" (εἰς ὑπακοὴν πίστεως) from "among all the Gentiles" (ἐν πᾶσιν τοῖς ἔθνεσιν) (v. 5). Much debate has surrounded the first clause, particularly on how πίστεως functions as a genitive.[7] Thomas Schreiner suggests that the genitive is functioning either subjectively or appositionally.[8] The first would place emphasis on ὑπακοὴν ("obedience"), rather than on faith. That is, "[The subjective genitive] sense would be the obedience that springs from or flows from faith."[9] If so, this would mean that "obedience" and not necessarily "faith" is what Paul wanted "to bring about among all the Gentiles." On the other hand, one could translate πίστεως "epexegetically, i.e., 'obedience which consists in faith.'"[10] This would mean that the "obedience," which Paul was so adamant about producing, is simply "faith" itself. Perhaps, though, Don Garlington's question is appropriate: "Is the significance of ὑπακοὴ πίστεως exhausted by treating it as a genitive of apposition?"[11]

6. Paul's introductory remarks are packed with insight that should be considered when investigating other portions of the letter. Cf. Young, "Romans 1.1–5," esp. 279–80, who thinks 1:1–7 illuminates 1:16–17. See also Fitzmyer, *Romans*, 232–33.

7. See e.g., Schreiner, *Romans* [2nd ed], 40; Schreiner, *Romans* [1st ed], 35. See also Garlington, *Obedience of Faith*; Garlington, *Faith*, esp. 10–31; Moo, *Romans* [2nd ed], 49–51; Moo, *Romans* [1st ed], 51–53; Mounce, *Romans*, 62–63; Fitzmyer, *Romans*, 235–36.

8. He calls these the "two most likely options" (Schreiner, *Romans* [2nd ed], 40; Schreiner, *Romans* [1st ed], 35). It is helpful to restrict discussion on the function of the genitive to that of the subjective genitive and the genitive of apposition, as Garlington (*Faith*, 14) says, "It should be noted that the [grammatical] terminology varies among individual writers. . . . In fact, it will be seen that some of the grammatical options differ in name only."

9. Schreiner, *Romans* [2nd ed], 40; Schreiner, *Romans* [1st ed], 35.

10. Mounce, *Romans*, 62n13. Cf. Wright, *Romans*, 420.

11. Garlington, *Faith*, 16.

Indeed, one wonders if *any* exclusive understanding of ὑπακοὴν πίστεως exhausts the significance it was meant to convey. Accordingly, it has been suggested Paul might have meant "both ideas."[12]

Indeed, there lacks warrant to think Paul implied one at the expense of the other (i.e., a subjective genitive or genitive of apposition). Nothing in the immediate context (1:1–7) or the greater literary context (e.g., chs. 2; 6–7; 12–15) contradicts such a conclusion.[13] Understanding ὑπακοὴν πίστεως as a reference to initial saving faith seems to preserve Paul's emphasis on faith itself,[14] thus keeping in line with his quite negative response to Israel's unbelief in their Messiah in Romans 9:30—10:4. Conversely, v. 6 reveals Paul's eagerness to "bring about the obedience of faith" (v. 5) in his own recipients, "those in Rome" (v. 7), lending to the idea that the phrase itself is more nuanced.[15]

Thus, in the end, I think the following can be said about ὑπακοὴν πίστεως: (1) It entails *initial* faith in Christ and (2) *continual* obedience among those of faith. The first exhibits the genitive of apposition, the second the subjective genitive. Thus, ὑπακοὴν πίστεως ought to be understood as both/and.[16] The temptation to argue for one interpretation at the detriment of the other must be resisted.[17] Garlington rightly states that "Paul has chosen to coin an *ambiguous* phrase expressive of two ideas: the obedience which consists in faith, and the obedience which is the product of faith . . . [and that] the 'genitive of apposition' and 'genitive of source,' while not inappropriate in themselves, are to be rejected as too restrictive."[18]

Moreover, ὑπακοὴν πίστεως becomes less obscure when the discussion moves beyond lexical denotations (e.g., the subjective or appositional elements) and onto the important storied connotations (e.g., the implications

12. Schreiner, *Romans* [1st ed], 35. In his second edition, Schreiner appears to give more weight to the subjective genitive than he did previously (*Romans* [2nd ed], 40). See also Mounce, *Romans*, 62n13. Cf. Wedderburn, *Reasons for Romans*, 97.

13. This point is highlighted in the shift of thought that takes place at Rom 12. After his lengthy exposition of God's plan of redemption (Rom 1:1—11:32) followed by a doxology (11:33–36), Paul begins his exhortation to obedience in Rom 12:1.

14. E.g., Rom 3:21–28.

15. Garlington, *Faith*, 20, concurs. Cf. Wedderburn, *Reasons for Romans*, 97–99.

16. Cf. Gorman, *Crucified Lord*, 347.

17. See the comments on Benno Przybylski in Garlington, *Faith*, 30n86.

18. Garlington, *Faith*, 30. Cf. Moo, *Romans* [2nd ed], 50–51; Moo, *Romans* [1st ed], 52–53. Garlington, *Faith*, 30, summarizes that "On the level of the grammatical, although tags can be applied to πίστεως only with some reservation, the category which best conveys his intentions is 'adjectival genitive'; that is, πίστεως is descriptive of ὑπακοὴ in a manner to be defined by the larger context and in keeping with the most pertinent exegetical data."

and assumptions that exist behind the text). What might Paul have been assuming in the phrase "obedience of faith," and what is the significance of bringing "all the Gentiles" (ἔθνος in v. 5) into it?[19] Paul, arguably, used this phrase (and its immediate context) as part of a much larger working narrative and utilizes it "to encapsulate a world of thought."[20] It is true that in his introduction (specifically v. 7), Paul "draws upon concepts evocative of Israel's relationship to Yahweh and applies them to *all* the Romans, the κλητοί of Jesus Christ."[21] Paul's employment of beliefs and hopes which were once entirely exclusive to the Jews is now, mysteriously at this point, given to those who come in by "the obedience of faith." Garlington comments further:

> The letter's opening paragraph is paralleled by 1:16–17, which is normally perceived to be the letter's thematic statement. However, in distinction to many traditional approaches to Romans, I take the theme to be *the revelation of the righteousness of God in the gospel to all who believe*—the Jew first but also the Greek. As such, 1:16–17 is the functional equivalent of 1:5, "the obedience of faith among all the nations."[22]

That Paul is expanding the rights exclusive to covenanted Israel to "the nations" is supported when one observes the connection between ὑπακοή (occurring in v. 5) with שׁמע.[23] The *Shema*, as a prayer with its strict focus upon monotheism, was foundational for God's covenant people Israel.[24] Specifically, the reception history regarding the conceptual association between ὑπακούειν and שׁמע in the Septuagint cannot go unnoticed either.[25]

19. See Novenson, "Jewish Messiahs," esp. 369–72, who convincingly argues that Paul's mission to the Gentiles was grounded upon his christological convictions.

20. Garlington, *Obedience of Faith*, 14. Cf. Wright, (*Romans*, 420), who detects "overtones . . . in this dense phrase." Garlington, *Obedience of Faith*, 11–13, makes several observations from the Old Testament about the significance of "obedience." He also (12) brings to light the fact that "obedience" has much to do with the theme of covenant. It will be important, then, to link the thought-world of Rom 1:5 with Rom 2. Cf. Schreiner, *Romans* [2nd ed], 39–40; Schreiner, *Romans* [1st ed], 34, who observes both important and upcoming narrative themes at work in Rom 1:5.

21. Garlington, *Faith*, 45. See also Garlington, *Obedience of Faith*, 238–42.

22. Garlington, *Faith*, 45; see also 46–47.

23. Wright, *Romans*, 420. Cf. Dunn, *Romans 1–8*, 17, who discusses the link between ὑπακοή and שׁמע.

24. On the importance of the Shema to Judaism, and Paul's use of it in 3:29–30, cf. the discussion in Moo, *Romans* [2nd ed], 272–74; Moo, *Romans* [1st ed], 251–52.

25. "The frequent use of ὑπακούειν for שׁמע in the LXX shows how strongly the idea of hearing is still present for the translator in the Gk ὑπακούειν. Hence ὑπακούειν and ὑπακοή as terms for religious activity are always to be thought of within the sphere of

The question, then, needs to be asked: Is Paul's use of "the obedience of faith" drawing upon a larger covenant narrative?[26] An affirmative answer to this question becomes clear when Paul refers to the *Shema* in the context of covenant (un)faithfulness later on which, interestingly, is similar to Rom 1:5 in that it, too, is part of a discussion concerning Gentile inclusion (e.g., Rom 3:1–3, 29–31; cf. Rom 1:5).[27] Therefore, by seeing ὑπακοή in Rom 1:5 as being linked to the Shema, one can reasonably assume that when Paul uses ὑπακοή, he has in mind a specific *covenant* obedience—or simply, covenant faithfulness of the Jewish sort.[28]

In light of Gadamer's hermeneutic, it is helpful to say that Paul's understanding of ὑπακοὴν πίστεως is what it is as a result of being in dialogue with its Jewish horizon. He never negates this horizon, but rather proceeds with it, as we have seen above. That said, his concept of faith-obedience is not a mere duplicate of that original horizon of understanding. While he does not invalidate the original horizon, he does proceed *beyond* it in an act of genuine *fusion* between that of his own horizon and that of the Jewish covenant. That Paul is, indeed, *going beyond* (what Gadamer has called a "fusion of horizons") is evident when one observes how the concept of faith-obedience itself is for Paul christologically modified, as we will see below.

Romans 1:16–17

The concept of faith emerges once again in Rom 1:16–17, where Paul quotes Hab 2:4. Everything about this quotation has been debated among scholars.[29] From the phrase ἐκ πίστεως εἰς πίστιν (often translated "from faith to faith") to the use of ὁ δίκαιος ("the just" or "the Righteous One"?) to the

---

a religion which receives the divine Word by hearing and then translates it into action" (Kittel, "Ἀκούω, κτλ.," 1:224). See also Garlington, *Obedience of Faith*, 11.

26. As in e.g., Garlington, *Obedience of Faith*, 247.

27. Wright, *Romans*, 420. See also 482.

28. All of this is in keeping with Paul's broader concern about the issue of faithfulness—both human and divine. Wright (*Romans*, 420) keenly observes, for example, that "[Roman 1:18—3:20] though, is not simply about 'the human plight.' It is about God's own problem and gives a preliminary statement of God's way of dealing with it. God created humans to bear the divine image within the creation and called Israel to shine the divine light into the dark world. Faced with human rebellion and Jewish faithlessness, will God abandon these projects?" Thus, Paul's concern is twofold: (1) How are Jews and Gentiles to be considered faithful/obedient and (2) how will God prove *his* own faithfulness?

29. Moyise, *Paul and Scripture*, 73, is correct to observe that the Habakkuk quotation here (and in Gal 3:11) "has had an enormous influence on the interpretation of Paul."

questions about Paul's source text—his use of Habakkuk is full of riddles. A glance at the texts reveals the issues, as seen in the following table.

Rom 1:17 δικαιοσύνη γὰρ θεοῦ ἐν αὐτῷ ἀποκαλύπτεται ἐκ πίστεως εἰς πίστιν, καθὼς γέγραπται·	Hab 2:4b (LXX)	Hab 2:4b (MT)
ὁ δὲ δίκαιος ἐκ πίστεως ζήσεται.	ὁ δὲ δίκαιος ἐκ πίστεώς μου ζήσεται.	וצדיק באמונתו יחיה

First, let us consider ἐκ πίστεως εἰς πίστιν, which leads into the quotation (v. 17a). It is best to translate the phrase as "from faithfulness to faithfulness."[30] Moreover, at the very least, in the first instance of πίστις, God's own faithfulness is in view.[31] This would distinguish πιστεύοντι in v. 16, where human faith is obviously in view, from πίστις in v. 17a (in either the first or both instances—depending, again, whether God's faithfulness is in view in the second instance). The former is a description of how one receives the benefits of the saving power of God; the latter, by contrast, is a description of what the gospel is in its broad essence, namely, the revelation of the "righteousness of God." This "righteousness of God," moreover, epitomizes the faithfulness of God: The Gospel itself is a revelation of God's own righteousness, a display of God's faithfulness. There are two reasons to prefer this interpretation. First, it accords with the equation of righteousness language with faithfulness in Rom 3 (see below). Second, this interpretation serves to make sense of the subsequent Habakkuk citation, to which we now turn.

In v. 17, Paul follows ἐκ πίστεως εἰς πίστιν with καθὼς γέγραπται· Ὁ δὲ δίκαιος ἐκ πίστεως ζήσεται. The introduction to the quotation, καθὼς γέγραπται, suggests that for Paul the prepositional phrase is based upon

---

30. Contra Fitzmyer, *Romans*, 263, who suggests either a progression of faith or else something like "faith and nothing but faith" (my words).

31. Contra Shreiner (*Romans* [2nd ed], 79; Shreiner, *Romans* [1st ed], 72), who sees human, not divine, faith as the focus. See also Moo (*Romans* [2nd ed], 78–80), who sees ἐκ πίστεως as "'from' the faith of the Jews" and εἰς πίστιν as "'to' the faith of the Gentiles" (80). This view is different than the one proposed in the first edition of his commentary (Moo, *Romans* [1st ed], 76). Wright, *PFG*, 1466, sees the first as a reference to God's faithfulness and the second as a reference to human faithfulness. Cf. Gorman, *Crucified Lord*, 350; Young, "Romans 1.1–5," 281. See also Moyise, "Quotations," 20–21.

Scripture itself, namely, Hab 2:4.[32] Moreover, the evidence suggests that the original text (LXX) read ὁ δὲ δίκαιος ἐκ πίστεώς μου ζήσεται, and should be translated "but the righteous will live by my faithfulness."[33] Thus, Paul, in distinction to the LXX, does not include μου in his quotation.[34] The noticeable difference between the LXX and the MT is that, in the former, the first person is used to clarify faithfulness, while the latter has a third person suffix to אמונה. As a result of Paul's omission, Moo says that his text follows the MT closer, suggesting that it is nearer to its meaning than to the LXX's.[35] This conclusion, however, is not persuasive since divine and human faithfulness cannot, in this context at least, be played off against each other (see below).

Some scholars opt for the idea that human faith is in view because of the way they understand the connection between v. 16 and v. 17. For instance, Schreiner dismisses the thesis that divine faithfulness (whether God's or Christ's) is in view because of how he understands v. 16, that is, how it—speaking as it does of *human* faith—is seen as the definitive way to interpret v. 17.[36] It is undoubtedly true that v. 16 concerns human faith, but it is not necessary to think v. 17 does so as well. It is possible, after all, that Paul switches his emphasis from human faith as a response to the Gospel in v. 16 to God's own faithfulness in one (or both) instances of πίστις in v. 17.

Francis Watson thinks the structure of Paul's wording will not allow for the idea of a divine faithfulness view. Though admitting ἐκ πίστεως can denote faithfulness, he is not content with such a view due to the fact Paul says nothing explicit in that regard.[37] He says "a reference here to divine faithfulness would require other indications in the context and it is just these that

---

32. See Watson, *Paul and the Hermeneutics of Faith*, 38–45. Though Watson's understanding of the quotation itself is not to be preferred, his insights into the dependence between the quotation and its antecedent are. See also Campbell, "Faithfulness of Jesus," 58.

33. Both Göttingen and Rahlfs have μου after πίστεώς. See Stanley, *Paul and the Language of Scripture*, 83–84. See also Koch, "Der Text von Hab 2 4b," who concludes that ὁ δὲ δίκαιος ἐκ πίστεώς μου ζήσεται represents "der älteste und ursprüngliche Text" (84). On the two different ways one can translate Paul's ἐκ πίστεως so as to modify either δίκαιος or ζήσεται, see Moo, *Romans* [2nd ed], 81–82; Moo, *Romans* [1st ed], 77–78. Cf. Schreiner, *Romans* [2nd ed], 81–82; Schreiner, *Romans* [1st ed], 74. Cf. also Young, "Romans 1.1–5," 280, who takes ζήσεται as a reference to Christ's resurrection.

34. On the use and omission of μου in the LXX MSS, see Stanley, *Paul and the Language of Scripture*, 83–84. See also Fitzmyer, "Paul and the Dead Sea Scrolls," 606n15.

35. See his discussion in Moo, *Romans* [2nd ed], 80n252; Moo, *Romans* [1st ed], 76–77n65. Cf. Fitzmyer, "Paul and the Dead Sea Scrolls," 606.

36. Schreiner, *Romans* [2nd ed], 79; Schreiner, *Romans* [1st ed], 72–74.

37. Watson, *Paul and the Hermeneutics of Faith*, 46.

Paul fails to provide in his interpretive gloss [i.e., 1:17a]."[38] Watson asserts that the lack of explicit use of phrases like "the faithfulness of God" make it "unlikely that this is intended in 1:17."[39] Maintaining the divine faithfulness view, he says, would "require a reader who is hypersensitive to what is only implicit in the citation—that the 'faithfulness' in question is God's or Christ's—while ignoring the explicit contextual interdependence of citation and antecedent. A reading is to be preferred that can make sense of that interdependence."[40] It is difficult, however, to see how this is ultimately convincing.[41] Watson seems to make a sweeping assumption, namely, that only explicit features of a text are allowed to convey genuine meaning, or, at the very least, these features are to be preferred over the implicit ones. Either way, such claims are hard to defend.[42]

Furthermore, Schreiner is mistaken to suggest that, just because Paul failed to include μου that Paul therefore "intended to eliminate [the] possibility" that God's faithfulness would be in view.[43] One wonders if it is too strong to speak of *impossibility*. Could it not have been the case that God's faithfulness was implied? Is it not possible that the implied portions of the original text remain integral to the meaning Paul finds in it?

38. Watson, *Paul and the Hermeneutics of Faith*, 46.

39. Watson, *Paul and the Hermeneutics of Faith*, 46.

40. Watson, *Paul and the Hermeneutics of Faith*, 46.

41. Although, seeing this as a reference to Christ's faithfulness is, as Wright (*PFG*, 1470) has said, "probably a bridge too far." Cf. Campbell, "Faithfulness of Jesus," esp. 64–66; Young, "Romans 1.1–5"; Gorman, *Crucified Lord*, 350.

42. He is correct, however, to maintain the integrity of the interdependence between the citation and its antecedent. The way he goes about this, though, is in my mind somewhat problematic. He thinks the interdependence cannot be maintained by any view but his own precisely because he already assumes what the antecedent needs to say based upon his views about the citation (and vice versa). In my estimation, it is the sort of assumptions he maintains that causes him to run afoul. See, e.g., Watson, *Paul and the Hermeneutics of Faith*, 45–46, esp. n54, where his particular translation of the quoted Habakkuk text is integral to his argument. He opts for "'The one who is righteous by faith will live' rather than, 'The righteous one will live by faith.'" He then sees "by faith," ἐκ πίστεως, in 1:17a as "scriptural" (45). He translates this antecedent as "by faith" because he is not comfortable with understanding the citation's "by faith," ἐκ πίστεως, as referring to divine faithfulness. The primary reason, it seems, is because of his views about the lack of certain explicit features in the antecedent (46; see above). Again, Watson is correct to highlight the interdependent relationship of text and antecedent (46), but his way of going about it does not strike me as the best option, as the Habakkuk text highlights God's own faithfulness—however implicitly, and this fact should be given full weight (see below).

43. Schreiner, *Romans* [2nd ed], 81; Schreiner, *Romans* [1st ed], 74.

In fact, it is likely. The original context of Habakkuk suggests that what is in view is about trusting in God's promise and covenant faithfulness.[44] The context of Habakkuk does suggest that, even if human faith/faithfulness were in view (per the MT), the implied (and underlying) contextual emphasis is indeed a trust upon God's own faithfulness.[45] Truly, the faithfulness *of* God gives foundation to any subsequent call for human faith/faithfulness *to* God.[46] It is not without reason, then, to suggest this is what Paul intended to convey as well. One wonders if strict attention to the text's denotations have concealed these connotations. Even if one were to follow the MT's rendering and, from there, argue that human faith/faithfulness was in view, one must not fail to see this as a response to an already-implied and an even more paramount emphasis regarding divine faithfulness. Arguably, *this* emphasis was operative in Paul's own rhetorical use of the quotation.

One might consider that the LXX emphasizes the divine foundation for a subsequent human response of faith/faithfulness, while the MT emphasizes the later (though without neglecting the former emphasis).[47] In fact, all of this seems congruent with how אמונה sometimes functions in other texts.[48] Divine and human faithfulness, therefore, should not be

---

44. See Wright, *PFG*, 1468–71. See also Hays, *Echoes*, 40, who sees the original context of Hab 2:4 as being a "response to the problem of theodicy, an implicit assertion of God's righteousness. The faithful community is enjoined to wait with patience for what they do not see: the appearing of God's justice. This hope God will not disappoint."

45. Even Watson, *Paul and the Hermeneutics of Faith*, 148, says, "Whether they think in terms of 'faithfulness' or 'faith', the prophet and the apostle are at one in their assumption that *emunah* and πίστις refers to the human response to the divine promise of definitive, eschatological saving action." This, arguably, demands to be pressed further so that the emphasis is upon God's faithfulness. Wright, *PFG*, 1467, is correct in his critique when he says that Watson fails to see how this saving action of God has to do with God's own covenant faithfulness. This is precisely my own present point. (Cf. Watson, *Paul and the Hermeneutics of Faith*, 148–49.) See also Hays, *Echoes*, 40–41, who insightfully posits that Paul perhaps draws on both traditions (MT and LXX) in order to render the question of "whose faithfulness?" as ambiguous to say, in effect, that "in the gospel *God's own righteousness* is revealed; and the gospel is the power of God for salvation *to everyone who believes*." Cf. Moyise, *Paul and Scripture*, 88.

46. See Wright, *PFG*, 1469. This idea fits quite well in Rom 1:16–17.

47. See again Hays, *Echoes*, 40–41, for a similar view. Wright, *PFG*, 1468, thinks it is possible the LXX's addition of μου reflects either the original Hebrew text (the change, he says, was perhaps due to "an easy orthographic slippage"), or because the LXX translator understood μου as a gloss of "the more natural reading." Cf. Moo, *Romans* [2nd ed], 81–82, esp. n256; Moo, *Romans* [1st ed], 78–79, esp. n69.

48. On this, cf. the observations in Moo, *Romans* [2nd ed], 81, esp. n256 (Moo, *Romans* [1st ed], 78n69), with my view that God's own faithfulness is very much in view in Rom 1:17. Cf. Schreiner, *Romans* [2nd ed], 81; Schreiner, *Romans* [1st ed], 74.

played off against each other.[49] Perhaps this is the reason why Paul eliminates μου in the first place.[50] Coupling this with the fact that elsewhere Paul parallels righteousness language with divine faithfulness in Rom 3:3 and 5 is something to keep in mind as well (more will be said on this below).[51] This parallel, I think, is essential for understanding the link between δικαιοσύνη and πίστις in 1:17. Thus, Paul must be seen as underscoring the faithfulness of God, *even if* human faith/faithfulness were in view on some level with the Habakkuk quotation.

Here is why all of this is important. In light of the above, one must conclude that Paul's idea of *faith(fulness)*, πίστις, is in full accordance with its source text. As he utilizes Habakkuk's text, he engages it with complete respect for its original horizon of understanding. That horizon consists of God's own faithfulness to bring about salvation *and* the human response of faith in God's act of bringing about salvation. And yet, even as Paul engages Habakkuk's horizon of understanding, he does so dialogically such that he brings to Habakkuk's text his own horizon of understanding. Paul's prejudgments—shaped as they were by his horizon—offer Habakkuk's text fresh proposals such that he (Paul) can re-author the source text to mean something *beyond* what Habakkuk himself had ever envisioned. Such interpretive moves are not unilateral re-authoring such that Paul imposes on the text whatever he wishes. This is instead *dialogical* re-authoring—something of which I will have more to say throughout this book.

In what way does Paul re-author the meaning of Habakkuk's text? The answer to this question is clear: Paul employs Habakkuk's text, which originally spoke of human and divine faith(fulness), in order to recontextualize it such that he can now speak of human faith *in* the person of Jesus Christ and God's faithfulness *through* the person of Jesus Christ. Originally, the oracle urged one to have faith in God's faithfulness as he (God) predicted the Babylonian onslaught and their subsequent demise. And yet, when it comes to Paul and the meaning he finds in this text, "faith(fulness)" is reoriented around Christ. All of this becomes clear when we examine the parallel text of Rom 3:21–22.

49. Again, see Wright, *PFG*, 1469. Cf. Garlington, *Obedience of Faith*, 10–11.

50. Contra Moo (*Romans* [2nd ed], 80n252; Moo, *Romans* [1st ed], 77n65), who thinks Paul's "deliberate omission" is "to facilitate his application of the verse" and hence to diverge from the LXX.

51. Cf. Schreiner, *Romans* [2nd ed], 75; Schreiner, *Romans* [1st ed], 68–69.

Romans 3:21–22

Though a fuller treatment of this passage will be given later, it is important to sneak in a word or two presently about how it clarifies Paul's interpretive posture toward Hab 2:4 in Rom 1:17. In 3:21–22, Paul says even though the Torah and the prophets have played a role in bearing witness to the "righteousness of God," it is nonetheless the case that this righteousness "has been manifested apart from the Torah" itself (v. 21). Instead, says Paul, it has been revealed "through the faithfulness of Jesus Christ (πίστεως Ἰησοῦ Χριστοῦ) to all the ones who believe" (v. 22). The translation "faithfulness of Jesus Christ" makes the best sense here.[52] If we rendered the phrase as "faith in Jesus Christ," this would make the following phrase, "to all the ones who believe," redundant.[53]

It is important to note that 3:21–22 exhibits striking similarities to 1:17, with both passages considering the same Jewish concepts, namely, righteousness and faithfulness. Campbell is not off the mark to describe these two passages as "sibling texts, if not twins."[54] The parallel is quite significant, for it sheds light upon how Paul reads Hab 2:4. Where Rom 1:17 speaks somewhat generally about the revealing of the righteousness of God "by faithfulness," Rom 3:22 speaks much more specifically about the nature of this faithfulness—namely, that it is "through the faithfulness of Jesus Christ" that God's righteousness has been made known. This reveals, I think, the hidden christological prejudgment behind Paul's interpretation of Hab 2:4 in Rom 1:17.[55]

The result is that a fusion between the horizon of the Jewish concept of faith itself and Paul's christological horizon has taken place. In this way, the *faithfulness of God* is recontextualized. And the way in which such recontextualization is supported is by the particular interpretive posture that Paul takes up with respect to the scriptural text he cites. The divine faithfulness of which Paul speaks about in Rom 1:17 was based upon his particular—and, in light of 3:21–22, his *christological*—rereading of Hab 2:4.[56]

---

52. Contra Matlock, "Saving Faith," 79–81, 86–89, I take πίστεως Ἰησοῦ Χριστοῦ subjectively. See again Campbell, "Faithfulness of Jesus," esp. 60, where he discusses the link between 3:21–22 and 1:17. Cf. Cho, "Christology of Romans," 43–46; Gorman, *Crucified Lord*, 358–59.

53. Wright, *Justification*, 203.

54. Campbell, "Faithfulness of Jesus," 60. I do not track with Campbell in everything he argues in this essay, though most of his thoughts on this issue are rather insightful.

55. That the "construction is christocentric," see the discussion in Campbell, "Faithfulness of Jesus," 61–66.

56. That Paul's concept of πίστις is christologically reconstrued is most clearly

RIGHTEOUSNESS AND TORAH

The pattern of christological reconstrual continues beyond the concept of faith and can be detected in other concepts, most notably *righteousness* and *law*(-keeping). This is in large part due to the fact that all three—faithfulness, righteousness, and law—are all deeply-intertwined concepts for Paul, though not without distinction of course. For example, as we have already seen, "the righteousness of God" is said to have been revealed through divine faithfulness (1:17; 3:21–22). And yet these two concepts (righteousness and faithfulness) are so deeply connected that Paul can virtually render them synonymous in the same breath (e.g., 3:3, 5). This being so, one thing to be noticed is that righteousness, like faithfulness examined above, also undergoes a dynamic reconstrual for Paul. Thus, much of what has already been said about πίστις above can be said about δικαιοσύνη. Because righteousness language and law-keeping language are themselves intertwined, I will treat them together below.

Romans 1:17 Revisited

Let us return briefly to Rom 1:17. God's righteousness is revealed "from faithfulness to faithfulness" (ἐκ πίστεως εἰς πίστιν).[57] This phrase, we recall, is based upon the quotation from Hab. 2:4. Moreover, this divine faithfulness anticipated the parallel discussion in 3:21–22, where Paul's christology is most explicit with regard to the concept of faith. As such, Paul's Habakkuk quotation therefore assumed this christological basis by understanding divine faithfulness by means of Christ's own faithfulness. In this sense, πίστις in Habakkuk 2:4 was christologically reconstrued. So far, so good.

The same idea holds for the concept of righteousness. The proximity of δικαιοσύνη to πίστις in these passages makes this evident. Righteousness, like faith, means what it does for Paul precisely because of his christological prejudgments. This idea is not controversial. Most readers of Paul will of course note that Paul's concept of righteousness takes on a christological significance. And yet what often is controversial is the very thing that undergirds this same christological significance, namely, that Paul's primary mode of interpretation is itself christological. The fact is that Paul's interpretive posture enables his reconstruals of these concepts. For example, Paul is only capable of reconstruing *faith* and *righteousness* because of the meaning

---

observed in the retelling of the story of Abraham in Rom 4. I will postpone that discussion for the next chapter.

57. See again the discussion above.

he finds in Hab 2:4, which has been interpreted by him christologically. Thus, the meaning of these concepts is dependent, on some level, upon the meaning he finds in Scripture. This can be seen in more detail in Rom 2, where *Torah-keeping* and *righteousness* are both front and center.

Psalm 61:13 in Romans 2:6

After his thorough indictment of humanity (1:18–32), Paul turns his gaze toward those within the covenant family, that is, toward the Jew (2:1–29). He begins by warning his interlocutor that, despite having the law as a means to judge others, the interlocutor himself should be on guard because he too partakes in the same wicked practices and is therefore in danger of the final judgment (vv. 1–5). Paul follows this warning with a quotation from Ps 61:13 (LXX), saying, "He will repay each according to his works," ὃς ἀποδώσει ἑκάστῳ κατὰ τὰ ἔργα αὐτοῦ (Rom 2:6).[58] This quotation serves to undergird Paul's idea of righteousness and law-keeping further down. I will reserve comments, therefore, about the sort of meaning Paul finds in this verse until we can get the full sweep of Paul's line of thought that extends through 2:29.

After v. 6, Paul goes on to elaborate the specifics of the relationship between the final judgment and works: Those people who, "by good-working endurance" (καθ᾽ ὑπομονὴν ἔργου ἀγαθοῦ), seek "glory and honor and immortality," God will grant eternal life (v. 7). But "wrath and fury" await those who are selfish, to those who are disobedient to the truth and committed "unrighteousness" (ἀδικία; v. 8). This wrath, says Paul, is for "all people who are workers of evil" (πᾶσαν ψυχὴν ἀνθρώπου τοῦ κατεργαζομένου τὸ κακόν; v. 9). And this eternal life, he continues, is for "all those who do good" (παντὶ τῷ ἐργαζομένῳ τὸ ἀγαθόν; v. 10). Paul states twice that such judgment is irrespective of persons, whether Jew or Greek (vv. 9–10). This displays God's impartiality in judgment (v. 11).

Paul brings everything to head in v. 13, where he states, "For it is not the hearers of the law who are righteous before God, but the doers of the law will be declared righteous." It is not clear at this point what, exactly, Paul means by "doers of the law" (οἱ ποιηταὶ νόμου).[59] What is clear, however,

---

58. Cf. Ps 62:13 (MT): בִּי־אַתָּה תְשַׁלֵּם לְאִישׁ כְּמַעֲשֵׂהוּ. The NA28 lists this also as a quotation from Prov 24:12: ὃς ἀποδίδωσιν ἑκάστῳ κατὰ τὰ ἔργα αὐτοῦ (Rahlfs); וְהֵשִׁיב לְאָדָם כְּפָעֳלוֹ (MT). Cf. Stanley, *Paul and the Language of Scripture*, 84n5, who does not include this as a quotation in his study.

59. I agree with Wright that a good approach to understanding v. 13 (indeed, all of vv. 12–16) is to start at vv. 25–29 and work backwards (see Wright, "Law in Romans 2," esp. 148–49). See also Halsted, "Intertextual Chaos?," 127–38.

is that this group of people will be declared righteous (δικαιωθήσονται).[60] Paul is not secretive about the identity of this group. They are "the Gentiles" mentioned in v. 14. Even though, says Paul, these Gentiles "do not naturally possess the law," they nonetheless "do the things of the law" (v. 14).[61] Those who do naturally possess the law are, of course, the Jews. Thus, while it is still not clear what Paul means by *doing the law*, his comments here do clarify the identity of both the *hearers* and *doers* of the law in v. 13. The "hearers of the law" are the Jews, while the "doers of the law" are Gentiles—and, as we will see, these Gentiles are specifically *Christian* Gentiles.[62] But still, what does it mean to be a *doer*?

Paul inches closer to clarity in v. 15. Whatever it means for a Gentile to be a law-keeper in vv. 13–14, it has to do with the fact that, somehow, "the work of the law is written on their hearts" (v. 15).[63] And yet, it is more than this. Paul says, "They [the Gentiles] *demonstrate* that the work of the law is written on their hearts" (v. 15; emphasis added). There are two ways to understand this, both of which should not be played off against each other. First, "demonstrate" implies good works.[64] This makes sense in light of the discussion in vv. 1–11 above. Second, it seems that it could also, along with this, mean something along the lines of *showing their covenant member-ship*.[65] In other words, these Gentiles "demonstrate" that the law has been written on their hearts by means of some *sign* or *symbol* of their covenant status. Originally, of course, the sign of the covenant was circumcision (Gen 17:11).

And yet physical circumcision cannot be what Paul means here. The reason is that just a few verses down, Paul says this is the very thing the Gentiles lack and nonetheless fulfill the requirements of the law *without* being circumcised:

> After all, indeed, circumcision is profitable if you keep the law. But if you break the law, your circumcision becomes un-circumcision. If, therefore, the uncircumcised person keeps the righteous requirements of the law, is it not the case that

60. That this is not "hypothetical justification," see Bird, *Saving Righteousness of God*, 169.

61. On φύσει in v. 14, see the discussion in Wright, "Law in Romans 2," 146–47; Halsted, "Intertextual Chaos?," 131–32. Cf. Fitzmyer, *Romans*, 309–10.

62. See Bird, *Saving Righteousness of God*, 170–72; Wright, "Law in Romans 2," 148–49.

63. On the issue of "conscience" in v. 15, see Wright, "Law in Romans 2," 148.

64. See the discussion in Jewett, *Romans*, 214.

65. This follows Wright's construal of the situation. See e.g., Wright, "Law in Romans 2," 141.

his uncircumcision will be counted as circumcision? And the person who is uncircumcised by nature but keeps the law will judge you who, though having the written law-code and physical circumcision, are a breaker of the law. After all, a person is not a Jew outwardly, and neither is circumcision an outward thing in the flesh. But Jewishness is invisible, and circumcision is a matter of the heart, in the Spirit, not of the written law-code, whose praise is not from people, but from God. (Rom 2:25–29)

Paul clearly intends for this discussion (vv. 25–29) to clarify, and be in continuity with, his earlier discussion examined above (esp. vv. 12–24).[66] That being said, it seems we can reach a few conclusions about what, exactly, Paul means by Gentiles becoming *doers of the law*. First, it does *not* mean that they keep every detail of every command of the law itself because circumcision, being one of the commands of the law, is not required to be a *doer*.[67] The fact that Paul can say a person can *keep* the law without being physically circumcised is telling, not least because the word he uses for "keep" is τελέω, implying completion and fulfillment (v. 27). But how? The answer is that Paul envisions a christological basis for such fulfillment. He says later, for example, that "Christ is the completion [τέλος] of the law leading to righteousness to all who believe" (Rom 10:4). In fact, if Paul is drawing upon Deut 10:16; 30:6 and Jer 4:4 as the backdrop for his discussion about heart circumcision (which seems likely), he seems to be reading these texts in view toward, and therefore in dialogue with, his christological prejudgments.[68]

Thus, Paul's discussion in Rom 2 is but an anticipation for a wider, more complete discussion elsewhere (e.g., 10:4).[69] That being so, we can tentatively conclude that Gentiles are declared "righteous" because of their doing/fulfilling/completing the law on a christological basis.[70] This entails most fundamentally their faithfulness and obedience to Christ (Rom 1:5). Tellingly, Paul states so much when he mentions Christ's role at the final

66. As Wright has argued (see again Wright, "Law in Romans 2"). See also Bird, *Saving Righteousness of God*, 170–71.

67. Wright, "Law in Romans 2," 140–41.

68. Cf Fitzmyer (*Romans*, 322–23), who comments that Paul "appeals to the OT idea of the circumcision of the heart" but also that this concept "takes on a new nuance; it is not just a spiritual circumcision of the human heart, but one that springs from the Spirit of Christ himself."

69. So Wright, *Romans*, 149.

70. Again, the mirroring of the discussion in Rom 2:12–15 with 2:25–29 with 10:4 evidences this fact.

judgment, where the verdicts of *righteous* and *unrighteous* will be given "through" him (2:16).[71]

Now that we have Paul's line of thought mapped out, let us revisit the scriptural quotation in Rom 2:6. Paul quoted this Scripture as an implicit support for his notion that, at the final judgment, every person will receive his or her just desserts. This would not have been controversial to his imagined Jewish interlocutor. A "judgment according to works" was, we might say, Theology 101 for Judaism. On the surface, then, Paul's quotation seems relatively benign. And yet, appearances can be misleading. As we have seen, Paul grounds his notion of "doing the law"—and the resulting righteousness that is acquired at the final judgment by such doing—*not* on the Torah as normally conceived, but rather upon a christological reconstrual of it. In some sense, then, Paul's understanding of what it means to keep the law is creative. What *this* means, therefore, is that Paul's use of Ps 61:13 is itself rather creative in terms of the meaning he reads into it. Recall that Paul cites this verse as support for his notion of a judgment according to works. Once again, the verse says: "He will repay each according to his works" (Ps. 61:13). We must ask, in light of what we have seen in Paul's larger discussion in Rom 2: What does Paul take "works" to *mean* in the quotation? In order for the quotation itself to work in Paul's larger argument, we must see it as being christologically reconstrued. In other words, Paul does not employ it to mean just *any* works, or even Torah-oriented works, but rather christologically-oriented works.

In this sense, then, Paul's interpretation cannot be reduced down to a mere "cut-and-paste" event. He does not, in other words, simply *read the text straight*, as if he could do so without making interpretive choices free from pre-understandings. And yet, neither does he obliterate the text's original meaning or disrespect its original horizon. Rather, he wants it to speak into the present. Therefore, a better way to understand the situation is to say that Paul's christological horizon fused with the text's original horizon, creating a fresh and radically new meaning. As I have said before, and as I will continue to say in the pages ahead, we can describe Paul's interpretations as instances of *dialogical re-authoring*.

---

71. Though I disagree with much of his overall construal of the situation, cf. Dunn (*Romans* 1–8, 106), who seems to suggest that the gospel and christology played a hermeneutic role of sorts in developing Paul's own understanding of the law and the final judgment.

Isaiah 52:5 in Romans 2:24

Thus far, we have addressed 2:1–16 and 2:25–29, leaving aside for a moment the important section in the middle, namely, vv. 17–24. It is here where Paul focuses his attention most explicitly on those Jews who would hypocritically boast in their election ("But if you call yourself a Jew and rely on the law and boast in God" [v. 17]). Thinking they are in a position of righteous primacy—being a "guide to the blind," a "light to those in darkness"—Paul's Jewish interlocutor must be confronted with the fact that he, too, is guilty of sin (vv. 18–22). As a result of his sinful state, the interlocutor and those like him are actually profaning the name of God. "You who boast in the law," Paul says, "dishonor God by breaking the law" (v. 23). To back this claim up, Paul quotes from Isaiah: "For as it is written, the name of God is blasphemed among the Gentiles because of you" (v. 24).

Rom 2:24	Isa 52:5c (LXX)
τὸ γὰρ ὄνομα τοῦ θεοῦ δι᾽ ὑμᾶς βλασφημεῖται ἐν τοῖς ἔθνεσιν, καθὼς γέγραπται	δι᾽ ὑμᾶς διὰ παντὸς τὸ ὄνομά μου βλασφημεῖται ἐν τοῖς ἔθνεσι

Several textual differences can be observed, a full discussion of which need not occupy us presently.[72] However, two stand out. First, that Paul alters the first-person "my name" (τὸ ὄνομά μου) to become "the name of God" (τὸ ὄνομα τοῦ θεοῦ) is to clarify, and perhaps highlight, the fact that it is the divine name itself that is profaned.[73] Second, that Paul would move this alteration to the front of his quotation serves to emphasize his larger point, namely, that his Jewish counterparts, through their "hypoctricial deeds . . . have caused the Gentiles to cast aspersion on the name of the God they profess to serve."[74] Thus, despite their boast of being "guides to the blind" (2:19), the Jews actually have misled the Gentiles.

What is interesting, however, about Paul's quotation is that the meaning Paul finds in it is not on par with Isaiah's original context. Hays is rather blunt when he calls Paul's interpretation "a stunning misreading of the text," saying,

> In Isaiah, the quoted passage is part of Yahweh's *reassurance* of Israel in exile: precisely because Israel's oppressed condition allows the nations to despise the power of Israel's God, the people

---

72. For a thorough discussion, see Stanley, *Paul and the Language of Scripture*, 84–86.

73. Stanley, *Paul and the Language of Scripture*, 86.

74. Stanley, *Paul and the Language of Scripture*, 85.

can trust more surely that God will reveal himself and act to vindicate his own name. Thus, Paul transforms Isaiah's oracle of promise into a word of reproach.[75]

But Hays is quick to vindicate Paul. He says that Paul's "provocative misreading" was only "provisional" in nature.[76] Hays points to Paul's later use of Isa 52:7 in Rom 10:15, where Paul shows that he is well aware of the hope-filled nature of the passage in question.[77] Hence, however one might describe Paul's quotation in Rom 2:24, one could not accuse him of being ignorant of the original meaning. Hays thinks that Paul's quotation is employed as part of the "rhetorical structure" of the entire letter in such a way that requires multiple readings in order to gain the sense Paul intended.[78] As I understand Hays, the idea is that Paul's quotation serves to invite the reader to *initially* feel the weight of Israel's despondency due to their own unfaithfulness. However, once the reader continues through the rest of the letter—not least through chapters 10-11—the salvific, loving nature of God's faithfulness is reclaimed. At that point, presumably, the original (and true) intent of Isaiah will be clearly seen.[79]

Hays' approach is insightful on a number of fronts. First, it reveals Paul to be exactly who he is—namely, a keen thinker and faithful reader of Scripture. Hays rightly presents Paul as someone quite capable of presenting

75. Hays, *Echoes*, 45. Cf. Wagner, *Heralds*, 176–77, who thinks the original context of Isaiah (LXX) does, in fact, serve as a "word of *judgment* on Israel" (177). This absolves Paul from the charge of taking Isaiah out of context. Wagner's reasons for thinking this is because the LXX adds to the MT an overt accusation against Israel (δι' ὑμᾶς) and heightens the problem by explicitly specifying that the dishonoring of God's name is "among the Gentiles" (ἐν τοῖς ἔθνεσι). Wagner also notes that the LXX has "[introduced] a complaint by Israel against the Lord" in v. 5 (θαυμάζετε καὶ ὀλολύζετε). This presumably adds to their guilt (177). Wagner, however, seems to be overstating his case. Moyise points out, for example, that Wagner does not adequately take into account the "pathos used to describe Israel's plight" that surfaces in the language of despair in vv. 3-4. Moyise suggests further that, due to textual difficulties, it is difficult to assert with confidence what the MT and LXX are actually communicating, thus putting into doubt Wagner's notion that the LXX depicts a complaint from Israel against God. As Moyise (*Evoking Scripture*, 46) states, the MT and the corresponding LXX translation are notoriously difficult to understand.

76. Hays, *Echoes*, 45.

77. Hays, *Echoes*, 45. He adds: "If he [Paul] reads Isa. 52:5 as a reproach, it is a reproach only in the same way that the historical event to which it refers was a reproach: a heightening of the tension of grace, a painful reminder of the discrepancy between human unfaithfulness and the faithfulness of God who will never abandon his covenanted people" (45–46).

78. Hays, *Echoes*, 46.

79. See the entire discussion in Hays, *Echoes*, 44–46.

sustained arguments that are rich in content, stringing them along in a complex and yet clearly organized manner. Second, Hays is right to absolve Paul from the charge of being ignorant of the original context, presenting the citation of Isa 52:7 in Rom 10:15 as evidence.

The difficulty I see in Hays' approach, however, is that it seems to ignore what Paul is doing within the context of Rom 2. He is right to highlight the larger context of Paul's discussion (e.g., Rom 10–11), as well as perhaps the requirement for multiple readings to draw out the quotation's full force. In doing so, though, I fear he essentially mutes the function of the quotation once those multiple readings and the overall rhetorical strategy has been taken into account.[80] Hays' approach, therefore, struggles to account for how the quotation can function as a genuine indictment against the Jewish interlocutor regarding specifically the charge of hypocrisy in Rom 2:17–23. The quotation must still have its full effect even after the reader gets to Rom 10–11, as well as after multiple readings have been conducted. In other words, even if the quotation was, on some level, employed as part of some larger rhetorical strategy, one would still need to account for how it can, at the same time, serve as a basis for a charge against the hypocritical Jew in Rom 2.[81]

To see how Paul can interpret the quotation the way he does, we need to pay attention to the point of the quotation. That point, initially, is to highlight the notion of Jewish unrighteousness. Paul needs to do this *so that* he can reorient focus toward the righteousness of Christ. In doing so, however, Paul is not merely arguing from *plight to solution*. He is, instead, dialogically recontextualizing the plight in light of the solution (and vice versa).[82] To see how this works out, it must be noted how the plight in question in Rom 2:17–23 is something that would have received a two-sided response from the Jewish interlocutor. On the one hand, he would have affirmed that the Jewish nation was not sinless.[83] On the other hand, he would have offered

80. In his critique of Hays' (and Wagner's) "innovative ways of reading Paul's quotations," Moyise (*Evoking Scripture*, 45) is right to say that it leaves the impression that most of Paul's readers would actually have misunderstood Paul's intention "until their monographs were published"!

81. See the critique in Moyise, *Evoking Scripture*, 33–48, esp. 37–38, 45–48.

82. The "plight to solution" or "solution to plight" debate has been brewing ever since the publication of E. P. Sanders' groundbreaking work *Paul and Palestinian Judaism*, where he famously argued for the latter. See Sanders, *Paul and Palestinian Judaism*, esp. 442–47, 474–75, 490. Cf. Wright, "Law in Romans 2," 144.

83. The notion of the *sinlessness* of Israel would not have been entertained by either Paul *or* the interlocutor. On this, cf. the discussion in Wright, "Meaning of Romans," esp. 495–502, who says "The 'boast' of 'the Jew' in 2.17 is not the boast that says, 'I am not a sinner like these gentiles.' It is the boast which says, 'I am the God-given

a rejoinder by saying this fact would not have been considered a defeater because the Torah had included the sacrificial system as recourse to sin and would have, accordingly, absolved Israel of the sin of which Paul accuses.[84] Given this, the purpose for which Paul's argument in Rom 2:17–23 is employed (i.e., to point Jews to the God-ordained solution that is in Christ) should not be seen as standing on its own. In other words, *if* all Paul had intended was to convict Israel of sin and, from there, lead them to Christ as a result, the argument would have been unconvincing. It is hard to imagine that Paul would have argued in this manner, which leads me to think this was not his point to begin with.

So what is Paul doing? Assuming that Paul's charge of sinfulness would have been uncontroversial to his sparring partner, it seems best to understand the charge itself (which culminates in the Isaiah quotation in v. 24) not so much as the conclusion of an argument but rather something more along the lines of a shared premise. What Paul does, then, is exploit this shared premise for his own (already assumed) christological ends. The fact of Israel's sin does not, in and of itself, establish for Paul the righteousness of Christ. The fact of Israel's sin does, however, establish for Paul the notion that a real and present problem for Israel exists if she wants to see herself as faithful in her task to be the promised solution to the world.[85] Thus, Paul can exploit this problem of unfaithfulness so that he can highlight what has been revealed *ab extra* the Torah, namely, the faithfulness of Christ as the display of God's righteousness.[86] The fact that Paul will soon speak to this

---

solution to their problem'" (495). Moreover, Paul is not saying every Jew is guilty of the list of charges in 2:17–23. This is a *national* and *corporate* charge of the nation as a whole. Thus, Wright (*Paul and His Recent Interpreters*, 205) says: "The point is not . . . that 'all Jews' committed adultery or robbed temples or whatever. That would indeed be a 'crude attack', and ineffective at that, since it could easily be avoided by pointing to Jews who were obviously not guilty of these sins (people like Paul himself in Philippians 3.4–6). . . . The point is that 'the Jew', here apostrophized in the singular but referring to Israel as a whole, really had received the divine call to be the *solution* to the problem sketched in 1.18—2.16. For this remarkable plan to work, however, Israel would have needed to be perfect, and this was clearly not the case." See n86 below.

84. Wright, "Meaning of Romans," 496.

85. The very thing for which Wright argues. See Wright, "Meaning of Romans," esp. 495–502.

86. Wright brings a plethora of insights to the table regarding the argument in Rom 2:17–24. In "Meaning of Romans," he adequately fends off those scholars who think that Paul, in Rom 2:17–24, is engaging in a battle with a Jewish interlocutor about the sinfulness of Israel as if this was a novel idea (see 495–509). Wright argues that, while *sin* is certainly a component of the argument, it is not the main focus. The focus is instead, he claims, the vocation of Israel—that she is the answer to the problem of human sin (see 495–97). Moreover, this absolves Paul from the charge of posing a faulty argument, Wright says (496–97). After all, says Wright, how could Paul claim individual Jews are

in Rom 3:21–22 lends to the idea that he is currently thinking along these lines.[87] And the fact that Paul has already had this in mind ever since Rom 1:17—a verse, we recall, that anticipated and assumed the christological details explicated in 3:21–22—only reinforces this conclusion.

In essence, Paul understands the plight of Israel in light of the solution—that is, in light of the revelation of Christ's faithfulness. But Paul also understands the christological solution to be situated within the matrix of the Jewish plight itself. As a result, that plight informs Paul's understanding of his christology such that it is situated within the *Jewish* narrative. This prevents Paul's christology from becoming an a-historical and un-situated reality. In this way, Paul's interpretive approach is dialogical, and the circular approach itself is fundamental to the structure of his understanding of the situation.

What does this have to do with the quotation of Isa 52:5 in Rom 2:24? Everything, in fact. I think a strong case could be made that Isaiah's originally-intended oracle of comfort was reinterpreted by Paul as having the meaning of condemnation in precisely the same way his vocational understanding of Jewish unfaithfulness in vv. 17–23 unfolded. Recall again that the quotation in v. 24 serves as the climax of the charge of vv. 17–23. By

---

sinful given that there was in place a solution to sin in the Torah, namely, the sacrificial system? The Paul of Phil 3:6, says Wright, would agree that, yes, 'the Jew' is sinful, but the Torah solves that problem (496). To think otherwise would naturally lead to thinking Paul's argument is faulty, as some scholars seemed to have done (see 496n24). Wright, seeking to correct this way of thinking about Rom 2:17–24 and thus absolve Paul from criticism, argues that Paul's focus is not on sin but on vocation (497). In this way, Wright better situates Paul's argument. However, I am hesitant to conclude that he goes far enough. It seems to me that his argument kicks the can down the road: If Israel's vocation has been impeded due to her sin—and if that is the focus—then conceivably the sacrificial system would suffice to take care of even *that* problem. At any rate, it seems that what Paul is doing is exploiting the shared fact of Israel's sin only to highlight his fundamental prejudgment, which governs his entire argument—a prejudgment which is nothing less than *the revelation of the righteousness of God through the faithfulness of Jesus Christ, who (per Wright) gets the Jewish vocation back on track*. Cf. the discussion in Sanders, *Paul and Palestinian Judaism*, 499, where he says, "Paul actually came to the view that all men are under the lordship of sin as a reflex of his soteriology," and how Paul employed the shared fact of human sinfulness out of convenience for the purpose of furthering his main point. He says elsewhere that Paul "reasoned to sin's dominion as the reverse of his soteriology and Christology, and he was then easily able to work 'sinning' in" (501). In this vein, inserting human sinfulness into his argument is for Paul "only a corollary of his main theme" (484; see also 555).

87. It will not do to say that Paul's statement about the manifestation of righteousness through Christ in 3:22 is something Paul *concludes* after an extended discussion about the plight of sin (1:18—3:20). We must remember that Paul began with this christological understanding from the outset—all the way back in Rom 1:16–17. It serves, therefore, as a key pre-understanding in subsequent discussions beyond that point.

way of the quotation, therefore, Paul heightens the situation of exile to focus on one particular facet of that original situation, namely, Jewish unfaithfulness *in the sense of failing to be a light to the Gentiles*. When the quotation itself is understood through the lens of Israel's calling (i.e., Israel being a solution to the world's problem), the fact that Paul is emphasizing Jewish unfaithfulness *vis-à-vis* Christ's faithfulness becomes clear.[88] Admittedly, this would not be the first thing a reader of Isaiah would notice apart from the christological fore-structure of understanding that Paul has launched in Rom 1:16–17. Perhaps that is the point. Paul's reinterpretation of the oracle is able to take on fresh meaning precisely because he expects his readers to assume certain christological beliefs—details that, again, gain visibility later in places like 3:21–22 and elsewhere.[89] Paul can find the meaning he does in Isa 52:5 precisely because his interpretive lens blurs the irrelevant features of the text's original meaning, allowing what is relevant to his argument to rise to the surface. On this, one recalls Gadamer's notion that all interpretation is situational and, as such, necessarily requires the interpreter to emphasize and/or de-emphasize certain elements of the text—not in order to muzzle the text's message, but instead to let it speak afresh into a new situation.[90] The same is true for Paul. The quotation serves a larger purpose—as yet another cog in the wheel—for his project of recontextualizing concepts like "faithfulness" and "righteousness" in light of what God has done in Christ.

All of this is quite similar to what takes place in Rom 3:4, where Paul quotes Ps 50:6 (LXX) in order to reinforce his particular christological understanding of righteousness.

Psalm 50:6 (LXX) in Romans 3:4

To set up the quotation, it is important to remember that chapter 3 has as its focus the faithfulness of God. God's faithfulness is questioned because of the covenant unfaithfulness and disloyalty on the part of some Jews.[91]

---

88. On Wright's insights into Israel's vocation and calling, see again n83 and n86 above.

89. See again Hays, *Echoes*, 45, where he speaks of the "heightening of the tension of grace." Without negating my criticisms above, I nonetheless concur that Hays is not far off the mark on his general idea.

90. See chapter 3 above.

91. On the debates surrounding 3:1–8, see Moo, *Romans* [2nd ed], 187–90. Here Moo observes "two broadly different approaches to the text" (188). He calls the first view the "traditional model," which sees the first part of vv. 1–8 as focusing upon the Jewish people, while the latter half is broadened to include all of humanity (188–89). The other way of viewing this text, according to Moo (and the one which he believes to be "nearer

Paul continues in Rom 3 with the same line of thought in 1:17—2:29. And then comes the important question: "What, therefore, is the advantage of the Jew? Or what value is there for circumcision?" (3:1). This question is in response to what came before, which will be more clearly seen when we examine 2:25–29 below.[92] At any rate, Paul answers the interlocutor's question in the affirmative, saying, "they were entrusted [πιστεύω] with the oracles of God" (v. 2). This is a reference to how the Jews were entrusted with the task of bearing witness to the world, that is, to the Gentiles.[93] The immediate follow-up question is, "What if some were unfaithful [ἀπιστέω]? Does not their unfaithfulness [ἀπιστία] bring to nothing the faithfulness [πίστις] of God?" (v. 3).

Observing the reoccurrence of πιστ- words in vv. 2–3 is instructive, for they display the interconnectedness of the passage better than what a typical English translation does, as in v. 2, where "entrusted" appears in English as an entirely different sort of word than "faithful" or "faithfulness."[94] That said, "faithfulness," both Israel's and God's, is the center of Paul's diatribe.[95] While "unfaithfulness" can be seen as a reference specifically to not having faith in Jesus,[96] it remains preferable to see "unfaithfulness" as the failure to carry out the divine mission of being "the light of the world," the very thing they were entrusted to do.[97] This, of course, was due to their own sinfulness, which undermines their "boast" in 2:17 and 23a, as they too are corrupt (vv. 21–24).[98] Does, then, Jewish unfaithfulness render God's faithfulness invalid, or put another way, does Jewish unfaithfulness "cause [God's faithfulness] not to function"?[99] If it is true that the covenantal promise was "*to bless the world through Israel*," and if God decides to bless the world in a different way—in a way that "bypasses Israel"—it would be true therefore,

to the truth"), is that the entire passage (vv. 1–8) is focused on the Jewish people. Under this account, vv. 5–8 "do not take up a general objection to the fairness and consistency of God, but affirm the faithfulness of God to Israel or the 'right' of God to judge even his own covenant people" (189) (cf. Moo, *Romans* [1st ed], 177–80). Generally speaking, I also believe the second view is closer to the mark. Cf. Gorman, *Crucified Lord*, 356.

92. Jewett, *Romans*, 241. Cf. Stuhlmacher, *Romans*, 51–52.

93. Wright, *Romans*, 453. Cf. Garlington, *Faith*, 54–55; Stuhlmacher, *Romans*, 52, takes this as a reference to "commandments." Cf. Fitzmyer, *Romans*, 326–27. See also, Wright, "Meaning of Romans," esp. 490–95.

94. That Paul intends a "play on the concept of πίστις," see Dunn, *Romans 1–8*, 131.

95. Cf. Moo, *Romans* [2nd ed], 187–90; Moo, *Romans* [1st ed], 178–80.

96. Jewett, *Romans*, 244; cf. Fitzmyer, *Romans*, 327; Dunn, *Romans 1–8*, 131–32.

97. Wright, *Romans*, 453. See also Wright, "Meaning of Romans," 491, 497–99.

98. Wright, "Meaning of Romans," 497.

99. Fitzmyer, *Romans*, 327, has "ineffective." See the entry on καταργέω in L&N 76.26.

as Wright maintains, that "he [God] stands convicted of unfaithfulness: un-faithfulness . . . not in relation to his promise *to* Israel, but to his promises *through* Israel for the world; promises to bless the world *by this means rather than some other.*"[100] Paul's response is μὴ γένοιτο (3:4a).[101]

To support this, Paul quotes Ps 50:6 (LXX). The quote is skillfully bookended between vv. 1–3 and v. 5. Thus, before we examine it more closely, we need to say a thing or two about the function of v. 5 in order to get the full scope of the rhetorical weight Paul places upon the quote.

In v. 5, Paul explains what he means by "faithfulness" in vv. 2–3. "But if our unrighteousness demonstrates God's righteousness, what shall we say?" (v. 5a). Here "righteousness" is set in direct parallel to the "faithfulness" spoken about in v. 3, and "unrighteousness" in v. 5 is also linked with "un-faithfulness" mentioned in v. 3.[102] The concept of righteousness is for Paul tied to the concept of "faithfulness," not least to covenant and obedience.[103] Thus, a continuity of thought ought to be observed, flowing backward from "un/righteousness" (ἀδικία and δικαιοσύνην in 3:5a) to "un/faithfulness" (ἀπιστέω, ἀπιστία, and πίστις in 3:3) to "decrees of the law" (δικαιώματα in 2:26) to the "righteous" (δίκαιοι in 2:13).

How do these observations impact how we understand Paul's use of Ps 50:6 in Rom 3:4? By equating righteousness with faithfulness, Paul narrows his focus once more onto a particular feature of the original text in order to highlight something much broader, something which goes *beyond* the original text's original horizon. Though, as we will see, it does not go *against* the text's original horizon. It is worth quoting the entirety of Rom 3:1–3, followed by the quotation and then v. 5. This will allow us not to lose the forest for the trees.

> What, therefore, is the advantage of the Jew? Or what value is there for circumcision? Much in every way. First, after all, they were entrusted with the oracles of God. What if some were unfaithful? Does not their unfaithfulness bring to nothing the faithfulness of God? Absolutely not! But let God be true and every person a liar, just as it is written: (Rom 3:1-4a)

---

100. Wright, "Meaning of Romans," 492.

101. On the "triple theme" at work here concerning continuity between Paul's Gos-pel and God's covenant with Israel, see Dunn, *Romans 1–8*, 132. On μὴ γένοιτο, see Fitzmyer, *Romans*, 327–28.

102. Dunn observes this link as well. See Dunn, *Romans 1–8*, 134.

103. Wright, *Romans*, 453; cf. Moo, *Romans* [2nd ed], 198–200; Moo, *Romans* [1st ed], 189–91.

Τί οὖν τὸ περισσὸν τοῦ Ἰουδαίου ἢ τίς ἡ ὠφέλεια τῆς περιτομῆς;
πολὺ κατὰ πάντα τρόπον. πρῶτον μὲν [γὰρ] ὅτι ἐπιστεύθησαν
τὰ λόγια τοῦ θεοῦ. τί γάρ; εἰ ἠπίστησάν τινες, μὴ ἡ ἀπιστία
αὐτῶν τὴν πίστιν τοῦ θεοῦ καταργήσει; μὴ γένοιτο· γινέσθω δὲ
ὁ θεὸς ἀληθής, πᾶς δὲ ἄνθρωπος ψεύστης, καθὼς γέγραπται·

Rom 3:4b Ὅπως ἂν δικαιωθῇς ἐν τοῖς λόγοις σου καὶ νικήσεις ἐν τῷ κρίνεσθαί σε.	Ps 50:6 (LXX) ὅπως ἂν δικαιωθῇς ἐν τοῖς λόγοις σου καὶ νικήσῃς ἐν τῷ κρίνεσθαί σε.
So that you might be justified in your words and will prevail when you judge.	So that you might be justified in your words and might prevail when you judge.

But if our unrighteousness demonstrates God's righteousness,
what shall we say? That God is unrighteous to inflict wrath (I
speak in human terms)? (Rom 3:5)

εἰ δὲ ἡ ἀδικία ἡμῶν θεοῦ δικαιοσύνην συνίστησιν, τί ἐροῦμεν;
μὴ ἄδικος ὁ θεὸς ὁ ἐπιφέρων τὴν ὀργήν; κατὰ ἄνθρωπον λέγω.

Paul employs Ps 50:6 (LXX) as a proof text for his claim that God's
faithfulness cannot be subverted by Jewish unfaithfulness, that is, by their
failure to be faithful stewards of "the oracles (τὰ λόγια) of God" (Rom 3:2b).
The original context of Ps 50 (LXX) records David's confession of sin (50:3–
6a). By his confession, God himself is justified (δικαιωθῇς), that is, shown to
be in the right (50:6b). In other words, because David acknowledges his sin
truthfully, God's own words of judgment against him are vindicated.[104] This
does not mean that David makes God righteous or that God's righteousness
per se is dependent upon David's confession. It does mean, however, that
God's *being seen as righteous* is, in this particular instance, dependent upon
David's coming into line with God's own words (λόγοις) of judgment. This
has a slightly different feel to it than the way Paul understands the quote.
Stanley is right to observe, for example, that in Ps 50, it is God's judgment
against sin that needs vindication, not "his faithfulness to his people," as in
Rom 3:3.[105] Moreover, for Paul, the quotation is proof that God's status of
"righteous" is not dependent upon Jewish obedience or even their acknowledgement of faithlessness (as with David). In fact, for Paul, God's

---

104. Cf. Stanley, *Paul and the Language of Scripture*, 86–87.

105. Stanley, *Paul and the Language of Scripture*, 86, says: "In Ps 50 (51 MT), it is
Yahweh's judgment against sin and not his faithfulness to his people (Rom 3.3) that
stands in need of vindication."

righteousness is secure *despite* Jewish faithlessness or any acknowledgment of the same. So, what is going on?

To answer that question, we first need to see that by quoting a passage such as Ps 50:6, where δικαιόω is the focus with respect to God, Paul equates the concept of God's being seen as righteous with God's being seen as faithful. Thus, δικ- language and πίστ- language once again run alongside each other, thus reinforcing what we have already observed above regarding Rom 3:3 and 5. This leads, secondly, to the answer as to how Paul could use a text that originally spoke of God's justification by means of human (i.e., David's) agency and employ it in such a way that God's justification is *not* dependent upon human (i.e., Jewish) agency. The reason is because Paul assumes a scenario where God's righteousness has already been revealed in a new, surprising sort of way. For Paul, we recall, *God's righteousness is revealed by faithfulness* (Rom 1:17). Or more specifically, as he says later in 3:21–22, "God's righteousness is manifested . . . through the faithfulness of Jesus Christ."

In this way, therefore, we can account for Paul's revisionary use of Ps 50:6. Paul's concept of "God's righteousness" is interpreted through the lens of his christological prejudgment. This interpretive lens blurs anything irrelevant (and thus not applicable) to Paul's situation, thereby bringing into focus what *is* relevant for his purposes—namely, the righteousness of God. In this way, the horizon of the Jewish text has undergone fusion with Paul's christological horizon such that what results is a new, fresh, and creative understanding. Thus, the text is not interpreted in a "cut-and-paste" sort of way. Paul is not a literalist. But neither is he a relativist. He does not bring upon the Jewish text his prejudgments such that the latter swallows the former. To the contrary, Paul is in *dialogue* with the Jewish text. He and the text engage in a series of questions and answers, hermeneutically speaking. The text is the answer to the question of Paul's christological convictions, thus rooting the Christ-event in the salvation-history of the Jewish tradition. The reverse is likewise true: Paul's christological convictions are the answer to the text's questions, thus allowing the text's message to find fulfillment and meaning.

The Catena of Quotations in Romans 3:10–18

A careful look at the first of several quotations Paul employs in Rom 3:10–18 continues to hint in this same direction.[106] In that first quotation, taken from Ps 13:1, notice how Paul inserts δίκαιος in place of χρηστότητα below (v. 10):

---

106. On the issues and debates surrounding how, when, and by whom the citations were combined, see Stanley, *Paul and the Language of Scripture*, 87–89. Following Koch, Stanley

Rom 3:10 καθὼς γέγραπται ὅτι	Ps 13:1c (LXX)
οὐκ εστιν δίκαιος οὐδὲ εἷς,	οὐκ ἔστιν ποιῶν χρηστότητα, οὐκ ἔστιν ἕως ἑνός.

Thus, where the LXX has "there is no one who does good," Paul has "there is no one who is righteous" (v. 10). As Stanley has quipped, this substitution "could hardly be more Pauline."[107] It is true that Paul's move here would not be out of line with its original context.[108] That said, given the context of Rom 3, the addition nonetheless may very well expose the fact that Paul's christological prejudgment is operative here. Before I say why, it is important to make a couple of observations to set the context.

First, the string of quotations in 3:10–18 is not simply about the sinfulness of humanity. The point behind the quotations is to reinforce all that was said in 3:1–9 about Jewish unfaithfulness *vis-à-vis* God's faithfulness. Rom 3:1–9 is not about "a general set of questions about God and human beings. It is, very specifically, about the failure of Israel to carry out the commission with which they had been 'entrusted', and about the fact that God's plan to save the world through Israel is going ahead anyway—though Paul has not yet explained how that can be the case."[109] There is no reason to think the quotations that follow in vv. 10–18 are outside of that discussion.[110]

Second, it should be recalled that Paul's discussion in 3:3–5 was such that he showed how (un)faithfulness ran parallel to the concept of (un)righteousness. This was seen when vv. 3 and 5 were compared to one another, especially so when we noted how these two verses bookended the quotation of Ps 50:6 in v. 4. All of this should be factored in by the time we arrive at 3:10, where Paul quotes Psalm 13:1 in such a way that he substitutes out "does good" for "is righteous." One should also keep in mind how the concept of righteousness (and justification) will undergo an important christological recontexualization just several verses after this. The importance of how he follows his catena of quotations with vv. 19–22 cannot be missed and should be factored into our analysis.

Note, for instance, how Paul says, "And we know that whatever the law says, it says to those under the law, in order that every mouth may be

---

thinks the citations were combined by Paul prior to the composition of Romans (89).

107. Stanley, *Paul and the Language of Scripture*, 90.

108. Stanley, *Paul and the Language of Scripture*, 90.

109. Wright, "Meaning of Romans," 495.

110. See again Wright, "Meaning of Romans," 495, and what he takes the role of the catena to be playing in 3:10–18.

stopped and the whole world may be subject to God" (v. 19).[111] Given that Jews (which includes the psalmist!) lived "under the law," and given that the law itself provided recourse for sins through the sacrificial system, it is difficult to imagine how the psalmist would have understood his original words to be the grounds for bypassing of the law in order to gain righteousness—the very trajectory that Paul takes with the catena of quotations.[112] "Therefore, by works of the law no flesh will be justified ($\delta\iota\kappa\alpha\iota\acute{o}\omega$) before him, for through the law comes knowledge of sin" (3:20).[113] Then Paul goes on to add—quite explicitly—that righteousness has been reconceptualized christologically: God's righteousness ($\delta\iota\kappa\alpha\iotao\sigma\acute{u}v\eta$) shines through the faithfulness of Christ (3:21–26).

What we can conclude, then, is that the status of not being "righteous" in Rom 3:10—which, again, is *Paul's* word inserted into Ps 13:1—must itself be taken in the christological sense, the fullness of which is not explicated until 3:21–22. Not being righteous is not so much about a failure to keep the law as it is to not be in Christ.[114] After all, Paul was *not* saying that righteousness could not be gained prior to the Christ-event by obedience to the Torah. Elsewhere he says that he had, in fact, gained it (Phil 3:6).[115] Presumably, then, he would not have denied the same for the psalmist. Paul's horizon is not detached from this same Jewish tradition, but he is reconfiguring it: *He is slowly and intricately now tracing everything onto a christological map.* Paul wants the Ps 13:1 quotation to speak into this new reconfiguration. In doing so, it continues the discussion of Rom 3:1–5—that is, into the situation of Israel's failure to fulfill her vocation. As a result of that failure, she is

111. On "law" in 3:19, see Rosner, *Paul and the Law*, 30–31.

112. This insight comes from Wright ("Meaning of Romans," 497), who raises the point, saying: "Even the catena of biblical passages on the universality of sin (3.19), might be thought inadequate: devout Israelites penned those accusations, and presumably exempted themselves." See the context of this discussion on 495–502.

113. Paul may very well be drawing from Ps 142:2b LXX (ὅτι οὐ δικαιωθήσεται ἐνώπιόν σου πᾶς ζῶν.) in 3:20a (see Käsemann, *Romans*, 88; Fitzmyer, *Romans*, 337; Schreiner, *Romans* [2nd ed], 176). If so, his use of πᾶσα σάρξ in the place of πᾶς ζῶν is important, as it highlights Paul's polemic against "the fleshly distinctives of which the loyal Jew makes boast, particularly his circumcision 'in the flesh' . . ." which speaks of the "nationalistic, or ethnic narrowing of the terms of God's righteousness" (Dunn, *Romans 1–8*, 155). Note that Stanley, *Paul and the Language of Scripture*, 99n43, does not include it among the quotations he examines given his "strict guidelines" for what counts as a citation.

114. I do not want to overplay the distinction. I realize, for example, that *not being able to keep the entire law* is on Paul's mind (e.g., Rom 2:25–29). That being said, this does not seem to be the main point for Paul.

115. See again the stimulating discussion in Wright, "Meaning of Romans," 496, which has served as a catalyst for my thoughts here.

unrighteous (3:5). Paul thus employs Ps 13:1 to speak to *that* fact. In order to do that, he must insert δίκαιος in place of χρηστότητα in the quotation. This insertion serves for Paul as a hint of, and anticipation for, the explicit, christologically-reconfigured righteousness of 3:21–22, thus linking that passage with the discussion in 3:1–5.[116]

The Shema in Romans 3:30

Everything that has been said above about faith, righteousness, and Torah-keeping can be summarized in Paul's allusion to Scripture at the end of chapter 3. In Rom 3:30, he alludes to a portion of the Shema. In context, he says:

> Where, then, is boasting? It is excluded. By what law? A law of works? Not at all, but rather by a law of faith. After all, we consider that a person will be justified by faith apart from works of law. Or is God only of the Jews and not also of the Gentiles? Yes, he is also a God of the Gentiles, *since God is one* (εἴπερ εἷς ὁ θεὸς), he will justify the circumcised by faith and the uncircumcised through faith. Do we, therefore, abolish the law through faith? By no means! Rather, we maintain the law (vv. 27–31).[117]

The point that Paul makes is that God accepts Gentiles *qua* Gentiles. They do not, in other words, need to perform works of the law in order to be declared righteous. This argument began in 2:12–29.[118] It is recalled that at 2:12–16, Paul had made the case that Gentiles could be declared righteous despite not being in natural possession of the law, that is, by birth. Nevertheless, Paul argued, these Gentiles could become doers of the law (vv. 13–14). As we saw, this did not imply that these Gentiles would begin carrying out works of the law and, as a result, be declared righteous. To the contrary, Paul says these same Gentiles complete the law *without* being circumcised—which was one of the works of the law (2:25–29, esp. 27). The main idea here—and it runs through 3:1–26—is that God accepts Gentiles

---

116. Given that this first quotation sets the tone for the rest, the other quotations in the catena naturally fall into line, packing the same rhetorical punch for which Paul employs them. A few of these following quotations undergo the typical Pauline alterations, but they are inconsequential and therefore contribute little for the present discussion. It is unnecessary, then, to explicate all the textual details and features of each. On this, see Stanley, *Paul and the Language of Scripture*, 93–99.

117. Emphasis added. Deut 6:4b LXX: Ἄκουε, Ἰσραήλ· κύριος ὁ θεὸς ἡμῶν κύριος εἷς ἐστιν.

118. In fact, the argument began at 1:16 and continued up to the present passage.

as Gentiles and does not favor the Jewish nation with respect to righteousness.[119] Thus, *works of the law*, those works which distinguish the Jew from the Gentile, are no longer what brings about a status of righteousness.[120] This, again, is the entire argument from 1:16—3:26, and our present passage quoted above naturally resumes this entire line of thought.

Thus, Paul can ask (and then answer): "Where, then, is boasting? It is excluded" (v. 27). This boasting, which should be understood as boasting-as-the-favored-covenant-nation, is not excluded through a law of works, but rather through a law of faith (v. 27).[121] The reason, of course, is simple: It was the very "law of works" that fueled the boast to begin with (2:17-20). The "law of faith," however, is what excludes boasting. The reason is that it, by definition, assumes everyone—Jew and Gentile—to be on equal terms. This leads Paul to remind his readers what he has already concluded previously: "After all, we consider that a person will be justified by faith apart from works of law" (v. 28). Again, "works of law" must be seen as those works which segregate Gentile from Jew; otherwise, as Wright has quipped, the question in v. 29a is a non sequitur: "Or is God only of the Jews and not also of the Gentiles?"[122] Paul's reply is that yes, God is also a God of the Gentiles (v. 29b). And this reply is backed by a partial allusion to Deut 6:4. Paul's logic here is that, because "God is one," he will have universal concern for all, and not just one group of, humanity. The way God accomplishes this is, once again, by faith (v. 30). This "faith" does not "abolish," but rather "maintains," the law itself (v. 31). This comment is on par with what he has already said before: That Gentiles *qua* Gentiles can actually become *doers of the law* and, hence, "righteous" and "justified" (2:13-14) and thereby *complete* the law's requirements (2:26-27) apart from the *works of the law* (3:20) precisely because *the righteousness of God has been revealed through the faithfulness of Jesus Christ* (3:21-22).

Thus, Paul's appeal to the monotheism of Deut 6:4 serves as a yet another scriptural basis for his larger project of recontextualizing the concepts of faith, righteousness, law-keeping in a decidedly christological sort of way. After all, each of these things are what they are for Paul *because* of what he believes God has done through Christ. Commenting on 3:29-30, Wright summarizes

---

119. See 2:11; 3:22.

120. See again, Wright, "Law in Romans 2," 141. On "righteousness" and "covenant *membership*," see Wright, "Justification: Yesterday, Today and For Ever," 430.

121. On boasting, see Dunn, *Romans 1-8*, 185–86; cf. Schreiner, *Romans* [2nd ed], 212–13. On the debates about "law of faith," see Rosner, *Paul and the Law*, 119–21.

122. Wright, "Justification: The Biblical Basis," 31.

This is one of Paul's most obvious evocations of the *Shema*. His point, echoing Zechariah 14.9, is that the unity of God himself grounds the unity of the community. And the community in question here consists of those marked out by *pistis*, 'faith', the faith which is the answering 'faith' to 'the faithfulness of the Messiah' in 3.22, which is itself the outworking of God's own faithfulness, his truthfulness and justice.[123]

Wright goes on to add that "Jewish-style monotheism . . . [has been] re-thought from top to bottom around the events concerning Jesus."[124] In this way, then, Paul enters into dialogue with Deut 6:4, allowing the horizon of Jewish monotheism to fuse with the horizon of his christological prejudgments.

SUMMARY

In this chapter, we have seen how Paul addresses the question of faithful-ness, righteousness, and law-keeping—all three of which are integral to the story of Israel. Through scriptural quotations, Paul claims to find an answer to the question in the revelation of Jesus Christ. Likewise, the question of the revelation of Jesus Christ finds its own answer in the *Heilsgeschichte* of Israel, embodied as it is in her texts. In this way, his interpretive approach has been dialogical through and through. Moreover, there is a noticeable newness and creativity that can be detected in the meaning Paul adduces. His christological prejudgment serves as an interpretive lens through which the text he reads can be brought to bear upon his present circumstances. That lens blurs the irrelevant out of view so that what is relevant can come into focus. The result is a newness—a sort of re-authoring that is what it is because of this dialogical nature of the interpretive event itself.

---

123. Wright, *PFG*, 641.
124. Wright, *PFG*, 641–42.

Chapter 5

Jewish Stories Retold (Romans 4–8)

Tradition is not simply a permanent precondition; rather, we produce it ourselves inasmuch as we understand, participate in the evolution of tradition, and hence further determine it ourselves.

HANS-GEORG GADAMER[1]

INTRODUCTION

In the last chapter, it was observed that the concepts of faith, righteousness, and Torah-keeping have undergone revision via Paul's use of Scripture. His interpretations, moreover, were shown to be what they were due to his christological prejudgments and the dialogical character of the interpretive event itself. As I will show in this chapter, this same pattern continues throughout Rom 4–8. For example, in the Abraham story in Rom 4, the three concepts mentioned above continue to be recontextualized. Similar to Rom 1–3, the meaning Paul finds in the Abraham story is integrally informed by his christological prejudgments, as we will see. This pattern of christological interpretation continues with other Jewish stories in Rom 5–8 as well, namely, those stories of Adam and the Exodus. We begin first with Abraham.

1. Gadamer, *TM*, 293.

THE ABRAHAM STORY

The Abraham story, as told in Rom 4, can be divided up into two sections: vv. 1–12 and vv. 13–25. In the first section, Paul employs Abraham as a proof that righteousness comes by faith, not works. To do so, he presents scriptural texts for consideration. His argument, however, should not be seen as merely a text-based argument—that is, as exegesis (strictly speaking). If it were, then his argument fails, as we will see. By highlighting this fact, clues will emerge that suggest his argument assumes a christological framework. In the second section, this christological framework becomes more visible as details surface regarding the way Paul retells the Abraham story by priming it to concur with his christological fore-structure of understanding. At the end of the retelling, Paul's christological prejudgments will have appeared, shedding light on the argument as a whole and on the way Paul discovers meaning in Scripture.

Romans 4:1–12

With the Abraham story, Paul puts into antithesis faith and works. "What, therefore, shall we say was found by Abraham, our forefather according to the flesh (κατὰ σάρκα)? For if Abraham was justified by works (ἐξ ἔργων ἐδικαιώθη), he had something to boast about, but not before God" (4:1–2).[2] Here, σάρκα is understood negatively.[3] Moreover, the phrase "by works" (ἐξ ἔργων) is a shorter version of the phrase ἐξ ἔργων νόμου which occurred in 3:20.[4] This phrase (ἐξ ἔργων νόμου in 3:20) points back to the discussion about circumcision of the flesh in 2:28 (σαρκὶ περιτομή), which is its functional equivalent.[5] Thus, Paul is not speaking of "works" in a general sense, but in a specific, Jewish cultic sense.[6] One cannot say, then, that "merit theol-

2. Wright, "Meaning of Romans," 505–6, connects "boast" here back to the boasting in 3:27 and 2:17–24. On the question of who is intended to have been seen as introducing the story of Abraham (whether Paul or his interlocutor), see Jipp, "Rereading the Story of Abraham," esp. 220–21; cf. Hays, *Echoes*, 54–55. See Dunn, *Romans 1–8*, 199, on κατὰ σάρκα. Cf. Moo, *Romans* [2nd ed], 281–82 (Moo, *Romans* [1st ed], 259–60); Juncker, "Children of Promise," 142n39. See Fitzmyer, *Romans*, 371–72, on the MSS issue. Cf. my translation of 4:1 with Jipp, "Rereading the Story of Abraham," 227.

3. Contra Jipp, "Rereading the Story of Abraham," 228.

4. Dunn, *Romans 1–8*, 200. On works, cf. Schreiner, *Romans* [2nd ed], 226–27; Moo, *Romans* [1st ed], 217–18.

5. Note that σαρκὶ περιτομή in 2:28 is tied back to those who, by nature, "have the law" and those who are merely "hearers of the law" in 2:13–14. The progression of Paul's working narrative, therefore, is clearly seen.

6. Contra Schreiner, *Romans* [2nd ed], 226–27; Schreiner, *Romans* [1st ed], 217–18.

ogy" is inherent to the discussion, as Paul's primary issue is "with the works of covenant loyalty . . . [and] Paul's opposition to Jewish covenantal nomism can be reduced to his insistence on *Christ-fidelity vs. Torah-fidelity*."[7] This claim is substantiated by the topic of circumcision in 4:9–12.[8]

In order to exploit the details of the Abraham story to his advantage, Paul observes how Abraham was "counted" righteous not by works, but by believing God (vv. 3–5).[9] To do this, he offers a quotation from Gen 15:6, saying, "For what does the Scripture say? 'But Abraham believed God and it was counted [λογίζομαι] to him as righteousness'" (Rom 4:3).[10] This discussion is itself buttressed by a quotation from the Psalms (vv. 6–8).[11]

Rom 4:7–8	Ps 31:1–2 (LXX)
7 μακάριοι ὧν ἀφέθησαν αἱ ἀνομίαι καὶ ὧν ἐπεκαλύφθησαν αἱ ἁμαρτίαι·	1 Μακάριοι ὧν ἀφέθησαν αἱ ἀνομίαι, καὶ ὧν ἐπεκαλύφθησαν αἱ ἁμαρτίαι·
8 μακάριος ἀνὴρ οὗ οὐ μὴ λογίσηται κύριος ἁμαρτίαν.	2a μακάριος ἀνήρ, οὗ οὐ μὴ λογίσηται κύριος ἁμαρτίαν,
	2b οὐδέ ἔστιν ἐν τῷ στόματι αὐτοῦ δόλος.

The fact that Paul introduces this quotation in v. 6, where he says it speaks of *righteousness* being counted to a person *apart from works of law*, is quite telling—not least because this is not what the psalm actually says. In fact, the psalmist goes on to say that it is his law*lessness* (ἀνομία) that he has confessed and which was forgiven: τὴν ἁμαρτίαν μου ἐγνώρισα καὶ τὴν ἀνομίαν μου οὐκ ἐκάλυψα ("I acknowledged my sin and I did not hide my lawlessness"; 31:5). There is no indication, then, that the psalmist would have concluded that works of law were not required for a righteous status.[12]

---

7. Garlington, *Faith*, 6–7. Cf. Wright, "Justification: Yesterday, Today and For Ever," 433–34.

8. Contra Schreiner, *Romans* [2nd ed], 227; *Romans* [1st ed], 218.

9. See Juncker, "Children of Promise," 131–60, for how the motif of the paternity of Abraham is consistent between the substance of Rom 4 and Gal 3. (Gen 15:6 is also cited in Gal 3:6.)

10. Gen 15:6 (LXX): καὶ ἐπίστευσεν Ἀβράμ τῷ θεῷ, καὶ ἐλογίσθη αὐτῷ εἰς δικαιοσύνην. There are no substantive textual issues or differences regarding Paul's use of Gen 15:6 that I need to highlight. On Paul's use of δὲ instead of καὶ, see Stanley, *Paul and the Language of Scripture*, 99–100.

11. On how significant, or perhaps insignificant, this citation is to Paul's overall argument, see Dunn, *Romans 1–8*, 230. Concerning Paul's use of *gezerah shavah* with his citation, see: Fitzmyer, *Romans*, 375–76; Barrett, *Romans*, 85; Longenecker, *Romans*, 499.

12. Stanley (*Paul and the Language of Scripture*, 101) draws attention to the fact that Paul stops his quotation at Ps 31:2a, leaving off οὐδέ ἔστιν ἐν τῷ στόματι αὐτοῦ

What, then, is Paul's interpretive logic? It seems that Paul conflates the status of forgiveness and the covering of sin in Ps 31:1 (ἀφέθησαν and ἐπεκαλύφθησαν) with the status of righteousness given to Abraham in Gen 15:6 (δικαιοσύνην). He can do this, apparently, because both passages contain the *Stichwort* λογίζομαι, which knits them together.[13] It is important to note that, as Paul conflates these things, he is already anticipating (and assuming) the conclusion of his argument from Genesis 15:6 and 17:11— namely, that Abraham was reckoned as "righteous" prior to being circumcised (see below). When this is considered, the way Paul finds the meaning he does in Ps 31:1-2 becomes clear: If Abraham can be counted "righteous" before performing works of the law, then, *mutatis mutandis*, works of the law are also not necessary for David's own status of being not counted as sinful and, hence, receiving "righteousness" (v. 6). Thus, Paul's interpretation of Ps 31:1-2 is dependent upon his assumptions about *how* and *when* Abraham attained righteousness.

The details of those assumptions are disclosed in the argument that Paul lays out in vv. 9–11. By comparing the events of Abraham's justification in Gen 15:6 with the events of Abraham's receiving the sign of circumcision in Gen 17:11, Paul is able to show quite easily that Abraham's righteous status was given *prior* to his circumcision, not during or after it (vv. 9–10). In this way,

> Paul's argument is straightforward: the event of which Gen 15:6 speaks precedes the event described in Gen 17:23-27. Paul insists on separating into distinct phases what his fellow Jews, and no doubt he himself previously, had always taken as a whole . . . by narrowing the issue to circumcision as such, Paul takes up a strong position, and one difficult to contest. For the evidence of Scripture is that Abraham was reckoned righteous, accepted in covenant relationship by God, prior to his being circumcised and without reference to circumcision. That one fact is sufficient to establish the point that God's righteousness was not

---

δόλος. He surmises that this line would have little "usefulness" to him, saying, "Indeed, the parallel that it presents between maintaining a pure mouth (v. 2b) and having one's sins overlooked by the Lord (v. 2a) might have suggested to some exactly the kind of 'works-righteousness' that Paul is at much pains to root out" (101). While I agree that Paul deliberately cut off the quotation where did, I do not think he did so for the reasons Stanley thinks. The reason is because, first, Paul's argument has not been against works *per se*, but rather against *works of the law*, that is, those works exclusive to Israel's identity (cf. Rom 2:6-29; 3:27-29). Second, the reason he cuts off the quotation at v. 2a is because he wants to bring attention to λογίσηται, a *Stichwort*, which will link this quotation to the Gen 15:6 passage that was cited a few verses earlier.

13. So Fitzmyer, *Romans*, 375–76; Longenecker, *Romans*, 499.

dependent upon works of the law, or any cultic observance, in the case of Abraham. And if Abraham is the paradigm for God's dealings with humankind, including his covenant dealings with the seed of Abraham, that also means that God's acceptance in general is or at least can be "apart from works."[14]

Indeed, this is the *shape* of Paul's argument. That said, there is more to the *content* of Paul's argument than merely the fact that he exploits the timing of events in Gen 15 and 17. Otherwise, how could his argument have been persuasive? Paul's interlocutor could have responded that it is nonsense to say just because the Torah divides Abraham's covenant status (i.e., "righteousness") from its sign (i.e., "circumcision") into two different events that the Torah's own command to circumcise has itself been abolished as a result. The fact that the thing signified precedes the sign itself does not negate the other fact that the Torah goes on to command circumcision anyway. If it were the case that circumcision had been abolished on the grounds Paul gives, then he might be forced to conclude that the command to circumcise was never (or should never have been) in force. These are the sort of charges one could imagine being lobbed at Paul *if* his argument was merely based on textual exegesis. But it is difficult to imagine that Paul would have proceeded in this way, leaving himself open to such conclusions.

How might we solve the riddle? Clues begin to emerge once we notice the purpose for which Paul employs the story in the first place. Paul desires to show that Abraham would become "the father of all those who believe without being circumcised, so that righteousness would be counted to them also" (v. 11b).[15] Here Paul refers to Gentiles, though Jews are within his purview as well. He says that Abraham would also "be father of the circumcised, to those who do not merely have circumcision but who also follow in the path of the faith our father Abraham possessed while uncircumcised" (v. 12). Here Paul refers to Jews. Thus, the larger picture is clear: Paul employs the Abraham story *for* the purpose of helping the Roman church to see how, and *from* the perspective of an apostle who has seen how, unity has been achieved for all believers *in Christ*—whether Jew or Gentile. This

---

14. Dunn, *Romans 1–8*, 231.

15. I do not intend to oversimplify things. Jipp ("Rereading the Story of Abraham") is, perhaps, right to call attention to the fact that Paul's use of the story is "complex" and that he is addressing multiple topics (218). However, I do not think this precludes the idea that Paul is pursuing one line of thought, namely, the multi-ethnic vision of the church in Christ. All of the various topics Jipp mentions that are in play in Rom 4 (see p. 239) remain, arguably, in service to validating this vision. At times, Jipp seems to isolate Rom 4 into sections that, at least on the surface, appear to be too segregated. See e.g., how he understands the relationship between 4:22 and 4:3 regarding the Gen 15:6 citation (Jipp, "Rereading the Story of Abraham," 237n33).

christological emphasis goes a long way in pointing us in the right direction in our effort to determine how Paul interprets the story the way he does.

Romans 4:13–25

Paul continues his discussion about Abraham's faith in vv. 13–16, juxtaposing it to relevant questions about the Mosaic law and how it could not bring about the promised inheritance—namely, the inheritance of the world.[16] If it could, says Paul, then "faith is emptied" (v. 14). This would mean that the significance of Abraham's faith itself was a moot point in the history of redemption—something Paul will not entertain. It is no moot point, says Paul. What matters most is that people—whether Jew or Gentile—participate in the faith of Abraham, and in this sense, Abraham is the "father of us all" (v. 16).[17] This idea is followed with, and reinforced by, a scriptural citation from Gen 17:5: "Just as it is written: 'I have made you a father of many nations'" (v. 17a).[18] It is important to state the obvious at this point, namely, that Gen 17:5 does not say anything about Abraham becoming the father of many nations apart from the implied natural, biological process.[19] Moreover, it says nothing about faith *apart from works* being the means by which those outside his family can become his offspring.[20] That being so, Paul must be reading even this part of the Abraham story in a way that is not merely exegetical in nature.

It is in v. 17 where Paul takes the discussion for a decisive turn. This move is rather creative, and it reveals his most basic interpretive prejudgment. In essence, what Paul begins to do at this point is prime the Abraham

16. See Forman, "Politics of Promise" on the phrase "inherit the world." Cf. Juncker, "Children of Promise," 144–46. It is true that Paul's reading of "offspring" in this passage is not overtly christological like it is in Gal 3:16, as his attention centers on the "collective" aspect of the believing community (Moo, *Romans* [2nd ed], 299; Moo, *Romans* [1st ed], 274). However, it would be a mistake to think christology is entirely absent (hermeneutically speaking; see below)—not least because the corporate and the individual, the *ekklesia* and the *christos*, cannot be played against each other as if the two are not, in Pauline thought, closely intertwined (see e.g., 1 Cor 12:12–13, 27).

17. On ἐκ πίστεως Ἀβραάμ in v. 16b, see Jipp, "Rereading the Story of Abraham," 231–33.

18. Rom 4:17a: καθὼς γέγραπται ὅτι πατέρα πολλῶν ἐθνῶν τέθεικά σε. (Gen 17:5 LXX: ὅτι πατέρα πολλῶν ἐθνῶν τέθεικά σε).

19. E.g., see Gen 17:6, 15–20. Cf. the discussion in Jipp, "Rereading the Story of Abraham," 233–35.

20. It is true that those outside his family receive the mark of circumcision (Gen 17:12–13). That said, the text differentiates these outsiders from Abraham's offspring, who alone receive the inheritance (v. 12; see also vv. 7–8).

story for his readers, creatively retelling it, so that it will accord with his christological convictions, thus revealing his own interpretive approach— one that has been operative since Rom 4:1.

With regard to "faith," for example, we note first what Paul means with respect to *Abraham's* faith. Dunn describes it (and the substance of vv. 17b–21) accurately and simply: "Abraham's faith was nothing other than unquestioning trust in God's power."[21] Thus, Abraham's faith was not lacking a proper object, but was rather a faith placed in the divine promise and, hence, *in* the God who can be trusted.[22] It was a faith in God's ability to bring "life to the dead," a faith in the "one who calls the things that do not exist to have existence" (17b). That Paul mentions Abraham's belief that God is the τοῦ ζῳοποιοῦντος τοὺς νεκροὺς is evidence that Paul seeks to find correspondence between God's giving life to both Abraham's dead body and Sarah's dead womb *and* God's raising Jesus from the dead.[23] Moreover, Paul draws a parallel between Abraham's *faith* that God could raise his and Sarah's dead body and the Christian's *faith* that God raised Jesus from the dead. In this way, the words of Gen 17:5, quoted in Rom 4:17, are given life themselves: The promise of Abraham's universal fatherhood finds the meaning it does because it is interpreted *from* a christological fore-structure of understanding. Likewise, the quotation in Rom 4:18 ("So shall your off-spring be"; οὕτως ἔσται τὸ σπέρμα σου; Gen 15:5 LXX) is interpreted as a reference to believers in Christ.

All of this is made explicit in vv. 19–25. Despite Abraham's aged body and the impossibility of Sarah to carry a child, Abraham believed God could fulfill the promise with full hope and expectation (vv. 18–21). In fact, Paul describes Abraham's self-perception of his own body as not merely as something *aged* but as something *dead* (νενεκρωμένον). Likewise, Paul says Abraham viewed Sarah's womb as "dead" (νέκρωσιν). One might translate this as "barren," but this would fail to capture how Paul primes the Abraham story so that a connection can be made between Abraham's faith in the God who raises the dead and the faith of the Christian who believes God raised Christ from the dead.[24] This connection is explicit in vv. 22–24, where Paul

21. Dunn, *Romans 1–8*, 236.

22. Moo, *Romans* [2nd ed], 308–9; Moo, *Romans* [1st ed], 282–83. See also Dunn, *Romans 1–8*, 239.

23. That this is a reference to Abraham and Sarah's body is clear from Rom 4:19, where Paul makes the connection explicit (see Fitzmyer, *Romans*, 386; Longenecker, *Romans*, 518–19). This could also be a reference to the tradition that stated Abraham believed God could raise Isaac from the dead when he went to sacrifice him, a tradition appearing in Heb 11:19.

24. Jipp, "Rereading the Story of Abraham," 235, says: "The language of νέκρωσιν is

says it was Abraham's faith that counted as righteousness (v. 22). He adds further: "'It was counted to him' was not written for him only, *but also for us*" (vv. 23–24a; emphasis added). Paul's hermeneutical assumption is that the text of Gen 15:6 (indeed the entirety of the story itself) was written for the present.[25] Paul narrows down this assumption—by which he had been operating all along[26]—to a specific group, namely, the believers in Jesus the Messiah: "To those whom it will be counted, to those who believe on the one who raised Jesus our Lord from the dead (ἐκ νεκρῶν), who was delivered up for our trespasses and was raised for our justification" (vv. 24b–25). Thus, this hermeneutical assumption has a christological basis, being centered around the one who was raised from the dead, ἐκ νεκρῶν.[27]

Again, this language echoes Rom 4:17 and 19 where Abraham believed in the resurrecting power of God "who gives life to the dead, τοὺς νεκροὺς" (v. 17; νεκρόω and νέκρωσις in v. 19).[28] The correspondence of language is potently suggestive: Those who possess similar faith are considered children of Abraham (v. 16).[29] Indeed, Abraham's faith for Paul finds its present parallel in the Christian's faith.[30] This faith has a specific object, which is God, specifically in his "life-giving power" as it relates to the resurrection of Christ.[31] From an interpretive standpoint, one must notice how the en-

---

shocking in that it is not the typical way to describe the natural decay of sexual organs or a female's barrenness, but is rather a word reserved for a corpse. . . . Paul has deliberately chosen to use these words of death in order to underscore the continuity between Isaac's miraculous birth and Jesus' (and 'our') resurrection from the dead."

25. This is not unlike what we see in the Scrolls. I address these and similar issues, in Halsted, "Intertextual Chaos?," 141–88. See also Jewett, *Romans*, 340, who says Paul was "following the tradition of Jewish hermeneutics"; Barrett, *Romans*, 388. Cf. Holt and Spears, "Ecclesia," 76–77.

26. See Moo (*Romans* [2nd ed], 312; *Romans* [1st ed], 287), who says, "The conviction expressed in vv. 23–24 that what is written in Genesis about Abraham has relevance to the Christian believer has been the implicit assumption of the whole of chap 4."

27. Cf. Holst, "Meaning of 'Abraham Believed God,'" 325; cf. Fitzmyer, "Paul and the Dead Sea Scrolls," 604–5; Jipp, "Rereading the Story of Abraham," 228–31.

28. Thus when Holst ("Meaning of 'Abraham Believed God,'" 325) attempts to subsume christology under a broader theological category, seemingly because in the Abraham story, "Faith is emphatically in the *God* who raised Jesus," is to perhaps miss the point. Of course, it is true that here God (and not Christ *per se*) is the object of faith for both Abraham and Paul. But one should be hesitant to play the two against each other. Paul is, after all, reading this story as a *Christian*.

29. See Juncker, "Children of Promise," 134, who comments on the Abrahamic sonship of the Gentiles in Gal 3:7 (where Gen 15:6 is cited, as in Rom 4:3).

30. So Fitzmyer, *Romans*, 388: "Paul sees an exact correspondence between Abraham's faith and the faith of all Christians." See also Moyise, *Paul and Scripture*, 38; Jipp, "Rereading the Story of Abraham," 237–38.

31. Bird, *Saving Righteousness of God*, 146.

tire discussion—not least with respect to *faith*—takes on a christological emphasis for Paul. In this vein, Garlington's comments are helpful. He says,

> One of the most striking phenomena of the extant letters is that [Paul] nowhere debates the meaning of faith with his opponents. Faith as such was never a point of controversy.... What is radical about Paul, however, is *faith's object*—Christ. Apart from the scandal of a crucified Messiah, the deciding factor, to coin a phrase, was Paul's "Christological eschatology."[32]

Though Garlington is correct, there might be a better way to describe the situation. If by "the meaning of faith" he means the *structure* of faith (i.e., the mechanics of it, how it functions, that it entails assent, loyalty, fidelity, etc.)—which is what I take Garlington to mean in light of his larger discussion about faith's relationship to obedience—then I concur. But when it comes to a discussion about the *meaning* of faith, we need to take our cues from Gadamer, namely, that this would entail something significant with respect to both *understanding* and *application* together. In other words, *faith* for Paul means what it does precisely because of how he applies the concept in light of his christological prejudgments. As such, then, faith becomes a concept that has undergone redefinition precisely because it has been applied to a new setting. And this application is mediated by the meaning Paul claims to find in his scriptural quotations.

That it is the case *faith* has undergone change is clearly seen when we attend to the way Paul interprets the story itself in light of his concerns about circumcision. Notice once again something important about the way Paul argues from the Abraham story. Recall how I said above that the shape of Paul's argument (i.e., that justification is on the basis of faith) is indeed rooted in Scripture by pointing out that the timing of Abraham's justification in Gen 15 preceded the work of circumcision in Gen 17. But again, this cannot account for the entirety of Paul's interpretation. Paul's argument, instead, stands insofar as his christological horizon of understanding is in place. The Scripture, by itself, cannot establish Paul's claim here (i.e., that circumcision as a command is no longer in force) since the fact that Abraham was deemed righteous prior to circumcision was true even when the command for circumcision was in force prior to the Christ-event—as even Paul would surely agree (cf. Gal 3:23–29). In other words, just because Paul can show in Scripture that Abraham was justified by faith prior to receiving the command of circumcision does not mean by itself that the command

---

32. Garlington, *Faith*, 18–19. This is part of a larger discussion about "faith" and "obedience," which begins on 17. See also Garlington, *Obedience of Faith*, 9–13. Cf. Fitzmyer, *Romans*, 388. See again my discussion on "faith" in the previous chapter.

of circumcision is no longer in force. This much is true—unless, of course, Paul assumed that his readers would share his prejudgment that the meaning of faith has now been re-centered around the resurrected Christ. Without Paul's *christological* prejudgment in place, then, the rhetorical force of his argument is severely weakened.[33] In fact, it fails altogether. Thus, Joshua Jipp is right to say that

> Based on Paul's double reference to "deadness" in 4.19, his characterization of God as "giving life to the dead" in 4.17b, and his emphasis on Jesus' resurrection "from the dead" (ἐκ νεκρῶν) in 4.24b–25, it appears likely that Paul's interpretation of the Abraham story is being construed according to his Christological presuppositions. . . . Appeals to Gen. 17 and the binding necessity of circumcision may be overwhelmed, therefore, if the essential components of the story of Abraham prefigure and correspond to that of Christ.[34]

Thus, Paul's argument *from* Scripture is what it is because of what he brings *to* Scripture, namely, his christological prejudgments. This dialogue between text and interpreter results in a fresh and revisionist understanding of the text and the concept of faith.[35] For Paul, the Abraham story speaks, but it speaks to new purposes and into new horizons.[36] Perhaps it is

33. This arguably solves a dilemma pointed out by Stanley, *Arguing with Scripture*, 151–53, in his evaluation of the rhetorical strategy of Paul's use of the Abraham story in Rom 4. Stanley is correct to say that "a more skeptical member" of an "informed audience" (a hypothetical category employed by Stanley as part of his larger project; see 68–69) would have found a problem in Paul's handling of the story (151). After all, Paul fails to mention, in line with Jewish custom, the essential relationship between Abraham's faith and his latter action—not least the "covenantal context" of the rite of circumcision (151–52, esp. 38). Such a skeptic, then, would easily find Paul's reading difficult. But again, as I propose above, the essence of Paul's exegesis here is not divorced from its most fundamental element: christology. When this element is granted full attention, and when this is understood as falling under the category of a prejudgment (*Vorurteil*; in Gadamer's sense), the problem found in Stanley's otherwise helpful rhetorical analysis is relieved. Thus, Stanley's idea that because of "the ready availability of an alternative reading" on the part of an "informed audience" therefore "suggests that Paul did not expect the Romans to conduct a careful verse-by-verse analysis of his argument" ought to be reconsidered (153).

34. Jipp, "Rereading the Story of Abraham," 235–36. See also 237 about Paul's "prior Christological commitments."

35. Though I do not agree with his views about the "interlocutor" in Rom 4:1, cf. Jipp's ("Rereading the Story of Abraham," 227) comments on 4:16–25: "Paul's exegesis of the Abraham story is indebted to his Christological commitments even though he remains tied to the Genesis narrative, which is absolutely necessary if he is to give a *scriptural* response to the interlocutor's question."

36. Cf. the discussion in DiMattei, "Narratives," 78–79, 86–92.

wise, then, to follow Steven DiMattei's advice and begin calling this the "Abraham-Christ story."[37] He says that

> In Rom 4, . . . where Paul seemingly invokes the narrative details of Sarah's miraculous pregnancy after having been sterile for so long, while simultaneously noting that Abraham was well beyond his youthful prime, we find that the narrative details and the context within which this story is re-presented are laden with extrabiblical themes and details—themes and details that we actually find in the recontextualized story that Paul is narrating. This is especially visible in Paul's choice of vocabulary: Sarah's "dead" womb and Abraham's "dead" body (4:19); and the God who "brings to life the dead" (4:17). Certainly there is an intensified interest in the narrative details here, but these narrative details do not belong to the biblical story per se nor to its context, but to the Abraham-Christ story.[38]

In this vein, therefore, Paul's hermeneutic is not a mere exercise in repeating the historical facts of the text; he is doing more: he is *interpreting* them. And when one takes into account Gadamer's insights about the nature of understanding itself, Paul's revisionist interpretation is afforded philosophical clarity—and perhaps, if we dare, even legitimacy.

The Abraham story, moreover, centered around the plot of how "Abraham believed God, and it was counted to him as righteousness" (4:3). Yet, as we have already seen, Paul understood "righteousness" as having been revealed "through the faithfulness of Jesus Christ" (3:22).[39] The Abraham story found completion in this revelation.[40] It is true for Paul that the faith Abraham exhibited "foreshadows" the faith of a Christian, as Fitzmyer says.[41] It is equally true that Paul reads the entire Abraham story *from* the position of Christian faith. This is the point of vv. 23–25: The Abraham story is to be read not merely as an artifact of history, but *for* the present

---

37. DiMattei, "Narratives," 91

38. DiMattei, "Narratives," 91.

39. See previous chapter.

40. So DiMattei, "Narratives," 92: "There is no longer an Abrahamic narrative in Genesis that can be separated from the historical narrative of Paul's own time. We must now speak of an Abraham-Christ narrative. One does not exist apart from the other; it is one narrative history. It starts with Abraham and has its ending (*telos*) in Christ. In short, it is an extrabiblical narrative. . . . In Paul's view, the proper and perhaps the only context within which to read the Abrahamic story is no longer to be found exclusively in Genesis; the proper context is the one provided by Christ. Paul might have called this 'lifting the veil' of Scripture."

41. Fitzmyer, *Romans*, 388.

situation—with believers in Christ as the focus. Paul finds in the Abraham story a correspondence of details that allows him to see the Abraham story as an answer to the question of his christological horizon (vv. 17, 19, 24–25). Likewise, Paul sees believers in Christ as children of Abraham (vv. 16–17), which shows that he understands his christological horizon as the answer to which the Abraham story was a question.[42] Here one ought to recall Gadamer's notion of question-and-answer, the core of his dialogical hermeneutics. This is exactly what we see with Paul's own interaction with the Abraham story.

That Paul's christology is supplementing the Abraham story and is operating hermeneutically is best seen when compared to a reading of the same story in Sir 44:19–21. There the Abraham story is told in such a way that

> Torah and circumcision are the central features, along with Abraham's near-sacrifice of Isaac (Genesis 22, which is absent from Romans 4). Sirach also highlights Abraham's faith(fullness) (εὑρέθη πιστός *heurethē pistos*, "he was found faithful," 44:20), but this does not have the sense of "believing the promise" that Paul has drawn out. The two belong on the same map; *but Paul's new construal, his new way of telling the story, grows directly out of what he now believes about God because of the events concerning Jesus*, resulting in the establishment of the Jew-plus-Gentile family with faith as its central demarcating feature.[43]

It can be said, then, that the hermeneutical assumption from which Paul read the Abraham story is christological, for Paul's particular reading of these texts is contingent upon this conviction. For without it, his reading simply does not work. In fact, his conviction enables his interpretations. Thus, it functions as a *Vorurteil*.[44]

---

42. Recall chapter 3 and how, for Gadamer, interpretation is dialogical.

43. Wright, *Romans*, 498; emphasis added. Cf. Gorman, *Crucified Lord*, 360–61; Jipp, "Rereading the Story of Abraham," 222–24. Elsewhere, Wright, *PFG*, 850, says that "Abraham's faith in God the creator, the life-giver, is thus well *re-expressed* in terms of Christian faith in the raising-Jesus God" (emphasis added). See also Moyise, *Paul and Scripture*, 33–34.

44. See again chapter 3 above on Gadamer's concept of *Vorurteil*. Cf. Moyise, *Paul and Scripture*, 45, about Paul's "christological 'reconfiguration.'"

Conclusion

What we have seen above reveals that Paul continues his pattern of recontextualization in the Abraham story. Specifically, Paul's approach to it was christological such that it can be re-presented to the Roman community about matters relating to faith and works of the law. Moreover, Paul's particular reading of the Abraham story was not unidirectional in that he merely imposes upon it his christological assumptions. To the contrary, Paul's approach is better described as dialogical—a question-and-answer posture toward the story itself. In this way, Paul's christological prejudgments are not left in historical isolation but are, rather, enfolded within the Jewish story itself and *vice versa*. In this way, the story was able to take on fresh meaning for the Roman believers. In light of Gadamer's theory, we might describe Paul's use of the Abraham story as an act of *fusion of horizons*.

THE ADAM STORY

Paul picks up the Adam story in Rom 5:12–21 to further his christological discussions, which came to the forefront in Rom 4:24–25. He segues into this with a discussion about the result of justification, namely, "peace with God" (v. 1).[45] Believers can now have hope, he says, in their suffering because God's love has been revealed to them—indeed, it has been "poured" into them—through the Spirit (vv. 2–5). This love, moreover, is christological: It is demonstrated through the death of Christ (vv. 6–8). It is through this Christ-shaped love that believers can have hope for *future* salvation, even as they possess *present* reconciliation (vv. 9–11).

Paul transitions to the Adam story in vv. 12–21 where he juxtaposes it with his christological beliefs that were expounded in vv. 9–11. He does so without any explicit quotation from Genesis, though allusions are clearly present.[46] The purpose for which he utilizes Adam is straightforward. His point is to show that, even before the law was given, "death reigned from Adam to Moses" (Rom 5:14a). And even when the law came from Moses, it served to officially *count* sin (Rom 5:13) thereby leading to the *increase*

---

45. On the well-known textual issue regarding ἔχομεν/ἔχωμεν in v. 1, see Longenecker, *Romans*, 548–49.

46. NA28 documents no explicit quotations in Rom 5. Stanley (*Paul and the Language of Scripture*, 102–3) likewise notes no quotations. On the allusion to the Adam story, see Dunn, *Theology*, 95. Longenecker (*Romans*, 541–43) notes the infrequency of scriptural quotations in Rom 5–8. He offers a brief synopsis of the ways scholars have made sense of this, as well as other "differences" Rom 5–8 has with respect to Rom 1–4 and 9–11 specifically (542). See also Wright, "New Exodus."

of the problem of sin (Rom 5:20). Paul, once again, exploits the fact of human sinfulness for his present purposes, much like he did in Rom 3 (see previous chapter). The Adam story, then, does not mark a shift in Paul's thinking. Rather, it is a continuation of the stream of thought that came before (Rom 1:16—4:25).

On this, several things ought to be noted. First, Paul takes Adam to be the progenitor of sin (vv. 12a, 19).[47] As a result of this, second, Adam is understood to be progenitor of death and condemnation (vv. 12bc, 15–18).[48] Although, Paul does not seem to lay *all* responsibility upon Adam. Individual sinners are to blame for death as well: "Death spread to all men," Paul says, "because all sinned" (Rom 5:12c).[49] Third, Adam is employed by Paul as a τύπος, a "type," of Christ (v. 14).[50] For Paul, Christ is shown—*and assumed from the outset*—to be the solution to the plight of Adam (vv. 15–21). As we will see, Paul will creatively retell the story of Adam in order to conform to this assumption.

An important question emerges at this point. Was Paul arguing from plight to solution *or* solution to plight? It seems the best answer is not so much either-or, but essentially both-and.[51] Paul's use of the Adam story is very much like his use of the Abraham story: It is dialogical, an interpretation that is back-and-forth in terms of question-and-answer (in the way Gadamer envisioned). This allows Paul to creatively reconceptualize the Adam story in light of his christological convictions, as we will see below.[52]

To show this, we start with how Paul understood Adam to be a "type" of Christ. Paul grounds this understanding in the contrasts that he sees existing in Christ when Adam is placed in parallel: Christ's "grace-gift" is unlike Adam's "trespass" (vv. 15, 20); Christ grants "justification" where

---

47. Rom 5:12a: "Through one man, sin came into the world" (δι' ἑνὸς ἀνθρώπου ἡ ἁμαρτία εἰς τὸν κόσμον εἰσῆλθεν).

48. Rom 5:12b: "And through sin, death" (καὶ διὰ τῆς ἁμαρτίας ὁ θάνατος). Much debate has centered around vv. 12, 18–19 with respect to the so-called doctrine of "original sin." On this, see Venema and McKnight, *Adam*, 183–88; Dunn, *Theology*, 94–97; Campbell, *Paul and the Hope of Glory*, 67.

49. On the debates regarding the meaning of the phrase "because all sinned," ἐφ' ᾧ πάντες ἥμαρτον, see Moyise, *Paul and Scripture*, 26; Dunn, *Romans 1–8*, 273–74; Longenecker, *Romans*, 587–92.

50. On Paul's use of τύπος κτλ, see the helpful discussion in Bates, *Hermeneutics*, 133–48.

51. Cf. the discussion in Moyise, *Paul and Scripture*, 24–30; Venema and McKnight, *Adam*, 181, who say, "One could argue that Paul *began with Christ* and found opposites in Adam just as easily as one could argue that he *began with Adam* and found opposites in Christ." See again chapter 4nn82–83, 86–87, above.

52. Cf. Moyise, *Paul and Scripture*, 29–30.

Adam ushered in "condemnation" (vv. 16, 18); Christ brought "life" where Adam passed on "death" (vv. 17, 21); Christ was obedient, while Adam was disobedient (v. 19).[53]

Here Paul's dialogical approach to the Adam story is rather clear. On the one hand, for example, note how the Adam story informs his christological convictions. Adam brings *death*, the negation of life, by means of his trespass/disobedience (vv. 12–14, 17). Here, Paul alludes to Adam's sin in the garden, specifically to the "function of the tree of life in Genesis 2–3."[54] Because Paul places the Christ event within that story—by means of the various Adam-Christ parallels discussed above—the story itself serves to raise his christology out of historical isolation and embed it within the Jewish story itself. Thus, for Paul, the Christ event is in continuity with the original Jewish story of humanity (Gen 2–3). In this way, Paul's christological convictions are informed. On the other hand, note how Paul's christological convictions inform his understanding of the Adam story. Paul does not merely rehash the story's every detail. In fact, he purposely leaves out important details to conform to what he already believes about the Christ event.

Observe, for example, what he omits from the story: Nowhere in Rom 5:12–21 does he mention Eve.[55] This is obviously important because she, not Adam, was the first person to sin.[56] And so, technically, it was Eve and not Adam through whom "sin came into the world" (Rom 5:12). It is certainly not the case that Paul is ignorant of the chronology of the situation. In other texts, for instance, it is evident Paul is aware of the chronological sequence—that Eve's sin, not Adam's, came *first* (e.g., 2 Cor 11:3; 1 Tim 2:14).[57] In these instances, Paul elevates the chronological priority of Eve's

53. Cf. Moyise, *Paul and Scripture*, 25.

54. Dunn, *Theology*, 95.

55. Venema and McKnight, *Adam*, 173, 183.

56. Venema and McKnight, *Adam*, 183.

57. Venema and McKnight, *Adam*, 183n28; Dunn, *Theology*, 82n11. Dunn (*Theology*, 99) says Paul may very well be echoing Eve's words later on in Rom 7. As evidence, Dunn points to God's warning in Gen 2:17 ("For the day you eat from it, you will certainly die"), the serpent's deceptive response to Eve in this regard in Gen 3:4 ("You will not certainly die"), and Eve's confession to God in Gen 3:13 ("The serpent deceived me [ἠπάτησέν με] and I ate). He then compares this to Paul's statement in Rom 7:11 ("For sin, seizing an opportunity through the commandment, deceived me [ἐξηπάτησέν με] through it.") He says (99), "Thus it was that the commandment which had been intended to regulate life (Gen. 2.16–17) became the means of death (Rom. 7.10, 13)." If Dunn is correct to draw these connections (and I think it is reasonable to think he is), then it reveals all the more that Paul is aware of Eve's chronological priority in the origins of human sin.

sin to make various points—all in line with the sequence of the Gen 3. The fact that Paul does not do so in Rom 5 suggests that his exclusion of Eve is deliberate and that his Eve-less retelling of the story is constrained by the christological point that he wants to make, namely, that Adam—being the first human—is an archetype for all humans everywhere.[58]

On this, Dunn says that "Paul encapsulates all human history under the two archetypal figures (note the double 'all' of 5.18)—Adam and Christ—as embodying, in effect, the only two alternatives which the gospel opens to mankind."[59] Thus, Paul omits Eve from the Adam story, *not* because he is ignorant of the story's chronological features, but rather because he needs to reconstruct a singular "Adam" with which he can juxtapose— and therefore *highlight*—the solution of Christ in a one-to-one comparison. In this way, "Paul *uses* Adam to bolster his Christology and to magnify the accomplishments of Christ."[60] The reason why he wants to do this is because his same train of thought continues from Rom 4 (and for that matter from 1:16–17)—namely, that fidelity to Christ, not the Torah, is what is at stake. For example, in his retelling of the Adam story, Paul says, "But the law came in order to increase the trespass" (Rom 5:20). The reason is because of what he says prior: "For up until the law [was given] sin was in the world, but sin is not counted where there is no law" (Rom 3:13). The insertion of "law" in 5:20, despite appearing out of place, serves to keep his overall line of thought at the forefront, namely, that the law cannot justify. Up until the Adam story, the focus for Paul has always been on the primacy of Christ over Torah observance, and there is no reason to think the same idea is not still operative in chapter 5. As I said above, the Adam story has been creatively employed by Paul in order to *continue* highlighting Christ's primacy over law. In this way, Paul's christology informs the way he retells the Adam story in order to speak of the supremacy of Christ over Torah observance.

The above observations are best seen when we compare Paul's use of Adam to another contemporaneous text that does the same.[61] For example, consider Sirach.[62] We read that obedience to the commandments leads

58. In his deliberations about the historical Adam, Scot McKnight (in Venema and McKnight, *Adam*, 93–191) often (and rightly) notices the mysterious absence of Eve in various retellings of the Adam story in both Paul's writings and Jewish writings.

59. Dunn, *Theology*, 94.

60. Venema and McKnight, *Adam*, 181.

61. McKnight speaks helpfully about the "variety of Adams (and Eves)" that exist in various Jewish texts (see Venema and McKnight, *Adam*, 146 and 147–69). See also Dunn, *Theology*, 84–90.

62. Also known as Ecclesiasticus, the author of which is Ben Sira. For simplicity, and in accordance with customary practice, I use "Sirach" to refer to the book and "ben

to wisdom (Sir 1:26). Likewise, the one "who holds to the law will obtain wisdom" (Sir 15:1).⁶³ Thus, keeping (and meditating on the commandments of) the Torah and proper interpretation of the Torah are both paramount in the pursuit of wisdom (Sir 6:37).⁶⁴ In this same vein, the primacy of keeping the law is also important with respect to the relationship between humans and sin. The commandments themselves are put forward as the alternative to human sin. For example, in Sir 15:11–20, the charge that God has caused people to sin is dismissed on account of human free will (vv. 11–13).⁶⁵ We read that it was God "who created man in the beginning, and he left him in the power of his own inclination" (v. 14).⁶⁶ Moreover, this freedom of the will exists for all people: "If you will, you can keep the commandments, and to act faithfully is a matter of your own choice" (v. 15).⁶⁷ The choice is between "life and death" (v. 17). Here, "life" is connected to keeping the commandments in v. 15.⁶⁸

Dunn muses on what seems to be a lack of a theology of the fall in Sirach.⁶⁹ He observes, for example, how the human "inclination" is not itself "evil."⁷⁰ In fact, as Sir 17:6 shows, it is "something positive."⁷¹ Free choice allows the person to "beware of all unrighteousness" (Sir 17:14a) and to embrace obedience to the Torah in order to gain wisdom and life (Sir 1:26; 15:1, 15–17; 17:6–14b). Dunn looks at Sir 17:1–2, where an "echo" is made

---

Sira" to refer to the author. For Greek and Hebrew editions of Sirach, I use the Göttingen LXX and Beentjes, *The Book of Ben Sira in Hebrew* (hereafter BBS), respectively. For an overview of Sirach, see DeSilva, *Apocrypha*, 153–97.

63. Unless indicated otherwise, all translations from Sirach are from the NRSV.

64. See Crenshaw, *Sirach*, 720; Skehan and Di Lella, *Ben Sira*, 264; DeSilva, *Apocrypha*, 176–78.

65. See the discussion in Skehan and Di Lella, *Ben Sira*, 271–72.

66. Sir 15:14 (LXX): αὐτὸς ἐξ ἀρχῆς ἐποίησεν ἄνθρωπον καὶ ἀφῆκεν αὐτὸν ἐν χειρὶ διαβουλίου αὐτοῦ. For ἐξ ἀρχῆς, cf. BBS: מבראשית in MSS A and Bmg (MS B has הוא מראש). For, διαβουλίου αὐτοῦ, cf. יצרו (MS A). On the extra colon in MSS A and B (not translated in the NRSV), see Skehan and Di Lella, *Ben Sira*, 269. See DeSilva (*Apocrypha*, 187–88), who observes the echo to Gen 1:1 in v. 14. This, he says, would perhaps lead listeners to consider Gen 3:1–8, where humanity freely chose evil.

67. See DeSilva, *Apocrypha*, 188, who notes that v. 15 speaks of the freedom of "every person." See also DeSilva's discussion how this relates to Sir 33:11–13, a passage that seems to nullify human free choice and responsibility (see 188, 196).

68. On the connection between Sir 15:15–17 to Deut 30:19, see DeSilva, *Apocrypha*, 162.

69. Dunn, *Theology*, 84–85.

70. Dunn, *Theology*, 84–85. Cf. Crenshaw, *Sirach*, 724–25.

71. Dunn, *Theology*, 85. Sir 17:6 (LXX): διαβούλιον καὶ γλῶσσαν καὶ ὀφθαλμούς, ὦτα καὶ καρδίαν ἔδωκεν διανοεῖσθαι αὐτοῖς.

to Gen 3:19, where Adam is said to have been cursed with hardship and death.[72] And yet, he says, even here ben Sira does not give "any hint that this was originally a word of judgment."[73] This is similar, he says, to Sir 40:1–11, in which Gen 3:19 is once again alluded. Here the discussion about hard labor, the anxieties of life, and the fear of death are depicted as nothing more than "the common lot" of all people.[74] This leads Dunn to a preliminary conclusion, namely, that in Sirach there *seems* to be no focus on anything like original sin, in which all people receive a "consequent punishment."[75]

And yet, he notes one exception. Ben Sira does, in fact, make a rather tantalizing statement about how sin and death entered into the world: "From a woman sin had its beginning, and because of her we all die" (Sir 25:24).[76] This is a clear allusion to Eve and her sin in the garden, and ben Sira casts the blame for human sin on her, not Adam.[77] In Sir 40:1–11, where Adam is mentioned in connection with the curse motif of Gen 3:19, Eve is never mentioned, only Adam. And yet even there, Adam is not blamed for the curse.[78]

---

72. Dunn, *Theology*, 84–85. Skehan and Di Lella, *Ben Sira*, 281, posits that Sir 17:1 is "based" upon Gen 3:19 and Gen 2:7. Sir 17:1 (LXX): Κύριος ἔκτισεν ἐκ γῆς ἄνθρωπον καὶ πάλιν ἀπέστρεψεν αὐτὸν εἰς αὐτήν. Gen 3:19 (LXX): . . . τοῦ ἀποστρέψαι σε εἰς τὴν γῆν, ἐξ ἧς ἐλήμφθης· ὅτι γῆ εἶ καὶ εἰς γῆν ἀπελεύσῃ.

73. Dunn, *Theology*, 85.

74. Dunn, *Theology*, 85.

75. Dunn, *Theology*, 85.

76. Dunn (*Theology*, 85) says, "Ben Sira knew (and at least drew upon) the tradition that death was the consequence of an original sin." Dunn cites parallels such as Wis 2:23–24 ("for God created man for incorruption, and made him in the image of his own eternity, but through the devil's envy death entered the world, and those who belong to his party experience it" [NRSV]), as well as from Paul (2 Cor 11:3; 1 Tim 2:14). On this, see Winston, *Wisdom*, 121–23; Kolarcik, *Wisdom*, 464–65.

77. Skehan and Di Lella, *Ben Sira*, 348–49. It should be noted, however, that there is dispute about whether Eve is referenced here. See e.g., Ellis ("Eve") who argues the Hebrew text will not permit the view that Eve is the reference. She does, however, think the Greek text would permit such a view (see 741–42n45). Ellis thinks a more likely candidate for the reference in the Hebrew text is Hesiod's Pandora (735–42). Ellis' textual insights are valuable, but I do not find all of her conclusions convincing. See also DeSilva, *Apocrypha*, 162 (see also 182n31). Sir 25:24 (LXX): ἀπὸ γυναικὸς ἀρχὴ ἁμαρτίας, καὶ δι' αὐτὴν ἀποθνῄσκομεν πάντες. BBS (MS C): מאשה תחלת עון ובגללה גועני יחד.

78. Venema and McKnight, *Adam*, 154. McKnight observes how, for ben Sira, individual humans (and not Adam) are blamed for their own sin (154). He also observes how, in Sir 49:16, Adam goes on to be "sketched as more than a little superior to all human beings" (154–55). Thus, far from being devalued, Adam is raised to prominence.

Important observations ought to be made at this point. Ben Sira clearly blames humans for the existence of sin.[79] Specifically, he blames individuals for their own sin (Sir 15:11–20). This is similar to Paul, who likewise places blame on humans for sin—not least the individual person (Rom 5:12).[80] However, one clear difference emerges: Whereas Paul blames Adam for human sin (with no mention of Eve), ben Sira blames Eve (with no mention of Adam).[81] One can only speculate why ben Sira singles out Eve (and not Adam), but it should be clear why Paul single's out Adam (and not Eve): Paul believes Jesus is launching a new epoch, a new sort of humanity (cf. 1 Cor 15:21–22, 45–49).[82] To illustrate this belief, he needs to single out humanity's *paterfamilias* for comparative purposes. Adam might not have been the first to sin, but he was the first human (genealogically speaking).[83] This shows that Paul's primary concern was not primarily about the precise origins of sin (if it were, surely Eve would have been mentioned). Neither is it Paul's point to discuss how sin has been passed down to others through the ages.[84] His point, rather, was to extol the person of Christ as the solution to the plight of humanity, which is embodied in Adam—the first human archetype.[85] Christ, for Paul, is the second—and *better*—human archetype (cf. 1 Cor 15:45–47).[86] In this way, the purpose *for* which, and the assumption *from* which, Paul employs the Adam story is christological. And because of his christological prejudgments, Paul could retell the Adam story the way he did—singling out Adam with no reference to Eve.

That Paul's christology is functioning here as a key prejudgment is substantiated when we note further comparisons with ben Sira. But first, recall

---

79. Crenshaw, *Sirach*, 724. See DeSilva, *Apocrypha*, 165, who notes that this is an element of distinction between Sirach and apocalyptic texts—the latter of which, for example, often place blame for evil on non-human forces. In this respect, DeSilva says Ben Sira "appears to be correcting" these ideas (165).

80. Note again "Because all sinned," ἐφ' ᾧ πάντες ἥμαρτον (Rom 5:12).

81. See again Rom 5:12 and Sir 25:24. Cf. Wis 2:23–24.

82. See Dunn (*Theology*, 94), who says Paul puts forward Adam and Christ as an "epochal choice between death and life." In his commentary, Dunn (*Romans 1–8*, 271) speaks of "two epochs instituted by Adam and Christ." See also McKnight's discussion about this in Venema and McKnight, *Adam*, 180–82.

83. This does not refer to what many today call "the historical Adam." On this, I follow McKnight (Venema and McKnight, *Adam*, 144–46, 176) who speaks of the "*genealogical* Adam" (144).

84. This explains, perhaps, why Paul is vague and unclear on *how* sin is passed down. That Paul is unclear in this regard, see McKnight's musings in Venema and McKnight, *Adam*, 183–88, esp. 183–84.

85. On Adam as an archetype, see Walton, *Adam and Eve*, 70–91.

86. On Adam and Jesus as archetypes, see Dunn, *Theology*, 94.

the motive for Paul's use of the Adam story. It was to show that, even before the law was given, "death reigned from Adam to Moses" (Rom 5:14a). Paul juxtaposes this with his long-running polemic against "works of the law" (which began in Rom 1:16–17), saying that even when the law did come with Moses, it only served to officially *count* sin (Rom 5:13) thereby leading to the *increase* of the problem, not to its solution (Rom 5:20).[87]

With this in mind, consider again ben Sira. For him, the solution to human sinfulness resides in obedience to the commandments. This is what it means to choose "life" (Sir 15:15, 17). This is in stark contrast to Paul, who offers a christological solution to the problem of human sinfulness. It is Christ who brings life (Rom 5:17). Paul does not merely argue *for* this idea; he argues *from* it, too. In fact, the assumption is made explicit from the outset, present *before* he even begins telling the Adam story (e.g., Rom 5:6–11). Paul therefore assumes christology in much the same way that ben Sira assumes the efficaciousness of fidelity to the Torah as the way to life.[88]

And here is the point: Because of what Paul already believes about Christ—particularly about his resurrection and, hence, his status as the second and last human archetype (1 Cor 15:21–22, 45–49)—he needs a genealogical first human archetype to which he can compare Christ.[89] This archetype could not be Eve (though she was the first to sin). It could only be Adam, given that he is the genealogical first archetype in Jewish tradition (Gen 5:1). Thus, Paul retells the original story of the first human pair in a way that he can legitimately say that "sin came into the world through one man" (Rom 5:12), even though this is not technically precise given that Eve, not Adam, was the first to bring sin into the world.[90] But due to his christological prejudgment, Paul's interpretive lens blurred that which was irrelevant to the story (i.e., Eve's chronological priority) so that it could recede from view. This allowed what was relevant to his christological retelling to emerge from the shadows of the Adam story (i.e., Adam's genealogical priority) so that the end result might be *meaning* and *understanding*.

---

87. See Wright ("New Exodus," 167), who, commenting on 5:20, says, "the arrival of the Torah strikes a negative, not a positive, note."

88. In this vein, Paul reveals himself to be most at odds with ben Sira's Torah-centered approach. For ben Sira, Torah was the alternative to sinfulness, bringing life (Sir 15:15–17). For Paul, Torah increased the presence of sin, bringing death (Rom 5:20–21a), and it is Christ who brings life (Rom 5:21b).

89. On the genealogical Adam, see n83 above.

90. To be even more precise, it was the serpent who introduced sin. See Wis 2:23–24.

Conclusion

In light of these observations, we can conclude two things. Firstly, Paul's christological horizon is clearly in play, just as one might expect (he is an interpreter, after all!). The apostle's prejudgments about the Christ event enable his subsequent judgments about the Adam story. The story itself was employed to continue his stream of thought about the primacy of Christ over and against "works of the law," which began in Rom 1:16–17. Paul's interpretations, therefore, were *creative*. But Paul's reading of the Adam story was not a one-way street such that he was merely reading *into* the story his own assumptions. To the contrary, his reading was dialogical in that the Adam story could also inform, and give shape to, his christology: Paul's christology is itself contextualized within the matrix of the Torah's own story of Adam. In light of Gadamer's theory, we might say that Paul's understanding of the Adam story was what it was due to a *fusion of horizons*—the horizon of the story (and text of Genesis to which Paul alludes) *and* his Christian horizon.

THE EXODUS STORY

N. T. Wright has long argued that a "new Exodus" theme runs prominently through Rom 6–8.[91] At first glance, this might appear to be a remarkable claim—not least because Paul quotes just two Old Testament texts in these three chapters.[92] In all reality, however, Paul does not need to appeal explicitly to the Old Testament in order to communicate a new Exodus theme. Paul, after all, is quite capable of alluding to the stories and texts of Israel without feeling the need to say explicitly that he is doing so.[93] Paul's im-

---

91. See e.g., Wright, *Romans*, 508–14; Wright, *PFG*, 1013–26, 1070; Wright, "New Exodus" (esp. 162–63). Wright ("New Exodus") argues this motif actually begins in chapter 3 (164–66). Wright's thesis is not without precedence. He states, for example, that his approach bears resemblance to the proposals put forward by Sylvia Keesmaat and Frank Thielman (he cites "Exodus Tradition" and "Story of Israel," respectively)— though he readily admits his own views are still quite unique (see 161). (Keesmaat's dissertation was subsequently published in JSNTSup; see Keesmaat, *Paul and His Story*). Additionally, Wright says he relies on the insights of Hays (*Echoes*) (161). At any rate, I am indebted to Wright's unique approach to Rom 6–8 with respect to the "new Exodus" motif explored below. In what follows, then, my arguments depend on, and are inspired by, his insights.

92. According to Stanley (*Paul and the Language of Scripture*, 103), there are two: Exod 20:17/Deut 5:21 in Rom 7:7 and Ps 43:23 in Rom 8:36. This is congruent with NA28.

93. E.g., Rom 2:15 (cf. Jer 31:33); Rom 2:25–29 (cf. Deut 10:16; 30:6; Jer 4:4).

mersion in the Old Testament is so thorough, in fact, that the stories about which they speak easily make their mark in all that he writes—the Exodus story being no exception. Wright summarizes how the Exodus story leaves its mark on Rom 6–8:

> In Romans 6, those who are "in the Messiah" are brought from slavery to freedom; in Romans 7, the story takes us to Mount Sinai; then in Romans 8, with echoes of the Galatians [4:3–7] passage, the Messiah's people are "led," not by the cloud and fire, but by the Spirit, and, assured of that "sonship" which is itself an Exodus-blessing, they are on the way to the "inheritance."[94]

Some scholars, however, are not convinced of this idea.[95] However, I think there are enough allusions present in Rom 6–8 to warrant Wright's conclusion of a new-Exodus reading. Thus, in what follows, I will assume Wright's thesis as foundation of sorts for my own argument—namely, that Paul continues his pattern of retelling the stories of Israel in a way that is consistent with, and yet creatively distinct from, the original stories themselves. My larger project, though, should not be forgotten, one that is worth repeating presently: Gadamer's interpretive theories account for—that is, they offer philosophical-hermeneutic justification for—Paul's creative retelling of these stories, not least the Exodus story. That is my larger aim. While my investigations must necessarily move from tree to tree, I encourage the reader not to lose sight of that forest.

To proceed, it is best to examine 1 Cor 10:1–13, where Paul's employs the Exodus for exhortatory, typological, and christological purposes.[96] It is there, arguably, where Paul's use of the story is most clear. A quick survey will reveal some of Paul's key prejudgments, and hence his interpretive approach, thus setting the stage for a new Exodus reading of Rom 6–8.

---

94. Wright, *PFG*, 1070. Elsewhere, Wright ("New Exodus," 163) cautions not to look for "slavish typology in which he [Paul] merely reproduces the earlier story point by point."

95. E.g., Moo, *Romans* [2nd ed], 319n14, says, "Paul alludes to many of the key events of Israel's history in these chapters, but he does not provide enough convincing allusions to suggest that this history guides the development of these chapters." Cf. Sanders, *Paul and Palestinian Judaism*, 511–13.

96. On 1 Cor 10 and its relationship to the new Exodus theme in Rom 6–8, see Wright, *PFG*, 1070.

1 Corinthians 10:1–13: The Typological and Christological Exodus

This passage is rich in content on many levels, and it is therefore worth quoting the relevant sections:

> For I do not want you to be ignorant, brothers and sisters, that all of our fathers were under the cloud and passed through the sea, and all were baptized into Moses in the cloud and in the sea, and all ate the same spiritual food, and all drank the same spiritual drink. For they drank from the spiritual rock that followed them. And the rock was Christ. However, God was not pleased with the majority of them, for they were struck down in the wilderness. But these things happened as examples (τύποι) for us so that we might not lust after evil things as they lusted. Do not be idolaters as some of them were, as it is written, "The people sat down to eat and drink and stood up to dance." We must not become sexually immoral as some of them engaged in sexual immorality and in one day, twenty-three thousand fell. . . . But these things came about as an example (τυπικῶς), and they were written down as instruction for us—to those upon whom the end of the ages has come. (1 Cor 10:1–8, 11)

There are several points to make. First, note how Paul connects Christian baptism with the Exodus event.[97] This is perhaps an understandable thing for Paul to do. After all, the rite of baptism, as practiced by the followers of Jesus, was rooted in the ministry of John the Baptist—a ministry that arguably saw itself as participating in a "new-exodus movement," one that "gathered people in the wilderness and looked for signs of salvation."[98] Indeed, both baptism and the eucharist are here "Exodus derivatives."[99] These Christian elements are derived from the Exodus event such that the latter gives narrative shape to the former. And yet, there is certainly more to say than just this. Baptism and the eucharist are themselves christologically-shaped realities and, as a result, serve to inform the retelling of the Exodus

97. Cf. the discussions in Garland, *1 Corinthians*, 449–52; Ciampa and Rosner, *First Corinthians*, 446–48.

98. Wright, *Romans*, 534. He adds: "There is every reason to suppose both that Jesus himself saw John's baptism as the starting-point for his own work, not just chronologically but thematically, and that the earliest church likewise looked back not just to Jesus but to Jesus as the leader of the movement that had begun with John's baptism. Christianity was a new-exodus movement from the beginning; baptism in the earliest church, we must assume, retained this character and overtone" (534).

99. Wright, *PFG*, 1070. See also Wright, *Romans*, 533–34, especially as it relates to Rom 6.

story itself. In this sense, Paul's christological assumptions and the original Exodus story engage in a dialogical relationship, both informing the other such that the result is a Christ-Israel reformulation. Paul's Christ, in other words, does not exist in historical isolation but *within* the story of Israel, and the story of Israel exists now *within* a christological structure.[100] In this sense, Paul "christologizes" the Exodus story and "exodusizes" the Christ story.[101] The result is *Horizontverschmelzung*.[102]

Second, that this is happening is perhaps most clear in 1 Cor 10:4, where Paul speaks of the "rock" that brought water to Israel.[103] The "rock" is interpreted christologically.[104] Thus, Paul reads the person of Christ *into* the wilderness episode. His point, once more, is to show that the ministry of Christ exists in continuity with the Exodus event itself and vice versa. Neither the Christ event *nor* this particular Exodus event exist in isolation—not least with respect to each other. They are mutually-interpreting events for Paul.[105]

Third, the Exodus is understood *typologically*—as an example, a pattern—with which the Christian community can compare themselves (note vv. 6, 11; τύποι and τυπικῶς, respectively).[106] But it is not a story that merely

100. Cf. the discussions in Baron and Oropeza, "Midrash," 64–65; DiMattei, "Narratives," 81–83.

101. Cf. Garland, *1 Corinthians*, 452; Hays, *Echoes*, 97–98.

102. See again chapter 3 above.

103. See Exod 17:6; Num 20:7–11. On the rock *following* the people of Israel, Paul may be borrowing from Jewish tradition (e.g., t. Sukkah 3:11). See Ciampa and Rosner, *First Corinthians*, 450; Garland, *1 Corinthians*, 455–56. Cf. Thiselton, *First Corinthians*, 727–28.

104. Cf. Thiselton (*First Corinthians*, 727–30), who discusses the possibility that Paul might have drawn on Wisdom tradition. He reasons that *"Paul informs his own Christology by drawing explicitly on traditions of preexistent Wisdom from the OT Wisdom literature* (e.g., Proverbs 8) and hellensitic Judaism of the first century" (728). He says further that "Paul could take for granted a background about the role of divine Wisdom as protector, guide, and nourisher of Israel in the wilderness which could readily be applied to the preexistent Christ" (728–29). He points to texts like Wis 10:15–18, where Wisdom herself is said to have led Israel through the Red Sea. Similarly, Wis 11:4 provided Israel with water (729). See also Dunn, *Theology*, 266–81. There is no doubt that Paul was drawing on the Wisdom tradition, as well as on OT texts that spoke of God as rock, as Garland (*1 Corinthians*, 457) has observed. But this does not negate (but rather highlights) the fact that Paul was reading *into* these OT texts his present christological assumptions. On this see, cf. Bates' (*Hermeneutics*, 148) discussion about the "hermeneutical priority of the present." Cf. Baron and Oropeza, "Midrash," esp. 73–75, who explains Paul's interpretation in terms of *gezerah shavah*. DiMattei ("Narratives," 70) questions whether Paul uses τύπος as a reference to Christ being "the rock" (10:4).

105. Cf. Hays, *Echoes*, 100; Bates, *Hermeneutics*, 148.

106. Cf. Ciampa and Rosner, *First Corinthians*, 443, who describe it as "typological

stands in the past that can offer moral principles for subsequent application only after the story has been explained and understood historically. To the contrary, for Paul, the story is a living story precisely because the story itself has been reread christologically.[107] In this vein, we note how the water the people of Israel drank was "spiritual drink" (πνευματικὸν πόμα) from the "spiritual rock" (πνευματικῆς πέτρας) and that "rock was Christ" (v. 4). *That* story, says Paul, offers "τύποι *for us* so that *we* might not lust after evil things as they lusted. . . . *We* must not become sexually immoral as some of them engaged in sexual immorality" (vv. 6, 8).[108] The "us" and the "we" refer, of course, to those who are in Christ, to those who drink "the cup of blessing" and are thereby *participants* in the body of Christ (vv. 14–22).[109] The christological rereading of the Exodus story enables the bridge to be built from Jews who drank the water from the rock in the wilderness to the Christians who drink the cup at Corinth. All of this works for Paul because he already believes that "the end of the ages has come" in and through the person of Christ (v. 11).[110]

Thus, we see Paul's dialogical hermeneutics in full view: The Exodus story was reread in light of Christ *and* Christ (embodied in the church) is himself reread in light of the Exodus story. For Paul, the Exodus, therefore, is a *typological* and *christological* Exodus. Thus, Paul's reading only works *if* one shares his christological assumptions—not least with respect to how he believes Christ has ushered in a new age (v. 11).[111]

As we turn back to Rom 6–8, we ought to keep the above observations in mind, namely, that: (1) Paul thinks Christian baptism and the Exodus story exist on the same narrative plane; (2) Paul rereads the Exodus story in light of Christ even as he understands his christological assumptions to be shaped by the story itself; and in this way, (3) the Exodus story can be creatively applied to the Christian community. In what follows, then, I will

---

(ecclesiological) interpretation." Cf. also Dunn, *Theology*, 279–80; Hays, *Echoes*, 91–104, esp. 91. On an extended discussion on "typology," especially as it relates to 1 Cor 1:1–11, see Bates, *Hermeneutics*, 133–48; DiMattei, "Narratives," esp. 59–75.

107. Cf. Bates, *Hermeneutics*, 147–48.

108. Cf. the discussion in Ciampa and Rosner, *First Corinthians*, 444.

109. And participants in baptism, as we see in Rom 6. See below.

110. Cf. the discussion in Baron and Oropeza, "Midrash," 64–65, 71.

111. On this passage and its relation to how Christ has "inaugurated" the new age, see Wright, *PFG*, 1070 (see also 552). On how Paul reads within a "contemporized eschatological context"—not least with respect to 1 Cor 10:11—and how this compares with the Pesharim, see DiMattei, "Narratives," 79, 86–92. DiMattei ("Narratives," 77) has an interesting take on the role Paul's christology plays within his hermeneutic. My more substantive interaction with his views on this matter can be found in chapter 8 below.

offer a sketch of Rom 6–8, highlighting the relevant allusions and echoes to the Exodus to show that here, too, Paul is alluding back to that story—albeit in christological form, much like he does in 1 Cor 10.

Romans 6: End of Slavery

We begin by noting what is missing, namely, explicit scriptural citations to the Exodus. And yet, the allusions are very present. In fact, the Exodus story, as we will see, is a *retold* story, one that "remains decisive" to the message of the chapter itself.[112]

Paul begins with a question: "What, then, shall we say? Should we remain in sin so that grace might abound?" (v. 1). The question elicits a strong response from Paul: μὴ γένοιτο ("By no means!"). The reason is because "we have died to sin," and the idea of still living in sinfulness is therefore unintelligible (v. 2).[113] This *death to sin* has been actualized through the event of baptism (v. 3).[114] But baptism does not merely unite the person into Christ's death, but also into Christ's resurrection (v. 4ab). This *death-and-resurrection-through-baptism*, says Paul, is the basis for the new type of living: "so also we might walk in newness of life" (v.4c). In this way, baptism legitimates Paul's answer (μὴ γένοιτο) to the question of whether or not it was permissible to continue living in sin.

Notice something important. This same issue—leaving behind sin, being united to Christ through the sacrament—is similar to what we have already seen in 1 Cor 10.[115] We recall that Christian baptism was linked there to the Exodus story, where Israel *passed through the sea*, an event understood by Paul as a "baptism" (vv. 1–2). It was through their "baptism" that Israel herself was freed from the slavery of Egypt. After the end of her slavery, Israel was encouraged never to look back, though of course she often did (e.g., Exod 16:1–3; Num 11:4–5; 14:3–4). Because of the narrative continuity assumed by Paul—by means of his christological prejudgments—the Corinthians should themselves never look back.

We see the same in Rom 6: Union with Christ through baptism is the foundation for the Christian's leaving behind a life of sin, indeed, of slavery. Notice how the sinful life is described, namely, as the life that is *enslaved*,

---

112. Wright, *Romans*, 547.

113. Cf. Wright's comments on v. 13 (*Romans*, 542).

114. That baptism here is literal (i.e., the "physical rite" itself) and not metaphorical, see Wright, *Romans*, 533.

115. Wright, *Romans*, 533–34.

δουλεύω (v. 6).[116] Sin has the ability to *reign* (βασιλεύω) and *exercise lordship* (κυριεύω) over people (vv. 12 and 14, respectively).[117] Because of sin, death too has the ability to "exercise lordship," κυριεύω (v. 9). And yet through the death and resurrection of Christ, death's lordship—its reign of terror—has been conquered (vv. 9–11).[118] Anyone united with Christ through baptism has been united in his death and resurrection and should therefore not turn back to sin's captivity (vv. 9–16).

Moreover, Christians united with Christ through baptism have been liberated, that is, "set free" (ἐλευθερόω), from slavery to sin so they are now "enslaved to righteousness" (ἐδουλώθητε τῇ δικαιοσύνῃ) (v. 18).[119] The basic idea is that Christians should not go back to their past life of sin but should move into a life of "holiness" (ἁγιασμός; v. 19). The culmination (τέλος) of the life of holiness, of righteousness—brought about by the death and resurrection of Christ *through baptism*—is entrance into the life of a better age: ζωὴ αἰώνιος (vv. 22–23). Here Paul rehashes what he has already said in v. 4. There, baptism into Christ was said to bring the new life (ἐν καινότητι ζωῆς περιπατήσωμεν). This post-baptismal new life speaks of new creation and may very well be an allusion to Israel's post-Red-Sea-crossing (and

116. On Paul's ὁ παλαιὸς ἡμῶν ἄνθρωπος in v. 6, and how it connects back to Rom 5:12–21 and therefore communicates "Adamic solidarity," see Wright, *Romans*, 539. He says, "In baptism the whole person leaves the Adam-world for good, leaves it by death, a final one-way journey" (539). On the connection between chapters 5 and 6, see also *Romans*, 546–47.

117. On "the notion of realm" in vv. 12–14 and how sin's realm is at war with God's realm, see Campbell, *Paul and the Hope of Glory*, 68–69

118. Commenting on v. 14, Campbell (*Paul and the Hope of Glory*, 69) says the verse "reminds believers that their allegiance to God, their lord, cancels sin's legitimacy as ruler over them. Sin will not rule over them because they no longer belong to the realm ruled by sin." Cf. Käsemann (*Romans*, 179): "Paul does not regard obedience as a possibility, expression, or variation of freedom. He regards freedom as the determinative relation of Christian obedience vis-à-vis the world. It is presupposed here as elsewhere that a person belongs constitutively to a world and lies under lordship. With baptism a change of lordship has been effected. . . . The new Kyrios sets those who are bound to him into freedom from powers and necessities."

119. Here, the continued use of *slavery* (δουλ-) language appears confusing on first glance. Paul continues with the language of *slavery*, however, not to suggest that Christians have traded out one evil master out for another, one reign of terror for a similar one (albeit with a new master). Paul continues with the language of slavery, he says, due to the limitations of his audience (v. 19). On this see, Wright, *Romans*, 544–45. Wright says, "Since Paul's basic point throughout is the exodus motif of the freeing of the slaves, he is well aware that suggesting an alternative slavery is in principle odd, and is only introduced to make the point of the alternative allegiance more sharply" (545).

subsequent post-wilderness-journey) entrance into the promised land.[120] But is this a stretch?

I do not think it is. In fact, this would make sense of Paul's working narrative thus far. Following Wright's lead, let us consider once more Paul's use of the Abraham story in Rom 4. He observes how one of Paul's favorite Abraham texts is located in Gen 15, a chapter that, interestingly, forecasts Israel's enslavement in Egypt *and also* tells of their deliverance and entrance into, and possession of, the promised land (Gen 15:13–14, 18).[121] There we read,

> And it was said to Abram, "Know for certain that your offspring will be a sojourner in a land not their own, and they will *enslave* (δουλώσουσιν), mistreat, and humiliate them for four hundred years. But the nation they serve as slaves (ᾧ ἐὰν δουλεύσωσιν) I will judge. And after these things, they will come out here with many items." . . . On that day, the Lord arranged a covenant with Abram, saying, "To your offspring I will give this land." (Gen 15:13–14, 18a LXX; emphasis added)

Wright thinks Paul has this text in mind when he (re)tells the Abraham story in Rom 4, where Christ is said to fulfill the covenant promises made to the patriarch.[122] Wright also observes (per the text above) that the covenant promise to Abraham entails (among other things) the Exodus.[123] So, his logic goes as follows: (1) The covenant with Abraham entails the fulfillment of the Exodus (Gen 15:13–14, 18); (2) The covenant with Abraham is fulfilled in Jesus (Rom 4); therefore, (3) Jesus brings the Exodus to complete fulfillment.

This plot is remarkably similar to what we observe in Rom 6–8: The "structure [of] the path of the people of God from slavery in Egypt to inheritance in the land of promise" is the same structure—with all the relevant key words, terms, and concepts being employed—that Paul outlines in his "exposition of the Christian's status, hope and vocation."[124] That exposition is most visible in a place like Rom 6:19–23, where the path takes on the following scheme: Those once *enslaved* to a *slave-master* have been *set free* by Christ and therefore should enter into a *new* type of *life*. This, says Paul, is the Christian's blueprint—or better, *map*—for leaving the old life behind. Terms like "slavery," then, are not plucked out of thin air, nor are they

---

120. Wright, "New Exodus," 164, 167–68.

121. Wright, "New Exodus," 164.

122. Wright, "New Exodus," 164.

123. Wright, "New Exodus," 164, 166.

124. Wright, "New Exodus," 164.

employed as part of a "slave market illustration taken from the Hellenistic world," as Wright says.[125] To the contrary, the metaphors and the text itself,

> cries out to be interpreted in terms of the exodus. And when we find that the key event through which slavery is abandoned and freedom is gained consists of passing through the water, re-enacting the death of Jesus, which was already interpreted in terms of Passover imagery, the case can be closed. Exodus is not a distant echo here. It is a main theme.[126]

Indeed, such talk of slaves and their being set free ought to harken the reader back to the Exodus story.[127] It is difficult to imagine how Paul—steeped as he was within the Jewish stories and texts—could use such highly-charged terminology and *not* have intended to refer to the Exodus. In fact, it seems to me that its unlikelihood is such that those who wish to argue against the Exodus motif bears most of the burden of proof.

Romans 7: The Law at Mount Sinai

With the insights gleaned from 1 Cor 10 and Rom 6, we are now ready to move onto Rom 7. Wright suggests that, if Paul has just alluded to Israel's exit from the land of Egypt in Rom 6, then one might also look for him to discuss the giving of the law at Mt. Sinai.[128] The reasons are obvious: First, the major event that followed Israel's exit from Egypt was, in fact, the giving of the law. Second, because Paul has argued at length from 1:16—6:23 that Christ and not the law is what reveals the righteousness of God and grants justification, it would seem that, at some point soon, a discussion about what role the law itself played in salvation history is necessary.

Here is how it plays out: Rom 7 can be divided into three parts, namely, (1) vv. 1–6; (2) vv. 7–24; and (3) v. 25. The first and third of these are what I will call the framing sections. These frame the middle section such that they set the terms of the debate for it. The "terms" are nothing other than Paul's christological convictions. As we will see below, vv. 1–6 reveals that Paul's christology, as a working prejudgment, is calling the shots. In vv. 5–6 of this section, Paul opens with what might be understood as a *reductio ad absurdum* argument, which is employed to deconstruct the notion that the law

---

125. Wright, *Romans*, 534. See also Wright, "New Exodus," 162. Cf. Thielman, "Story of Israel," 186–87.

126. Wright, *Romans*, 534.

127. Wright, "New Exodus," 162.

128. Wright, *Romans*, 550; Wright, "New Exodus," 162–63.

can be appealed to as a means to righteousness (at least intelligibly so), thus reinforcing his already-assumed christology. These opening verses prepare the reader for the middle section (vv. 7–24), which serves to extend Paul's *reductio* argument. Once the *reductio* has done its job, Paul concludes with the third section (v. 25), where he issues a final christological statement.

Romans 7:1–6

Paul begins with, "Or do you not know, brothers and sisters—I speak, after all, to those who know the law—that the law has dominion [κυριεύω] over a person so long as he lives?" (7:1). The fact that the law is said to exercise *lordship* (κυριεύω) is revealing in light of what Paul has already said in Rom 6 about slavery and the dominion of sin, and I will have more to say about this below. But first we should note the "or" (ἤ) in v. 1. The word is quite instructive, as it demands the reader link the ensuing discussion back to 6:23.[129] In fact, it demands a link be made back to the entire discussion of Rom 6, which itself is an extension of his larger argument that began in 1:16—namely, that Christ is the one through whom God has accomplished his purposes. Paul's long-running argument has shown that Christ has (1) revealed God's righteousness in the face of Jew and Gentile unrighteousness (1:16—3:31); (2) fulfilled the Abrahamic promise (ch. 4); (3) launched a new humanity (ch. 5); and (4) set the captives free (ch. 6). Throughout these sections, Paul has interacted routinely with the topic of *law* and how it relates to his christology. This is most visible in chapters 1–4.

But "law" and its oft-associated terms (e.g., circumcision, works) appear to take somewhat of a backseat in chapters 5–6. Paul, for example, only mentions "law" and "lawlessness" a handful of times.[130] That said, it would be a mistake to think the Torah has been completely sidelined, pushed as it were to the peripheral edge in these chapters due to its irrelevance for the discussions there. In fact, as we will see, Paul's discussion about slavery in Rom 6 primes the reader for the discussion about the law in Rom 7.[131] Once again, the "or" that introduces the topic of law in v. 1 is, in all reality, a reminder that what has already been said is still in play when he discusses

129. Wright (*Romans*, 558) follows the connection specifically back to Rom 6:6, 14–15 and 5:20.

130. E.g., Rom 5:13, 20; 6:14–15, 19.

131. On this, see Wright, *Romans*, 549. He says, "In particular, this passage [7:1—8:11] stands at the heart of the great section, chaps. 5–8. If the two very different paragraphs of chap. 5 form a foundation, and chap. 6 an initial platform built on that foundation, 7:1—8:11 must be seen as the main part of the building."

the law in Rom 7. But what does Paul have to say about the law in Rom 7 that has not already been said in Rom 1:16—4:25? As it turns out, a lot.[132] But Paul could not get to the discussion in Rom 7 until after his discussion of slavery in Rom 6.[133] This will become evident in what follows.

Paul begins chapter 7 with an explanation that one is only obligated to the Torah if the person is alive (v. 1). This is based on an analogy from marriage (vv. 2–3).[134] A wife, he says, is only obligated to her husband while he lives, but if he dies, then her obligation is nullified. She is then free to marry someone else (vv. 2–3). Likewise, says Paul, those committed to Torah-observance ought to come to terms with what, exactly, Christ's death has brought about: "You have also died to the law through the body of Christ in order to belong to another, to the one who was raised from the dead" (v. 4). Thus, Paul's marriage analogy is itself based on Paul's christological assumptions. Paul concludes, then, that the Christian is not obligated to the law in the same way the widow is no longer obligated to her deceased husband. Though his analogy is awkward, Paul's point is clear: Christ's death has brought about a change in one's relationship to the Torah.[135] But we must pay attention to the way Paul argues. He is *not* merely arguing from plight to solution. Again, Paul's christology is more operative than this would allow. Because his working assumption is that believers have been incorporated into Christ's death and resurrection for sins, they are therefore freed from the law (vv. 4–6). But Paul does not end here; he has much more to say in vv. 7–24.

Before we get to that passage, however, we have to focus deeper on what is happening in vv. 4–6. Recall that Paul has already argued that those who have been baptized into Christ's death are raised to new life and hence out of the slavery of sin (Rom 6).[136] But now, he proceeds to advance the discussion to a startling conclusion in v. 4: Those baptized can also escape not just the sin of slavery, *but also Torah observance itself.*[137] By saying this, Paul is not saying the law is sinful. He explicitly denies this (see vv. 7–12). What he does think, however, is that law is a type of slave-master and that

132. On how Rom 7 is not "a mere aside" to his overall argument, see Wright, *Romans*, 549

133. Wright (*Romans*, 549) is correct to say Paul has been anticipating the discussion in Rom 7 all along, offering "hints" leading up to it.

134. On Jewish and Roman marriage/divorce laws, practices, and customs, see Dunn, *Romans 1–8*, 359–61.

135. On the "epochal shift" that Christ has accomplished, see Dunn, *Romans 1–8*, 361–62.

136. See esp. Rom 6:3–11.

137. On baptism here, see Dunn, *Romans 1–8*, 361.

adherence to the works of the law is a type of slavery itself.[138] How so? The problem, he says, is that the law—precisely because it is holy—arouses sin, activating it to full affect. This is the moment when Paul begins his *reductio*. He says,

> For while we were in the flesh, our sinful passions, aroused through the law, were at work in our members in order to bear fruit to death. But now, we have been released [καταργέω] from the law, having died to what held us captive [κατέχω], so that we can serve [δουλεύω] with newness of the Spirit and not according to the old letter. (Rom 7:5–6)

Notice how the law is contextualized in terms of the all-too familiar language of slavery: It holds captive; it is something from which people need release (v. 6).[139] It should not be surprising that Paul equates the Torah with slavery, as he does this same thing elsewhere. For example, consider Gal 4:21–31. There Paul interprets Hagar (the slave) to be an allegory of the Mosaic Covenant, represented by Mt. Sinai, the place where the law was given (vv. 21–25). Hagar, says Paul, represents the "present Jerusalem," that is, those who insist on law-keeping as a means to righteousness (v. 25). Because Hagar is enslaved (δουλεύω), so also are her Torah-observant children (v. 25). The entire discussion is summed up in Gal 5:1, where Paul proclaims Christ as the one who sets people free from their slavery. As a result of this freedom, Christians should not go back to "a yoke of slavery" (ζυγῷ δουλείας).

In Rom 7, the same idea is in play. The deliverance from captivity—that is, from law—takes place through death, namely, the death of Christ (vv. 4–6). That the law is a slave-master, from which Christ offers escape, is quite clear from the start, namely, in v. 1, where Paul spoke of the law as a lord (κυριεύω). As I said above, this is quite revealing in this context, as it serves to link Paul's present discussion about the law's power to enslave with his previous discussion about sin's (and death's) own enslaving power in Rom 6.[140] The entire discussion of Rom 7, then, continues that narrative of slavery, only this time with the Torah's own role in the enslavement process being highlighted. Paul claims it is Torah that *arouses* sin (v. 5). Paul's overall logic is clear: If sin is slavery (6:16), and if the Torah arouses

138. This is not unlike his argument in Gal 4:21–31.

139. In v. 6, it should not be missed that "serve" (δουλεύειν) in the phrase "serve with newness of the Spirit" ought to be carried over to the final phrase: "and not [serve] according to the old letter."

140. Cf. esp. with κυριεύω and βασιλεύω in Rom 6:9, 14 and 12, respectively. Cf. also Dunn, *Romans 1–8*, 359.

JEWISH STORIES RETOLD (ROMANS 4–8) 153

sin (7:5), then we need release from the dominion of Torah itself (7:1, 6).
For Paul to say these sorts of things would have been controversial—indeed,
"outrageously provocative."[141] And Paul knows it. This leads us to the second
section, namely, vv. 7–24, where Paul extends his *reductio* argument in order to reinforce his conclusions above.

Romans 7:7–24

He immediately follows up with a question: "What, then, shall we say? That
the law is sin? By no means!" (v. 7a). The reason Paul speaks of the Torah
in such provocative terms is because he wants to christologically retell the
Exodus story.[142] He wants to reread the old story which spoke of slavery
and rescue, the story of Israel being freed from bondage and subsequently
given the law as a prized gift. Earlier, Paul had taken issue with those who
hypocritically "rely on the law" as the supreme source of revelation and enlightenment—the "embodiment of knowledge and truth" (Rom 2:17–20).
In Rom 7, that issue is once more revisited, though with more flare. Paul
not only wants to reinforce his earlier claim that the law is not the definitive revelation of the righteousness of God (Rom 3:21–22), but also that the
law—despite being a good thing—has itself contributed to the problem of
enslavement (Rom 7:1, 7–12). He needs to enter that discussion at precisely
this point because of all that he has said in Rom 6, where Paul interpreted
baptism as the solution to slavery, as the new Exodus from a different sort of
Egypt (Rom 6). Thus, by the time he gets to Rom 7, Paul assumes he needs
to say a thing or two about the giving of the law at Sinai—the next major
event after Israel left Egypt through their passing through the waters of the
Red Sea. This is the narrative in which Paul is working. But he also knows
that, in order to advance his larger argument (i.e., that works of the law are
not the path to righteousness), he needs to discuss the events at Sinai (i.e.,
the giving of the law) in such a way that, after his discussion is finished, all
appeals to the law and to law-keeping will be rendered unintelligible. And in
order to do *that*, he shows that Sinai was an event that actually contributed
to the problem of enslavement.

He continues with this line of thought in v. 7b, where he discusses explicitly the giving of the law. He does so in order to explain the law's purpose
and function. This is his immediate focus. He says, "But in fact, if it were not
for the law, I would not have known sin. After all, I would not have known

141. Wright, *Romans*, 561.

142. That the new Exodus motif runs through vv. 7–25, and that Paul's use of "I" fits
within that motif, see Wright, *Romans*, 552.

about coveting unless the law had said, 'You shall not covet.'" (v. 7b).[143] This quotation, taken from Exod 20:17/Deut 5:21, is the only explicit quotation from the Old Testament in Rom 7.[144] But the lack of citations is irrelevant, as this particular quotation is intended to represent the giving of the law in its entirety.[145] Käsemann's observations support this idea. He says that it was a standard belief among some Jews that the prohibition against coveting embodied the "core and sum of the law" and that Paul was following suit.[146] With his quotation, then, Paul wants his readers to grasp the big picture—that is, the giving of the law at Sinai.[147]

Paul employs the quotation to further his immediate argument, namely, to show that the law functioned to reveal sinfulness. But it cannot be missed how this particular point serves to advance his larger aim, which is twofold: (1) The law, despite its being a good thing, only served to increase enslavement and (2) because of this, rescue from the law's dominion is necessary. By arguing that the giving of the law served to compound and complicate Israel's enslavement, Paul's discussion is primed such that he can now present Christ as the better alternative to law (explicitly so in v. 25). Thus, Paul's christology is not so much the conclusion to his argument as it is his alternative solution that is presented once the *reductio* has deconstructed the old paradigm. In order to make room for his already-assumed christology (vv. 1–6), Paul must deconstruct the paradigm of law-keeping down to unintelligibility.

This deconstruction continues in the same vein through vv. 8–12, though with more detailed explanation: The law is not sin, he says, but it serves to raise up the sin within the person. Paul explains: "But sin, seizing an opportunity through the commandment, brought about in me all kinds of covetousness" (v. 8a).[148] Moo observes the irony of it all, saying, "Paradoxically, what sin produces by taking advantage of the commandment is just what the commandment prohibited: 'all kinds of coveting.'"[149] Without

---

143. On covetousness as the "root of all sin" in Jewish thinking, see Dunn, *Romans 1–8*, 380. Cf. Käsemann, *Romans*, 194.

144. See the NA28. On the shortened form of the quotation, see Stanley, *Paul and the Language of Scripture*, 103.

145. See Schreiner, *Romans* [2nd ed], 367.

146. Käsemann, *Romans*, 194.

147. Wright, *Romans*, 563. When coupled with v. 11, Wright thinks the Fall is being alluded to in v. 7b, as well (563–64).

148. The syntactical function of the phrase "through the commandment" (διὰ τῆς ἐντολῆς) in vv. 8, 11 is debated. On this, see Schreiner, *Romans* [2nd ed], 365n32. On the link back to the quotation in v. 7, see Käsemann, *Romans*, 194.

149. Moo, *Romans* [2nd ed], 460.

the law, sin remains dormant—or, in Paul's words, sin is "dead" (νεκρός) until the law brings it to the surface (v. 8b). As a result, the law brings about death, though it originally intended to bring life (vv. 9–10).[150] It does this by deceptively exploiting the opportunity by way of the commandment itself (v. 11).[151] Again, all of this strikes a tone of controversy. Schreiner is correct when he says, "Paul's analysis would have been shocking to his Jewish contemporaries, since he claims that the Torah doesn't prevent sin but augments it."[152] And yet, Paul is quick to say this fact does not undermine the holiness, righteousness, or goodness of the law (v. 12). Indeed, it is not the law *per se* that leads the sinner to death; it is the sin within that does this. The law merely causes the sin to become visible (v. 13).[153] The law is an "instrument" that sin uses to wreak havoc.[154]

This leads to vv. 14–24. We should not see this section as a digression. It is certainly not a discussion about Paul's personal struggle with sin.[155] To the contrary, Paul is simply utilizing an autobiographical mode of argumentation to advance the argument of vv. 1–14.[156] Verses 14–24 serve to substantiate his argument that the law is insufficient with respect to solving the sin problem. But again, there is more than just the sin problem. The problem of sin in vv. 14–24 must be interpreted in light of all that has been said already—in Rom 6 and 7:1–14. Thus, the "sin problem" here is really about the *enslavement*

150. On how the law was intended to bring about life, see the discussion in Dunn, *Romans 1–8*, 383–84. Wright sees an allusion to the golden calf episode in v. 9, as well as in the surrounding passage. He says, "There may be an allusion, here and indeed throughout this passage, to the fact that, in the exodus story, the giving of the commandments was the moment when Aaron and the children of Israel made the golden calf—the incident to which some subsequent rabbinic writing looked back with sorrow as the time when Israel imbibed iniquity" (Wright, *Romans*, 563). See also Moo, *Romans* [2nd ed], 461.

151. In v. 11 (and v. 7b), Wright (*Romans*, 563–64) suggests Paul is alluding to both Mt. Sinai and the Fall in Gen 3. This make sense of Paul's larger argument, especially given that his discussion of Adam in Rom 5 is integral to the whole of Rom 6–8. On Adam, cf. the discussion in Käsemann, *Romans*, 194–98.

152. Schreiner, *Romans* [2nd ed], 366–67.

153. In this way, then, Paul understands Torah to be a *good* thing. Wright is correct to observe that Paul does not seek to present Torah in exclusively negative terms. Instead, Paul ultimately wants to vindicate Torah's divinely-ordained purpose and function within salvation history—not least with respect to pointing to the cross. On this, see Wright, *Romans*, 551, 565–66; Wright, "New Exodus," 163.

154. Schreiner, *Romans* [2nd ed], 370.

155. On this section, much ink has been spilled. For an overview about the much-debated "I," see Schreiner, *Romans* [2nd ed], 377–91. In the end, I think Wright's narrative approach to this question is correct. See Wright, *Romans*, 549–57, 565–72, esp. 565, 567.

156. Cf. the discussion in Wright, *Romans*, 552–53.

problem and, hence, about the *new Exodus* in Christ already assumed in vv. 1–6. Paul alludes to this very thing when he says, "For we know that the law is spiritual, but I am fleshly, sold under sin" (v. 14).[157]

As we have already seen in 7:1–14, the law, far from being able to rescue from slavery, actually intensifies the slavery—and this fact leads to the struggle and frustration that Paul laments in vv. 14–24. This lament adds force to his already-operative *reductio ad absurdum* argument against law-keeping. The *reductio* itself, armed with the rhetorical power of vv. 14–24, allows Paul to lead his Torah-observant readers to the dead-end road, phrased as it is in the form of both lament and question: "I am a wretched person! Who will rescue me from this body of death?" (v. 24).[158]

Romans 7:25

This, in turn, leads him to his final conclusion, the very thing he has been assuming and leading up to all along, namely, his christological convictions: "Thanks be to God through Jesus Christ our Lord! So, then, on the one hand, I myself serve the law of God with my mind, but with my flesh I serve the law of sin" (v. 25).[159] Paul is here, of course, anticipating chapter 8, where the resurrection and the new life are discussed as the final answer to the problem of enslavement, sin, and death.[160] But even here, the larger picture cannot be missed: Paul seeks to subvert the traditional Exodus narrative by suggesting that another, much more effective, Exodus is required. And that new Exodus, as we have already seen, is brought about through Christ. To make the case for the new Exodus, the *reductio* was introduced in vv. 5–6 and extended throughout vv. 7–24. This, again, served to reinforce Paul's already-assumed christology in vv. 1–4.

157. This is a strong hint that Paul is thinking of Israel's story, of their bondage in Egypt. Wright, commenting on v. 14, says, "The point he is making is that the 'I,' the Jew, Israel 'according to the flesh' (cf. 9:5; 11:14; 1 Cor 10:18), belongs within the Adamic solidarity, still held as a slave within the 'Egypt' of sin and death; and that the law, in its promise of life, is ontologically as well as morally mismatched with Adamic humanity, Israel included. The problem is not the Torah, but the sort of person 'I' am" (Wright, *Romans*, 566).

158. On the "I" as a "rhetorical feature" and "device," see Wright, *Romans*, 553.

159. It is important to note that Paul is not finished. He does not, in other words, conclude that everything ends finally in a stalemate—as if one should be content with the struggle, leaving behind the "flesh" as an irrelevant bygone that one will soon escape. The resolution, in fact, continues and is resolved in chapter 8, where the problem of the "flesh" and the "body of death" (vv. 24–25) is solved at the resurrection to come (8:11, 23).

160. See Wright, *Romans*, 571.

What seems to be decisive, then, for Paul is just that—namely, christology. Through Christ, slavery—and hence, law—ends (cf. 10:4). Whereas the original Exodus story spoke of the leaving behind slavery in order to embrace a Torah-based life, Paul deconstructs the Torah-based life as no life at all—but rather as one that actually leads back to slavery. Thus, Paul offers a retelling such that Christ, not the Torah, delivers Israel from slavery precisely because he, and not the Torah, sufficiently dealt with the problem of sin.[161] In this way, the Exodus story in Rom 7 continues to be christologically interpreted, just as it was in Rom 6. Similarly, Paul's christology also continues to be interpreted in light of the Exodus. We see once again that Christ's death and resurrection are not isolated events; they are, instead, events existing in continuity with the story of Israel. Those who have been baptized into Christ have gone through the waters of sin, death, and slavery and emerged out of that realm and into the realm of new life.

Romans 8: The Promised Land

In chapter 8, we continue to encounter the language of the Exodus with familiar terms like *freedom* and *slavery*. Paul also brings to the fore other highly-evocative concepts such as *sonship* and *Spirit*. He says, "For the law of the Spirit of life in Christ Jesus" (ὁ γὰρ νόμος τοῦ πνεύματος τῆς ζωῆς ἐν Χριστῷ Ἰησοῦ) has served to "set you free from the law of sin and death" (ἠλευθέρωσέν σε ἀπὸ τοῦ νόμου τῆς ἁμαρτίας καὶ τοῦ θανάτου) (8:2). The γὰρ introduces the verse to back up the claim of v. 1, which speaks of there being no condemnation against those who are in Christ.[162] The phrase "the law of sin and death" (v. 2) picks up from the previous discussion in 7:23–25.[163] There the sin/death problem—and hence the *enslavement* problem—was discussed, along with Paul's christology, which was given as the solution to the problem. When we arrive at Rom 8:2, Paul adds an important layer to the christology of Rom 7:25, saying it is "the law *of the Spirit* of life in Christ Jesus" (8:2; emphasis added). Paul had employed language of the Spirit prior to this, but in v. 2 he qualifies the freedom gained through Christ as the work of the Spirit (v. 2).[164]

161. On the "tension" between the original Exodus and the new Exodus, see Wright, *Romans*, 550–51.

162. So Moo, *Romans* [2nd ed], 496.

163. Recall "law of sin" in v. 23. On v. 2, see the discussion in Moo, *Romans* [2nd ed], 496–500, esp. 499.

164. E.g., Rom 1:4, 11; 2:29; 5:5; 7:6, 14. On what, exactly, characterizes this freedom, see Moo, *Romans* [2nd ed], 499–500.

The reason Paul does this is because he is continuing his retelling of the Exodus.[165] Having spoken about enslavement in chapter 6 and the subsequent giving of the law in chapter 7, he needs to turn to that moment in Israel's Exodus when they were led by God through the wilderness.[166] For Paul, "the Spirit takes the role, within the new wilderness wanderings of the liberated people of God, that in the exodus story was taken by the pillar of cloud and fire."[167] Thus, just as the pillar of cloud and fire led the people away from Egyptian bondage, so also "the Spirit of life in Christ Jesus" can set the captives free from the bondage of sin and death (v. 2). That Paul has in mind the Exodus story and that the Spirit occupies for Paul the role of the pillar in that story is substantiated by the fact that Paul can speak of the Spirit leading, or bringing out, believers from slavery.[168] Paul says, for example, that "those who are led (ἄγω) by the Spirit of God are the sons of God" (v. 14).[169] Given that ἄγω is used to describe God's leading Israel through the wilderness in the relevant Old Testament passages, Moo thinks it might be the case that Paul is alluding to that story.[170] We see, for example, the following:

> For the Lord your God leads (εἰσάγω) you into a good and plenty land. (Deut 8:7)

> The Lord your God, who led (ἐξάγω) you out of the land of Egypt, out of the house of slavery, who led (ἄγω) you through that great and fearful wilderness. (Deut 8:14b–15a)

> And he led (ἄγω) you forty years in the wilderness. (Deut 29:5)

---

165. On v. 2 and its continuation of the new-Exodus motif, see Wright, *Romans*, 576.

166. See e.g., Exod 13:17–22; 14:19–20; Num 14:14. It should be noted that Wright ("New Exodus," 163) sees 7:1—8:11 as a whole unit, which, he says, speaks about "the arrival at Sinai and the giving of the Torah."

167. Wright, *Romans*, 581. Wright continues: "Once again Paul, as a theologian in the strict sense (that is, one who thinks and writes about God), is innovating appropriately from within the Second Temple Jewish tradition. The result, as in a more compressed form in Gal 4:4–7, is that the one God of Jewish monotheism now begins to be known in three usually (though not always) distinct ways. Though Paul does not use the language of 'person' to distinguish these three ways, he sets up a universe of discourse within which some such development would ultimately appear necessary" (581). See also Wright, "New Exodus," 163.

168. Wright, "New Exodus," 163.

169. Longenecker (*Romans*, 702) thinks v. 14 might be an "early Christian confessional affirmation."

170. Moo, *Romans* [2nd ed], 521. Moo points to Deut 8:5, 15; 29:4; 32:12.

The Lord alone led (ἄγω) them, and no foreign god was with them. (Deut 32:12)

In light of this, Paul's description of believers in v. 4 makes sense. He describes them as those "who walk not according to the flesh but who walk according to the Spirit" (περιπατοῦσιν; v. 4).[171] Given that these verses occur within the context of being led out of sin and death, and hence out of slavery (vv. 2–13), and given further the link to select passages in Deuteronomy (see above), they should be seen as echoes to the Exodus itself, where God leads the people up from slavery.[172]

Moreover, that Paul has in mind the Exodus event is further substantiated by the way the Spirit is said to indwell believers. In vv. 9–11, he says,

> But you are not in the flesh but in the Spirit, if indeed the Spirit of God dwells (οἰκεῖ) in you. But if anyone does not have the Spirit of Christ, he is not his. But if Christ is in you, the body is on the one hand dead because of sin, but on the other hand, the Spirit is life because of righteousness. But if the Spirit who raised Jesus from the dead dwells (οἰκεῖ) in you, he who raised Jesus from the dead will give life also to your mortal bodies through his Spirit who dwells (ἐνοικοῦντος) in you. (Rom 8:9–11)

This passage should be seen as an echo back to passages that speak of the tabernacle and the temple as God's dwelling place.[173] Moreover, when we take into account how Paul brings the language of *sonship* into play, particularly with respect to being "led by the Spirit," in vv. 14–15, the link to the Exodus is once again strengthened.[174] "For all who are led by the Spirit of God are sons of God (υἱοὶ θεοῦ). For you did not receive the spirit of slavery again to fear, but you received the Spirit of sonship (υἱοθεσίας), by whom we cry, 'Abba! Father!'" (Rom 8:14–15).[175] It is the Spirit who assures believers they are the "children (τέκνα) of God" (vv. 16–17). These are important observations because it is the Exodus event that proves vital for Israel's

171. Cf. Deut 23:14, where God himself is said to have walked among the encamped people of Israel. Because of God's presence—his walking about the people—Israel must maintain holiness. "Because the Lord your God walks (ἐμπεριπατεῖ) among your encampment to deliver you and hand over your enemy before your face, your encampment shall be holy, so that he does not see among you any shameful deed and turn back from you."

172. Not least to passages such as Exod 13:17–22; 14:19–20; Num 14:14.

173. Wright, *Romans*, 583. On tabernacle/temple texts, see e.g., LXX Exod 25:7; Num 9:15; Deut 23:18; 3 Kgdms 3:2; 8:10; 12:27.

174. Wright, "New Exodus," 163. See also Moo, *Romans* [2nd ed], 521.

175. On υἱοθεσία and the concept of adoption in the Greco-Roman world, as well as the way αββα functioned within Jewish circles, see Longenecker, *Romans*, 702–6.

self-understanding as *sons* and *children*. For example, in a speech to Moses, God describes Israel as his "firstborn son" who he seeks to rescue: "But you will say to Pharaoh, 'Thus says the Lord, "Israel is my firstborn son." And I have said to you, "Let my people go so that they might serve me"'" (σὺ δὲ ἐρεῖς τῷ Φαραὼ Τάδε λέγει κύριος Υἱὸς πρωτότοκός μου Ἰσραήλ· εἶπα δέ σοι Ἐξαπόστειλον τὸν λαόν μου, ἵνα μοι λατρεύσῃ; Exod 4:22–23a LXX).[176]

Furthermore, we should note two key terms Paul employs together in his retelling, namely, the Spirit's *dwelling* (οικ-) in vv. 9–11 and the spirit of *slavery* (δουλ-) in vv. 14–15. The Spirit's dwelling in the believers is what grants them freedom from slavery (v. 2). This is reminiscent of an Old Testament precedent that routinely unites these concepts together. For example, in a variety of texts, it was common to refer to the flight from Egypt as coming "out of a house of slavery" (ἐξ οἴκου δουλείας).[177] Paul's retelling is similar: Believers in Christ dwell in the *house* of *freedom* by means of the Spirit, through Christ.

Thus, again, Paul is operating on the same narrative plane as the original Exodus story. But he is not simply retelling that story in a cut-and-paste sort of way. He is, rather, retelling the story by *interpreting* it (in the way Gadamer means). To illustrate this, consider the passage quoted above (vv. 9–11). There Paul equates "Spirit of God" with "Spirit of Christ." By making this move, Paul christologizes the Exodus story itself, as he reads Christ back into the original story. This should not be surprising, as he does something similar in 1 Cor 10 (see above). On this, Wright is not off the mark when he says, "The story of the exodus formed the backdrop to the Jewish expectation that the covenant God would once again act within history to deliver Israel. Paul has retold the story of the exodus, the freedom story, demonstrating that the Egypt of sin and death has been decisively defeated through the death of the Messiah, and that the Spirit is now leading God's redeemed people to their promised inheritance."[178]

In the section that extends from vv. 18–25, Paul employs the same Exodus language as before—only this time applying it beyond just the individual believer and to the entire created order itself. The point is to show that the new Exodus of God's people has cosmic effect.[179] He says, "For with eager expectation the creation waits longingly for the revelation (ἀποκάλυψιν)

---

176. See also Hos 11:1 MT (כי נער ישראל ואהבהו וממצרים קראתי לבני). On the allusion to Exod 4:22, see Moo, *Romans* [2nd ed], 521.

177. See e.g, LXX Exod 13:3, 14; Deut 5:6; 6:12; 7:8; 8:14; 13:10. See also Sarna, *Exodus*, 65.

178. Wright, *Romans*, 585. On "inheritance," see Moo, *Romans* [2nd ed], 521.

179. Wright, "New Exodus," 163. Wright (163) connects the renewal of creation with the believer's "inheritance" (Rom 8:17).

of the sons of God (τῶν υἱῶν τοῦ θεοῦ)" (v. 19). The reason is because the well-being of the created order itself is dependent upon the freedom gained by the sons of God: "The creation itself will be set free (ἐλευθερωθήσεται) from the enslavement (δουλείας) of corruption and enter into the freedom (εἰς τὴν ἐλευθερίαν) of the glory of the children of God" (τῶν τέκνων τοῦ θεοῦ) (v. 21).[180] This revealing of the sons of God *as sons*, and the ultimate freedom they will gain, is climaxed in their resurrection: "We wait longingly for sonship (υἱοθεσίαν), the redemption of our bodies" (v. 23).

This new Exodus, then, has not been consummated. This much is evident in how Paul follows with an exhortation to patiently hope for what is to come (vv. 24–25). The character of such hope is none other than the prayerful reliance on the ongoing ministry of the Spirit (vv. 26–27). The basis of this hope, moreover, is christological—that is, in the God who, even in ages past, has always centered his final Exodus around the person of Christ (vv. 28–30). Here Paul calls Christ the "firstborn (πρωτότοκον) among many brothers" (29). This is a strong echo back to a text we have already examined, namely, Exod 4:22b: "Israel is my firstborn son (Υἱὸς πρωτότοκός)."[181] Thus, Paul conceives of Christ as the firstborn son of God, who experiences the harsh reality of this world's enslaving corruption (i.e., his crucifixion/death) *and* the freedom from that slavery into newness of life (i.e., his resurrection/life). That Christ is called the "firstborn among many brothers" (v. 29) emphasizes the incorporative aspect of his ministry—namely, that those baptized into him can, at last, experience the Exodus they need as well: Resurrection and new life (Rom 6:5–11; 8:1–11, 23).

This makes the echo back to Exod 4:22 all the more important. In the next verse, we read how Israel needs to be released for the purpose of engaging in service to God: "Let my people go so that they might serve me" (Ἐξαπόστειλον τὸν λαόν μου, ἵνα μοι λατρεύσῃ; v. 23a LXX).[182] Thus, if Christ, as God's "firstborn" (Rom 8:29), has brought about the new Exodus, the wider structure of Paul's thought becomes clear: The people of God, embodied in God's "firstborn" (Christ), are now freed for service—for λατρεία. This is the very thing Paul will say in the opening lines of Rom 12:

180. "When Christians are finally redeemed, Paul is saying, then the land—only now, in this case, the whole cosmos—will be redeemed" (Wright, "New Exodus," 163).

181. Commenting on v. 29, Dunn (*Romans 1–8*, 485) says "Since a corporate dimension is in view (Christ as eldest of many brothers) Paul was also probably mindful of the fact that Israel was also called God's 'firstborn.'" See also the helpful discussion in Schreiner, *Romans* [2nd ed], 445–46.

182. See Sarna, *Exodus*, 24, who says, "The first-born son in Israel was regarded as being naturally dedicated to God and in early times had certain cultic prerogatives and obligations. It is this that informs the concomitant demand of verse 23 that Israel be allowed to worship in the wilderness."

"Therefore, I appeal to you, brothers and sisters—by the mercies of God—to present (παραστῆσαι) your bodies as a living sacrifice, holy and pleasing to God, which is your reasonable service (λατρείαν)" (Rom 12:1). In fact, this is the very thing Paul has already said: "Present (παραστήσατε) yourselves to God as those who have come from death to life" (Rom 6:13). Never mind what happened previously, says Paul, when sin acted as lord (κυριεύσει; v. 14), at a time when "you once presented your members as slaves (δοῦλα) to uncleanliness and lawlessness" (v. 19a). Now that the christological Exodus has happened, now that freedom has been gained, it is time to *serve* God in that freedom. I will have much more to say about this new christological ethics—this new way to live—in chapter 7 below. At present, it is enough to say that Paul's vision for the new life is what it is precisely because of his christologically-shaped retelling of the Exodus. And as such, that new life corresponds directly to Israel's promised land—to which they were led by the pillar, which for Paul is the Spirit.

It is important to highlight one more echo back to that story, one that occurs in the final section of Rom 8. In vv. 31–39, Paul ends his carefully-constructed essay on a high note. His point, it seems, is to reassure his audience that the individual and cosmic salvation that he has just explicated will, in fact, come to pass. Nothing, he says, "is capable of separating us from the love of God that is in Christ Jesus our Lord" (v. 39). This reassurance is needed because the final salvation has yet to arrive, and the Exodus has yet to be fully consummated. Thus, Paul is under no illusion that the present world has finally been freed, that all is well. Paul can speak, for example, of "the sufferings of the present time" (v. 18). He can hear the deep groans of creation, as well as the cry of the saints as they await the final restoration (vv. 22–23). Though the final Exodus is yet-to-be, it still remains the object of hope (vv. 24–25).

Hope and reassurance are indeed precious commodities in a world stuck in the mire of pain, and Paul is quick to recognize the need to keep them at the fore. And that hope is based upon the firm foundation of his christology: "He did not even spare his own son, but gave him up for us all. How will he not also with him graciously give us all things?" (v. 32). In other words, because God has already demonstrated his love through the giving of his son, it follows that *all* the promises of final restoration will be accomplished. And yet Paul is quite adamant that present threats remain. To fortify the hope and assurance of the Roman community, Paul addresses these threats directly in vv. 35–36. These are the "sufferings of the present time" (v. 18) that appear to threaten the people of God: *tribulation, distress, persecution, hunger, nakedness, danger,* and *sword* (v. 35).[183] Threatening as they may be, they pose no ultimate threat to the relationship that has been fostered through Christ between God and his people.[184] In fact, such perils for the Christian find scriptural support for Paul in Ps 43:23, which he quotes,

Rom 8:36	Ps 43:23 LXX
καθὼς γέγραπται ὅτι ἕνεκεν σοῦ θανατούμεθα ὅλην τὴν ἡμέραν, ἐλογίσθημεν ὡς πρόβατα σφαγῆς.[185]	ὅτι ἕνεκα σοῦ θανατούμεθα ὅλην τὴν ἡμέραν, ἐλογίσθημεν ὡς πρόβατα σφαγῆς.

In this quotation, Paul has in mind those persecutions believers undergo due to their commitment to Christ.[186] The "your" in the opening lines "for your sake" (ἕνεκα/ἕνεκεν σοῦ) ought to be read as a reference to Christ.[187] To support this, one might compare 2 Cor 4:10–11, where Paul speaks of "always carrying in the body the death of Jesus, so that the life of Jesus in our body might be made visible. For we who are living are constantly being given over to death for Jesus' sake (διὰ Ἰησοῦν), so that also the life of Jesus might be made visible in our mortal flesh." In this way, Paul's interpretation of the psalm is christological. The aim behind such an interpretation is, like the message of 2 Cor 4:10–11, to assure believers that suffering in this age is the path to proclaiming the life and resurrection of Jesus—and hence, to serve as a preview for what is to come when they, too, are resurrected.

In light of this fact, then, Paul can speak of believers as being "beyond conquerors" (ὑπερνικῶμεν) with respect to their suffering and tribulation.[188] This, he says, is possible through "the one who loves us" (v. 37). And *this* love is secure and cannot be broken by anything or any being (vv. 38–39). It is interesting how Paul mentions here "angels," "rulers," "powers"—as well as

183. Käsemann (*Romans*, 249) is correct to identify this "seven-membered list" as a reference to persecutions Christians experience and hence not as a reference to simply the hardships of life. That Paul's list is "drawn from some early Christian confessional portion," see Longenecker, *Romans*, 757.

184. See the helpful discussion in Käsemann, *Romans*, 247–49, esp. 247.

185. On Paul's use of ἕνεκεν, see Stanley, *Paul and the Language of Scripture*, 103.

186. On the function of the quotation, see Käsemann, *Romans*, 249. Longenecker (*Romans*, 757) thinks this psalm was part of the "early Christian confessional portion" alongside the list of v. 35b.

187. Käsemann (*Romans*, 249) calls ἕνεκεν σοῦ an "undoubtedly christological introduction."

188. Longenecker (*Romans*, 758) considers the "triumphal affirmation" of v. 37b to have come from an "early Christian confessional" source.

"height" and "depth" in vv. 38–39.[189] It is best to take these as references to
supernatural beings who, with sinister aims, seek to threaten the well-being
of God's people.[190] If that is the case, a link could be made back to the Exodus even here. The Exodus itself, after all, was originally depicted within the
context of battle against the gods of Egypt.[191] Moreover, this aspect of divine
judgment upon the gods continued to be told in various Jewish writings.[192]
In similar fashion, then, Paul may very well be alluding to the conquering of
the gods in vv. 37–39—only this time within the context of the new Exodus
through Christ.[193]

The point, then, is that nothing that appears to pose a threat to the
people of God—whether Pharaoh, the gods, sin, death, angels, or rulers—
can ever succeed in keeping God's people from attaining the resurrection to
eternal life, that is, entrance into their promised land (vv. 18–25).[194] For it
is the "love of God in Christ Jesus" that guarantees the new Exodus (v. 39).
Specifically, Paul retells the Exodus story in light of what God has done in
Christ's resurrection through the Spirit (v. 11). "The specific argument of
chapter 8 then winds to its glorious close, held in place and given coherence
and theological power by the Exodus story, now rethought in and through
Jesus and the Spirit."[195]

Conclusion

If it is indeed that case that Paul retells the Exodus story in Rom 6–8 (and,
in fact, we have seen in our analysis above that there is good reason to
think so), then this section offers yet another example of Paul engaging in

189. On the rhetorical style of vv. 38–39 and its similarity to Hellenistic practices,
see Longenecker, *Romans*, 758–59.

190. See Campbell, *Paul and the Hope of Glory*, 71–72, 101–2.

191. See e.g., Exod 12:12 ("For I will pass through the land of Egypt that night, and I
will smite all the first-born in the land of Egypt, both man and beast; and on all the gods
of Egypt [MT: וּבְכָל־אֱלֹהֵי מִצְרַיִם; LXX: καὶ ἐν πᾶσιν τοῖς θεοῖς τῶν Αἰγυπτίων] I will ex-
ecute judgments: I am the LORD" [NRSV]). See also Num 33:1–4. Sarna (*Exodus*, 56)
says, "God's power to take Israel out of Egypt manifests His own exclusivity, mocks the
professed divinity of the pharaoh, and exposes the deities of Egypt as nongods." See also
Boyd, *Crucifixion*, 823; Strawn, "Pharaoh," 635.

192. See e.g., Sarna, *Exodus*, 56n35, who points to texts like Wis 12:23–27 and Jub
48:5. See also Wis 11:15–20. Cf. the discussions in DeSilva, *Apocrypha*, 128; Kolarcik,
Wisdom, 535–44.

193. On Paul's understanding of the supernatural powers, see Heiser, *Unseen
Realm*, 326–31.

194. Wright, "New Exodus," 167–68.

195. Wright, "New Exodus," 163.

dialogical interpretation. Paul's christological convictions do not overpower and completely rewrite the Exodus story; they enhance it, expand it, and re-envision its scope to include all of Abraham's children. The hermeneutic key is his christology, at least in the sense of being a prejudgment, a *Vorurteil*. The back-and-forth, question-and-answer approach that Paul employs allows the Exodus story to take on incredibly new meaning—specifically, Christian meaning. But it does not do so in a way that renders the original story obsolete. It is still the *Jewish* story, but retold in light of Christ. Moreover, Paul's christology is itself read in light of that story. This, once again, allows for Paul's christology to emerge out of historical isolation and thus exist within the matrix of the Jewish hope, embodied as it was within her stories and texts.

SUMMARY

In this chapter, I have shown that Paul continues his larger project of recontextualization. Like his reinterpretation of key Jewish concepts in Rom 1–3, Paul continues this pattern by retelling key Jewish stories. I have examined the Abraham story, the Adam story, and the Exodus story. In each of these, Paul's christological fore-structure of understanding was predominant. It afforded him a certain interpretive posture such that, in his retelling of the stories, conclusions with fresh insights could be attained. We have seen that Paul's christology functioned, often, as a key prejudgment (*Vorurteil*). In keeping with the way Gadamer's concept *Vorurteil* functions, we have noted how Paul does not merely impose upon these stories his own assumptions such that nothing material of the original stories remain. To the contrary, Paul's christology entered into a dialogical relationship with the stories such that both—Christ and the stories—become both answers and questions to the other. In this way, neither Paul's Christ nor the Jewish stories become isolated realities, but rather mutually-interpreting ones. Thus, both are affirmed and respected as "other," and all the while, both together render something fresh in the act of application. The process, then, is dialogical, but the net result is fresh meaning. In this vein, Paul's approach to the stories ought to be described as *dialogical re-authoring*.

Chapter 6

Election and Renewal (Romans 9–11)

If we want to do justice to man's finite, historical mode of being, it is necessary to fundamentally rehabilitate the concept of prejudice and acknowledge the fact that there are legitimate prejudices.

Hans-Georg Gadamer[1]

INTRODUCTION

It is an understatement to say that Rom 9–11 is dense—whether in regard to scriptural quotations or theology. As a result, the scholarly debates are endless, and it would be impossible for me to cover everything. The discussions below, then, are necessarily selective. In what follows, I simply wish to trace the very thing that has preoccupied us thus far, namely, how Paul continues his pattern of recontextualization—rereading key concepts and scriptural texts in light of what he believes God has done through Christ such that he can adduce fresh meaning.

One key concept that Paul reconfigures is "election." As we will see, Paul's christology serves to guide him in his reconfiguration of election.[2]

1. Gadamer, *TM*, 278.

2. This is a major theme in the work of Wright, who describes "the doctrine of election" in Paul as something "reconfigured around the Messiah" (Wright, *PFG*, 860).

But once again, the reverse is true: The Jewish idea of election will also play a significant role in recontextualizing his christology. Both are mutually-interpreting, as Paul sets things up such that both can engage in hermeneutic dialogue. This, once again, is the advantage of using Gadamer's hermeneutic theory. We can utilize his concept of prejudgment, *Vorurteil*, as a way of identifying and situating Paul's christology within his interpretive activity. And this, in turn, reveals the dialogical characteristic of Paul's reading of the Old Testament. In this vein, I hope to show that in chapters 9–11, Paul continues to engage in what I have been calling "dialogical re-authoring."

EXEGESIS: RECONFIGURING JEWISH ELECTION

In Rom 9:1–13, Paul runs through a variety of scriptural texts to pave the way for his christological reconfiguration of election. This is followed by vv. 14–29, a discussion in which Paul offers supporting arguments to his exegetical conclusions reached in vv. 1–13. It should be noted from the outset that, despite appearances to the contrary, the exegesis of vv. 1–13 (and that of vv. 14–29) are not intended to do all the work with respect to Paul's view of election itself. In simple terms, this long section functions as a sort of interpretive *prolegomena*. In other words, vv. 1–29 set the stage for the substance of the core of the argument which appears later, beginning in 9:30 and stretches to 11:6.

Paul begins by expressing his grief over Israel's unbelief in 9:1–5—a grief that is heightened, he says, given the fact Israel had been granted privileges.[3] He mentions privileges such as "sonship," "glory," "the covenants," "the giving of the law," "the worship," "the promises," and "the patriarchs" (vv. 4–5a). "But," says Paul, "it is not as though the word of God has failed" (v. 6a). How so? Even though Israel has failed to believe, their unbelief is not because "God's word has failed; for God has always specified one son and not the other, one twin and not the other, one small group while the rest fell away, one tiny remnant while the rest were lost to view"[4] and so, for Paul, "not all who are descended from Israel (ἐξ Ἰσραὴλ) are those who belong to

---

See also: "Christology, in the several senses that word must bear, is the first major lens through which Paul envisages the ancient doctrine of Israel's election" (816); and: "Paul is neither denying the election of Israel as the focal point of God's worldwide saving plan nor reducing it to a secondary place. He is interpreting it in the light of the Messiah's death" (1199).

3. Cf. Ticciati, "Election," esp. 259, in view of her larger project; Gorman, *Crucified Lord*, 380.

4. Wright, *Romans*, 634.

Israel" (6b).[5] Thus, not everyone who is a physical descendant of Abraham (σπέρμα Ἀβραὰμ) is included among the children (τέκνα) of Israel (v. 7a).

To support this assertion, Paul quotes from Gen 21:12. "But (ἀλλά), in Isaac your offspring will be called (κληθήσεταί)" (v.7b).[6] This quotation is explained in v. 8: "That is, it is not the children of the flesh who are the children of God, but the children of the promise who will be counted as offspring."[7] Verse 7 ought to be seen as an echo back to Rom 2:12–29. In both places, the questions are: *Who are the people of God, and how are they classified as such?*[8] In Rom 2:13 and 28–29 it is "the doers of the law" and the circumcised in heart, respectively, who are classified as the people of God.[9] In 9:7 Paul continues this discussion, though providing more detail. Paul says the true descendants are those who are "children of the promise." This refers to the promise of providing Abraham a son through Sarah, which is recorded in Gen 18:14—a verse Paul quotes in v. 9.[10] It reminds the reader of 4:13–25, where Abraham believed God and was given a righteous status. Coupled with the use of καλέω in the Gen 21:12 quotation in 9:7, Paul's initial train of thought becomes quite clear: God elects on the basis of divine calling and promise, not on ethnicity and, hence, not on Jewish works of the law.

That this is what Paul is saying is seen best in vv. 10–13, where the story of Jacob and Esau is given. Before these twins could do "good or bad" (v. 11), and "in order that God's purpose of election might stand," he chose one over the other—Jacob over Esau (vv. 12–13). This "doing" (πραξάντων) "good or bad" (v. 11) is clarified in v. 12: "not by works, but by the one who calls" (οὐκ ἐξ ἔργων ἀλλ' ἐκ τοῦ καλοῦντος).[11] This must refer to "works of the law" in the Jewish sense.[12] Like Paul's point with the Abraham story (concerning a specific prescription of the law, namely, circumcision in 4:10–12), the same narrative is still at work: Covenant status (those who are truly "Israel," v. 6) is

---

5. On defining the second use of "Israel" in 9:6b, see Juncker, "Children of Promise," 143.

6. Gen 21:12 (LXX): ἐν Ἰσαὰκ κληθήσεταί σοι σπέρμα.

7. Σάρξ in v. 8 is used disapprovingly as in Rom 2:25–29; cf. 3:20.

8. See also Bird (*Saving Righteousness of God*, 74), who says the same question "permeates" ch. 4.

9. See Gorman, *Crucified Lord*, 381, on the link to 2:28–29.

10. In v. 9, Paul quotes (κατὰ τὸν καιρὸν τοῦτον ἐλεύσομαι καὶ ἔσται τῇ Σάρρᾳ υἱός) from Gen 18:14 (LXX) (εἰς τὸν καιρὸν τοῦτον ἀναστρέψω πρὸς σὲ εἰς ὥρας, καὶ ἔσται τῇ Σάρρᾳ υἱός). On the textual differences, see Stanley, *Paul and the Language of Scripture*, 103–5.

11. Gorman, *Crucified Lord*, 381.

12. Contra Schreiner, *Romans* [2nd ed], 488n38.

conferred *prior* to the giving of the law. Thus, for Paul, observing the law no longer functions as the instrument by which the people of God are identified. Before Jacob or Esau could do "anything good or bad" (v. 11), a status of "loved" (ἀγαπάω) was given to Jacob, though he was younger than his brother (vv. 12–13). Thus, covenant love and covenant status precede "doing good" (v. 11), i.e., "works" [of the law] (v. 12).

Moreover, that "works of the law" primarily mean those ordinances which separate Jews from the nations is clear when one takes into account the passage quoted in 9:12b, namely, Gen 25:23, where the distinction between "nations," ἔθνη, and "peoples," λαοὶ, is clearly made, which is "precisely the point at issue: the identity and status of two eschatological nations or peoples."[13] To support this assertion, Paul quotes from Mal 1:2–3 in v. 13, saying, "Just as it is written: 'Jacob have I loved, but Esau have I hated.'"[14] The important thing to note here is the primacy of "love" in Rom 9:13 and its connection to "calling" in 9:12.[15] Furthermore, in the context of Malachi, Esau is used as an epithet for Edom (Mal 1:4–5). Thus, divine "love" and "hatred" refer specifically to the status of different peoples[16]—specifically, to their covenant status. Paul's discussion, therefore, is not an excursus about individual election but is, rather, a continuation of his thought about the corporate identity of the people of God.[17] By drawing on the stories of the patriarchs in vv. 7–13, Paul builds his case for why "election" comes apart from the works of the law—even for the Jewish people. But that argument is not yet settled. Like his use of the Abraham story in Rom 4, Paul's argument here cannot rest on exegesis alone. After all, just because it can be shown that covenant status was granted to the patriarch apart from the works of the law does not mean, therefore, that one is not obligated to perform those works. If *this* is the substance of Paul's argument here, then he exposes himself to the charge that the works of the law should never have been in force.[18] Paul's

13. Juncker, "Children of Promise," 153. Paul says: ὁ μείζων δουλεύσει τῷ ἐλάσσονι (9:12b). LXX: Δύο ἔθνη ἐν τῇ γαστρί σού ἐστιν, καὶ δύο λαοὶ ἐκ τῆς κοιλίας σου διασταλήσονται· καὶ λαὸς λαοῦ ὑπερέξει, καὶ ὁ μείζων δουλεύσει τῷ ἐλάσσονι (Gen 25:23).

14. Paul: καθὼς γέγραπται· τὸν Ἰακὼβ ἠγάπησα, τὸν δὲ Ἡσαῦ ἐμίσησα (Rom 9:13). LXX: Ἠγάπησα ὑμᾶς, λέγει κύριος, καὶ εἴπατε Ἐν τίνι ἠγάπησας ἡμᾶς; οὐκ ἀδελφὸς ἦν Ησαυ τῷ Ιακωβ; λέγει κύριος· καὶ ἠγάπησα τὸν Ιακωβ, τὸν δὲ Ησαυ ἐμίσησα καὶ ἔταξα τὰ ὄρη αὐτοῦ εἰς ἀφανισμὸν καὶ τὴν κληρονομίαν αὐτοῦ εἰς δόματα ἐρήμου (Mal 1:2–3). On the quotation, see Stanley, *Paul and the Language of Scripture*, 105–6.

15. Cf. Stanley, *Paul and the Language of Scripture*, 106. On "love" and "calling," cf. Rom 9:25 below.

16. Juncker, "Children of Promise," 154.

17. For a different view, see Piper, *Justification of God*, esp. 47–73.

18. See again the discussion about Paul's use of the Abraham story in chapter 5 above.

exegesis, then, can only go so far. As I will show below, what supplements Paul's exegesis, and what Paul is anticipating in the latter part of Rom 9, is his christology—the linchpin of his reading of Scripture.

In light of his discussion in vv. 6b–13, Paul recognizes that a question will emerge in the mind of his interlocutor: "What, therefore (οὖν), shall we say? Is there unrighteousness with God?" (v. 14ab). The οὖν serves to connect with the previous thoughts, not least with v. 6 and is parallel to 3:5.[19] Is there ἀδικία with God? For Paul, the answer is, "By no means! (v. 14c). We should understand the question itself to be motivated by the fear of where Paul's argument seems to be leading: *If* Israel under the Torah was excluded from the covenant promises because she has clung to Torah and not Christ (recall Rom 3:20; 7:7–10), and *if* Gentiles have been included in the covenant promises even though they do not have the Torah but have Christ (recall Rom 2:12–29)—in other words, *if* "not all who are descended from Israel are those who belong to Israel (v. 6b)—then it makes sense why Paul's interlocutor would question the righteousness of God in v. 14. But, again, Paul is quick to shoot the suggestion down: μὴ γένοιτο, "By no means!" (v. 14c).

He confirms this answer with two Old Testament texts, which he quotes in tandem: Exod 33:19 and Exod 9:16. In the first quotation, Moses is told that mercy depends upon divine prerogative—the conclusion of which, according to Paul, is that mercy is not conditioned by human performance (vv. 15–16).[20] In the second quotation, Pharaoh is told that he is only being raised up to display the glory of God's salvation of Israel—the conclusion, too, being that God's mercy and hardening are *God's* prerogative (vv. 17–18).[21]

It is important to note the function of these quotations in Paul's argument. First, they should be seen as paired quotations, both playing a significant role in advancing Paul's reconfiguration of election. In the first quotation (Exod 33:19), the revelation of God's goodness and mercy is granted freely to Moses. In Paul's argument, this overwhelming act of the

---

19. Wright, *Romans*, 638. See also Schreiner, *Romans* [2nd ed], 494–95.

20. Paul: τῷ Μωϋσεῖ γὰρ λέγει· ἐλεήσω ὃν ἂν ἐλεῶ καὶ οἰκτιρήσω ὃν ἂν οἰκτίρω. (Rom 9:15). LXX: καὶ ἐλεήσω ὃν ἂν ἐλεῶ, καὶ οἰκτιρήσω ὃν ἂν οἰκτίρω. (Exod 33:19).

21. Paul: λέγει γὰρ ἡ γραφὴ τῷ Φαραὼ ὅτι εἰς αὐτὸ τοῦτο ἐξήγειρά σε ὅπως ἐνδείξωμαι ἐν σοὶ τὴν δύναμίν μου καὶ ὅπως διαγγελῇ τὸ ὄνομά μου ἐν πάσῃ τῇ γῇ (Rom 9:17). LXX: καὶ ἕνεκεν τούτου διετηρήθης, ἵνα ἐνδείξωμαι ἐν σοὶ τὴν ἰσχύν μου, καὶ ὅπως διαγγελῇ τὸ ὄνομά μου ἐν πάσῃ τῇ γῇ (Exod 9:16). For a discussion about the textual differences, see Stanley, *Paul and the Language of Scripture*, 106–9. On Pharaoh's *hardening*, see the discussion in Wright, *Romans*, 639, especially where he says Paul is not arguing that "God has the right to show mercy, or to harden someone's heart, out of mere caprice. Nor is it simply that God has the right to do this sort of thing when someone is standing in the way of the glorious purpose that has been promised" (see also 676–78).

giving of mercy anticipates the inclusion of the Gentiles, which Paul will mention in vv. 25–26. In the second quotation (Exod 9:16), Pharaoh is told that he has been hardened for the purpose of revealing God's saving activity to Israel at the Exodus. This quotation, ironically, anticipates the role Israel's own hardening plays in revealing the saving activity of God with respect to the Gentiles. This will not, of course, be the final word. For in the great plan of God, Paul believes that the salvation of the Gentiles will serve to bring in—and hence reverse the hardening of—the Jews (Rom 11:11–36).[22]

Second, I would like to suggest that Paul employs these quotations, and finds the meaning he does in them, precisely because of what he already believes about the reconfiguration of election. Even though Paul has kept in mind their original meaning, he nonetheless employs them within a new matrix of thought—one that envisions and anticipates what he already thinks about Christ with respect to election, that is, to the identity of the people of God. The reader, of course, must be patient. Paul has not yet revealed what, exactly, serves as the *crux* of his thought.[23] This will come about shortly, namely, when Paul explains the role christology plays in the stumbling (and hence, hardening) of Israel, beginning in v. 30.

This brings us to the discussion that continues through vv. 19–23. There Paul speaks of God who, as the "potter," has the right to do as he wills with "clay" (v. 21). This aside serves to support the assertions made in vv. 14–18. The entire discussion—spanning as it does from vv. 15–23—is once again employed to answer the question posed in v. 14: "Is there ἀδικία with God"? This question, we recall, was put forward because of v. 6b. In fact, Paul's long-running argument demands the question be dealt with: *If* not everyone who happens to be a descendant of Israel is really to be counted as "Israel" (v. 6b), and *if* Jewishness is defined as a circumcision of the heart (2:28–29), and *if* Jewishness is not defined by nature—by those who have the law, hearing it regularly (2:12–13)—then perhaps the promises of God have failed; perhaps he is *unfaithful* to his promises to Israel and hence, unrighteous, ἀδικία. Again, Paul answers this charge directly by citing examples of how God's mercy, calling, and faith have been how God's redemptive story has always worked (vv. 7–13), and this is supported by the discussion in vv. 14–23. On one level, then, Paul is not saying anything that a faithful Jew would consider controversial—*yet*, that is. Where Paul is

---

22. See again Wright, *Romans*, 639.

23. Or has he? Paul's christological hermeneutic has been quite active up to this point, as I have already shown.

headed, though, will prove highly controversial: Election is now reworked around Christ (see below).[24]

After rebuking his interlocutor, Paul asks: "What if God, although desiring to show his wrath and make his power known has endured with much patience vessels of wrath prepared for destruction—even in order to make known the riches of his glory for vessels of mercy, which he prepared for glory?" (vv. 22–23).[25] The question is left hanging, but the phrase "vessels of mercy" is picked up and identified in v. 24 as those who are called by God.[26] Moreover, the "called" are not just the Jews, but also the Gentiles: "Even us (ἡμᾶς), who were called, not only from the Jews but also from the Gentiles" (v. 24).[27] To make this argument—namely, that God has called Gentiles and Jews—Paul offers quotations from Hosea and Isaiah, respectively. With the Hosea quotations, Paul seeks to buttress specifically his argument for Gentile covenant inclusion—an argument, we recall, that commenced all the way back in chapter 1.[28] The quotes are lifted from Hosea 2:25 and 2:1 (LXX):[29]

24. Cf. Wright, *PFG*, 1186–87, who sees the question of v. 14 as being one a Gentile Christian would ask given that Israel has behaved so badly—why are *they* the chosen people? Thus, according to Wright, Paul is in this section silencing all such arrogance. I do think this idea captures Paul's train of thought, as Rom 11:18 makes clear. However, one should not miss the fact that the polemic runs both ways—to the Jew and Gentile. Indeed, that Paul is continuing his polemic against Jewish works of the law in this section is clear (see e.g., v. 11). Thus, Paul's aim here is to reconfigure how election functions with respect to non-kosher Gentiles. First, since 9:14 and 9:6 are linked back to 3:3–5 (and that back to the argument of ch. 2), then the argument that begins in v. 6 should still be seen as continuing the same line of argument—namely, to reorient what it means to be the people of God. Second, the argument in Rom 9 itself includes a provocative statement about the inclusion of Gentiles in 9:24–26, which no doubt would have, as Wright admits (1185, 1187), stirred Jews to cry foul (and not so much Gentiles!). The fact is that vv. 24–26 are *no* mere aside (as Wright seems to suggest) to the greater narrative; rather, it is perhaps a climactic part of it. And so, I do think Paul is even at this point in his argument seeking to reconfigure the Jewish doctrine of election (contra Wright, *PFG*, 1187).

25. I take the participle as a concessive. Regarding the different views, see Wright, *Romans*, 641.

26. Wright, *Romans*, 642.

27. For the view that ἡμᾶς in v. 24 encompasses both believing Gentiles and believing Jews, see Juncker, "Children of Promise," 156. On Rom 9:6–29, cf. Ticciati, "Election," 259–61, and her larger discussion.

28. Specifically, in Rom 1:5. Cf. Koch, *Schrift*, 173.

29. On the two quotations as "Zitatkombination," see Fuß, *"Dies ist die Zeit,"* 173–74. Cf. Koch, *Schrift*, 166–67, 172–74. On the *Zitateinleitung*, "as even in Hosea he says," see Fuß, *"Dies ist die Zeit,"* 181–82.

Rom 9:25b	Hos 2:25b LXX
καλέσω τὸν οὐ λαόν μου λαόν μου καὶ τὴν οὐκ ἠγαπημένην ἠγαπημένην	καὶ ἐλεήσω τὴν Οὐκ ἠλεημένην καὶ ἐρῶ τῷ Οὐ λαῷ μου Λαός μου εἶ σύ
Rom 9:26	Hos 2:1cd LXX
καὶ ἔσται ἐν τῷ τόπῳ οὗ ἐρρέθη αὐτοῖς· οὐ λαός μου ὑμεῖς, ἐκεῖ κληθήσονται υἱοὶ θεοῦ ζῶντος.	καὶ ἔσται ἐν τῷ τόπῳ, οὗ ἐρρέθη αὐτοῖς Οὐ λαός μου ὑμεῖς, κληθήσονται καὶ αὐτοὶ υἱοὶ θεοῦ ζῶντος.

As we saw in chapter 1, Paul's use of Hosea turns out to be problematic. In the original context, we recall that Hosea's oracle prophesied about a time when rebellious Israel would return to YHWH, nowhere mentioning the inclusion of Gentiles. Yet, Paul employs the Hosea quotations to argue for just that—the inclusion of the Gentiles.[30] Thus, the meaning Paul sees in these texts is different from the meaning of the original context.[31]

Furthermore, one senses the creative freedom Paul felt when certain alterations to the text are observed, as is seen for example when Paul's quotation in v. 25 is compared to the LXX.[32] The differences between the wording in Paul's quotations and the original text are well-documented; I note only those that are relevant for our purposes.[33] First, Paul has replaced

30. E.g., Moo, *Romans* [2nd ed], 632; Moyise, *Paul and Scripture*, 78. Cf. Wagner, *Heralds*, 86. Wagner may be overstating his case when he says that Paul understood the Hosea quotations to speak also of Jewish inclusion (86). It seems that the chiastic structure beginning in v. 24 precludes this. On this, Wagner (79) thinks the issue is quite a bit more "complex" and "multilayered" than basing everything on this chiasm. Cf. Stanley, *Paul and the Language of Scripture*, 109; Hays, *Echoes*, 66–67.

31. Cf. DiMattei, "Narratives," 78–79. That Paul interprets the Hosea texts as referencing the Gentiles (and not Jews like the original context) becomes quite clear when one notices how the Hosea quotations are followed by quotations from Isaiah. In v. 27, Paul introduces the Isaiah quotations with, "But [δὲ] Isaiah cries out concerning Israel." The disjunctive δὲ clearly distinguishes the Isaiah citations from the Hosea citations that precede them. On this, cf. Jewett, *Romans*, 601. Thus, the implication is that, while Paul employs the Isaiah citations "concerning Israel," he was all the while employing the Hosea citations *concerning the Gentiles* (so Moo, *Romans* [2nd ed], 632; cf. Moyise, *Paul and Scripture*, 78.) This, moreover, comports well with Paul's statement in v. 24, namely, that God has "called" people from "not only the Jews, but also from the Gentiles" (I do not think the text supports the view of Jewett, *Romans*, 600, namely, that the Hosea quotations refer not just to the Gentiles but also the Jews—that is, to the "mixed community of the church"). The quotations from Hosea are therefore meant to explain the scriptural basis for his claim that God has called "Gentiles," while his citations from Isaiah have the same function with respect to the Jews (on this, see the section "Die Entfaltung von Röm 9,24 in 9,25–29" in Fuß, *"Dies ist die Zeit,"* 173).

32. On how "Paul uses the Greek scriptures exclusively," see Bates, *Hermeneutics*, 42–43.

33. Regarding the wording of Paul's quotations, see Stanley, *Paul and the Language of Scripture*, 109–13. Cf. Fuß, *"Dies ist die Zeit,"* 170–92.

ἐρῶ, "I will say," with καλέσω, "I will call."[34] Second, whereas the Hosea text began with, "And I will have mercy," Paul has turned the original text around so that he can begin with his new term, καλέσω.[35] This allows for the two quotations to be bookended with the concept of the divine calling.[36] Third, Paul omits the verb ἐλεήσω.[37] Presumably, this is for the purpose of emphasizing the "call" of God, such that "I will call" does the verbal work for both clauses.[38] For Paul, of course, God's "calling" is a driving motif (especially in Rom 9),[39] and it seems that he adapts the quotation to fit within his own context.[40] Fourth, Paul substitutes ἠγαπημένην for ἠλεημένην.[41] The insertion of "loved" will prove significant (see below).

Regarding Paul's interpretation of Hosea, Stanley makes an interesting comment, saying, "Though the violence of the reinterpretation is undeniable, the smoothness of the resultant 'quotation' is a sure indicator of the remarkable literary artistry with which the Pauline interpretation has been incorporated into the very wording of the text itself."[42] While I readily agree that Paul's use of Hosea is artistic, for reasons given below, I am not

34. That this is a Pauline substitution, see Stanley, *Paul and the Language of Scripture*, 110. See also Fuß, *"Dies ist die Zeit,"* 175; Jewett, *Romans*, 600; Koch, *Schrift*, 166–67.

35. On the "rhetorical" function of this, see Stanley, *Paul and the Language of Scripture*, 110.

36. Stanley, *Paul and the Language of Scripture*, 110. He says, "The choice of καλέσω also highlights the thematic unity of the two citations as applied here to the Gentiles, as the idea of 'calling' both opens and closes the citation in its new Pauline form." Regarding the second quotation, Wagner (*Heralds*, 84–85n127) thinks Rom 9:26 originally read ἐὰν κληθήσονται (as in e.g., 𝔓[46] F G ar b d* sy[p]) instead of ἐρρέθη αὐτοῖς (as in e.g., ℵ A D K L P Ψ, et al.). If Wagner's reading is correct, then when combined with the geographical references (ἐν τῷ τόπῳ/ἐκεῖ), οὗ ἐάν renders the quotation "into a more expansive prophecy. . . . *Wherever* people are estranged from God, there God is now actively calling out a people for himself" (Wagner, *Heralds*, 85). Cf. Stanley, *Paul and the Language of Scripture*, 113.

37. Stanley, *Paul and the Language of Scripture*, 111–12. On the issue of variant texts regarding ἐλεήσω and ἀγαπήσω in the LXX, see 112.

38. Stanley, *Paul and the Language of Scripture*, 111–12; Wagner, *Heralds*, 80–81.

39. Fuß, *"Dies ist die Zeit,"* 177; Hays, *Echoes*, 66; Kujanpää, "From Eloquence to Evading Responsibility," 198–99.

40. Cf. the discussion about "Die syntaktisch beherrschende Funktion von καλέσω" in Koch, *Schrift*, 105.

41. It is possible that Paul's *Vorlage* read ἀγαπήσω τὴν οὐκ ἀγαπημένην, as several variants vouch for this reading (Göttingen LXX notes B V 407 Co Aeth[P] Cyr.[P]Hil). Stanley (*Paul and the Language of Scripture*, 112) thinks, therefore, that Paul's Hos 2:25 text aligned with these variants. On the other hand, Wagner (*Heralds*, 81) thinks that enough evidence exists to ascribe the substitution to Paul (see esp. n120). I am more persuaded by the latter than the former.

42. Stanley, *Paul and the Language of Scripture*, 112.

convinced "violence" is an adequate description of Paul's application of the prophet. The foundation of Paul's hermeneutic seems to be operating under the radar, so to speak. Thus, once we unearth the base structure of his reading, the details will come to light.

The textual features noted, it is clear that Paul thinks believing Gentiles are now part of the Jacob community of the "loved," and not part of the Esau community of the "hated," that is, of the rejected.[43] Käsemann is not far off the mark when he says that Paul's interpretation is "provocative" and that he employs the quotations "with great audacity" since "he takes the promises to Israel and relates them to the Gentile-Christians."[44] In light of these considerations, we must ask: What is one to make of Paul's novel interpretation of Hosea? There is no doubt Paul is creative, on some level, in his reading.[45] Yet, at the same time, it must be noted that Paul also claims to be arguing *from* Hosea. Can Paul's reading, then, be rightly described as interpretive "violence"?[46]

There are reasons to think such a conclusion is unwarranted. We should allow for Paul's insertion of "call" (καλέσω) into the quotation (v. 25) to have its full effect. When we do, it shows how Paul's train of thought is still on the same track of his prior discussions. It seems apparent, for instance, that the insertion of καλέσω in v. 25 serves to form a "verbal interplay" with v. 24 (Οὓς καὶ ἐκάλεσεν).[47] And yet, I think such "verbal interplay" goes beyond just v. 24. We find, for example, that the divine calling was brought to the fore in v. 12, where Paul argued that God's people are not identified on the basis of "works" (ἔργων) but on the basis of "the one who calls" (καλοῦντος).[48] Similar to what we observe in Rom 9:25, the discussion of *calling* in v. 12 is likewise coupled with the concept of divine *love* (ἠγάπησα) in v. 13 via the quotation from Mal 1:2.[49] It seems, then, that the *calling* of the Gentiles in vv. 25–26 (via the Hosea quotations) should not strike us as

43. Rom 9:13. On this, see Jewett, *Romans*, 598.

44. Käsemann, *Romans*, 274. To support his claims, Käsemann compares Paul's use of Hosea to texts like Jub 2:19 and 4 Ezra 6:55, 59; 7:11.

45. Cf. DiMattei, "Narratives," 78.

46. Stanley, *Paul and the Language of Scripture*, 112.

47. Stanley, *Paul and the Language of Scripture*, 110. Stanley goes on to say that such "verbal interplay" is "typically Pauline, designed to bring citation and 'interpretation' into closer verbal agreement. The effect is to impress upon the hearer the appropriateness of the citation for its present use." See also Wagner, *Heralds*, 80.

48. See Wagner, *Heralds*, 80. It should be recalled that "works" here ought to be seen as "works of the law." See above.

49. Cf. the discussion in Jewett, *Romans*, 600 (and 576, 579–80) about the Stichworte "call" and "love."

all that surprising, for Paul has already stated in vv. 12–13 how the people of God are identified—namely, through the divine call itself. He has said the same thing in v. 7 via the quotation from Gen 21:12, where it is said that "through Isaac your offspring shall be called (κληθήσεται)."[50]

What is surprising, however, is that whereas Israel ("Jacob") is called and loved, leaving the Gentiles ("Esau") to exist within the group of those "not called" and "not loved" (vv. 11–13), Paul startles his readers in v. 25 with the claim that it is precisely the "not called" who are called; it is those who are "not loved" who are now loved. This is a point Ross Wagner has made, calling Paul's interpretation "shocking."[51] Wagner says that Paul's quotations of Hosea serves to dismantle "the logic of exclusion" when it comes to the Gentiles, saying, "In this way, Paul subverts any conception of Israel's election that would deny the blessing of Abraham to Gentiles *qua* Gentiles"[52] Wagner thinks Paul's interpretive moves follow a certain pattern, something he calls a "hermeneutic of reversal," where Paul "consistently seizes on such negative appellations as 'not my people . . . not loved' as hermeneutical warrants for finding references to Gentiles in scripture."[53] He continues, saying,

> This bold move reveals one of Paul's fundamental interpretive strategies: Israel's scriptures are read as testimony to the surprising reversal wrought by God's grace, in which those apparently outside the scope of God's mercy are included among the people God has redeemed himself. Paul's hermeneutic of reversal is far-ranging and profound in its effects, necessitating

---

50. See Wagner, *Heralds*, 80.

51. See Wagner, *Heralds*, 82: "In Romans 9:24–26, those whom God has 'called,' who formerly were 'not loved', are given a new name, 'beloved.' This transformation of 'not loved' to 'beloved' recalls Paul's earlier discussion of Jacob and Esau (τὸν Ἰακὼβ ἠγάπησα, τὸν δὲ Ἡσαῦ ἐμίσησα), where ἀγαπάω belongs to a cluster of terms (including καλέω) within the semantic field of election (Rom 9:11–12; cf. 11:28). By echoing the earlier allusion to the Jacob/Esau story in this way, Hosea's words intimate a reversal of the divine exclusion of Esau (= the Gentiles) from God's mercy. The shocking nature of this interpretive move should not be minimized." Steve Moyise ("Hosea as a Test Case," 49) thinks Paul's Hosea quotations are "less shocking" when one considers that, first, Paul obviously does not think Hosea's original prophetic message (i.e., that wayward Israel will be re-included) is not going to be fulfilled, as the discussion in Rom 11 makes clear. Second, Paul also believes the inclusion of the Gentiles will actually serve to bring about the re-inclusion of Israel (per Rom 11). Moyise says even though this sort of scheme is not something Hosea knew about or anticipated, it does resolve a bit of the tension in Paul's application to the Gentiles.

52. Wagner, *Heralds*, 82–83.

53. Wagner, *Heralds*, 83. He points to passages such as Rom 9:25–26, 30; 10:19–20; 15:21.

a radical rereading of texts foundational to Israel's understanding of election.[54]

The question must be asked, then: On what grounds can Paul do this?[55] Setting that question aside for a moment, we must point out first that what Paul has done in vv. 7 and 12–13 has been to craft an argument carefully to show that it is not physical descent, but rather divine calling, that determines the identity of the people of God. But he has done so subtlety and, from the Jewish perspective, uncontroversially. There is nothing odd or debatable about the fact that God has called Isaac over Ishmael or Jacob over Esau.[56] It seems that Paul has not said anything controversial thus far with his use of καλέω—at least not in the discussion of vv. 7–23. But given that this discussion occurs within a larger context, with more ambitious aims—namely, Gentile inclusion through Christ—the seemingly unbenign nature of the discussion turns out itself to be just as controversial. So, the question still lurks: On what grounds can Paul use Hosea—and hence, the entire discussion of election in vv. 7–23—to show that the outsiders are now, surprisingly, *insiders*?

The answer, I think, lies in places where Paul has used καλέω prior to Rom 9. For example, in Rom 8:30, Paul has employed the concept of calling in an explicitly controversial way (from a Torah-observant Jew's perspective). It was there, after all, where the divine calling was mentioned within a thoroughly christological context (see vv. 31–39). The same must also be said about his use of καλέω in his unique development of the Abraham story, which was grounded upon a christological foundation (see 4:17–25). If such a link between Paul's use of Hosea can be linked back to the discussions of Rom 8:30–39 and Rom 4:17–25, then it is not unreasonable to think Paul's use of Hosea is likewise grounded upon the same christological foundation.

That Paul had in mind the Abraham story is substantiated by the fact that Hos 2:1a alludes to the Abrahamic promise: "And the number of the sons of Israel was as the sand of the sea, which cannot be measured or

54. Wagner, *Heralds*, 83.

55. Wagner (*Heralds*, 89) thinks the answer to this question is found in the quotation from Isaiah 10:22 in Rom 9:27, where Paul, he says, "conflates" Isaiah and Hosea 2:1a. But one must remember that Wagner assumes Paul quotes Hosea to refer to Gentiles *and* Jews—a thesis of which I am not persuaded (see 86–89). At any rate, I am not sure how the reference to Isaiah helps make sense of Paul's use of Hosea as warrant for *Gentile* inclusion (leaving aside the question whether Paul's Hosea quotation refers to Jews, too). Hermeneutically (in the Gadamerian sense), there seems to be something more fundamental at work with how Paul understands election—not least with respect to the inclusion of Gentiles via the Hosea quotation.

56. See Wright, *PFG*, 1184–86, and the surrounding discussion.

numbered" (cf. Gen 22:17).[57] True, Paul does not quote this part in Rom 9:26, but that is inconsequential given the next quotation in vv. 27–28, which is often recognized by scholars as a conflated quotation of both Isa 10:22–23 and Hos 2:1a.[58]

Rom 9:27–28	Hos 2:1a/Isa 10:22a LXX
27a Ἠσαΐας δὲ κράζει ὑπὲρ τοῦ Ἰσραήλ·	
27b ἐὰν ᾖ ὁ ἀριθμὸς τῶν υἱῶν Ἰσραὴλ ὡς ἡ ἄμμος τῆς θαλάσσης,	Hos 2:1a: Καὶ ἦν ὁ ἀριθμὸς τῶν υἱῶν Ἰσραηλ ὡς ἡ ἄμμος τῆς θαλάσσης, ἢ οὐκ ἐκμετρηθήσεται οὐδὲ ἐξαριθμηθήσεται Isa 10:22a: καὶ ἐὰν γένηται ὁ λαὸς Ἰσραηλ ὡς ἡ ἄμμος τῆς θαλάσσης
27c–28 τὸ ὑπόλειμμα σωθήσεται· λόγον γὰρ συντελῶν καὶ συντέμνων ποιήσει κύριος ἐπὶ τῆς γῆς.	Isa 10:22b–23: τὸ κατάλειμμα σωθήσεται· λόγον γὰρ συντελῶν καὶ συντέμνων ἐν δικαιοσύνῃ, ὅτι λόγον συντετμημένον ποιήσει ὁ θεὸς ἐν τῇ οἰκουμένῃ ὅλῃ.

The numerous textual details need not detain us.[59] The fact that Paul blends Hos 2:1a with Isa 10:22–23 immediately after his Hos 2:1b quotation in the previous verse puts to rest the idea that Paul would not have had the Abrahamic promise in mind all along—not least with the respect to Gentile inclusion in Rom 9:25–26. And if that is the case, then the christological fore-structure of understanding that governed his use of the Abraham story in chapter 4 ought to be carried over into chapter 9 as well. Much more will be said about the function of christology below. Presently, however, we only note the general point that Paul is making thus far: Election has been re-configured such that (1) Gentiles *qua* Gentiles are now "called" and "loved" (9:25–26)—just like God *called* Abraham (4:17–19), just like he *called* the descendants of Isaac (9:7), and just like he *called* and *loved* Jacob (9:12–13); and (2) that Israel herself is not necessarily part of the people of God by virtue of her ethnicity.[60] This does not mean, of course, that Israel *qua* Israel

57. Hos 2:1a (LXX): Καὶ ἦν ὁ ἀριθμὸς τῶν υἱῶν Ἰσραηλ ὡς ἡ ἄμμος τῆς θαλάσσης, ἢ οὐκ ἐκμετρηθήσεται οὐδὲ ἐξαριθμηθήσεται; Gen 22:17a (LXX): ἦ μὴν εὐλογῶν εὐλογήσω σε καὶ πληθύνων πληθυνῶ τὸ σπέρμα σου ὡς τοὺς ἀστέρας τοῦ οὐρανοῦ καὶ ὡς τὴν ἄμμον τὴν παρὰ τὸ χεῖλος τῆς θαλάσσης.

58. See Wagner, *Heralds*, 90–92; Stanley, *Paul and the Language of Scripture*, 114–15.

59. For an excellent analysis, see Stanley, *Paul and the Language of Scripture*, 113–19.

60. See again Rom 9:6b.

is excluded.[61] It does mean, however, that if she is to be included, she will need to be part of the "remnant" (ὑπόλειμμα), which Paul speaks of in v. 27 via Isa 10:22.

In the next quotation, which occurs in v. 29, Paul once again invokes Isaiah, only this time the remnant is identified as a "seed." Paul says, "And just as Isaiah foretold, 'Unless the Lord of the Sabbath had left (ἐγκατέλιπεν) us a seed (σπέρμα), we would have become as Sodom and would have been made like Gomorrah'" (v. 29, quoting Isa 1:9).[62] Paul's quotation of Isa 1:9 in v. 29 serves to tie the previous quotations of Isaiah (vv. 27–28) and Hosea (vv. 25–26) to that of his larger argument by use of the *Stichwort* σπέρμα. Previous uses of the word are telling, as they weave the thread of Paul's initial thoughts about election in the first half of Rom 9 all the way to key parts of the Abraham story in Rom 4. In Rom 9:7, Isaac—the son of promise—serves as the σπέρμα of Abraham and is the one through whom the covenant promises pass. Paul then strikes a contrast between the "children of the flesh (σαρκὸς)" and the "children of the promise (ἐπαγγελίας)" whereby he can find a larger principle, namely, that it is not the former, but rather the latter, who become beneficiaries of the covenant blessings—those who Paul says are "counted as offspring/σπέρμα"(v. 8). This anticipates the quotation in v. 29, where only a remnant of Israel are counted as σπέρμα. And because the Abrahamic covenant rests on ἐπαγγελία (promise) and not σάρξ (flesh), it is presumably open to Gentiles *qua* Gentiles—the very thing for which Paul argues through the voice of Hosea (vv. 25–26). But again, even here Paul does not appear to rest his case for Gentile inclusion on merely exegesis; something else seems to be going on.

In fact, there is: For the promise must be *believed*, accepted by faith. The ἐπαγγελία—around which election of the σπέρμα is centered—is for Paul refracted through a christological lens. This is evident when we take note of how these key words (σπέρμα in vv. 7–8, 29 and ἐπαγγελία in v. 8) are tied back to the Abraham story in Rom 4. There we read how "the promise (ἐπαγγελία) to Abraham and to his seed (σπέρμα)" came about "through the righteousness of faith" (4:13). The promise, therefore, is "to all the σπέρματι" of Abraham (4:16). But we recall from our earlier discussions that these key concepts (promise, offspring) are situated within an explicit christological context (see vv. 17–25). In other words, the promise has to be believed and *that* promise to all of Abraham's offspring is recontextualized

61. Though I do not agree with every facet of his argument, Wagner is to be commended for highlighting this fact in his approach to Rom 9:25–29. See Wagner, *Heralds*, 86–117, esp. 86–89.

62. LXX: καὶ εἰ μὴ κύριος σαβαωθ ἐγκατέλιπεν ἡμῖν σπέρμα, ὡς Σοδομα ἂν ἐγενήθημεν καὶ ὡς Γομορρα ἂν ὡμοιώθημεν.

around what Paul believes has been accomplished through the ministry of Jesus—specifically in regard to his death and resurrection.

Coming back to Rom 9, the same ideas are still in play. To be part of the remnant, the σπέρμα, is to be a beneficiary of the *promise* by way of faith in Christ. Thus, in his reconfiguration of the doctrine of election, Paul's christology plays a vital role. Though the hermeneutic role of Paul's christology has existed just below the surface of his exegesis in Rom 9, he has not left his readers entirely in the dark. As we have already seen, Paul's christology has shined through previous arguments (in places like Rom 4, especially). Since then, though, Paul has left a crumb trail of hints that nudge us back to places like Rom 8:30–39 and 4:13–25, where the divine call was openly situated within the matrix of christology.

In what follows, we will see how Paul explicitly brings his christological convictions to the fore in the argument that spans from Rom 9:30—11:6. Thus far in Rom 9 with the doctrine of election, we have seen mostly Pauline exegesis. In the next section, we will see what fundamentally grounds that exegesis, namely, his christology.

CHRISTOLOGY: ELECTION RECONFIGURED

Like his use of the Abraham story in Rom 4, Paul's reconfiguration of the doctrine of election cannot rest on simply exegesis. There seems to be something prior to exegesis that is operative. In other words, Paul's *judgment* that Gentiles are now included is not based merely on his exegesis of the details of the stories and texts of Israel. Indeed, those stories are necessary mediums through which his *prejudgments*—which are equally necessary to the interpretive process—must pass. Neither the Old Testament texts nor Paul's prejudgments can exist in isolation to one another. While both are necessary, neither are sufficient when left alone. What is required, therefore, is *dialogical* engagement between the two. We have already seen how Paul's christology functions as a hermeneutical prejudgment in the last chapter, and we will see how it continues to work in the present context.

Take, for instance, the next section in Paul's argument: Rom 9:30—10:4. "What, therefore (οὖν), shall we say?" (9:30a). The οὖν serves to bridge the substance of the previous discussion to the following section—the latter of which sums up the former. His summary is quite simple: The Gentiles attained covenant status ("righteousness") while Israel did not (vv. 30b–32). On what grounds did both of these realities obtain? The Gentiles, he says "pursued . . . a righteousness that is by faith" (v. 30b), whereas Israel pursued righteousness based on the law, that is, based on "works" (ἐξ ἔργων; vv. 31–32a). Paul says the latter "stumbled on the stumbling stone" (προσέκοψαν τῷ λίθῳ τοῦ προσκόμματος; v. 32b). Paul then cites two passages—both of which he conflates into one quotation—from Isaiah to provide attestation for this stumbling: "Just as it is written, 'Behold, I lay in Zion a stone of stumbling and a rock of offense, and the one who believes upon him will not be put to shame" (καθὼς γέγραπτι· ἰδοὺ τίθημι ἐν Σιὼν λίθον προσκόμματος καὶ πέτραν σκανδάλου, καὶ ὁ πιστεύων ἐπ᾽ αὐτῷ οὐ καταισχυνθήσεται; v. 33).[63]

It is clear that Paul quotes these "stone" and "rock" passages christologically, for here he anticipates his discussion in Rom 10:9–11, where he again quotes from the last clause of Isa 28:16: "All who believe upon him will not be put to shame" (πᾶς ὁ πιστεύων ἐπ᾽ αὐτῷ οὐ καταισχυνθήσεται; 10:11).[64] The reference to Christ is clear in that context. Moreover, given that both Isa 28:16 and 8:14 are quoted in a similar discussion in 1 Peter 2 (vv. 6 and 8, respectively), it seems evident that "the early Church was particularly interested in these 'stone' texts as an explanation for belief and unbelief."[65] Thus, the deciding factor for Gentile inclusion and Jewish failure (spoken about in 30–32a) is how each group responded to "the stone/rock" in v. 33a.[66] The conclusion, again, is that the Gentiles believed "upon him," but the Jews did not. Thus, it seems that this "rock of offense" is the axis around which Paul's *ecclesiology* and *soteriology* rotate, being central to Paul's *hermeneutic*.[67]

Paul begins ch. 10 by saying that the Jews have zeal, "but not according to knowledge, ἐπίγνωσις" (v. 2). Some have argued that the zeal in question should be understood in terms of devotion to God, that is, "for God."[68] It is best, however, to see "zeal" as still having to do with the is-

63. Isa 28:16 (LXX): διὰ τοῦτο οὕτως λέγει κύριος Ἰδοὺ ἐγὼ ἐμβάλω εἰς τὰ θεμέλια Σιων λίθον πολυτελῆ ἐκλεκτὸν ἀκρογωνιαῖον ἔντιμον εἰς τὰ θεμέλια αὐτῆς, καὶ ὁ πιστεύων ἐπ᾽ αὐτῷ οὐ μὴ καταισχυνθῇ. Isa 8:14 (LXX): καὶ ἐὰν ἐπ᾽ αὐτῷ πεποιθὼς ᾖς, ἔσται σοι εἰς ἁγίασμα, καὶ οὐχ ὡς λίθου προσκόμματι συναντήσεσθε αὐτῷ οὐδὲ ὡς πέτρας πτώματι· ὁ δὲ οἶκος Ιακωβ ἐν παγίδι, καὶ ἐν κοιλάσματι ἐγκαθήμενοι ἐν Ιερουσαλημ. The intertextual details need not detain us at this point. For a helpful analysis, see Stanley, *Paul and the Language of Scripture*, 119–25. That Paul assumes a christological interpretation, see esp. 121–22. See also Moyise, *Paul and Scripture*, 81–82.

64. Moyise, *Paul and Scripture*, 82. On Paul's addition of πᾶς, see Moyise, "Hosea as a Test Case," 39. On his use of it, see Käsemann, *Romans*, 291–92; cf. Moo, *Romans* [2nd ed], 677.

65. Moyise, *Paul and Scripture*, 81–82.

66. Ticciati, "Election," 261.

67. Juncker ("Children of Promise," 157) calls 9:30–33 a "theological summation" of 9:6–29. Cf. the following statement by Holt and Spears ("Ecclesia," 78): "Paul reads the Scriptures ecclesially *because* he reads them christologically."

68. Ortlund, "Zeal," 26. See also Moo, *Romans* [2nd ed], 650–51. However, one should specifically understand this in the context of covenant: Dunn, *Romans*

sue of Jew-Gentile relations, that is, with ethnocentric concerns.[69] The γὰρ immediately following in v. 3 connects this "knowledge" with saying they are ignorant (ἀγνοέω) "of the righteousness of God, and seeking to establish their own, they did not submit to the righteousness of God" (v. 3).[70] Thus, the problem of Jewish zeal for righteousness "not according to knowledge" is that they have failed to understand the righteousness from God, since they have sought to "establish their own." Likewise, the γὰρ in v. 4 serves to connect it with v. 3: "For (γὰρ) Christ is the culmination (τέλος) of the law for righteousness to all who believe" (v. 4).[71] Here Paul seeks to explain the Jewish failure to "reach righteousness" (9:31)[72] and make explicit how this happened—that is, Paul seeks to describe the nature of their "stumbling" (9:33). The problem, then, is christological. Paul's understanding that the Jewish failure to "reach righteousness" was founded upon a fundamental prejudgment about faith in the Christ event and its unique role it has come to play in redemptive history. Christ, as "the culmination of the law for righteousness to all who believe,"[73] is Paul's way of explaining how the Gentiles have "attained righteousness" in v. 30—that is, *they have believed in Christ*.

If, for Paul, the Jewish problem of *exclusion* is christological, then the Gentile solution of *inclusion* is also christological. According to Paul, covenant status is found in "attaining righteousness," in reaching a point of culmination of the law, which was the entire point of Rom 2:12–29,[74] namely, that Gentiles could be considered part of God's covenant—circumcised (*spiritual*)—people.[75] Thus, the implicit features that served to enable the interpretations of key scriptural concepts and stories discussed in Rom 2:12–29 and 3:20–21 (as well as the Abraham, Adam, and Exodus stories in chs. 5–8) come to light once again in 9:32—10:4. Just as Paul's christological convictions grounded his revisionist understanding of these concepts and stories, Paul's christology is now reconfiguring the concept of election in Rom 9:1–29 via the discussion in 9:30—10:4.

But Paul's christological hermeneutic does not come to a screeching halt at 10:4. Indeed, it continues from 10:5–21—a dense passage, if there

---

9–16, 586–87. See also Morris, *Romans*, 378n5. See esp. Wright, *PFG*, 1169.

69. Contra Smiles, "Zeal," 282–99, esp. 285–86. Cf. Ortlund, "Zeal," 34–35, 37.

70. Cf. Ortlund, "Zeal," 34, who describes the "ignorance" in question as anthropological (i.e., their sinful state), christological, and salvation-historical.

71. Contra Heil, "Law." Cf. Morris, *Romans*, 402–5; Gorman, *Crucified Lord*, 383.

72. Wright, *Romans*, 656.

73. See again the discussion on *Vorurteil* in chapter 3.

74. Τελοῦσα is used Rom 2:27 in terms of Gentiles keeping and fulfilling the law, linking it to τέλος in 10:4 (Wright, *Romans*, 657).

75. Cf. Wright, *Romans*, 657–58.

ever was one. As we trot through the field of quotations throughout this section, it is important we keep in mind the function of the passage itself. That function, as I mentioned above, is to support and undergird Paul's conception of a christologically-reconfigured view of election in Rom 9:1—10:4. We can divide vv. 5–21 into two parts: vv. 5–17 and vv. 18–21. We will deal with each one in turn.

Romans 10:5–17

In vv. 5 and 6–8, respectively, Paul speaks of "the righteousness that is based on the law" and "the righteousness that is based on faith." On the first, Paul quotes from Lev 18:5, saying,

> For Moses writes about the righteousness that is based on the law: "The person who does them shall live by them."[76]

On the second, he quotes from select texts from Deuteronomy, saying,

> And the righteousness that is based on faith says thus: "Do not say in your heart: 'Who will ascend into heaven?'" (That is, to bring Christ down from heaven.)[77] Or, "'Who will descend into the abyss?'" (That is, to bring up Christ from the dead.)[78] But what does it say? "The word is near you, in your mouth and in your heart," that is, the word of faith which we preach.[79]

---

76. Rom 10:5: Μωϋσῆς γὰρ γράφει τὴν δικαιοσύνην τὴν ἐκ [τοῦ] νόμου ὅτι ὁ ποιήσας αὐτὰ ἄνθρωπος ζήσεται ἐν αὐτοῖς. Lev 18:5 (LXX): καὶ φυλάξεσθε πάντα τὰ προστάγματά μου καὶ πάντα τὰ κρίματά μου καὶ ποιήσετε αὐτά, ἃ ποιήσας ἄνθρωπος ζήσεται ἐν αὐτοῖς· ἐγὼ κύριος ὁ θεὸς ὑμῶν. Lev 18:5 (MT): וּשְׁמַרְתֶּם אֶת־חֻקֹּתַי וְאֶת־מִשְׁפָּטַי אֲשֶׁר יַעֲשֶׂה אֹתָם הָאָדָם וָחַי בָּהֶם אֲנִי יְהוָה. On textual issues, see Stanley, *Paul and the Language of Scripture*, 126–28.

77. Rom 10:6: ἡ δὲ ἐκ πίστεως δικαιοσύνη οὕτως λέγει· μὴ εἴπῃς ἐν τῇ καρδίᾳ σου· τίς ἀναβήσεται εἰς τὸν οὐρανόν; τοῦτ' ἔστιν Χριστὸν καταγαγεῖν; Deut 9:4 (LXX): μὴ εἴπῃς ἐν τῇ καρδίᾳ σου ἐν τῷ ἐξαναλῶσαι κύριον τὸν θεόν σου τὰ ἔθνη ταῦτα πρὸ προσώπου σου λέγων Διὰ τὴν δικαιοσύνην μου εἰσήγαγέν με κύριος κληρονομῆσαι τὴν γῆν τὴν ἀγαθὴν ταύτην· ἀλλὰ διὰ τὴν ἀσέβειαν τῶν ἐθνῶν τούτων κύριος ἐξολεθρεύσει αὐτοὺς πρὸ προσώπου σου; Deut 30:12 (LXX): οὐκ ἐν τῷ οὐρανῷ ἐστιν λέγων Τίς ἀναβήσεται ἡμῖν εἰς τὸν οὐρανὸν καὶ λήμψεται ἡμῖν αὐτήν; καὶ ἀκούσαντες αὐτὴν ποιήσομεν. That Paul has merged Deut 9:4 with 30:12 in Rom 10:6, see Stanley, *Paul and the Language of Scripture*, 129–30.

78. Rom 10:7: ἤ· τίς καταβήσεται εἰς τὴν ἄβυσσον; τοῦτ' ἔστιν Χριστὸν ἐκ νεκρῶν ἀναγαγεῖν; Deut 30:12–13 (LXX): οὐκ ἐν τῷ οὐρανῷ ἐστιν λέγων Τίς ἀναβήσεται ἡμῖν εἰς τὸν οὐρανὸν καὶ λήμψεται ἡμῖν αὐτήν; καὶ ἀκούσαντες αὐτὴν ποιήσομεν. οὐδὲ πέραν τῆς θαλάσσης ἐστὶν λέγων Τίς διαπεράσει ἡμῖν εἰς τὸ πέραν τῆς θαλάσσης καὶ λήμψεται ἡμῖν αὐτήν; καὶ ἀκουστὴν ἡμῖν ποιήσει αὐτήν, καὶ ποιήσομεν.

79. Rom 10:8: ἀλλὰ τί λέγει; ἐγγύς σου τὸ ῥῆμά ἐστιν ἐν τῷ στόματί σου καὶ ἐν τῇ

There is much to be said about the textual issues regarding Paul's quotations, but most of these need not preoccupy us presently.[80] One glaring question, however, does require attention: How does Paul intend for the quotation in v. 5 to relate to the quotations in vv. 6–8? There are two main options—namely, that they either (1) *contrast* or (2) *complement* one another.[81] James Dunn is an advocate for the former.[82] Several observations lead him to this view. Among these, he points specifically to the significance of ἐκ πίστεως, which introduces the second set of quotations. When coupled with righteousness language, the phrase is a "central motif" in Paul (he cites Rom 1:17 as an example).[83] As such, he says, the Lev 18:5 quotation—with its focus on *doing the law*—functions for Paul as a "foil" to the quotations in vv. 6–8.[84] Moreover, the fact that ἐκ πίστεως is preceded by δὲ in v. 6a substantiates this conclusion, namely, that what was said before in v. 5 is being contrasted.[85] He also points to Paul's discussion in Gal 3:10–12, where a "contrast involving a more polemical treatment of Lev 18:5 is clear."[86] Thus, that Paul is quite capable of viewing Lev 18:5 in negative light lends to the view that he is also doing so in Rom 10:5.

Ross Wagner represents the other view.[87] As evidence, he points primarily to the context of Rom 9:30—10:4.[88] Significant for him is the observation that Paul actually contrasts the law with works: Israel failed to attain the law (v. 31) precisely because she did not pursue it "by faith" but rather ὡς ἐξ ἔργων, a phrase which Wagner renders: "*as if* it were from works [which it is not]" (v. 32).[89] Thus, within the matrix of *faith*, and when "isolated from 'works,' the Law has a positive valence for Paul."[90] Indeed, Paul can say Christ is the τέλος of the law (10:4). Paul is not, after all, antinomian. And so the idea, Wagner says, is that "Paul contrasts 'God's

---

καρδίᾳ σου, τοῦτ' ἔστιν τὸ ῥῆμα τῆς πίστεως ὃ κηρύσσομεν; Deut 30:14 (LXX): ἐγγύς σού ἐστιν τὸ ῥῆμα σφόδρα ἐν τῷ στόματί σου καὶ ἐν τῇ καρδίᾳ σου καὶ ἐν ταῖς χερσίν σου αὐτὸ ποιεῖν.

80. For a detailed analysis, see Stanley, *Paul and the Language of Scripture*, 128–33.

81. See Wagner, *Heralds*, 159–60.

82. Dunn, *Romans 9–16*, 600–602. See also Rosner, *Paul and the Law*, 71–72, 139–42.

83. Dunn, *Romans 9–16*, 602.

84. Dunn, *Romans 9–16*, 602.

85. Dunn, *Romans 9–16*, 602.

86. Dunn, *Romans 9–16*, 602.

87. See his entire discussion in Wagner, *Heralds*, 157–68.

88. See Wagner, *Heralds*, 157–60.

89. Wagner, *Heralds*, 158.

90. Wagner, *Heralds*, 158. He says, "For Paul, the Law is rightly pursued only ἐκ πίστεως (through faith 'we establish the Law' [Rom 3:31])" (158).

righteousness'/'righteousness ἐκ πίστεως' not with 'righteousness from the Law,' but with Israel's 'own righteousness.'"[91] Thus, because Paul has (1) opposed law with works (vv. 31–32) and (2) understood faith to be the road to attaining the law, with Christ as its τέλος (9:32; 10:4), Paul recognizes that such controversial claims will need scriptural substantiation.[92] This is where the quotations in vv. 5–8 come into play. Wagner thinks the first quotation (Lev 18:5 in v. 5) is put forward to show that the law "intended to lead to *life*," that is, to "righteousness."[93] The second set of quotations in vv. 6–8 is used to show that "this righteousness to which the Law has been leading comes to focus in Christ."[94] In fact, it does more, says Wagner. With the second set of quotations (vv. 6–8), Paul "*redefines* 'doing'" in the first (Lev 18:5) quotation "*as* 'believing/trusting in what God has done in Christ.'"[95] In this way, any tension in v. 5 about a "righteousness that is based on the law" with respect to the quotations in vv. 6–8 is relieved.

While much evidence can be marshalled in favor of both views, I think Wagner's has more explanatory power for the larger context of Romans, especially so in light of some of Paul's idiosyncrasies regarding the law itself. Paul, for example, often draws a wedge between *works of the law* and *faith in Christ*.[96] But Paul can also speak positively about *doing the law*—even in christological contexts.[97] Moreover, Wagner's view also accounts better for the details of Paul's immediate context (9:30—10:4).[98] His insights on 9:32 and 10:4 are most significant in this regard (see above).

Keeping in mind all that I have said in the investigations of Rom 9:1—10:4, one immediately recognizes that the point of Rom 10:5–8 is quite simple: To provide scriptural attestation for a reconfigured concept of election. But again, it is not simply exegesis. Paul brings his christology to bear upon the text in a way that is reminiscent of his use of the Abraham story

91. Wagner, *Heralds*, 158. This, he says, "is fully in keeping with his redefinition of the Law apart from works" (158). See Rom 10:3.

92. Wagner, *Heralds*, 159.

93. Wagner, *Heralds*, 160–61.

94. Wagner, *Heralds*, 161.

95. Wagner, *Heralds*, 160. He adds: "Citing the words of the Law itself, Paul argues that the Law points to Christ as its goal and thus that the 'righteousness from the Law' finds its fulfillment in 'the righteousness from faith'" (160).

96. E.g., Rom 3:20–22; Rom 4:4–5.

97. E.g., Rom 2:13–16.

98. The weakest part of Wagner's argument is its congruence with Gal 3:10–12. However, I think Wagner is correct to point out how (1) the differing situations and contexts may play a role in explaining such incongruence and (2) that it is quite possible Paul's thought might have developed. See Wagner, *Heralds*, 158n121.

in chapter 4. Consider how Paul creatively weaves his assumptions about Christ into the second set of quotations. It is the "righteousness that is based on faith" that speaks the words of Scripture (v. 6a). The personification of faith-righteousness assumes, of course, a christological framework.[99] The notion of *ascending into heaven* in v. 6b influences Paul's interpolated notion about *descending into the abyss* in v. 7 in order to accommodate Paul's already-existing belief in the ministry of Jesus, not least his resurrection.[100] The follow-up to this is the final quote from Deut 30:14: "The word is near you, in your mouth and in your heart" (v. 8a). Paul defines this word as "the word of faith which we preach" (κηρύσσομεν; v. 8b). This, again, assumes the same christological framework of v. 6a.

While it is true that Paul glosses over Deuteronomy's emphasis on doing the law in his reformulated quotation, I do not think he is necessarily trying to suppress the notion of *doing the law* as much as he is reconfiguring it around the ministry of Christ.[101] One reason I have for thinking this is the fact that Paul has already said something similar in Rom 2:6–16. There Paul speaks positively of good works in general (vv. 6–7, 10–11). He can even speak positively about *doing the law* (vv. 13–16). So by the time we arrive at 10:5–8, we should not be quick to think Paul is giving the law a negative treatment. In fact, it makes more sense to think he is reconfiguring the law around his christology—something he seems to have been hinting at in 2:16, 3:31, and 10:4. In this vein, Wagner is correct to think the confessional statements in 10:9 govern Paul's interpretation of Deuteronomy in vv. 6–8. It is worth quoting him in full:

> Paul's two "creedal statements" in Romans 10:9 correspond closely to his interpretation of the two questions in Deuteronomy 30:12–13 (Rom 10:6–7). The confession, "Jesus is Lord," recalls the early Christian proclamation that Christ has been exalted to the right hand of God. It is this event that provides the most plausible background for Paul's fanciful interpretation of Deuteronomy 30:12 as a depiction of someone attempting to ascend to heaven to bring Christ down, as if there were anything left for him to accomplish on earth (Rom 10:6). Similarly, belief "that God has raised [Jesus] from the dead" echoes Paul's

---

99. Cf. Rom 3:21–22; 4:22–25; 9:30—10:4. Rosner (*Paul and the Law*, 139–42 [see also 142–58]) is correct to observe the *prophetic* function of the Deuteronomy quotations.

100. Stanley, *Paul and the Language of Scripture*, 131–32. See also Wagner, *Heralds*, 164.

101. Contra Rosner, *Paul and the Law*, 139–42. On this, the analysis in Wagner, *Heralds*, 159–68, is to be preferred.

version of Deuteronomy 30:13, where he finds a reference to bringing Christ up from among the dead (Rom 10:7). By linking his formulation of the gospel so closely to Deuteronomy 30:12–13, Paul supplies the answer to its insistent question: "Who?" There is no need to be chasing around heaven or the abyss, Paul responds, for by raising Christ from the dead and exalting him as Lord, *Israel's God* has already done everything necessary for salvation. The word is near. All that remains is to confess and believe.[102]

The confessional statement is followed by a brief explanation (v. 10), which is itself followed by a quotation from Isa 28:16. "For the scripture says, 'All who believe upon him (ἐπ' αὐτῷ) will not be put to shame'" (v. 11).[103] The insertion of "all" is most certainly Paul's doing, for it aids him in leveling the playing field, so to speak, between Jew and non-Jew.[104] There is "no difference" (οὐ διαστολὴ) between the two, for God is "Lord (κύριος) of all, being generous to all who call upon (ἐπικαλουμένους) him" (v. 12).[105] Paul finds warrant for this claim in a quotation from Joel 3:5. "For 'all who call upon (ἐπικαλέσηται) the name of the Lord (κύριου) will be saved'" (v. 13).[106] That Paul reads "Christ" into both the αὐτός in Isa 28:16 and the κύριος in Joel 3:5 is clear from v. 9, as well as the larger context of 9:33—10:10.

Paul continues next with a single train of thought that runs from vv. 14–17. If God is accessible to all who believe and call upon him (vv. 11–13), then Paul muses how this can obtain if they have not "heard" (ἤκουσαν) the news (v. 14a). Of course, to hear requires that someone be sent (ἀποστέλλω) who preaches (κηρύσσω) that news (vv. 14b–15a). A "connected chain of steps" that leads to salvation emerges: *Sending, preaching, hearing, believing,* and finally, *calling.*[107] This is followed by a quotation from Isa 52:7: "Just as it is written: 'How beautiful are the feet of those who preach the good news'" (v. 15b).[108] Moo is correct that the point of the quotation is twofold: (1) To

102. Wagner, *Heralds*, 167–68.

103. Rom 10:11: λέγει γὰρ ἡ γραφή· πᾶς ὁ πιστεύων ἐπ' αὐτῷ οὐ καταισχυνθήσεται. Isa 28:16 (LXX): καὶ ὁ πιστεύων ἐπ' αὐτῷ οὐ μὴ καταισχυνθῇ.

104. See Moo, *Romans* [2nd ed], 677–78; Stanley, *Paul and the Language of Scripture*, 133–34.

105. This echoes his previous arguments in Rom 2:11; 3:22, 29.

106. Rom 10:13: πᾶς γὰρ ὃς ἂν ἐπικαλέσηται τὸ ὄνομα κυρίου σωθήσεται. Joel 3:5 (LXX): καὶ ἔσται πᾶς, ὃς ἂν ἐπικαλέσηται τὸ ὄνομα κυρίου, σωθήσεται. Joel 3:5 (MT): והיה כל אשר־יקרא בשם יהוה ימלט.

107. Moo, *Romans* [2nd ed], 681–82.

108. Rom 10:15b: καθὼς γέγραπται· ὡς ὡραῖοι οἱ πόδες τῶν εὐαγγελιζομένων τὰ ἀγαθά. Isa 52:7 (LXX): ὡς ὥρα ἐπὶ τῶν ὀρέων, ὡς πόδες εὐαγγελιζομένου ἀκοὴν

legitimate preaching and (2) to show that God has done his part, namely, to send proclaimers.[109]

This leads Paul to bring up the fact that not everyone has "obeyed the gospel" (Ἀλλ' οὐ πάντες ὑπήκουσαν τῷ εὐαγγελίῳ; v. 16a).[110] Paul immediately quotes from Isa 53:1, saying, "For Isaiah says, 'Lord, who has believed our report?'" (v. 16b).[111] Verse 16 is most likely Paul's response to why many Jews have failed to attain salvation—many of them have failed to believe in the gospel.[112] Thus, the "chain of requirements leading to salvation" in vv. 14–15 has been broken.[113]

This makes sense as to why Paul immediately follows with a discussion about having *faith* in, and *hearing* the message of, Christ: "So then, faith comes by hearing, and hearing through the word of Christ (ῥήματος Χριστοῦ)" (v. 17).[114] The connection back to 9:30–33 cannot be missed: The problem of unbelief in Israel is that they have stumbled over the "stumbling stone" (9:33).[115] Moreover, v. 17 recalls how the discussion began. In v. 8, we recall, Paul wrapped up his quotation from Deut 30:14 ("The word is near you, in your mouth and in your heart") by explaining what he takes that "word" to be: "the word of faith (τὸ ῥῆμα τῆς πίστεως) which we preach"

εἰρήνης, ὡς εὐαγγελιζόμενος ἀγαθά, ὅτι ἀκουστὴν ποιήσω τὴν σωτηρίαν σου λέγων Σιων Βασιλεύσει σου ὁ θεός. Isa 52:7 (MT): מה־נאוו על־ההרים רגלי מבשר משמיע שלום מבשר טוב משמיע ישועה אמר לציון מלך אלהיך. There are many textual issues associated with this quotation. On this see, Stanley, *Paul and the Language of Scripture*, 134–41. Schreiner (*Romans* [2nd ed], 555) thinks Paul was dependent on the MT for his quotation. Dunn (*Romans 9–16*, 621) acknowledges the quotation is from Isaiah, but he also thinks an echo to Nah 2:1 can be seen.

109. Moo, *Romans* [2nd ed], 682.

110. The discussion of being *sent* (ἀποστέλλω) to *proclaim the gospel* (εὐαγγελίζω) to bring about *obedience to the gospel* (ὑπακούω, εὐαγγέλιον) in vv. 15–16 should all be seen as an echo back to Rom 1:1, where Paul introduces himself as an "apostle (ἀπόστολος) set apart for the gospel (εὐαγγέλιον) of God." See also v. 5, where Paul describes his "apostleship" (ἀποστολή) as a calling to bring about the "obedience (ὑπακοή) of faith" (cf. 16:26). See the discussions in Dunn, *Romans 9–16*, 621–23.

111. Rom 10:16b: Ἡσαΐας γὰρ λέγει· κύριε, τίς ἐπίστευσεν τῇ ἀκοῇ ἡμῶν; Isa 53:1 (LXX): κύριε, τίς ἐπίστευσε τῇ ἀκοῇ ἡμῶν; The fact that Paul can equate "obey" (v. 16a) with "believe" (v. 16b) provides yet further evidence that Paul's train of thought does *not* seek to oppose *doing/obedience* with *faith*—not least with respect to the quotations in vv. 5–8. On this, see the discussions in Dunn, *Romans 9–16*, 629; Schreiner, *Romans* [2nd ed], 556–57.

112. Moo, *Romans* [2nd ed], 682–83 (on "not all," οὐ πάντες, in v. 16 as litotes, see 283). See also Mounce, *Romans*, 212.

113. Moo, *Romans* [2nd ed], 682.

114. Moo, *Romans* [2nd ed], 683–84.

115. Moo (*Romans* [2nd ed], 682–83) is correct to link v. 16 back to Paul's discussion in 9:30.

(v. 8b). Thus, "the word of faith" (v. 8) and "the word of Christ" (v. 17) bookend the discussion. In this way, Paul interprets Isaiah's "report" (ἀκοή) christologically.[116]

Before we look at the last section of chapter 10 (vv. 18–21), we ought to pause and survey the forest so we do not get lost among the trees. Working backwards, the purpose of vv. 14–17 was to support the preceding passage (vv. 11–13) by outlining the necessity of preaching the gospel (or "word") of Christ (vv. 14, 17). Paul padded this discussion with quotations, thus affording the christological preaching ministry scriptural legitimacy (vv. 15–16). Preaching is required because of what Paul says in vv. 11–13, namely, that God's generosity is available to all people. There, two quotations from Joel and Isaiah served to support the christological/confessional statement of v. 9 (and Paul's commentary of it in v. 10). That statement, we recall, governed Paul's christological interpretation of the quotations taken from Leviticus and Deuteronomy in vv. 5–8. And *these* quotations were employed to reinforce the discussion in 9:30—10:4, where it was revealed that Paul's christology functioned as a key prejudgment in his reconfiguration of the Jewish notion of election. In this way, Paul does not leave his exegesis in Rom 9:1–29 to stand alone in isolation from his prejudgments. In other words, the discussion of 9:30—10:17 disclosed Paul's hermeneutical pre-commitments that were operative all along, thus legitimating the exegesis of the previous section.

Romans 10:18–21

In vv. 18–21, Paul begins a transition to a more focused discussion about the question of Israel, which will come to full bloom in chapter 11. There he will address Israel's status with respect to election. The transition begins in v. 18 with a question: "But I say, have they not heard (μὴ οὐκ ἤκουσαν)? Yes, they have (μενοῦνγε)" (v. 18a).[117] Moo thinks that here, as in vv. 14–15, Paul is asking in regard to all people, though he sees a "special reference to Israel."[118] I think something like this is correct. Paul does indeed have Israel in mind at this point, and he will focus directly on Israel's situation in the next verse.

116. See Longenecker (*Romans*, 855), who says Paul "interprets [Isa 53:1] in a Christian fashion not only by speaking of the necessity of 'faith' in the 'message' proclaimed by the preachers sent by God, but, more particularly, by identifying that 'message' as 'the word of Christ.'"

117. On μὴ οὐκ, see Longenecker, *Romans*, 855–56. Contra Dunn, *Romans 9–16*, 556, 623–24, I translate μενοῦνγε here as "Yes"—along the lines of "indeed."

118. Moo, *Romans* [2nd ed], 684.

At any rate, Paul follows the question with a quotation from Ps 18:5a: "Their voice has gone out into all the earth, and their words (ῥήματα αὐτῶν) to the ends of the inhabited world" (v. 18b).[119] Paul clearly applies this to the preaching of the Gospel of Christ. The "words" (ῥήματα) of the quotation connect easily back to "the word of Christ" (ῥήματος Χριστοῦ) in v. 17. Both of these echo back to Paul's discussion about preaching and hearing the gospel of Christ in vv. 14–16. And most importantly, the quotation is itself an echo of the quotation from Deut 30:14 in v. 8a, which Paul interpreted christologically: "The word (ῥῆμά) is near you, in your mouth and in your heart." Recall once more that Paul defined that *word* as "the word (ῥῆμά) of faith which we preach" (v. 8b).[120] Thus with respect to Paul's christological approach to adducing meaning from Scripture, I do not get the impression that much has changed with his quotation from Ps 18:5. Paul continues to read Scripture from the standpoint of a christological horizon of understanding.[121]

That Paul transitions to a more focused attention to Israel's predicament is evident in v. 19, where he calls out Israel directly. He says, "But I say, did Israel not know (μὴ Ἰσραὴλ οὐκ ἔγνω)?" (v. 19a).[122] The language suggests that Paul expects a positive answer of, "Yes, they did, in fact, know"— much like the question in v. 18a.[123] However, there may be more to the story than a simple "yes" (see below). Before we get to that, however, we must ask: What does Paul expect Israel to have known? Taking into consideration the biblical texts Paul cites in what follows, the answer appears on the surface

119. Rom 10:18b: εἰς πᾶσαν τὴν γῆν ἐξῆλθεν ὁ φθόγγος αὐτῶν καὶ εἰς τὰ πέρατα τῆς οἰκουμένης τὰ ῥήματα αὐτῶν. Ps 18:5 (LXX): εἰς πᾶσαν τὴν γῆν ἐξῆλθεν ὁ φθόγγος αὐτῶν καὶ εἰς τὰ πέρατα τῆς οἰκουμένης τὰ ῥήματα αὐτῶν. ἐν τῷ ἡλίῳ ἔθετο τὸ σκήνωμα αὐτοῦ·

120. Moo notices these connections, too. See Moo, *Romans* [2nd ed], 685n539. See also Wagner, *Heralds*, 184–85.

121. Longenecker (*Romans*, 856) describes Paul's use of Ps 18:5 (LXX) as a "Christianizing in a typically *pesher* fashion the words of a passage in the Jewish (OT) Scriptures that in their context of Ps 19:1–6 [18:1–5 LXX] extolled God's revelation of himself through his created world."

122. That Paul seeks to connect the question of v. 18a with v. 19a (and hence had in mind Israel in both places) is perhaps seen in the similarity of language: Ἀλλὰ λέγω, μὴ οὐκ (v. 18a); Ἀλλὰ λέγω, μὴ . . . οὐκ (v. 19a). On this, cf. Moo, *Romans* [2nd ed], 685. Furthermore, Moo is correct to notice that Paul's insertion of *Israel* between the two negative particles in v. 19a makes explicit what was implicit in v. 18a, namely, Israel herself, who is the "real subject in this paragraph" (686).

123. "Just as in his first question of 10:18, the apostle here again uses μή as an interrogative particle and οὐκ (sic) as a negative particle, and so again anticipates the positive response "Yes" (Longenecker, *Romans*, 856).

straightforward: Israel should have known, through her Scriptures, that God had always intended to bring Gentiles into the covenant.

On the other hand, the issue may be slightly more complex. What is interesting about Paul's question ("did Israel not know?") is that, unlike v. 18a, Paul never answers with an explicit μενοῦνγε. I do not think it is excluded because he necessarily expects a negative answer. It could be that he thinks the answer is along the lines of, "Yes, *but the issue is more complex.*" In other words, while Paul thinks Israel should have known about Gentile inclusion, he also thinks they have failed to listen to the testimony of Scripture because they are *not* (in one sense) "in the know" with respect to how God has accomplished Gentile inclusions through Christ. I think Moo sums up the situation well, and it is worth quoting him at length as an introduction to Paul's quotations in vv. 19–21. He says,

> What it was that Israel "knows," as the subsequent context suggests, is that God could very well act in such a way that the preaching of Christ would result in the inclusion of the Gentiles and in judgment upon Israel (see the OT quotations in vv. 19b–21). This Israel knows from her own scriptures; her ignorance, then (v. 3), consists in her willful refusal to recognize the fulfillment of these texts in the revelation of God's righteousness in Christ. Israel, Paul suggests, "sees, but does not perceive; hears, but does not comprehend" (Isa. 6:9; see Mark 4:12 and pars.; John 12:40; Acts 28:26–27).[124]

I think Moo is onto something. Despite the fact that Israel "knows" (or should have known) that God was going to bring about Gentile inclusion, she suffers from what we might call christological ignorance.[125] In other words, she refuses to know that Christ is the means by which God has brought about Gentile inclusion. This thesis would make sense of his earlier discussion in vv. 2–3. There Paul laments Israel's having "zeal for God, but not according to knowledge (ἐπίγνωσιν)" (v. 2). Israel is "ignorant (ἀγνοοῦντες) of the righteousness of God" (v. 3). That entire discussion, we recall, was explicitly christological in orientation (9:30—10:4).[126]

There is, therefore, a twofold focus to the passage: (1) Israel's knowledge about Gentile inclusion *and* (2) Israel's ignorance about the christological

---

124. Moo, *Romans* [2nd ed], 686. Cf. Longenecker, *Romans*, 857. See also Wagner, *Heralds*, 187–88.

125. The ambiguity about whether Israel "knows" (and the content about which she knows or does not know) explains, perhaps, the exclusion of μενοῦνγε in v. 19a.

126. Wagner (*Heralds*, 187–88) also notices the link between ἔγνω in v. 19a and the discussion in 9:30—10:4.

means by which that inclusion is obtained. Subsequently, a twofold response is in order. To show evidence for the first, Paul quotes from Deut 32:21 in v. 19b. For the second, Paul quotes from Isa 65:1–2 in vv. 20–21. We will look at each quotation in order.

The meaning Paul mines from Deut 32:21 is quite novel. Before we get to that, though, it is important to note a few textual differences that appear in Paul's quotation.

Rom 10:19:	Deut 32:21 LXX:
ἐγὼ παραζηλώσω ὑμᾶς ἐπ’οὐκ ἔθνει, ἐπ’ ἔθνει ἀσυνέτῳ παροργιῶ ὑμᾶς.	Κἀγὼ παραζηλώσω αὐτοὺς ἐπ’ οὐκ ἔθνει, ἐπ’ ἔθνει ἀσυνέτῳ παροργιῶ αὐτούς.

First, κἀγὼ is replaced with ἐγὼ at the beginning of the quotation.[127] Second, αὐτοὺς is replaced by ὑμᾶς.[128] This second change is designed to allow Moses himself to speak directly to the unbelieving Israel of Paul's day.[129] The evidence suggests that both of these changes originated with Paul himself.[130] The idea behind Paul's quote is to show that it had long been prophesied Gentiles would be factored into the equation.[131] Significantly, Paul introduces his quotation from Deut 32:21 with "Moses says," placing the foretelling of Gentile inclusion into one of Israel's "esteemed" religious authorities.[132]

But what is Paul intending with the quotation? On this, it is helpful to note that Paul alludes to Deut 32:21 in Rom 11:11–14, without citing that

127. Jewett, *Romans*, 645. He says, "The deletion of the 'and' in Paul's version is required because of the need to place the citation in a new context" (645).

128. On this, see Koch, *Schrift*, 110. Cf. Stanley, *Paul and the Language of Scripture*, 143.

129. Jewett (*Romans*, 645) says, "The result of this minor alteration is that Moses, the most authoritative voice in Jewish history, addresses his fellow adherent to the law in a direct manner."

130. See Stanley, *Paul and the Language of Scripture*, 142–44; Jewett, *Romans*, 645.

131. Wagner, *Heralds*, 197. Wagner says that the main reason for the quotation is not only to announce the salvation of the Gentiles but also that "God is doing this *for the sake of Israel's own salvation.*" On the important this quote has in Paul's larger argument, see Stanley, *Paul and the Language of Scripture*, 143–44.

132. Wagner, *Heralds*, 189. Wagner says (191), "It is not difficult to grasp the gist of Paul's quotation: Moses' words reveal that God is calling Gentiles to be a part of his people in order to make Israel jealous. Because God told them about this through Moses, Israel certainly 'has known' all along that God planned to pour out his mercy on Gentiles, as now is happening through the ministry of Paul." See also Jewett (*Romans*, 644), who notes that the use of Moses' name "lends additional warrant to the argument." See also Kujanpää, "From Eloquence to Evading Responsibility," 188–89.

text explicitly.[133] There Paul asks rhetorically, "Did they [Israel] stumble in order that they would fall? By no means! But rather by their trespass, salvation has come to the Gentiles in order to make them jealous" (Rom 11:11). It becomes clear in the following verses that Paul understands God's work to drive unbelieving Jews to jealousy is for the purpose of their redemption (vv. 13–14).[134] By granting salvation to the Gentiles, Israel will become jealous, paving the way for Israel's own salvation. Like the allusion in Rom 11:11, the quotation of Deut 32:21 in Rom 10:19b is meant to imply the same thing—only it is not so much Paul's point there to argue that Israel will be saved through the Gentiles' inclusion as it is that Gentiles are actually included at all.

That said, the jealousy motif in the original context of Deut 32:21 does not convey the precise soteriological overtones that Paul appears to read into them.[135] In fact, Paul's interpretation is a "radical re-reading" when compared to the original context.[136] Wagner describes the situation well:

> In the Song of Moses, the role of the nations is to punish Israel. It is their victories over God's people—attributed to God's transferral of favor from Israel to the nations—that make Israel jealous (Deut 32:21). But these nations themselves do not come to put their trust and allegiance in Israel's God; on the contrary, they remain reprehensible idolaters (Deut 32:27–33). Consequently, God reaffirms his election of Israel by rising up to defeat the nations who he has temporarily allowed to plunder his people (Deut 32:34–42).
>
> Paul's recontextualization of Deuteronomy 32:21 presents quite a different scenario, however. As Paul would have it, God is making Israel jealous not by allowing the Gentiles to oppress them, but by graciously embracing these strangers as his own and thereby stirring up in Israel a zeal to resume their proper places as God's people. In Romans 11, the Gentiles appear not as a divine scourge to be wielded for a time and then cast aside, but

133. Baker, "Paul and the Salvation of Israel," 474. See also Kujanpää, "From Eloquence to Evading Responsibility," 189.

134. Contra Baker, "Paul and the Salvation of Israel," 470–73.

135. Kujanpää, "From Eloquence to Evading Responsibility," 189.

136. Wagner, *Heralds*, 271. Wagner says Paul's "radical re-reading of Moses' Song [is] plausible only when seen through the eyes of one fully committed to the Gentile mission. That Paul accomplishes this remarkable reinterpretation of scripture by means of another verse of scripture (Isaiah 65:1) only reveals further the complexity of this dialectic, for Paul's reading of Isaiah 65:1–2 is itself inconceivable apart from his prior convictions and experiences as an apostle to the Gentiles."

as objects of divine mercy and instruments through whom God will ultimately bring salvation to Israel.[137]

Thus, Paul's soteriological argument relies upon a *creative* interpretation of Deut 32.[138] Simply put, Paul gives the text fresh meaning.

But what is the hermeneutic logic behind Paul's quotation? The answer is to be found in the quotations from Isaiah that occur in vv. 20–21, especially in the quotation of Isa 65:1 in v. 20. An argument can be made that Paul's Deut 32:21 quotation works only in light of an assumed hermeneutic logic that he brings to the Isa 65:1 quotation. In other words, I think Deut 32:21 has the meaning it has for Paul because of the fresh meaning Paul finds in Isa 65:1–2.[139] Speaking about the Gentiles, Paul says,

> But Isaiah is bold and says, "I was found by those who were not seeking me, I showed myself to those who did not ask for me" [quoting Isa 65:1]. But to Israel he says, "All day long I stretched out my hands to a disobedient and contrary people" [quoting Isa 65:2].[140]

Like his quotations from Hosea in 9:25–26, Paul's use of Isaiah is no less intriguing. This is especially so in regard to the textual differences.[141] Those differences are ripe for discussion, especially with respect to the role Paul might have played in intentionally changing them for his own purposes.[142] Regardless of the extent to which Paul altered the *wording* of the original text, the issue that remains most important for our purposes is the

---

137. Wagner, *Heralds*, 270–71 (regarding Deut 32:43, see 270n164).

138. Cf. Hays, *Echoes*, 160–64.

139. Cf. Wagner, *Heralds*, 271.

140. Rom 10:20–21: Ἡσαΐας δὲ ἀποτολμᾷ καὶ λέγει· εὑρέθην [ἐν] τοῖς ἐμὲ μὴ ζητοῦσιν, ἐμφανὴς ἐγενόμην τοῖς ἐμὲ μὴ ἐπερωτῶσιν. πρὸς δὲ τὸν Ἰσραὴλ λέγει· ὅλην τὴν ἡμέραν ἐξεπέτασα τὰς χεῖράς μου πρὸς λαὸν ἀπειθοῦντα καὶ ἀντιλέγοντα. Isa 65:1–2 (LXX): Ἐμφανὴς ἐγενόμην τοῖς ἐμὲ μὴ ζητοῦσιν, εὑρέθην τοῖς ἐμὲ μὴ ἐπερωτῶσιν· εἶπα Ἰδού εἰμι, τῷ ἔθνει οἳ οὐκ ἐκάλεσαν τὸ ὄνομά μου. ἐξεπέτασα τὰς χεῖράς μου ὅλην τὴν ἡμέραν πρὸς λαὸν ἀπειθοῦντα καὶ ἀντιλέγοντα, οἳ οὐκ ἐπορεύθησαν ὁδῷ ἀληθινῇ, ἀλλ' ὀπίσω τῶν ἁμαρτιῶν αὐτῶν. Regarding the introductory formula, see Kujanpää, "From Eloquence to Evading Responsibility," 195–97. On Paul's use of Second Isaiah in Romans, see Walters, "How Beautiful Are My Feet."

141. See the analysis in Stanley, *Paul and the Language of Scripture*, 144–47.

142. Commenting on Paul's use of Isa 65:1 in Rom 10:20, Jewett (*Romans*, 648) says, "Whether the sequence of Paul's citation is due to the existence of the A and Q versions, which may in fact have been influenced by Christian scribes, or to his recollection of the Hebrew word order, or to faulty memory, the citation as he provides it serves his purpose well."

fact that Paul altered the *meaning* of the text.[143] In the original context of Isa 65:1–2, both verses are "referring to the same subject (rebellious Israel)."[144] Paul, however, does not read them in this manner. For him, Isa 65:1 is understood as a prophecy about the inclusion of the Gentiles (Rom 10:20), while Isa 65:2 is for him a polemic against "contemporary Israel" (Rom 10:21).[145] Thus, Paul

> boldly bisects the quotation so that the first verse speaks of Gentiles, while only the second verse refers to Israel. Simultaneously, Paul transforms 65:1 from a declaration of condemnation for Israel into a proclamation of salvation for Gentiles, all the while continuing to read 65:2 as a severe censure of Israel's constant rebelliousness.[146]

As J. Edward Walters notes, Paul does not appear here to be "concerned about violating the 'original context' of the passage."[147] To make sense of this, Wagner claims the enigma of Paul's "brazen misreading" of this text can be accounted for by recognizing that "Paul's most common interpretive strategy" is to "[locate] Gentiles in negatively-phrased descriptions of people (often Israelites!) who are estranged from God."[148] Thus we recall, for Wagner, whenever Paul sees these "negatively-phrased descriptions" of people—even Israelites—in Scripture, Paul reads "Gentiles" into these descriptions.

While there is merit to this idea, I am not convinced that his solution solves the entire problem—at least from a hermeneutic standpoint. It might be said that while Wagner's solution solves the "tendentious" appearance of Paul's exegesis,[149] it falls short in answering the prior question of the hermeneutic fore-structure of Paul's understanding and how *that* relates to his act

---

143. So Wagner, *Heralds*, 211: "The most notorious feature of Paul's quotation does not depend on an actual alteration of the words of his *Vorlage*, but rather on his interpretive comments."

144. Moyise, *Paul and Scripture*, 78. See also Wagner, *Heralds*, 211.

145. Wagner, *Heralds*, 205. He says: "What is, in Isaiah, an oracle about God's relentless pursuit of apostate Israel (65:1) becomes in Paul's hands a declaration of God's gracious acceptance of Gentiles. As if to add insult to injury, Paul then employs the very next verse (65:2) to paint a sharply contrasting picture of contemporary Israel as a people continually resisting God's grace." Cf. Jewett, *Romans*, 648.

146. Wagner, *Heralds*, 211.

147. Walters, "How Beautiful Are My Feet," 37.

148. Wagner, *Heralds*, 211–12. Wagner (212, 216–17) also sees Deut 32 as playing a role in how Paul came to understand Isa 65:1–2 in fresh ways. In fact, he sees these passages for Paul as "mutually interpreting" (216; see also 205).

149. Wagner, *Heralds*, 212. Cf. Bates, *Hermeneutics*, 273–75.

of application.[150] That is to say, it only tells us *what* Paul is doing, not *how* he can do what he is doing. That said, I think Wagner gets close to answering the "how question" when he says that Paul's hermeneutic is framed by his "missionary theology," which he says "exercises a profound influence on his interpretation of the prophetic text."[151] He is also correct to speak of Paul's "deep conviction that God is calling Gentiles as well as Jews to be his redeemed people in Christ" as a "hermeneutical lens" that guides him in discovering Gentiles within "divine oracles" that originally had Israel as the referent.[152]

This is surely correct. In fact, a close examination of Paul's quote in Rom 10:20–21 is most revealing in this respect, especially when we observe imbedded links to his other discussions. For example, consider again v. 20: "But Isaiah is bold and says, 'I was found by those who were not seeking (ζητοῦσιν) me, I showed (ἐμφανὴς) myself to those who did not ask for me'" (quoting Isa 65:1). But how did God show himself? Paul's use of ἐμφανής here is key, for it serves as a link to the previous discussion in 3:21–22: "God's righteousness has been shown/manifested (πεφανέρωται) . . . through the faithfulness of Jesus Christ." Thus, given the legitimacy of this link, there is no reason to think Paul's christology is not informing his interpretation of Isa 65:1. It seems clear that Paul finds in Isaiah a testimony about the manifestation of Christ.

There are other hints in the text that legitimate this link. For example, in the quotation, Isaiah supplies Paul with the twin concepts of *seeking* and *asking*—or, more precisely, the concepts of *not seeking* and *not* asking (v. 20). "Not seeking" recalls the earlier discussion in 9:30, where the Gentiles attained righteousness even though they were not pursuing (διώκοντα) it.[153] There Paul situated the Gentiles' non-pursuit of righteousness within a christological framework, which became most explicit in the quotations from Isaiah in v. 33. We recall that, contrary to the Gentiles, the Jews were "seeking (ζητοῦντες) to establish their own righteousness," a righteousness set in antithesis to "God's righteousness"—a righteousness which was configured around Christ (10:3–4). The second part of the Isaiah quotation in v. 21 also links back to that discussion: "But to Israel he says, 'All day long

150. To be clear, this is not a negative evaluation of Wagner's excellent work. I recognize Wagner's project was not a philosophical-hermeneutic investigation and did not, therefore, set out to ask these sorts of questions.

151. Wagner, *Heralds*, 211.

152. Wagner, *Heralds*, 211–12. Wagner (271) is correct when he says, "Paul's reading of Isaiah 65:1–2 is . . . inconceivable apart from his prior convictions and experiences as an apostle to Gentiles."

153. So Wagner, *Heralds*, 188.

I stretched out my hands to a disobedient and contrary (ἀπειθοῦντα καὶ ἀντιλέγοντα) people." Paul understands this to refer to Israel's disobedience *with respect to fidelity to Christ*, a topic he addressed in 9:30—10:4, 16–17.[154] These observations substantiate Wagner's claim above about what role Paul's christological beliefs play in his hermeneutic. Paul seems to reread Isaiah to accord with those beliefs.

Thus, it seems clear to me that Paul reads Gentiles into Isa 65:1 by means of his prejudgments concerning the Christ event, which has rendered both Jew and Gentile as neutral with respect to election. In this vein, a recap of Paul's line of thought is helpful. First, he has argued within mainstream Judaism that the Abrahamic covenant—the covenant that identified Israel as Israel, that is to say, that guaranteed their "election"—is based on God's call and love (9:1–24a). But after sneaking in not-so-subtle remarks about the inclusion of some Gentiles and the exclusion of some Jews (9:24b–29), it became evident rather quickly that Paul had, in fact, altered the logic of election somewhat. We quickly learned that Paul was actually operating from a *reconfigured* concept of election, one that was re-oriented around his prior belief that God had acted through Christ (9:30—10:17). Significantly in this regard, Paul believed that Christ has brought the law to completion (10:4). This fact alone effectively rendered Jew and Gentile to be on equal footing.

As a result of christologically neutralizing any ethnic priority with respect to election, Paul could reread not just the psalmist as speaking about the gospel of Christ (v. 18), but also Moses and Isaiah as texts that spoke of the inclusion of some Gentiles and the exclusion of some Jews (vv. 19–21). For Paul, then, it simply did not matter that a text like Isa 65:1 originally referred to Israel; it can now refer to Gentiles precisely because ethnic distinction in regard to election does not factor into the newly-reconfigured concept. In other words, Paul believed that through Christ God deals with *both* Jew *and* Gentile. For in quoting Isa 65:1 to say, "I showed (ἐμφανὴς) myself to those who did not ask for me" (v. 20), Paul echoes back to his previous discussion in 3:21–22, where he says, "the righteousness of God has been manifested (πεφανέρωται) . . . through the faithfulness of Jesus Christ for all who believe, *for there is no distinction*" (3:21–22).[155] Thus, the *manifestation* of Christ has served to dissolve distinction—not least, of course, with respect to election. As he says elsewhere, "So from now on, we regard nobody according to the flesh" (2 Cor 5:16).

154. See Wagner, *Heralds*, 214, who is correct to compare Isa 65:2 (Rom 10:21) with Paul's larger discussion about Israel's rebellion in Rom 10:1–3, 16.

155. Emphasis added.

In thinking this way, Paul does not mean to exclude Israel from being the recipients of mercy while Gentiles alone enjoy covenantal benefits (recall that both Jew and Gentile are on *equal* footing). For Paul will in fact go on to say that some Jews, like some Gentiles, are in fact objects of God's mercy, a point Paul will make in chapter 11. But in fact, Paul has already hinted in this direction with his use of Deuteronomy in Rom 10:19, a quotation discussed above but left unexplained until we could first examine the quotations in vv. 20–21.

As I said above, this was necessary because the key to unlocking the riddle of Paul's use of Deut 32:21 in Rom 10:19 is found in his interpretation of Isaiah in vv. 20–21. The key to that, we recall, was his christological prejudgment. I think Paul's christological (and hence neutralizing) prejudgment is also operative in his reading of Deut 32:21. The fact that its original context spoke not about Gentile inclusion, but rather Gentile persecution of Israel, as the means by which Israel would become jealous is for Paul incidental to what he considers to be the main point of that passage. The main point is simply that Gentiles spurn Israel to jealousy. That Paul already envisions the inclusion of the Gentiles has been established on other grounds (e.g., by means of his christology operating through the Isa 65:1 quotation). Thus, Paul is free to see the Gentiles as being able to spurn Israel to jealousy in another way—namely, *by being included in the covenant.*

Paul's christology, as a prejudgment, once again blurs what is irrelevant in the text and allows that which is relevant to emerge into full view. None of this is to suggest that Paul is violently forcing his christology onto the scriptural texts. If we approach the issue through Gadamerian eyes, this becomes clear. As I have mentioned throughout this study, Paul's christology routinely enters into a dialogical relationship with the text of Scripture—both of which have their own "say" and thus make their own contribution to the discovery of meaning. The meaning which emerges from this dialogical relationship is, nonetheless, something *new*—something *fresh* and *novel*.[156] The contingency of Paul's reading situation demands that this be so, and his christological prejudgments make this possible.

With Paul's christological understanding of election established, deep questions emerge for Paul's interlocutor. *If* the logic of election has been reconfigured around Christ, and *if* the net result is that there is no difference in the way God relates to people—whether Jew or Gentile—then what about the Jews? Has God abandoned his people? These are the questions Paul takes up in chapter 11.

---

156. Recall Gadamer's concept of "application." See chapter 3 above.

THE MYSTERY OF ELECTION

Paul opens the chapter with a question: "I say, then, has God rejected his people?"—a question which is followed by his typical answer: μὴ γένοιτο ("by no means!") (v. 1a).[157] Elaborating on this, Paul says first that God has obviously not forsaken his people, leaving them behind in the abyss of forgottenness since, after all, he himself is a Jew: "For even I myself am an Israelite, from the offspring of Abraham, of the tribe of Benjamin" (v. 1b). In other words, because some Jews like himself are recipients of the grace in Christ, it cannot follow God has abandoned his people.[158] In this regard, Paul's forthrightness is clear in the next verse, where he says, "God has not rejected his people whom he foreknew" (v. 2a). The words "God has not rejected his people" (οὐκ ἀπώσατο ὁ θεὸς τὸν λαὸν αὐτοῦ) are probably taken from either Ps 93:14 or 1 Kgdms 12:22 (or both).[159] Either way, they serve as an "emphatic denial" of the initial question in v. 1a.[160] Paul's addition of "whom he foreknew (προέγνω)" is interesting. Schreiner is correct that προέγνω is antonymic to ἀπώσατο.[161] Moreover, Cranfield is correct to deny the so-called "restrictive sense" of προέγνω—namely, that this refers to the elect *within* Israel—and ought to be taken as a reference to "Israel as a whole."[162] Paul's point, it seems, is fairly straightforward: If God has elected the nation of Israel (and he has), then the nation of Israel has not, and will not ever be, abandoned by God.

Paul finds support for this idea in a story that comes from 3 Kingdoms. From this story he lifts two quotations and places them in vv. 3–4. The story is about Elijah, who flees from Jezebel, who had threatened to kill him (3 Kgdms 19:1–3). Elijah was subsequently frightened by her threat

157. Fitzmyer, *Romans*, 603, thinks Paul has reworked the quotation from Psalms (in v. 2) and used it in v. 1 as the opening question.

158. See Cranfield, *Romans*, 543, who says, "In support of his emphatic denial of the possibility that God has cast off His people Israel Paul cites the fact of his own Jewishness (God would hardly have chosen a Jew to be His special apostle to the Gentiles, had He cast of His people, the Jews)."

159. Ps 93:14 (LXX): ὅτι οὐκ ἀπώσεται κύριος τὸν λαὸν αὐτοῦ; 1 Kgdms 12:22 (Rahlfs): ὅτι οὐκ ἀπώσεται κύριος τὸν λαὸν αὐτοῦ. Stanley (*Paul and the Language of Scripture*, 147n215) does not include this as a quotation in his study. Moo (*Romans* [2nd ed], 692n574) offers reasons why Paul might have been quoting either Psalms or 1 Kingdoms. In the end, I suspect Paul might have been referring to both in his quotation (as does Dunn, *Romans 9–16*, 636).

160. Fitzmyer, *Romans*, 604.

161. Schreiner, *Romans* [2nd ed], 566. That said, I do not adhere to the further implications Schreiner draws with respect to "foreknow."

162. Cranfield, *Romans*, 545. See also Dunn, *Romans 9–16*, 636; Moo, *Romans* [2nd ed], 692–93.

and escapes quickly to Mt. Horeb (vv. 4–9). After finding a cave to stay in, the Lord speaks to him, saying, "What are you doing here, Elijah?" (v. 9). Elijah's answer is recorded in v. 10. After this, a short interval occurs, during which Elijah experiences the presence of the Lord in the sound of a low breeze (vv. 11–13a). The Lord then repeats the question: "What are you doing here, Elijah?" (v. 13b). Elijah's answer is recorded in v. 14 and is similar to the one he gave in v. 10.

It is Elijah's responses in 3 Kgdms 19:10 that Paul quotes in Rom 11:3.[163] Introducing the quotation, Paul asks, "Or do you not know what the Scripture says about Elijah, how he appeals to God against Israel?" (v. 2b). This is followed by the quotation (Elijah's reply): "Lord, they have killed your prophets, they have torn down your altars, and I alone am left—and they seek my life" (v. 3).[164] Paul then asks his readers, "But what was the divine answer? (v. 4a).[165] This is followed by a second quotation from 3 Kgdms 19:18: "I have reserved for myself seven thousand men, who have not bowed a knee to Baal" (v. 4b).[166] The point of the quotation is simple: To show that just because a majority of Israel has not obeyed the Gospel does not imply anything novel. Paul utilizes the quotation to prove that, even in Israel's early stories, God often dealt with but a remnant—a small group of faithful Jews. This much is evident from Paul's own interpretation of the verse: "So then, even at the present moment, there is a remnant—according to an election by grace" (v. 5). The prepositional phrase κατ' ἐκλογὴν χάριτος ("according to

---

163. Though v. 10 and v. 14 are nearly the same, it is clear Paul draws the quotation from v. 10. See Stanley, *Paul and the Language of Scripture*, 147, esp. n216.

164. Rom 11:3: κύριε, τοὺς προφήτας σου ἀπέκτειναν, τὰ θυσιαστήριά σου κατέσκαψαν, κἀγὼ ὑπελείφθην μόνος καὶ ζητοῦσιν τὴν ψυχήν μου; 3 Kgdms 19:10 (Rahlfs): καὶ εἶπεν Ηλιου Ζηλῶν ἐζήλωκα τῷ κυρίῳ παντοκράτορι, ὅτι ἐγκατέλιπόν σε οἱ υἱοὶ Ισραηλ· τὰ θυσιαστήριά σου κατέσκαψαν καὶ τοὺς προφήτας σου ἀπέκτειναν ἐν ῥομφαίᾳ, καὶ ὑπολέλειμμαι ἐγὼ μονώτατος, καὶ ζητοῦσι τὴν ψυχήν μου λαβεῖν αὐτήν. Cf. 3 Kgdms 19:14 (Rahlfs): καὶ εἶπεν Ηλιου Ζηλῶν ἐζήλωκα τῷ κυρίῳ παντοκράτορι, ὅτι ἐγκατέλιπον τὴν διαθήκην σου οἱ υἱοὶ Ισραηλ· τὰ θυσιαστήριά σου καθεῖλαν καὶ τοὺς προφήτας σου ἀπέκτειναν ἐν ῥομφαίᾳ, καὶ ὑπολέλειμμαι ἐγὼ μονώτατος, καὶ ζητοῦσι τὴν ψυχήν μου λαβεῖν αὐτήν. On the textual differences, see Stanley, *Paul and the Language of Scripture*, 147–51.

165. Rom 11:4a: ἀλλὰ τί λέγει αὐτῷ ὁ χρηματισμός. On ἀλλά and the hapax legomenon χρηματισμός, see Jewett, *Romans*, 656.

166. Rom 11:4b: κατέλιπον ἐμαυτῷ ἑπτακισχιλίους ἄνδρας, οἵτινες οὐκ ἔκαμψαν γόνυ τῇ Βάαλ; 3 Kgdms 19:18 (Rahlfs): καὶ καταλείψεις ἐν Ισραηλ ἑπτὰ χιλιάδας ἀνδρῶν, πάντα γόνατα, ἃ οὐκ ὤκλασαν γόνυ τῷ Βααλ, καὶ πᾶν στόμα, ὃ οὐ προσεκύνησεν αὐτῷ. On Paul's use of κατέλιπον, see Jewett, *Romans*, 657. On this, cf. Stanley, *Paul and the Language of Scripture*, 154.

an election of grace") is often translated as "chosen by grace."[167] Either way, Paul's point is the same, which is to reconfigure the *concept* of election itself.

One might become curious at this point how Paul could be reconfiguring the concept of election by appealing to historical and scriptural precedent. Is it not better, then, to say that Paul is not so much reconfiguring election as he is reviving it? The answer, ultimately, is no. On the one hand, of course, Paul does find continuity with Jewish stories (such as Elijah) in regard to remnant theology. But there is at the same time a profound discontinuity. As we have already said above, election for Paul has been reconfigured around the person of Christ. It is not that Paul has reconfigured election around grace that renders his concept of election different from what one sees in the story of Elijah. It is not as though Paul's readers did not know about Elijah's story or that the concept of remnant was foreign to second temple Jews. In fact, as both Moo and Jewett have pointed out, the structure of Paul's question in v. 2b suggests that Paul expected his readers to have *already* been familiar with the story.[168] So one should not imagine that Paul was, strictly speaking, teaching remnant theology for the first time. They were already familiar with that. And so, giving a brief lesson on the concept of "remnant" via a scriptural story was never Paul's aim. His intentions were much more radical: He wanted to show the Roman believers how the remnant theology they already knew about had been situated around the ministry of Christ.

Indeed, *the* pressing issue for Paul—not least with respect to questions about Israel's covenant status—was that remnant theology is now christologically reconfigured, that God's grace has been manifested *in* and *through* Christ. After all, it is Christ and not grace *qua* grace (or remnant theology *qua* remnant theology) that Paul says served as the stumbling stone—the axis around which election happens (9:33).

All of this leads into what Paul says next: "But if it is by grace, it is no longer by works—otherwise grace would no longer be grace" (v. 6). Here "grace" should be taken to be christologically reconfigured as in Rom 5, where God's own grace is virtually synonymous with the grace of Jesus Christ: The "grace of God" comes about "by the grace of the one man, Jesus Christ" (v. 15); likewise "grace" comes "through Jesus Christ" (v. 21). Moreover, "works" ought to be understood as a reference to works of the law— those works that identify Jews *as* Jews.[169] The fact that Paul uses "works" in shortened form (omitting "law") is not reason enough to think he does not

167. As in, e.g., the ESV.

168. Moo, *Romans* [2nd ed], 693; Jewett, *Romans*, 655.

169. Contra Schreiner, *Romans* [2nd ed], 569; Moo, *Romans* [2nd ed], 696.

have the "law" in mind.[170] Since Paul's focus in this chapter revolves around questions about the election of Israel as a distinct group is enough to suggest that the cultic aspects of the law are in view.[171] Dunn is therefore correct when he says,

> The context here confirms . . . that the "works" referred to are a way of understanding election which Paul firmly rejects (election of grace, not from works)—"works" understood as the hallmark of election, as that which marks out the elect as such. The point being that the remnant is not constituted as a group within Israel by their faithfulness to the law . . . but as a group sustained by God's grace; *that* is how election is to be understood and how it is sustained . . . χάρις by definition precludes the kind of limitation which ἐξ ἔργων involves.[172]

Thus, the point I wish to make is that Paul's use of the Elijah story (vv. 2b–4), and the subsequent interpretation he gives it—namely, that it speaks of divine *grace* (vv. 5–6)—assumes a christological framework.

That Paul is presupposing this framework is easily seen when we notice connections back to earlier discussions. Consider again 9:30—10:4, where Israel failed to attain righteousness because she pursued it "by works" (ἐξ ἔργων) and not "by faith" (ἐκ πίστεως) (v. 32).[173] Similar to how "faith" was set in opposition to "works" in 9:32, "grace" is set in opposition to "works" in 11:6. Given how "faith" is christologically oriented around the "stumbling stone" quotation in 9:33, "grace" also needs to be seen as christologically oriented in 11:6.[174] The link to 9:30—10:4 is also confirmed when we consider what Paul says in 11:7a: "What, then? Israel failed to obtain what it was seeking (ἐπιζητεῖ), but the elect obtained it." Here *seeking* is an echo back to 9:31 and 10:3a, where Israel pursued (διώκων) "a law of righteousness" but failed (v. 31) because they were "seeking (ζητοῦντες) to establish their own" (v. 3a). They did not "submit to the righteousness of God" (v. 3b), which Paul conceives of as being "manifested . . . through the faithfulness of Jesus Christ" (3:21–22). Given these multiple connections, one can reasonably conclude that Paul's christological prejudgments are still operative in

---

170. Contra Schreiner, *Romans* [2nd ed], 569.

171. Moo (*Romans* [2nd ed], 696) is open to this possibility, but quickly dismisses it in the end. See again the comments made by Cranfield (*Romans*, 545) on προέγνω in v. 2.

172. Dunn, *Romans 9–16*, 639.

173. Dunn (*Romans 9–16*, 639) also sees a link from 11:6 to 9:32.

174. This is seen clearly when we let Paul's earlier descriptions of "grace" in 5:15, 20–21 have their full force. On this, see above.

11:1–7a just as they were in 9:30—10:4. This means that the meaning Paul finds in his quotations are what they are because of his christological pre-judgments. The concept of election, derived as it was from the Elijah story in particular, is itself christologically reconfigured.

Unsurprisingly, the same can be said about the quotations in vv. 8–10. Paul segues into them in v. 7, which echoes his earlier discussion that began in 9:30 and continued to 10:3.[175] He says, "What, then? Israel failed to obtain what it was seeking (ἐπιζητεῖ), but the elect obtained it. But the rest (οἱ λοιποὶ) were hardened." To support this, Paul introduces two quotations. The first is a composite of Deut 29:4 and Isa 29:10, the second comes from Ps 68:23–24.

> Just as it is written,
> God gave them a spirit of stupor, eyes that do not see (βλέπειν)
> and ears that do not hear (ἀκούειν), until this very day. (v. 8)[176]

> And David says,
> Let their table be a snare and a trap and a stumbling block
> (σκάνδαλον) and a retribution to them; Let their eyes be dark-
> ened (σκοτισθήτωσαν) so they do not see (βλέπειν) and bend
> their back always. (vv. 9–10)[177]

Paul quotes these passages in order to tie his present discussion back once again to his previous discussions—specifically to that of 9:30—10:4 and 10:14–18. The links are obvious. The mention of the "stumbling block" (σκάνδαλον; v. 9) immediately draws us back to the "stone of stumbling and a rock of offense" (λίθον προσκόμματος καὶ πέτραν σκανδάλου) and to its christological interpretation in the Isaiah quotation in 9:33.[178] Likewise,

---

175. Dunn, *Romans 9–16*, 648.

176. Rom 11:8: καθὼς γέγραπται· ἔδωκεν αὐτοῖς ὁ θεὸς πνεῦμα κατανύξεως, ὀφθαλμοὺς τοῦ μὴ βλέπειν καὶ ὦτα τοῦ μὴ ἀκούειν, ἕως τῆς σήμερον ἡμέρας. Deut 29:4 (LXX): καὶ οὐκ ἔδωκεν Κύριος ὁ θεὸς ὑμῖν καρδίαν εἰδέναι καὶ ὀφθαλμοὺς βλέπειν καὶ ὦτα ἀκούειν ἕως τῆς ἡμέρας ταύτης. Isa 29:10 (LXX): ὅτι πεπότικεν ὑμᾶς κύριος πνεύματι κατανύξεως καὶ καμμύσει τοὺς ὀφθαλμοὺς αὐτῶν καὶ τῶν προφητῶν αὐτῶν καὶ τῶν ἀρχόντων αὐτῶν, οἱ ὁρῶντες τὰ κρυπτά. On the textual differences, see Stanley, *Paul and the Language of Scripture*, 158–63 (see esp. 161 on πνεῦμα κατανύξεως).

177. Rom 11:9–10: καὶ Δαυὶδ λέγει· γενηθήτω ἡ τράπεζα αὐτῶν εἰς παγίδα καὶ εἰς θήραν καὶ εἰς σκάνδαλον καὶ εἰς ἀνταπόδομα αὐτοῖς, σκοτισθήτωσαν οἱ ὀφθαλμοὶ αὐτῶν τοῦ μὴ βλέπειν καὶ τὸν νῶτον αὐτῶν διὰ παντὸς σύγκαμψον. Ps 68:23–24 (LXX): γενηθήτω ἡ τράπεζα αὐτῶν ἐνώπιον αὐτῶν εἰς παγίδα καὶ εἰς ἀνταπόδοσιν καὶ εἰς σκάνδαλον· σκοτισθήτωσαν οἱ ὀφθαλμοὶ αὐτῶν τοῦ μὴ βλέπειν, καὶ τὸν νῶτον αὐτῶν διὰ παντὸς σύγκαμψον. On the textual differences, see Stanley, *Paul and the Language of Scripture*, 163–66.

178. Cf. Dunn, *Romans 9–16*, 650. See also Stuhlmacher, *Romans*, 165, regarding

Israel's *not hearing* (μὴ ἀκούειν) in v. 8, echoes back to 10:14–18, where *hearing* is taken to be *gospel hearing* (v. 16) and is therefore connected exclusively to the ministry of Christ (vv. 17–18).

It is important to realize, though, that Paul is not interested in rehashing those discussions for the sake of reminding his readers of what he has already said. Instead, in the quotations of 11:8–10, he seeks to build upon those previous discussions, adding yet another important layer as to why the majority of Israel has failed to find inclusion in the covenant.[179] As we have seen, the reason for their failure is christological (9:30—10:4). In v. 8, though, we can see how Paul raises the stakes. By tweaking the Deuteronomy quotation, Paul adds a layer to his overall point that is, in Dunn's words, "striking"—the result of which is the conclusion that God himself intended for this to happen all along; he played a role in Israel's rejection.[180] "*God* gave them a spirit of stupor, eyes that do not see (βλέπειν) and ears that do not hear (ἀκούειν), until this very day" (11:8; emphasis added).

This is a far cry, however, from certain theories regarding the predetermined destinies of individuals—theories that frequent many modern debates.[181] In speaking about "Israel," Paul does not intend for us to draw conclusions about the predetermined eternal fate of *individual* unbelieving Jews. Neither does he intend to speak of "Israel" as a *corporate* entity (in the sense of a conglomerate of individuals) whose eternal fate as a whole is in question. Paul is not, in other words, seeking to develop a stand-alone theology of eternal reprobation or anything of the sort.[182] The reason is simple: Those who are hardened are capable of coming to Christ—*even in their state of hardening*, as Paul will go on to say (11:1, 14, 23–24).[183] This fact is reinforced by his comments about the temporal (and redemptive!) aspect of Israel's hardening in vv. 11–12, 25, and 30–32. All of this suggests Paul is speaking about something other than eternal reprobation.

Instead, I think it is best to understand the problem of Israel's hardening in a christological sense. Paul has already identified Christ as the "stone of stumbling" and the "rock of offense" (πέτραν σκανδάλου)" in 9:33. As I have already said above, Paul is most likely indirectly referring back to this

---

the "offering table."

179. Dunn (*Romans 9–16*, 648) makes the same observation.

180. Dunn, *Romans 9–16*, 648–49.

181. See Wright, *Romans*, 676–78; on the "apocalyptic context" of divine "hardening" (see also 688). Cf. Moo, *Romans* [2nd ed], 698–99.

182. So Wright, *Romans*, 677. Contra Calvin, *Romans*, 416–17.

183. Wright, *Romans*, 677–78. He says, "As the next passage will make clear, Paul does not suppose that any particular ethnic Jews are subject to this condemnation; there is always room for them to come to faith" (678).

in the quotation from Ps 68 in 11:9, where the "table" becomes "a snare and a trap and a stumbling block (σκάνδαλον)." There are various opinions as to what is meant by "table," but it does seem to be a reference to either the sacrificial system[184] or to Jewish-only table fellowship.[185] I think a good case could be made for the latter. Either way, the point is that the very Torah that Israel pursued to gain righteousness ends up being a self-defeating endeavor because such a pursuit is disobedience and fails to see Christ as the culmination of the law (cf. 9:30—10:4; 11:31). Thus, the cause of Israel's rebellious status is her lack of faith in Christ and her pursuit of works of the law (11:23). Moreover, Schreiner is right to point out how select passages in Ps 68 are often alluded to or quoted in the New Testament as a reference to Christ[186] and how Paul himself interprets Ps 68:10b similarly in Rom 15:3.[187] In this way, "The curse pronounced on the psalmist's enemies, therefore, was applied to unbelieving Jews of Paul's day who rejected Jesus as their Lord and oppressed the church."[188] When it comes to hardening, then, it seems that God is the cause of Israel's hardening only in the sense that he has refocused election around Christ. This would mean that the combined quotations in v. 8 (which speak of God's agency in hardening Israel) is interpreted in light of the christologically-primed quotation of Ps 68 in vv. 9–10. The problem of hardening, therefore, is christological.[189]

Furthermore, it would be a mistake to ignore how "Israel" has a salvation-historical definition and function in the argument of Rom 11. In a sense, "Israel" refers not merely to ethnic Israel *per se* but rather to that redemptive entity through which God works to bring salvation to the entire world. On this, one must pay careful attention to Paul's illustration about the "olive tree" in which both ethnic Israel ("the natural branches") and Gentiles ("wild olive shoot") can be grafted—if they believe in Christ (vv. 17–24). As Michael Gorman says, "Paul understands the olive tree not as ethnic Israel but more broadly as God's covenant people rooted in Israel."[190] When, for example, Paul speaks about the Gentiles being "participants in the nourishing root of the olive tree" (v. 17), the reference to "root" is most likely a reference to the patriarchs of Israel—particularly to Abraham, who is the

---

184. Stuhlmacher, *Romans*, 165.

185. Wright, *Romans*, 677.

186. E.g., Ps 68:22 in Matt 27:34; Ps 68:10a in John 2:17; Ps 68:5a in John 15:25.

187. Schreiner, *Romans* [2nd ed], 573.

188. Schreiner, *Romans* [2nd ed], 573.

189. See the discussion in Wright, *Romans*, 677–78.

190. Gorman, *Crucified Lord*, 386.

initial recipient of the covenant promises of Israel.[191] It must not be missed, moreover, that ethnic Israel is *naturally* related to the olive tree and, hence, to the root (vv. 16, 21, 24). As a result, ethnic Israel, as a *broken-off branch* (vv. 19–21) and as a *re-grafted-in branch* (vv. 23–24), has an important role to play in the redemptive plan of God by fulfilling the Abrahamic covenant. Specifically, this covenant entailed both that Abraham's family would be *blessed* and that they would be a *blessing* to the nations (Gen 12:1–3).

It is important we elaborate further on this. With respect to Israel being a *blessing* to the world—to the nations—Paul clearly has this in mind throughout Romans. Paul is absolutely convinced that Israel's texts and stories foretell how God has manifested Christ *for the non-covenanted nations*, and he has done so *through* Israel.[192] In this way, Israel is indeed a blessing and thus fulfills the Abrahamic covenant. With respect to Israel being *blessed*, Paul very much envisions this as well and thus walks in step with the Abrahamic promises of Gen 12:1–3 even here. But the way Paul envisions Israel receiving the Abrahamic blessings is actually quite remarkable: *Israel is blessed by the Gentiles*—specifically by *Christian* Gentiles, who through Israel's own disobedience became included (hence *blessed* by Israel), which leads Israel herself to come back to the fold (hence a *blessing* to Israel).[193] In this sense, I think, "Israel" functions as a salvation-historical entity that is fundamentally defined by both its calling to *bless* and its status as being *blessed*—a calling and status of which is open both to Jews and Gentiles. In other words, for Paul "Israel" is defined by the Abrahamic covenant. In many ways, I think, this goes a long way in making sense of Paul's elusive claim that "all Israel will be saved" (Rom 11:26). To see how all this works, let us examine the following sections.

Romans 11:11–24

Paul is clear that Israel's stumbling is not final (v. 11a). The reason is because her stumbling had a redemptive purpose, namely, the redemption of the Gentiles (v. 11b). And this, says Paul, will serve "to make them [Israel]

191. Gorman, *Crucified Lord*, 386. Gorman says "the root" is "probably Israel, but perhaps the patriarchs or Abraham."

192. See e.g., Rom 1:1–5; 3:21–22; 4:11–12, 23–25; 9:25–26. Wright has convincingly made the case, I think, that a most important (but often neglected) narrative in Romans is "the story of the single-plan-through-Israel-for-the-world," which is specifically "the covenant"—something of which Paul believes has been fulfilled in Christ (Wright, *Justification*, 194; see also 194–207 and surrounding discussion).

193. This is the sort of construal that I understand Wright to make (see *PFG*, 1197–265, esp. 1199, 1203, 1230).

jealous" (v. 11c). In this way, Israel is both a blessing to the Gentiles and is blessed by the Gentiles. In this sense, Israel did not stumble "in order to fall (ἵνα πέσωσιν)." That Israel has not *stumbled in order to fall* is important for Paul because it would imply that God's own covenant promises to Israel had failed. One is reminded of Rom 9:6: "But it is not as though the word of God has failed (ἐκπέπτωκεν)." In this way, again, Israel herself serves as the embodiment of the entire salvation-historical plan of God. If she fails to be *blessed by* God and fails to be a *blessing to* the nations, then God's plan itself fails. But Paul interprets the phenomenon of Israel's unbelieving status in a way that fits into the salvation-historical scheme: Israel's reprobation is temporary. It is also redemptive for the sake of the Gentiles and, through their inclusion, redemptive for Israel's own inclusion. As Paul considers this, he celebrates what Israel's re-inclusion means in the grand scheme of things, thus leading him to boast in the role that his own ministry plays in the redemptive plan (vv. 12–16).

His considerations lead him to preempt (or perhaps respond to) the sensitive and at times unsettled nature of Jew-Gentile relations in vv. 17–24. On the surface, this might appear to be a discussion parenthetical to his stream of thought. Nothing, in fact, could be further from the truth. As we will see in the next chapter, Paul's arguments and interpretations have direct consequence for ethical considerations with regard to the believing community. But that discussion largely has to do with intramural disputes—clashes from within the church. In vv. 17–24, Paul's point is to caution believing Gentiles not to become "boastful" with respect to *unbelieving* Jews (v. 18). The point is that Gentiles ought to be humble and not "proud" (v. 20). The posture of humility, in Paul's thinking, is the only way to receive the blessing that comes from Israel.

Romans 11:25–36

To help the believing Gentiles not become "wise in [their] own mind," Paul tells them about the "mystery" (μυστήριον) of God's plan—namely, that Israel's hardening is "partial" (μέρους) (v. 25). By this, he means that it is temporary in that it is not necessarily complete or final, which is clear from Paul's use of the phrase "until the fullness of the Gentiles has come in" at the end of the verse.[194] By describing Israel's hardening as not cemented in stone, Paul simply means something along the lines of, "One should not be

---

194. Cf. Fitzmyer, *Romans*, 621. Cf. Wright, *Romans*, 688, who links v. 25 with v. 7. Contra Moo, *Romans* [2nd ed], 734, I do not think "fullness of the Gentiles" refers to a precise, predestined number of elect.

surprised that Jews begin believing in Christ." In other words, their rebellion is not sealed in the abyss of fate. This makes sense of what Paul has said
immediately prior: Gentiles should not only *not* be surprised, they should
also not arrogantly discount how easy it would be for Jewish re-inclusion to
occur. The Jews, after all, are the "natural branches" (vv. 17–24).

Paul then adds that "And in this way, all Israel will be saved" (v. 26).
Various answers have been proposed as to what Paul means by "all Israel."[195]
It seems best to take "all Israel" as a reference to the whole people of God—
Jew *and* Gentile. This would, of course, mean that "Israel" in v. 25 and "Israel" in v. 26 mean different things—a move some commentators do not
think works.[196] But in the end, Wright is correct to say that it does when one
considers especially Rom 9:6.[197]

But even then, it must not be missed that what is at stake is Paul's
resolve to settle the issue of "Israel" as a *perceived* failed eschatological plan
by which she will be blessed and a blessing. Thus, by "all Israel," Paul means
simply *all those who participate in the plan of being blessed* and of *being a
blessing.* In other words, God's plan to be *for* Israel by working *through* Israel
will not, in fact, fail. To accomplish *that* plan, God will graft in the Gentiles so that they, too, will be blessed and be a blessing to Israel (by stirring
the latter to jealousy). In this way, the word of God will have not "failed"
(9:6) and God will not have "rejected his people whom he foreknew" (11:2).
Through Israel's disobedience, God brings a blessing to the Gentiles. And
their inclusion brings about Israel's inclusion. In this way, God's promises to
Abraham are fulfilled. All of this recalls the discussion in Rom 3:1–5. There
Paul spoke about how Israel was "unfaithful" and "unrighteous" and how
this fact does not at all mean God's righteousness and faithfulness will fail
to deliver (3:3, 5). God's own righteousness, after all, has come "through the
faithfulness of Jesus Christ" (3:22). For Paul, Christ is that deliverer.

This fact, along with the claim that "all Israel will be saved" (v. 26), is
supported by a quotation which combines Isa 59:20–21 with Isa 27:9. "As it
is written: Out of Zion will come the Deliverer; he will remove ungodliness
from Jacob. And this is my covenant with them, when I take away their sins"
(Rom 11:26b–27).[198]

---

195. On various views, see Cranfield, *Romans*, 576.

196. So Cranfield, *Romans*, 576; Schreiner, *Romans* [2nd ed], 598.

197. "In particular, [Rom] 9:6 gives the lie to the constantly repeated assertion that
one cannot make 'Israel' in 11:26 mean something different from what it means in
11:25" (Wright, *Romans*, 690).

198. Rom 11:26b–27: καθὼς γέγραπται· ἥξει ἐκ Σιὼν ὁ ῥυόμενος, ἀποστρέψει
ἀσεβείας ἀπὸ Ἰακώβ. καὶ αὕτη αὐτοῖς ἡ παρ' ἐμοῦ διαθήκη, ὅταν ἀφέλωμαι τὰς ἁμαρτίας
αὐτῶν. Isa 59:20–21 (LXX): καὶ ἥξει ἕνεκεν Σιων ὁ ῥυόμενος καὶ ἀποστρέψει ἀσεβείας

Paul clearly has christology in mind—that is, *Christ* is the "Deliverer" foretold by the prophet.[199] It will be *through* Christ that Israel—by way of the Gentiles (themselves by way of Israel)—are finally saved. The logic of Paul's christologically-reconfigured election is that while unbelieving Jews are living contrary to the Gospel, they are still "beloved for the sake of the patriarchs" (v. 28). Even though these rebellious Jews (as hardened) are not, on the one hand, part of the "elect" (v. 7), they are still, on the other hand, identified as part of the elect because "the gifts and calling of God are irrevocable" (v. 29). What Paul means here is what I have pointed out above: "Israel" in this passage ought to be seen as the embodiment of the salvation-historical plan of God, which began with the Abrahamic promise. That plan consisted of Israel being both *blessed* and a *blessing*. That is why Paul can say what he does in vv. 28–29: Israel, outside of Christ, is not part of the elect in one sense, and yet in another sense they are because they, even in—especially in—their disobedience, are functioning as a *blessing* to the Gentiles. And the result of *that* (i.e., Gentile inclusion) will in turn prove to be God's way of causing Israel to be *blessed*. Here is how Paul puts it:

> For just as you [Gentiles] were once disobedient to God, but now have received mercy because of their [Israel's] disobedience, so also they have now become disobedient so that they might receive mercy through the mercy given to you. For God has consigned all to disobedience so that he might have mercy on all. (Rom 11:30–32)

This recalls vv. 11–12, where Israel's disobedience has brought "riches (πλοῦτος) for the world" and "riches (πλοῦτος) for the Gentiles." Both of these passages should be seen as an allusion back to the Abrahamic covenant (Gen 12:1–3).[200] What Paul has essentially done, therefore, in this long-winding passage (ever since Rom 9:6b) has been to reconfigure the concept of election around the reality of Christ.[201] But he has also done something else: He has provided an answer as to *how* Israel would fulfill the Abrahamic covenant—specifically how they would be *blessed* and how

---

ἀπὸ Ιακωβ. καὶ αὕτη αὐτοῖς ἡ παρ᾽ ἐμοῦ διαθήκη, εἶπε κύριος· τὸ πνεῦμα τὸ ἐμόν, ὅ ἐστιν ἐπὶ σοί, καὶ τὰ ῥήματα, ἃ ἔδωκα εἰς τὸ στόμα σου, οὐ μὴ ἐκλίπῃ ἐκ τοῦ στόματός σου καὶ ἐκ τοῦ στόματος τοῦ σπέρματός σου, εἶπε γὰρ κύριος, ἀπὸ τοῦ νῦν καὶ εἰς τὸν αἰῶνα. Isa 27:9 (LXX): διὰ τοῦτο ἀφαιρεθήσεται ἡ ἀνομία Ιακωβ, καὶ τοῦτό ἐστιν ἡ εὐλογία αὐτοῦ, ὅταν ἀφέλωμαι αὐτοῦ τὴν ἁμαρτίαν, ὅταν θῶσι πάντας τοὺς λίθους τῶν βωμῶν κατακεκομμένους ὡς κονίαν λεπτήν· καὶ οὐ μὴ μείνῃ τὰ δένδρα αὐτῶν, καὶ τὰ εἴδωλα αὐτῶν ἐκκεκομμένα ὥσπερ δρυμὸς μακράν.

199. Fitzmyer, *Romans*, 624.

200. See also Rom 10:18.

201. See again n2 above.

they would be a *blessing*. Ironically, they would be both *through* their disobedience. For Paul, God does not merely work in spite of Israel's (and the Gentile's) disobedience; he works through it. In this manner, God fulfills the promises to the patriarchs. Thus, in Rom 9:6b—11:32, we have Paul's reconfiguration of election. By that I mean not merely how Paul has reconfigured its *foundation* (on christology) but also how that foundation has itself served to reconfigure the vision of the *function* of election (through Jew/Gentile rebellion *and* inclusion). This realization leads Paul to conclude his long-running argument by way of a doxology:

> O, the depth of riches (πλούτου) and wisdom (σοφίας) and knowledge (γνώσεως) of God! How unfathomable are his judgments and how inscrutable are his ways! *For who has known the mind of the Lord or who has become his counselor or who has given to him that he would be repaid? For from him and through him and to him are all things.* To him be glory for the ages! Amen. (Rom 11:33–36)

There are two brief remarks I wish to make regarding the doxology and the quotes embedded therein. First, that Paul quotes in this passage from Isa 40:13 and Job 41:3 seems clear.[202] The opening line of the doxology contains key terms that are meant to sum up the major points of Paul's previous discussion. Consider, for example: "riches," "wisdom" and "knowledge" (v. 33). The "riches" of God's wisdom, despite being about just that—*God's* wisdom—echo the description in v. 12 about God's blessings that have come on the Gentiles as "riches" (πλοῦτος) as a result Israel's failure to believe.[203] Likewise, "wisdom" appears to be a reference back to the "mystery" of God's redemptive plan of which Paul speaks in v. 25.[204] Lastly, God's "knowledge" is extolled in the doxology as a reference back to God's foreknowledge of his

---

202. Italicized portions indicate a quotation. Stanley (*Paul and the Language of Scripture*, 171n298) thinks Paul has quoted these biblical texts, though does not include it in his study since it does not meet his criteria for analysis. Rom 11:34–35: τίς γὰρ ἔγνω νοῦν κυρίου; ἢ τίς σύμβουλος αὐτοῦ ἐγένετο; ἢ τίς προέδωκεν αὐτῷ, καὶ ἀνταποδοθήσεται αὐτῷ; Isa 40:13 (LXX): τίς ἔγνω νοῦν κυρίου, καὶ τίς σύμβουλος αὐτοῦ ἐγένετο, ὃς συμβιβᾷ αὐτόν; Job 41:3 (LXX): ἢ τίς ἀντιστήσεταί μοι καὶ ὑπομενεῖ, εἰ πᾶσα ἡ ὑπ᾽ οὐρανὸν ἐμή ἐστιν; MT: מי הקדימני ואשלם תחת כל־השמים לי־הוא. Scholars have noticed the issues related to Paul's quote from Job 41:3, since it and the LXX (and the LXX and MT) do not match. See e.g., the discussions in Jewett, *Romans*, 719–20; Fitzmyer, *Romans*, 635; Cranfield, *Romans*, 591; Moo, *Romans* [2nd ed], 761n909. In the end, I think Moo is correct that the idea Paul himself has translated from the Hebrew is "probably the best option" (*Romans* [2nd ed], 761n909).

203. See Cranfield, *Romans*, 589, who rightly connects πλοῦτος to vv. 31–32.

204. See Dunn, *Romans 9–16*, 699.

people (e.g., v. 2).[205] In this way, Paul extols the wisdom of God that establishes Christ as the foundation for election, praising God who has worked to bring mercy to Jew *and* Gentile. Hence, the doxology is itself a response to Paul's christological reconfiguration of election. This means that the quotations that serve as the heart of the doxology have taken on a christological orientation: Scripture supports Paul's contention that the way in which God brings salvation to Jew and Gentile is itself abundantly *rich*, surpassing in *wisdom*, and beyond human *knowledge*.

SUMMARY

In this chapter, I have shown how Paul has embarked on a program of recontextualizing the concept of election. He has done this by employing scriptural quotations, embedding them within his arguments. These quotations were often interpreted creatively, thus allowing Paul to adduce fresh meaning from them. We saw, moreover, how Paul's interpretations were refracted through the lens of his christology. Consistent with what we have seen in other parts of Romans, this has a double benefit for Paul. On the one hand, it allows him to adopt a fresh vision for the Jewish concept of election—not least with respect to its definition and function within the salvation-historical plan of God. This allows scriptural texts he quotes in support of election to take on concrete and relevant meaning for the Christian community in Rome. On the other hand, it also allows his own christology to be informed and situated. In this way, the ministry of Christ avoids abstraction and detachment from its Jewish horizon. The ministry of Christ thus circumvents an ahistorical existence. It is, in fact, a ministry that is situated within Jewish history. Paul, as a reader, thus engages Scripture dialogically—posing questions to, and answering questions from, the Old Testament text with respect to his christological convictions. It is in this vein that I employ, among other things, Gadamer's concept of horizon and prejudgment: It gives the modern reader clarity on how Paul can, at the same time, argue from Scripture even as he reconfigures it.

---

205. Dunn, *Romans 9–16*, 699.

Chapter 7

A New Way to Live (Romans 12–16)

Our knowledge of law and morality too is always supplemented by the individual case, even productively determined by it.

Hans-Georg Gadamer[1]

INTRODUCTION

In this chapter, we turn our attention to the final section of Romans, namely, chapters 12–16. Just as Paul has dialogically reconfigured Jewish concepts and stories by means of his particular horizon of understanding, he continues this pattern of interpretation in his closing chapters—only this time with respect to Christian conduct and living. As we will see, Paul does so by engaging key Jewish texts and recasting them within a new, situation-driven matrix. Paul's interpretive logic continues to be christo-logical, as we will see. In what follows, I focus on three concerns that Paul has, namely, *unity*, *ethics*, and *mission*—all of which have a basis in Paul's Christian reading of the Old Testament. Though all three of these concerns are intertwined with another, I will treat each one separately.

In the first section, I sketch Paul's vision for *unity* in the church, observing how that unity has as its foundation christology. This section is

1. Gadamer, *TM*, 34.

necessarily brief, written only to show the shape of Paul's vision for the believing community. The second section on *ethics* seeks to build upon the first. Because Paul does not believe the church's unity is automatically realized but is instead something that must be nurtured through right conduct, the section on ethics will serve to fill out the details of the first section. The third section, which discusses *mission*, will be the natural concomitant to the first two sections. As we will see, Paul's communal and ethical vision for the church flows downstream from what he believes about his christologically-oriented Gentile mission.

CHRISTOLOGICAL UNITY

In the section that spans from Rom 12:1–13 and 14:1—15:13, Paul focuses his attention on the pressing issue of unity within the church.[2] The Christians at Rome, he says, ought to consider all that has been said about "the mercies of God" in the previous chapters and use it as a basis for a new way to live—not least in regards to unity with one another (12:1).[3] Paul is particularly concerned about Jew and Gentile unity within the Roman church specifically. He also has important things to say about Christians living in harmony with those outside the church. In the first two verses, no less than seven times does Paul employ the plural to address his readers:

> *Brothers and sisters*, I encourage *you all* through the mercies of God to present *your bodies* as a living sacrifice, holy and acceptable to God—which is the reasonable act of worship for *you all*. And do not let *yourselves* be conformed to this age, but let *yourselves* be transformed by the renewal of the mind so that *you all* can discern what the good and pleasing and complete will of God is. (Rom 12:1–2)[4]

2. Rom 12–16 can be divided into three sections: 12:1—15:13; 15:14—16:23; 16:25–27 (Schreiner, *Romans* [2nd ed], 621–784).

3. See e.g., Rom 9:15, 16, 18, 23; 11:30–32. See Fitzmyer, *Romans*, 637; Cranfield, *Romans*, 595–96. Stuhlmacher (*Romans*, 185) is correct when he says that 12:1—15:13 is no stand-alone discussion with respect to chapters 1–11. To the contrary, he says, what Paul seeks to do is show "how the life of the church can and should appear as a sign of the righteousness of God." See also Achtemeier (*Romans*, 195) who, commenting on vv. 1–2, says, "Life under the lordship of God means a life under the structuring power of grace. That power transforms not only individuals, but the individual's relationships to the community around them."

4. On the link vv. 1–2 have with Paul's previous argument in chapters 5–7, see Tobin, *Rhetoric*, 388–90.

The important thing to note here is that Paul encourages the Roman Christians to carry out their "act of worship" together in unity. While it is true Paul speaks of individuals presenting their own bodies as sacrifices, it is possible to see a collective emphasis such that all the bodies presented culminate into one, unified act of obedience: *All* are to present their *bodies* as a singular "living sacrifice" (θυσίαν ζῶσαν) (v. 1). Similarly, Paul cautions *all of them* not to be "conformed" (plural: συσχηματίζεσθε) to the age but to be "transformed" (plural: μεταμορφοῦσθε) by the renewing of the "mind" (singular: νοὸς) (v. 2). Paul most likely intends for each Christian to see his/ herself as part of a collective unity, bringing their bodies into submission to God as one, unified "sacrifice."[5] Each Christian ought to resist the world's pattern of living in order to adopt a singular *mindset* that allows for unity as a group.

In this way, vv. 1–2 serve as an introduction to vv. 3–8, where Paul remarks that the Christian should not think too highly of his or herself (μὴ ὑπερφρονεῖν παρ' ὃ δεῖ φρονεῖν). Instead, one should think reasonably (ἀλλὰ φρονεῖν εἰς τὸ σωφρονεῖν), according to the "measure of faith" God has granted (v. 3). This command occurs within the context of God's giving grace-gifts (χαρίσματα) to each Christian (vv. 6–8). The point here is simple: "If that Christian community responds appropriately to the structuring grace at work within it, what it will display in its life is unity."[6] A communal response is necessary, for Paul's most basic assumption is that each believer has a christological commonality with other Christians. For, as Paul says, even though there are "many members" (πολλὰ μέλη), there is still "one body" (ἑνὶ σώματι) (v. 4). That body is, of course, "one body in Christ" (ἓν σῶμά . . . ἐν Χριστῷ) (v. 5).[7] Thomas Tobin is correct when he says that "Christ is an active and central reality within the life of the community. The basis for the solidarity and harmony of the community is not primarily social but religious, in the sense that the community is rooted in its forming one body 'in Christ.'"[8]

---

5. See Fitzmyer (*Romans*, 638), who says, "The unity and harmony of the community demand that individuals realize that they are living in the new aeon and are to strive to overcome evil with good. The common pursuit of the good is expected of those who are members of the body of Christ and whose lives are to be a sacrifice offered to God."

6. Achtemeier, *Romans*, 196.

7. On Paul's conception of the church as "the body of the Christ," see Stuhlmacher, *Romans*, 190–91. See also Tobin, *Rhetoric*, 390–93, who tends to over-exaggerate the differences between Rom 12 and 1 Cor 12, not least with respect to the way Paul employs the concept of *the body of Christ*. That Paul is not preaching "uniformity," see Achtemeier, *Romans*, 196–97.

8. Tobin, *Rhetoric*, 391. See also 393.

Here Paul anticipates his discussion in Rom 15:5–6, where he says, "And may the God of perseverance and of encouragement give to you all a mindset of harmony (τὸ αὐτὸ φρονεῖν) for one another according to Christ Jesus so that in unity (ὁμοθυμαδὸν) you might with one voice glorify (δοξάζητε) the God and father of our Lord Jesus Christ." The discussion is quite similar to Phil 2:2, where Paul exhorts the believers to have "the same mindset" (τὸ αὐτὸ φρονῆτε), "the same love" (τὴν αὐτὴν ἀγάπην), to be of "one spirit" (σύμψυχοι), and "one mindset" (ἕν φρονοῦντες). The way of thinking that believers are supposed to have is, of course, christological: "You all have this mindset (φρονεῖτε) among yourselves, which also was in Christ Jesus" (v. 5). The fuel behind Paul's calls for Christian unity is genuine *love* (12:9–10) that reveals itself in action and "hospitality" (v. 13).

This love, moreover, is not to be shared only with believers but also with those outside of the church, as vv. 14–21 indicate.[9] Christians, for example, are to love their persecutors (v. 14). They are not to "give back evil for evil" but, instead, they are to "consider (προνοούμενοι) how to do good in the presence of all people" (v. 17). Paul encourages the believers to be "peaceable with all people" and to never retaliate against their enemies, doing "good" to them instead (vv. 18–21). Thus, while it is true Paul thinks in terms of *insiders* and *outsiders* with respect to the church and the world (as Rom 12:2 seems to indicate), the church is not to become a sect disassociated from the world. By showing unconditional love to outsiders (even to those outsiders who are actively persecuting the church), Paul envisions a church that lives in harmony with the outside world. This does not imply, of course, that Paul is encouraging the church to agree in totality with the ways of the world (again, recall Rom 12:2). He is, rather, encouraging the church to adopt a posture of humility toward the world. Thus, he can say: "Have the same mindset (τὸ αὐτὸ . . . φρονοῦντες) toward one another, not having a haughty mindset (ὑψηλὰ φρονοῦντες), but associate with the lowly; do not be wise in regard to yourselves (φρόνιμοι παρ' ἑαυτοῖς)" (v. 16).

The fact that v. 16 is wedged between the two sections—that is, between vv. 14–15 and vv. 17–21—that discuss how the church should relate to the world suggests that Paul intends for v. 16 to be taken as part of that same discussion as well.[10] If that is so, this means that the humble mindset (φρονοῦντες) of agreement Christians are to have "toward one another" most likely refers to their posture toward the unbelieving world; the "other" here may refer to unbelievers.[11] The use of the φρην-word group in v. 16 and

9. As is also recognized by Tobin, *Rhetoric*, 394–95.

10. See Cranfield, *Romans*, 643.

11. Cranfield, *Romans*, 642–43, thinks the command to agree with one another

in Phil 2:1–11 provides a helpful clue in this regard. In Philippians, Paul calls the church to maintain a Christ-like—and hence *servant-like*—posture and "mindset" (φρονεῖτε) toward others (Phil 2:5). In Rom 12, that same christological mindset is applied to outsiders. This same posture of humility, furthermore, also allows the church to live in concord with the pagan Roman government as much as possible (13:1–7). Thus, in the section that spans from 12:14—13:7, Paul's focus is on how the church ought to live, as best as possible, in harmony with those outside the church. And this harmony, Paul says, is rooted in "love" of neighbor (13:8–10). As we will see below, Paul's christological conception of *love* is the grounds for both the church's humble posture toward each other within the church and those outside the church. Presently, it is enough to note that Paul's vision for the church is unity—unity with insiders *and* with outsiders.

In the next section that encompasses 14:1—15:13, Paul revisits the topic of unity within the church, only this time he does so with regard to specific issues that confronted the Roman church. He divides the church between two groups: the "weak" (14:1) and the "strong" (15:1). At issue, it seems, is the controversy surrounding dietary regulations and other Jewish legal requirements like the observance of holy days—a controversy that was most likely occurring between Jews (the "weak") and Gentiles (the "strong") (14:2–3, 5–6).[12] Though gaining certainty about details on the issue at hand need not detain us, it seems likely that Paul identifies the "weak" as those who want to maintain forms of Jewish purity codes and regulations (vv. 2b, 5a).[13] The "strong" are those who do not feel the need to do so (vv. 2a, 5b). Paul tells the strong to "welcome (προσλαμβάνεσθε) the one who is weak in faith" (v. 1). He also exhorts them to "not judge" the weak in this regard because God himself, says Paul, "has welcomed" (προσελάβετο) the weak believer (v. 3). The command not to judge the weak is repeated in v. 13, where the command is grounded on the notion of Christian "love" (v. 15). The various views between the "weak" and the "strong" are not to become

---

refers to conduct among Christians. He is, however, convinced Paul is still primarily concerned about how the church's unity or disunity among themselves will impact those outside the church (as a parallel text, he cites John 17:20–23). Cranfield may be correct, especially given how closely it is related to the discussion in Phil 2, as he points out (642). Either way, the issue is incidental to my argument.

12. Longenecker, *Romans*, 995–96. See also Bird, *Anomlaous Jew*, 185–94; Käsemann, *Romans*, 364–69. Gorman (*Crucified Lord*, 398) is right to say that, while the controversy was probably marked out along Jew and Gentile ethnic lines, this does not necessarily mean that every Jew in the Roman church was "weak" or that every Gentile in the church was "strong." Cf. Tobin, *Rhetoric*, 404–10.

13. See the discussion in Käsemann, *Romans*, 368.

sources of schismatic disagreement (v. 1), but rather opportunities of "love" (v. 15) and "peace" and "edification of one another" (v. 19).[14]

In what would have been understood as a controversial move (from the perspective of law-abiding Jews), Paul goes on to say that "the kingdom of God is not about eating or drinking but about righteousness and peace and joy in the Holy Spirit" (v. 17). The point is that Paul envisions the church's unity as based on something other than Jewish purity laws. Paul clearly intends unity to have a christological foundation, as we have already seen in Rom 15:5–6 above.[15]

In chapter 16, Paul warns the Roman church to "avoid" those who swerve from "the teaching" and thereby create "divisions and stumbling blocks" (σκάνδαλα) in the church (v. 17). Such schismatic people, says Paul, "do not serve our Lord Christ," which implies they lack a christological basis for their own teaching (v. 18a). Instead, he says, such people serve their own "belly" (κοιλία) and "they deceive the unsuspecting hearts" of people, cunningly leading them astray (v. 18b).[16] The details of this text will be discussed in the next section below. I wish merely to note at present that Paul's vision of unity is here, once again, christologically founded.

The above has sketched out a twofold fact: In Rom 12–16, (1) Paul has a concern for church unity and (2) he believes that unity is founded upon christology. None of this is surprising or novel. But as we will see below, Paul's vision of unity is accomplished only when the believers follow his particular vision of ethics. His ethics, moreover, has the particular shape it does because of the way his assumed christology, working as an interpretive prejudgment, engages with key Old Testament texts in a dialogical sort of way. In the following section, we will see more specifically how Paul hermeneutically grounds his vision of unity in Scripture.

CHRISTOLOGICAL ETHICS

Paul's vision of unity entails a call to action, which in turn necessitates that he launch into a discussion about ethics. To be sure, Fitzmyer is correct that Paul's discussion is not an "ethical treatise" *per se*.[17] There is, however, a

14. See Longenecker, *Romans*, 996, who says "the apostle's purpose in all his exhortations was to restore peace and unity within the Christian congregations at Rome, and so to enhance an accurate expression of the Christian gospel in the city."

15. Because 15:5–6 occurs within the context of Paul's ethical admonishments, I will postpone further discussion on this for the section on ethics below.

16. On the link back to Rom 14:1—15:13, see Longenecker, *Romans*, 1081–82.

17. Fitzmyer, *Romans*, 638. Fitzmyer is, however, quite wrong to describe Paul as "somewhat rambling" in this section (638).

certain hermeneutic logic at work that, when understood, reveals a stream of thought that is consistent with his previous discussions in Romans. As we have already seen above, Paul calls for harmony to exist *both* between Christians within the church (12:3–13; 14:1—15:13; 16:17–20) *and* between the church and the unbelieving world (12:14—13:7).[18] In this section, I will show that Paul envisions such unity to be achieved through a christological ethic that is itself derived from his christological reading of the Old Testament.

In 12:14-21, where Paul begins to speak about the church's relationship with outsiders—specifically with persecutors—he encourages believers to maintain a posture of love. They are to "bless" and "not curse" (v. 14), show sympathy (v. 15), not be arrogant (v. 16), not "give back evil for evil" (v. 17), be peaceable as much as possible (v. 18), not take vengeance upon one's enemies (v. 19) but instead do good to them (vv. 20–21).[19] In this entire section, Richard Longenecker has argued that Paul appears to draw upon an early Jesus tradition—incorporating several "'sayings of Jesus' that had been enshrined in the consciousness of at least some of the earliest Christian congregations."[20] Specifically, he argues that a "paraphrastic rendering of a 'saying of Jesus'" occurs in the following verses: v. 14 (followed by Pauline comments in vv. 15–16); v. 17a (followed by Pauline comments in vv. 17b–18); v. 19a (followed by quotations from Deut 32:35 and Prov 25:21-22 in vv. 19b–20); and finally v. 21 (to which Paul adds no comment and, according to Longenecker, simply treats it "as a conclusion to his whole discussion of 12:14–21").[21] Indeed, when one compares Paul's exhortations with that of the synoptics (e.g., Matt 5:43–48; Luke 6:27–36), the evidence that he draws on the Jesus tradition is persuasive.[22]

With this in mind, we note specifically the exhortation of v. 19, namely, that persecuted Christians should not seek "vengeance" but instead should "give place for wrath" (v. 19a). This is followed by a quotation from Deut

18. See Tobin, *Rhetoric*, 394–95. He says Paul's exhortations "are, for the most part, either directly or indirectly social in orientation, either toward other members of the community or toward the outside world" (394); "Paul also emphasizes the importance of harmonious relations with the outside world" (395).

19. In view of his larger project, see Boyd, *Crucifixion*, esp. 725–26.

20. Longenecker, *Romans*, 939.

21. Longenecker, *Romans*, 940. Regarding the "sayings of Jesus," Longenecker (*Romans*, 940) traces them to their synoptic equivalents: v. 14 (Matt 5:44; Luke 6:27–28); v. 17a (Matt 5:39–42; Luke 6:29–30); v. 19a (the Old Testament quotations from Deuteronomy and Proverbs, says Longenecker, are considered to be "drawn by Jesus himself" and were presumably part of Q even though they do not appear in Matthew or Luke); v. 21 (Matt 5:38–48; Luke 6:27–36).

22. See also Moo, *Romans* [2nd ed], 799.

32:35 in the second half of the verse: "For it is written, 'Vengeance belongs to me; I will repay,' says the Lord."[23] In its original context, the quotation is part of a speech from God, who promises to avenge the enemies of Israel (Deut 32:35–43).[24] In this way, Paul sees the church as embodying the story of Israel. This should not be surprising for two reasons. First, Paul envisions the church as "one body in Christ" (12:5; cf. 1 Cor 12:27). Second, he understands Christ as the "son of God" and "firstborn" (1:4; 8:29)—both of which were descriptions of Israel (Exod 4:22). It is reasonable to conclude, then, that the quotation's meaningfulness is possible in light of Paul's interpretive posture, one that assumes an implicit christological fore-structure understanding. Through his dialogical hermeneutics, the story of Israel informs Paul's understanding of the believers at Rome in such a way that they do not exist in a historical vacuum, but rather in continuity with salvation history.[25] Similarly, the story of Israel itself takes on fresh meaning in light of how it lives on through the believers who are united together *in Christ*, the firstborn son of God.

The same must be said about the quotation taken from Prov 25:21–22, which Paul immediately cites after Deuteronomy. He says, "But instead, 'If your enemy is hungry, feed him. If he is thirsty, give him something to drink. For by doing this, you will heap coals of fire on his head'" (v. 20).[26] Being cited in tandem with his christologically-interpreted Deuteronomy quotation, Prov 25:21–22 serves Paul's purposes quite well. It voices the call to action—that is, what the Christians ought to be actively doing in response to persecution. Thus, if these observations are correct, we have a strong hint that Paul's ethical approach stems from his christological horizon of understanding. In a very real way, Paul's christology and the Jewish story are both

23. Rom 12:19b: γέγραπται γάρ· ἐμοὶ ἐκδίκησις, ἐγὼ ἀνταποδώσω, λέγει κύριος. Deut 32:35 (LXX): ἐν ἡμέρᾳ ἐκδικήσεως ἀνταποδώσω, ἐν καιρῷ, ὅταν σφαλῇ ὁ πούς αὐτῶν· ὅτι ἐγγὺς ἡμέρα ἀπωλείας αὐτῶν, καὶ πάρεστιν ἕτοιμα ὑμῖν. Deut 32:35 (MT): לי נקם ושלם. On Paul's Greek text and the MT, see Stanley, *Paul and the Language of Scripture*, 171–74. Cf. Moo, *Romans* [2nd ed], 805n248.

24. See Wagner, *Heralds*, 316–17 (esp. n38 in regard to God's vengeance on the enemies of Israel in Deut 32).

25. This recalls the olive tree metaphor in Rom 11:17–18.

26. Rom 12:20: ἀλλ' ἐὰν πεινᾷ ὁ ἐχθρός σου, ψώμιζε αὐτόν· ἐὰν διψᾷ, πότιζε αὐτόν· τοῦτο γὰρ ποιῶν ἄνθρακας πυρὸς σωρεύσεις ἐπὶ τὴν κεφαλὴν αὐτοῦ. Prov 25:21–22 (Rahlfs): ἐὰν πεινᾷ ὁ ἐχθρός σου, τρέφε αὐτόν, ἐὰν διψᾷ, πότιζε αὐτόν· τοῦτο γὰρ ποιῶν ἄνθρακας πυρὸς σωρεύσεις ἐπὶ τὴν κεφαλὴν αὐτοῦ, ὁ δὲ κύριος ἀνταποδώσει σοι ἀγαθά. In place of τρέφε, B has ψώμιζε. It is possible that B represents an alteration in order to conform to the Pauline quote (Moo, *Romans* [2nd ed], 805n251). See also Boyd, *Crucifixion*, 819–20n20.

integral with respect to not just how Scripture is to be interpreted *but also* with respect to how the Christian's life in the empire is to be interpreted.

This is seen clearly in Rom 13:8–14. Leading into that section, Paul exhorts the church to act rightly in the empire—to "do good," he says (v. 3). This specific command draws from the Jesus saying depicted in 12:21 (mentioned above): "Do not be conquered by evil but conquer evil with good." This ethic is not set in the abstract; Paul contextualizes it within a concrete political situation. One does "good," he says," by submitting to the government (v. 5)—not blindly, of course, but rather in the sense of paying one's "taxes" and "tolls/revenues" and in terms of giving "respect" and "honor" to proper authorities (v. 6–7).[27]

All of this is summarized in the concept of *love*: "Owe nobody anything, except to love one another" (v. 8a). He continues: "For the one who loves the other has fulfilled (πεπλήρωκεν) the law" (v. 8b). Paul then quotes four commandments from the Decalouge: "For the commandments: 'You shall not commit adultery; you shall not kill; you shall not steal; you shall not covet" (v. 9a).[28] Following this, he quotes Lev 19:18: "And if there are any other commands, they are summed up in this word: 'You shall love your neighbor as yourself'" (v. 9b).[29] His logic is stated in the next verse: "Love does no evil to one's neighbor. Therefore, love is the fulfillment (πλήρωμα) of the law" (v. 10). It appears, then, that Paul's use of "fulfill" goes something like this: Love fulfills the law in the sense that it renders any subsequent commands as redundant. If one loves another, they will not harm them; hence, so long as *love* is in place, commands not to harm others are unnecessary. But does this capture the entirety of Paul's thought?

---

27. Cf. the discussion in Jewett, *Romans*, 798–801.

28. Rom 13:9a: τὸ γὰρ οὐ μοιχεύσεις, οὐ φονεύσεις, οὐ κλέψεις, οὐκ ἐπιθυμήσεις; Deut 5:17–19, 21 (LXX): Οὐ μοιχεύσεις. Οὐ φονεύσεις. Οὐ κλέψεις; οὐκ ἐπιθυμήσεις τὴν γυναῖκα τοῦ πλησίον σου. οὐκ ἐπιθυμήσεις τὴν οἰκίαν τοῦ πλησίον σου οὔτε τὸν ἀγρὸν αὐτοῦ οὔτε τὸν παῖδα αὐτοῦ οὔτε τὴν παιδίσκην αὐτοῦ οὔτε τοῦ βοὸς αὐτοῦ οὔτε τοῦ ὑποζυγίου αὐτοῦ οὔτε παντὸς κτήνους αὐτοῦ οὔτε ὅσα τῷ πλησίον σού ἐστιν; Exod 20:13–15, 17 (LXX): Οὐ μοιχεύσεις. οὐ κλέψεις. οὐ φονεύσεις; Οὐκ ἐπιθυμήσεις τὴν γυναῖκα τοῦ πλησίον σου. οὐκ ἐπιθυμήσεις τὴν οἰκίαν τοῦ πλησίον σου οὔτε τὸν ἀγρὸν αὐτοῦ οὔτε τὸν παῖδα αὐτοῦ οὔτε τὴν παιδίσκην αὐτοῦ οὔτε τοῦ βοὸς αὐτοῦ οὔτε τοῦ ὑποζυγίου αὐτοῦ οὔτε παντὸς κτήνους αὐτοῦ οὔτε ὅσα τῷ πλησίον σού ἐστιν. On the differences in word order, as well as Paul's drawing on oral tradition, see Stanley, *Paul and the Language of Scripture*, 174–76. On the significance of the Decalogue for Judaism, see Stuhlmacher, *Romans*, 209.

29. Rom 13:9b: ἀγαπήσεις τὸν πλησίον σου ὡς σεαυτόν; Lev 19:18 (LXX): καὶ οὐκ ἐκδικᾶταί σου ἡ χείρ, καὶ οὐ μηνιεῖς τοῖς υἱοῖς τοῦ λαοῦ σου· καὶ ἀγαπήσεις τὸν πλησίον σου ὡς σεαυτόν· ἐγώ εἰμι κύριος. On the significance of this commandment within Judaism, see Stuhlmacher, *Romans*, 209.

The answer seems to be no. There is more to Paul's hermeneutic than merely the notion that the commandments have become redundant—and in that way *fulfilled*—once they are placed within the context of love of neighbor. For starters, as we will see below, there is much more to Paul's conception of what it means to *fulfill* the law than that. Indeed, Paul's notion of love should not be abstracted from the christological horizon of understanding in which he interprets it. Several observations to this end are in order. First, the preceding context is clear that the exhortations to love and care for others have a christological basis. In 12:3–13, for example, the church was told to use their gifts for others in light of their common union with Christ (vv. 3–8). This fact is clearly connected to the believer's calling to embody "sincere love" (v. 9), to "love one another" (v. 10), and to show "hospitality" (v. 13). Second, the Christian's ethic toward unbelievers was likewise based upon the Jesus sayings (vv. 14–21), within which were two quotations that were set within a christological framework (see above).

Third, when Paul speaks of how "the one who loves the other has fulfilled (πεπλήρωκεν) the law" (13:8b) and how "love is the fulfillment (πλήρωμα) of the law" (10b), he echoes back to his previous discussion in Rom 8: "For what the law was incapable of doing because of the weakness of the flesh, God has done by sending his own son in the likeness of sinful flesh and, concerning sin, condemned sin in the flesh so that the righteous requirement of the law might be fulfilled (πληρωθῇ) in us who walk (περιπατοῦσιν) not according to the flesh but according to the Spirit" (vv. 3–4).[30] Here we see much the same idea: *walking in step with the Spirit* runs parallel to *loving one's neighbor*. And just as *walking in step with the Spirit* is associated with Christ having "fulfilled" the law for believers in Rom 8:3–4, it would be a mistake not to see the same correlation in Rom 13:9–10.

Fourth, we ought to consider a parallel passage in Galatians, where a similar discussion—along with a quotation from Lev 19:18—also occurs.[31] Paul urges the Galatians to consider how the only thing that matters is "faith working through love" (5:6). He exhorts the believers to "become servants to one another through love" (5:13). The reason, he says, is because "the whole law is fulfilled (πεπλήρωται) in this one word: 'You shall love your neighbor as yourself'" (5:14, quoting Lev 19:18). He then urges them to "walk by the Spirit (πνεύματι περιπατεῖτε) and you will not gratify the lust

30. See Stuhlmacher, *Romans*, 210–11. He says, "in [Rom] 8:3ff. he emphasized that those who believe in Christ do not somehow exist in a state of lawless capriciousness, but in the freedom of fulfilling (the legal demand) of the Law by virtue of the sacrificial death of Jesus and the Holy Spirit which has been allotted to them" (210). See also Gorman, *Crucified Lord*, 396.

31. See Gorman, *Crucified Lord*, 396; Tobin, *Rhetoric*, 401–2.

(ἐπιθυμίαν) of the flesh" (5:16). He concludes his exhortations by saying "the ones who are of Christ Jesus have crucified the flesh with its passions and lusts (ἐπιθυμίαις). If we live by the Spirit, let us follow the Spirit" (5:24–25). Thus, Paul envisions the law as being fulfilled through the believer's *love*, as they walk in step with the *Spirit*, because they are in union with *Christ*. Paul simply does not envision a fulfillment of the law apart from his beliefs about Christ in Galatians. The same must be said, then, about Rom 13:8–10. There is no reason to think that Paul's christology is not playing a similar role there as it was in Rom 8:3–4 and Gal 5:6–25.

Fifth, we ought to recognize how the larger context of Rom 13:8–14 echoes the previous discussion in Rom 6—the latter of which is explicit in regard to how Paul envisions christology playing a role in living in holiness. "Therefore, we have been buried with him through baptism into death, in order that, just as Christ was raised from the dead by the glory of the father, so also we might walk (περιπατήσωμεν) in newness of life" (v. 4). What follows from this is a command to walk in holiness: "Do not let sin reign in your mortal bodies to obey its lusts (ἐπιθυμίαις)" (6:12). Paul says something similar at the end of Rom 13, just a few verses down from the Lev 19:18 quotation: "Let us walk (περιπατήσωμεν) properly as in the day ... clothe yourselves in the Lord Jesus Christ and make no provision for the flesh to lust (ἐπιθυμίας)" (vv. 13–14).[32]

In light of all this, we can conclude that Paul has not read Leviticus' command to love one's neighbor as fulfilling the law in that *love in general* renders the commandments redundant. Rather, the commandments are redundant (and hence *fulfilled*) precisely because the *love* in which believers walk, and in which they are united, is a christological love.[33] The commandments have not simply been supplanted by a greater ethic; they have been brought to completion because believers are united with Christ.[34] Thus, Paul can say a commandment like "You shall not covet (ἐπιθυμήσεις)" (13:9) has been "fulfilled" (πεπλήρωκεν) by love precisely because the believer is "clothed" in Jesus such that sinful "lusts" (ἐπιθυμίας) are left ungratified (13:14). The clothing image is a metaphor for the believer's union with Christ on the cross: "the ones who are of Christ Jesus have crucified the flesh with its passions and lusts (ἐπιθυμίαις)" (Gal 5:24).[35] And lest we forget,

---

32. That this was taken from an early baptism liturgy, see Tobin, *Rhetoric*, 403–4.

33. This is not to deny the important trinitarian aspect. See Gorman, *Crucified Lord*, 396–97: "Thus, for Paul the Son is both the source and the cruciform paradigm (as 15:3 will make clear) of love, yet only in connection with God as the provider of both the Son and the Spirit."

34. Cf. the discussion in Rosner, *Paul and the Law*, 195, in light of his larger project.

35. See Calvin (*Romans*, 490), who says that with this "metaphor . . . Paul had in

Paul believes it is the cross in which love was on full display: "But God commends his own love toward us in that, while we were still sinners, Christ died for us" (Rom 5:8). Thus, Christians "are to live out their community story freed from the deeds of the flesh, guided by the Spirit, and clothed in the narrative of cruciform love found in Christ."[36] In light of these observations, one should not assume that Paul discusses love in Rom 13:8–10 in abstraction from its christological context.

But the observations above are not the only clues that suggest Paul envisions ethics to be situated within a christological horizon. In the discussion that occurs in Rom 14:1—15:13, Paul's christological ethic is on full display. There Paul argues that those who are "weak in faith" (14:1) are to be accepted by those are "strong" (15:1). As mentioned above, the pressing issue that Paul addresses is the specific controversy over Jewish dietary regulations and Sabbath laws. Within the Roman church, some believers apparently felt the freedom to not abide by the cultic rituals while others felt an obligation to follow them. In the opening verses of chapter 14, Paul commands the libertarian-minded believers to "welcome" (προσλαμβάνεσθε) the weaker believers (v. 1). Neither the weak nor the strong are to judge or disdain the other (v. 2). All within the community are to be accepted by the community. The justification for this is found two verses down: "For God has welcomed (προσελάβετο) him" (v. 3).[37] The justification, then, is theological. *God* has accepted all believers. "The Lord," says Paul, "is able to make him stand" (v. 4).[38] But the most significant factor at work is not theological *per se*, but rather christological—a fact of which we will see momentarily.[39]

On this, Paul elaborates further, inching closer to the way in which God makes believers "stand." He says that each believer—whether they are part of the weak or the strong—should be "fully convinced in his own mind" with respect to whether to abide by the cultic rituals (v. 5). Whatever is decided, the sincere believer will do so in a spirit of thankfulness and sincere worship to God (v. 6). All believers, he adds, are under the lordship of

---

view the end of our calling; inasmuch as God, by adopting us, unites us to the body of the only-begotten Son, and for this purpose,—that we, renouncing our former life, may become new men in him."

36. Gorman, *Crucified Lord*, 397.

37. Even though the object "him" (αὐτὸν) is singular, there is little doubt Paul intends it as a reference to members of both groups. See Käsemann, *Romans*, 369. Contra Dunn, *Romans 9–16*, 803.

38. See the discussion in Longenecker, *Romans*, 997.

39. Observing the christological aspect is not without warrant among scholars. E.g., in Longenecker, *Romans*, 997–98, there is a section entitled "On the Christological Support That Paul Gives for His Exhortations and Appeals of 14:1—15:13."

Christ—whether in life or death, for every believer belongs to the Lord (vv. 7–8). And then Paul reveals his basic prejudgment on the matter: "For this reason Christ died and lived again—in order that he might be Lord of the dead and the living" (v. 9). What Paul means is that *the way in which* each believer can live (and die) to the Lord *with respect to eating or not eating* is by means of the death and resurrection of Jesus. *That* is the way "The Lord is able to make [the weak and the strong] stand" (v. 4). What this also means, then, is that judgments from believers who differ with others is prohibited. For if the believer stands *in the Lord*, then there can exist no tribunal of condemnation within the church. The only court in which a believer will *stand* before his or her judge is the Lord's court. Paul then asks:

> But who are you to judge your brother and sister? Or why do you show disdain for your brother and sister? For we will all stand before the judgment seat of God. For as it is written: "As I live, says the Lord, to me every knee will bow and every tongue will confess to God" [quoting Isa 45:23]. So then, each of us will give an account of his or herself to God. (vv. 10–12)[40]

Before we observe the features of this quotation, we must attend to its function in the argument. Paul quotes Isaiah in order to validate his thesis that judgment with respect to this issue is prohibited among Christians. It is prohibited because there is but one judge—namely, "the Lord" and "God" (vv. 3–4, 6–8)—in front of whom all will give an account. The quotation verifies this scenario, as it proclaims that such judgment before the Lord will, in fact, occur.[41] The quotation, then, provides scriptural warrant for Paul's assertion.

As to the quote's features, it must be admitted that Paul interprets it christologically. In other words, the one who speaks ("As I live, says the Lord, to me every knee will bow and every tongue will confess to God") is Christ.[42] In my view, Paul reads "Lord" and "God" in Isa 45:23 as a reference

---

40. Rom 14:11: γέγραπται γάρ· ζῶ ἐγώ, λέγει κύριος, ὅτι ἐμοὶ κάμψει πᾶν γόνυ καὶ πᾶσα γλῶσσα ἐξομολογήσεται τῷ θεῷ. Isa 45:23 (LXX): κατ᾽ ἐμαυτοῦ ὀμνύω Ἦ μὴν ἐξελεύσεται ἐκ τοῦ στόματός μου δικαιοσύνη, οἱ λόγοι μου οὐκ ἀποστραφήσονται ὅτι ἐμοὶ κάμψει πᾶν γόνυ καὶ ἐξομολογήσεται πᾶσα γλῶσσα τῷ θεῷ. Longenecker (*Romans*, 998, 1003) thinks Paul might be drawing from the Jesus tradition (see Matt 7:1, 3–5; Luke 6:37) in his opening question of v. 10 ("But who are you to judge your brother and sister?").

41. See Schreiner, *Romans* [2nd ed], 701.

42. Contra Käsemann, *Romans*, 373. Bates (*Hermeneutics*, 287–89) does not think this is an instance of prosopological exegesis, though he concludes "Paul is being playful with his sources" and is "deliberately and provocatively placing the Lord Jesus in the role of God" (287–88).

to Christ.[43] There are several reasons to think along these lines. We must first make some preliminary observations. Firstly, Paul has said that "God has welcomed" the believer (v. 3). Secondly, by "welcome," Paul intends to communicate more than divine hospitality but also divine acquittal with respect to the matter at hand (i.e., eating, drinking, observing Sabbath). This seems clear from v. 4, where Paul rebukes the would-be human judge: "Who are you to judge another servant? Before his own Lord (κύριος) he stands (στήκει) or falls. But he will stand (σταθήσεται), for the Lord (κύριος) is able to make him stand (στῆσαι)" (v. 4). And then Paul goes on to describe the believer's final judgment in terms of *standing*: "We will all stand (παραστησόμεθα) before the judgment seat of God" (v. 10). Paul seems to be saying that, in the present time, the believer can "stand" unconcemned with respect to whatever choice they make regarding eating or not eating *and*, at the final judgment, they will be found there to "stand" uncondemned as well. The assumption, it appears, is that the present judgment and the future judgment are linked. Thirdly, Paul uses "God" and "Lord" interchangeably with respect to whom the believer will stand. This is a simple, though important, observation to remember.

With these preliminary observations in mind, I can now make a few comments on why I think Paul interprets Isa 45:23 christologically. First, in vv. 6–8, Paul says all believers—regardless of what they decide regarding the issue at hand—are uncondemned since they live in a spirit of thanksgiving to "the Lord" with respect to their decision (v. 6). In this way, Paul says "we live to the Lord" and "we die to the Lord" (v. 8). Paul's use of *living* and *dying* to the Lord ought to be taken as a synonym for *standing* before the Lord in the present and future judgment (vv. 3–4, 10). Moreover, by "Lord" (v. 8), Paul clearly intends a reference to Christ, as the very next verse indicates: "For this reason Christ died and lived again (ἔζησεν)—in order that *he* might be Lord of the dead and the living" (v. 9; emphasis added). The idea is that the Lord in front of whom the believer stands (and will stand) is none other than the crucified and resurrected Christ. Thus, *through the death and resurrection of Christ*, the believer—whether they are on the side of the "weak" or the "strong"—can *stand* uncondemned. Because the quotation's references to "Lord" and God" have thus been recontextualized within the matrix of christology (vv. 10–11), so also the "God" who has "welcomed" the believer (v. 3) has been recontextualized within that same matrix.

Second, the opening line of the quotation, "As I live, says the Lord" (ζῶ ἐγώ, λέγει κύριος), appears to be a Pauline insertion—verbiage of which is

---

43. Contra Cranfield, *Romans*, 710.

not uncommon in the LXX (v. 11a).[44] Presumably, Paul employs this line because he wanted to link the quote back to the statement about Christ's resurrection in v. 9 (ἔζησεν), a move that would guarantee a christological reading of the quotation.[45] Third, the use of Isa 45:23 in Phil 2:10–11 ought to have some bearing on how we understand the quotation in Rom 14:11.[46] It is there where Paul quotes the so-called Christ hymn, with its insertion of references to Christ where references to "God" were originally: "In order that at the name of Jesus *every knee should bow*—in the heavens, on the earth, and under the earth—*and every tongue should confess* that Jesus Christ is Lord to the glory of God the Father" (Phil 2:10–11).[47] Given that Paul quotes the hymn approvingly, and given further the observations we have already made regarding the context of Rom 14:3–10, it is not a stretch to think Paul still has christology in mind when he quotes Isaiah in Rom 14:11.[48]

Here is why all of this is important. Paul's exhortation to "welcome" the one who is "weak in faith" (v. 1) is based upon the fact that "God has welcomed him" (v. 3). And, as we have seen, references to "God" and to God's having "welcomed" believers, have all been prejudged christologically by Paul.[49] Even Isaiah's text—cited as it was as scriptural support for the reality of divine judgment—has been prejudged in this manner. Thus, because

44. Stanley, *Paul and the Language of Scripture*, 176–77.

45. Contra Cranfield, *Romans*, 710. Bates (*Hermeneutics*, 288) rightly observes: "Surely it is not a matter of coincidence that just two verses prior to invoking the oath formula 'as surely as I live" via conflated citation, Paul has just discoursed on the very topic of *living* for the Lord, concluding: 'For this reason Christ died and *lived* [again], in order that also he might be the Lord of both the dead and the *living*' (Rom 14:9). In the immediate context in which the citation 'As surely as I live' is found, Paul has just emphatically stated that the Lord (Christ) is the one who lives."

46. On the use of Scripture in Philippians, see Fowl, "Scripture"; Bates, *Hermeneutics*, 288–89.

47. The quoted text is in italics. See Hays, *Reading Backwards*, 65–66.

48. Thus Stephen Fowl ("Scripture," 165) is only somewhat correct when he says "it is interesting to note that the authority and power that Paul attributes to God in Romans [14:11] he attributes here [in Phil 2:10–11] to Christ by invoking the same Old Testament text." Though the Rom 14:11 quotation lacks the same explicit attribution that is present in Phil 2:10–11, it is still very much there. Once the context of Rom 14:11 is taken into account, this becomes clear, as I have argued above. Bates (*Hermeneutics*, 288–89) is correct when he says "It is difficult to escape the conclusion that Paul somehow makes the Lord Christ the speaker of Isaiah 45:23 in Romans 14:11."

49. Paul's prejudgment here is not hidden, merely lurking behind the text. He makes it rather explicit in 15:7.

of the way he grounds his commands on his christological interpretation, Paul's *ethic* is not merely theological but likewise christological.[50]

But it is not just the first half of the discussion that evidences this (14:1–12); the second half does as well (14:13—15:7). After quoting Isa 45:23, Paul concludes that passing judgment upon other believers on the matter is not part of the new way to live. To do so is to "set a stumbling block or obstacle" in the path of a fellow believer (v. 13).[51] And, says Paul, if you cause a brother or sister to be "grieved" over the matter, then you are "no longer walking (περπατεῖς) according to love" (v. 15a). This "walking according to love" is understood christologically, that is, as *walking in accordance with what the crucifixion has accomplished*. He says, "Do not destroy the person for whom Christ died with your food" (v. 15b). He says later on, "Do not on the account of food destroy the work of God" (v. 20a). In other words, to "destroy" is to work against what the cross has brought about, namely, the acceptance of the other and unity within the community—all without respect to whether one eats or does not eat. What Christ has done on the cross has made such acceptance and unity possible. This is how Paul can say, "I know and am persuaded *in the Lord Jesus* that nothing is unclean (κοινὸν) in itself" (v. 14a). It is likely that Paul, in this verse, draws from the Jesus tradition—embodied in Matt 15:11–20 and Mark 7:15–23.[52] This would lend to my argument that the ethical stance Paul takes is rooted and grounded in his christology. Indeed, this would make sense of what Paul says a few verses later:

> For the Kingdom of God is not about eating and drinking but righteousness and peace and joy in the Holy Spirit. For *whoever serves Christ in this way* is pleasing to God and approved by people. *So then let us pursue* that which brings peace and the building up of one another. (vv. 17–19; emphasis added)

The call to harmony is rooted in one's service to Christ.[53] And the freedom one can have with respect to deciding whether to follow (or not follow)

---

50. Wagner (*Heralds*, 338–39) is right that the context of the quotation (that God will revive Israel and call the nations to himself) is key. Thus, he is correct to add: "Paul's citation invites those who hear the echoes of Isaiah's narrative to locate themselves imaginatively at the climactic moment of this story and to shape their communal life in light of what God has now accomplished for them in Christ" (Wagner, *Heralds*, 339). This confirms my point: Paul's christological horizon of understanding (via scriptural citation) informs the ethic that he demands of the Roman believers.

51. As in 14:10, Longenecker (*Romans*, 998, 1006) thinks Paul draws on the Jesus tradition (see Matt 18:7; Mark 9:42; Luke 6:37; 17:1–2) in v. 13.

52. Longenecker, *Romans*, 998, 1006–8.

53. Recall vv. 6–8.

the dietary laws, etc., is a personal matter (vv. 5, 22) so long, of course, it does not cause grievous offense to others such that they stumble and fall as a result (vv. 13b, 15, 20–21). So, whether one follows the dietary laws or feels the freedom not to follow them *or* if one sets aside the freedom they believe they have out of respect for others who do not share the conviction—all of these decisions are grounded in a conception of "love" that is christologically reconfigured.

Even though Paul is adamant about the believer's freedom and insistent that such freedom should never be discounted even by the so-called "weak" (vv. 14, 16, 22), Paul does emphasize to the "strong" that they are called to care for their counterparts (15:1). He says, "But we who are strong owe it to the weak to bear up their weaknesses and not to please ourselves. We must each please our neighbor for his good, to build him up" (vv. 1–2). Paul bases this command on what he believes about Christ. He says, "For even Christ did not please himself" (v. 3a). This statement is backed up by Scripture: "But as it is written: The reproaches of those who reproach you fell on me" (v. 3b, quoting Ps 68:10).[54] That Paul interprets this from the vantage point of his christological horizon of understanding is clear.[55]

On this, a few observations are in order. First, Paul clearly connects the command to the strong in vv. 1–2 to Christ's manner of life such that Paul's ethics are, once again, rooted in Paul's christological prejudgment (note γὰρ in v. 3).[56] And that prejudgment plays a role in bridging the gap between the historically-distanced text of Ps 68:10 and the situation at Rome. It is, therefore, a *christological* ethic. Second, this echoes much of what Paul has already said about neighborly love in 13:8–10 (cf. πλησίον in 15:2). There, we recall, Paul quotes Lev 19:18 in view of his christology as well. Third, that Paul's christology envelopes his horizon of understanding is clear from the verse that follows the quotation in v. 3: "For (γὰρ) whatever was written beforehand was written for *our* instruction so that by patient endurance

54. Rom 15:3: ἀλλὰ καθὼς γέγραπται· οἱ ὀνειδισμοὶ τῶν ὀνειδιζόντων σε ἐπέπεσαν ἐπ᾽ ἐμέ. Ps 68:10 (LXX): ὅτι ὁ ζῆλος τοῦ οἴκου σου κατέφαγέν με, καὶ οἱ ὀνειδισμοὶ τῶν ὀνειδιζόντων σε ἐπέπεσαν ἐπ᾽ ἐμέ.

55. Bates, *Hermeneutics*, 240–55, identifies this as an instance of prosopological exegesis, which is informed by, and situated within, Paul's apostolic-kerygmatic hermeneutic. Cf. Schreiner, *Romans* [2nd ed], 722n8; Campbell, *Hope of Glory*, 292.

56. "By reading this psalm text as an expression of Christ's freely chosen, prayerful attitude toward God, Paul encourages those who are strong to bear the burdens of others. Like Christ, who was 'strong' in position and status with God (2 Cor. 8:9; Phil 2:6), the strong can—indeed, must, if they are to live 'in accordance with Christ Jesus' (15:5)—put up with the failings of the weak by abstaining from meat and wine even while believing that their own normal culinary habits are not wrong" (Gorman, *Crucified Lord*, 401).

and comfort of the Scriptures *we* might have hope" (v. 4; emphasis added).[57] Paul's assumption is that the Christian community is an eschatological community—the Scripture speaks to *them* and for *them*. Thus, he can say in his final admonishment:

> And may the God of perseverance and of encouragement give to you all a mindset of harmony for one another *according to Christ Jesus* so that in unity you might with one voice glorify the God and father of our Lord Jesus Christ. *Therefore, welcome one another, just as Christ welcomed you* to the glory of God. (vv. 5–7; emphasis added)

Because Paul sees Christ's work as a *neutralizing* work (with regard to Jew and Gentile relations), the church can live in harmony together—even despite any deeply-imbedded disagreements about the law.[58] Paul's christological ethic is what makes possible the Christian unity he envisions. Contrary to what many of his Jewish contemporaries believed, Paul envisions unity irrespective of convictions about dietary regulations and the like. The point is simple: Jews and Gentiles are both welcomed by Christ and, as a result, they should be welcomed by the people of Christ. Paul's vision is fresh and startling—it's a *new way to live* in light of what Christ has accomplished in his death and resurrection.

The command in 15:7 ("Therefore, welcome one another, just as Christ welcomed you to the glory of God") is the conclusion of Paul's long-running argument that began in 14:1. In fact, the call to "welcome" each other bookends the entire argument (14:1; 15:7). In vv. 8–13, Paul concludes his argument by citing several Old Testament texts that reveal his belief that, in fact, Christ has indeed welcomed both Jew and Gentile. He begins with, "For (γὰρ) I say Christ has become a servant of the circumcised for the sake of the truth of God in order to confirm the promises of the patriarchs" (v. 8). The γὰρ serves to connect the following discussion with the previous one, specifically back to v. 7. When Paul speaks of Christ as a "servant of the circumcised," he means two things: (1) That Christ serves the Jews and (2) that Christ serves on behalf of the Jewish nation. This seems clear from how Paul speaks of Christ's service as one that *confirms* the promises of Israel's fathers. Here Paul has in mind the covenant promises made to Abraham and his descendants (Rom 4; 9:1–13). In this way, Christ serves the nation, namely, by bringing the promises to completion. But as Israel's Messiah, Christ is

---

57. On "instruction" (διδασκαλίαν) and its link to the wisdom motif, see the discussion in Rosner, *Paul and the Law*, 185–88.

58. See previous chapter.

someone who also serves the world on behalf of the Jewish nation.[59] This is evident from what Paul says in v. 9, which in Greek is part of the same sentence as v. 8 and should be read together: "For I say Christ has become a servant of the circumcised for the sake of the truth of God (ὑπὲρ ἀληθείας θεοῦ) in order to confirm the promises of the patriarchs and for the Gentiles to glorify God for the sake of mercy (ὑπὲρ ἐλέους)" (vv. 8–9).[60]

To say these two verses pack a lot of punch is an understatement. What Paul is saying is that because Christ's ministry to the Jews has confirmed the covenant promises (and hence established the truthfulness and faithfulness of God; 3:1–5, 21–22), mercy can now flow to the Gentiles. We can put vv. 8–9 like this: "Christ has become a servant of the circumcised" for two reasons: (1) "for the sake of the truth of God in order to confirm the promises of the patriarchs" *and* (2) "for the Gentiles to glorify God for the sake of mercy."[61] Obviously, Paul does not intend to communicate that only Gentiles are recipients of mercy.[62] One should not forget, after all, that Paul still has in mind the argument in Rom 11. Because God's mercy has come to the Gentiles by means of the Jewish nation (11:11, 18), mercy will come to the Jews once again (11:30) because they will be driven to jealousy by the Gentiles (11:11–14). Thus, in light of Rom 11, we can conclude that in v. 9, Paul is still thinking about how the mercy granted to Gentiles is designed to be a conduit through which mercy can rebound to the Jews.[63] In short, Christ is a servant *through* Israel and (via the Gentiles) *to* Israel. Thus, Paul is simply saying what he has already said previously: The Jew-Gentile relationship is, in all reality, mutually-supporting. If this captures Paul's train of thought, it makes sense why it would be raised here—the controversy depicted in 14:1—15:7 requires it.

To support his thesis in vv. 8–9 that Christ became a servant of Israel for the sake of Israel and for the sake of the Gentiles, he quotes a string of passages from the Old Testament—all of which are tied together with

---

59. Recall the discussion in the last chapter, specifically with regard to Wright's emphasis on how the covenant promises are *for* the world *through* Israel. See again chapter 6, n192 above.

60. Contra Bates, *Hermeneutics*, 291, I do not think Paul intends for the first clause ("Christ has become a servant") in v. 8 to be supplied by the reader at the beginning of v. 9 so that Christ becomes the subject of the latter (see also Bates' qualification on 298 about v. 9). On this, cf. Schreiner, *Romans* [2nd ed], 730.

61. Though my construal of vv. 8–9 was developed independently from his, see Schreiner (*Romans* [2nd ed], 728–30) who reaches the same conclusion.

62. Bates, *Hermeneutics*, 298.

63. Bates, *Hermeneutics*, 298.

reoccurring references to the "Gentiles."[64] Because he intends these to be treated as a unit of thought, I will reproduce the entire section in full, beginning once again with v. 8:

> For I say Christ has become a servant of the circumcised for the sake of the truth of God in order to confirm the promises of the patriarchs and for the Gentiles to glorify God for the sake of mercy, just as it is written:

> 'Therefore, I will confess you among the Gentiles, and I will sing praise to your name.' (v. 9b, quoting Ps 17:50)[65]

> And again it says,

> 'Rejoice, O Gentiles, with his people.' (v. 10, quoting Deut 32:34)[66]

> And again,

> 'Praise the Lord, all you Gentiles, and let all the peoples praise him.' (v. 11, quoting Ps 116:1)[67]

> And again, Isaiah says.

> 'The root of Jesse will come, the one who rises to rule the Gentiles—upon him the Gentiles will hope.' (v. 12, quoting Isa 11:10)[68]

Regarding the first quotation, it may be that Paul understands this as the voice of Christ with David being merely the mouthpiece.[69] If so, this

64. Käsemann, *Romans*, 386.

65. Rom 15:9b: διὰ τοῦτο ἐξομολογήσομαί σοι ἐν ἔθνεσιν καὶ τῷ ὀνόματί σου ψαλῶ. Ps 17:50 (LXX): διὰ τοῦτο ἐξομολογήσομαί σοι ἐν ἔθνεσιν, κύριε, καὶ τῷ ὀνόματί σου ψαλῶ. Cf. 2 Kgdms 22:50 (LXX); on this, see Stanley, *Paul and the Language of Scripture*, 179n329; Schreiner, *Romans* [2nd ed], 731.

66. Rom 15:10: εὐφράνθητε, ἔθνη, μετὰ τοῦ λαοῦ αὐτοῦ. Deut 32:34 (LXX): εὐφράνθητε, ἔθνη, μετὰ τοῦ λαοῦ αὐτοῦ.

67. Rom 15:11: αἰνεῖτε, πάντα τὰ ἔθνη, τὸν κύριον καὶ ἐπαινεσάτωσαν αὐτὸν πάντες οἱ λαοί. Ps 116:1 (LXX): Αἰνεῖτε τὸν κύριον, πάντα τὰ ἔθνη, ἐπαινέσατε αὐτόν, πάντες οἱ λαοί. On ἐπαινεσάτωσαν/ἐπαινέσατε, see Stanley, *Paul and the Language of Scripture*, 182.

68. Rom 15:12: ἔσται ἡ ῥίζα τοῦ Ἰεσσαὶ καὶ ὁ ἀνιστάμενος ἄρχειν ἐθνῶν, ἐπ' αὐτῷ ἔθνη ἐλπιοῦσιν. Isa 11:10 (LXX): Καὶ ἔσται ἐν τῇ ἡμέρᾳ ἐκείνῃ ἡ ῥίζα τοῦ Ιεσσαι καὶ ὁ ἀνιστάμενος ἄρχειν ἐθνῶν, ἐπ' αὐτῷ ἔθνη ἐλπιοῦσι, καὶ ἔσται ἡ ἀνάπαυσις αὐτοῦ τιμή. On the ἐν τῇ ἡμέρᾳ ἐκείνῃ, see Stanley, *Paul and the Language of Scripture*, 183; Jewett, *Romans*, 896; Dunn, *Romans 9–16*, 850; Wagner, *Heralds*, 318.

69. Bates (*Hermeneutics*, 292–304) takes this as an instance of prosopological

would be consistent with his christological interpretation of Ps 68:10 in Rom 15:3, and it might also make sense of his omission of the vocative "Lord," which was present in the original text.[70] On the other hand, it might make better sense to think Paul has his own apostolic voice in mind.[71] Although, it could be that Paul has in mind someone else, namely, David himself. Because David serves "as the representative and king of the people of Israel," perhaps the psalm is thereby "fulfilled as believing Jews sing among the Gentiles."[72]

Though I think the first option is the best, good arguments could be marshalled for the others. No matter which is chosen, though, one cannot escape the fact that Ps 17:50 is interpreted from Paul's christological horizon of understanding. If, on the one hand, the "I" is a reference to Christ, then this thesis is easily seen. If, on the other hand, the "I" is a reference to either Paul, David, or Israel, then it still cannot be denied that Paul's prejudgments regarding the ministry of Christ have been the lens through which the quotation has been read, justifying the reason for praise in the first place. After all, the quotation was employed to verify the statements Paul made about Christ's ministry in vv. 8–9a. Thus, the quotation does not so much prove anything as much as it supports Paul's (presupposed) christological prejudgments.[73] All of this is true whether or not the "I" or even the "you" in the quotation of v. 9b ought to be taken as a reference to Christ.

That Paul is reading the quotation in the manner I have described is seen again when one considers that the original verse occurs within the context of David's conquering the Gentiles. David says God will "rescue" him "from disputes with people (λαοῦ)" and that God will "install" him as "head of the nations (ἐθνῶν)," over a "people" (λαὸς) he "does not know about" — all of whom will be made into his servants (ἐδούλευσέν μοι) (Ps 17:44 LXX). David goes on to describe God as "the one who gives me vengeance" (ὁ θεὸς ὁ διδοὺς ἐκδικήσεις ἐμοὶ) and "the one who subjugates peoples under

---

exegesis. He says that "Paul does in fact see the Christ as the speaker and the addressee is God. . . . Although David remains the nominal speaker, for Paul, the Holy Spirit is speaking through David in the prosopon of the Christ, and for Paul, the Christ is the true speaker" (293) and "David was a vehicle through whom the Spirit spoke in the prosopon of the Christ, praising God" (302).

70. Stanley, *Paul and the Language of Scripture*, 180; Bates, *Hermeneutics*, 299.

71. Käsemann, *Romans*, 386. Käsemann links the quotation back to "For I say" in v. 8. See also Jewett, *Romans*, 894.

72. Schreiner, *Romans* [2nd ed], 732 and n19.

73. Although his comments are about Rom 15:12 specifically, I think Wagner's general point can apply here and elsewhere: "Paul's main concern in Romans 15:12 is not to 'prove' something about Jesus, but to show that scripture prophesies the inclusion of Gentiles in the worshiping community as a result of what God has done in and through Jesus Christ" (Wagner, *Heralds*, 323).

me" (ὑποτάξας λαοὺς ὑπ' ἐμέ) (v. 48). God, says David, will save him from his "angry enemies," "from those who rise up against" him, and "from the unrighteous man" (v. 49). It is for these reasons that David will confess and praise God "among the Gentiles" (v. 50). Thus, the original context does not seem to suggest the salvific tone that Paul gives it.[74] But Paul is reading in light of his own christological mission to the Gentiles—a mission that is characterized as one of inclusion and mercy for all.[75] To this end, texts from Deut 32 and Ps 116 have been inserted into vv. 10–11: The Gentiles, who have received mercy, are beckoned to join "the cosmic chorus of praise" along "with his people" (v. 10).[76] Indeed, "all the peoples" are called to praise him (v. 11).[77]

As for the quotation in v. 12, several important observations can be made. First, "the root (ῥίζα) of Jesse" looks back to Rom 1:3, where Jesus' Davidic lineage is mentioned (ἐκ σπέρματος Δαυὶδ).[78] Second, it may subtly recall the discussion in Rom 11:17 where Gentiles are described as those who "share in the rich root (τῆς ῥίζης τῆς πιότητος) of the olive tree."[79] Third, that "the root of Jesse" is one who "rises" (ἀνιστάμενος) may echo Rom 1:4, where Jesus's resurrection (ἀναστάσεως) was discussed.[80] Fourth, the fact that the quotation mentions how it is "upon him (ἐπ' αὐτῷ) the Gentiles will hope" recalls the quotations from Isa 28:16 in Rom 9:33 and 10:11: "the one who

74. Cf. Schreiner, *Romans* [2nd ed], 731–32, who says "that even in the OT context David's victories anticipated the greater victories of Jesus. Thus Paul would have understood David's headship over his enemies and their service to him as fulfilled in Jesus the Messiah. It is likely that the rule over the gentiles was understood to involve not just the judgment of nations but also, at least for some gentiles, salvation." Schreiner also points to the quotation in v. 12, which depicts the idea of *ruling* as "a saving event, since the gentiles put their hope in this ruler" (732). On this, see also Wagner, *Heralds*, 313. On how Jesus' "lordship has the quality of servanthood" in this context, see Jewett, *Romans*, 896.

75. E.g., Rom 9:23–26; 10:12; 11:11–12, 22, 31.

76. Jewett, *Romans*, 895. Jewett (895) says that "in contrast to the broad tradition of anticipating Gentile conversion as a form of social and political subordination to Israel, bringing their gifts to the Jerusalem temple, Paul envisions all nations rejoicing together, *with* each other rather than *above or below* each other with respect to honor, lending their varied voices to the cosmic chorus of praise." See also Wagner, *Heralds*, 316–17.

77. Regarding the quotation (Ps 116:1 LXX) in v. 11, Cranfield (*Romans*, 746) says, "With its repeated use of πᾶς, it stresses the fact that no people is to be excluded from this common praise of God."

78. See Jewett, *Romans*, 896. See also Cranfield, *Romans*, 747; Fitzmyer, *Romans*, 707–8; Stuhlmacher, *Romans*, 233; Wagner, *Heralds*, 319, 322.

79. Although, see Jewett, *Romans*, 896.

80. See Bates, *Hermeneutics*, 299 and n187; Dunn, *Romans 9–16*, 850; Jewett, *Romans*, 896; Wagner, *Heralds*, 319.

believes upon him (ἐπ' αὐτῷ) will not be ashamed." Thus, that Paul is interpreting the present quotation christologically is incontrovertible.[81]

After this quotation, Paul ends with a blessing: "May the God of hope
fill you with all joy and peace in believing so that you will abound in hope by
the power of the Holy Spirit" (v. 13). The call to "hope" and "joy" and "peace"
is the very thing the Jew-Gentile church of Rome needed to heed if they
were to realize the unity Paul envisioned. Paul's main concern, as we have
seen above, is that the church would maintain a humble, Christ-like posture
toward one another—something I have described as a "christological ethic."
This christological ethic, moreover, was advanced and legitimated by Paul's
christological interpretation of relevant Old Testament texts he employed to
this end. As we have seen, Paul's christological horizon of understanding was
the posture from which he read *Scripture* and the Roman church's *situation*.
Ross Wagner is correct to observe that "Paul's christology is everywhere presupposed in Romans, and it is not far from the surface in many of his appeals
to other portions of Isaiah in the letter."[82] Indeed, I would add that this is
true—in one way or another—for *all* his scriptural quotations.

CHRISTOLOGICAL MISSION AND MINISTRY

In this section, I show that Paul's call for unity in the Jew-Gentile church,
and his call to follow a christological ethic in order to achieve that unity,
flows directly out of what he believes about his own apostolic calling and
how *that* relates to God's plan of redemption foretold in the Scripture. This
observation will once again reveal what I have been saying thus far, namely,
that Paul's reading of the Old Testament is dialogical in nature such that
it allows him to walk away with new and fresh meaning—not least with
respect to the way the Roman church ought to live in relation to each other.

Paul says that the bold language in his letter is largely inspired by his
calling to the Gentiles:

> And I myself am convinced, my brothers and sisters, that you
> all are full of goodness, being filled with all knowledge being
> capable also to instruct one another. But I have written to you
> very boldly in some parts as a reminder because of the grace
> given to me from God to be a minister of Christ Jesus to the
> Gentiles, serving as a priest for the Gospel of God, so that the

---

81. "The quotation of Isaiah 11:10 in Romans 15:12 is notable because, of all the
Isaianic texts quoted by Paul in Romans, it is the one that most clearly reveals a 'christological' hermeneutic at work" (Wagner, *Heralds*, 318–19).

82. Wagner, *Heralds*, 323.

offering of the Gentiles might be acceptable, being sanctified in
the Holy Spirit. (15:14–16)

When Paul references these boldly-written parts, he likely refers to the
hortatory section of 12:1—15:13.[83] There his christologically-grounded ethic
was laid out to support the call to unity that began in Rom 12:3. If that is the
case, then as vv. 15–16 indicate, Paul considers the christological ethic he es-
pouses to flow downstream from his calling and mission to preach Christ to
the Gentiles. *If* Christ has opened the door to Gentile inclusion, and *if* Christ
has called him to preach to the Gentiles so they can hear of Christ and believe
in him (Rom 10:10–17), then it follows he must also defend their right to be
fully included into the life of the community of Christ (Rom 14:1—15:13).
And thus, Paul would need to base that defense upon the very christological
foundation that makes Gentile inclusion possible in the first place. This, as
we have seen above, is the very thing Paul has done. But the defense itself was
not *merely* christologically deduced. It was always in dialogue with Scripture.
In the present section (15:1–21), the same strategy is employed.

What is most interesting in this regard is how Paul describes himself
and his missionary endeavor. He is a "minister (λειτουργὸν) of Christ Jesus to the Gentiles" (v. 16a), who engages in the act of "serving as a priest
(ἱερουργοῦντα) for the Gospel of God" (v. 16b). He speaks of Gentile inclusion as an "offering" (προσφορὰ) that is "sanctified (ἡγιασμένη) in the
Holy Spirit" (v. 16cd). These words are packed with scriptural overtones,
each imbedded with significance derived from their cultic context—none of
which we can afford to ignore. Once the narrative weight of these terms is
reckoned with, Paul's own apostleship takes on added dimension.

Consider, for example, how Paul describes himself as a λειτουργὸν. The
word is used in the Old Testament LXX to describe Aaron's, and his sons',
priestly work (λειτουργεῖν).[84] Paul, likewise, sees his own apostolic mission
to the Gentiles as "serving as a priest" (ἱερουργοῦντα).[85] This shows, I think,
that Paul situated his ministry within a narrative continuity of Israel's cultic

---

83. Cranfield, *Romans*, 753. Contra Fitzmyer, *Romans*, 711, ἀπὸ μέρους refers to the
part of the letter Paul considers to have been written "boldly," not as reference to *part* of
the motive for which Paul has written (cf. Cranfield, *Romans*, 753). Thus, Käsemann (*Romans*, 391) says, "ἀπὸ μέρους adds a further restriction: not everywhere but in some places."

84. E.g., Exod 28:31, 39; 29:30; 30:20. Käsemann (*Romans*, 392) is correct to note
that even though λειτουργός does not necessarily imply cultic significance, it is qualified by ἱερουργοῦντα (which has obvious cultic overtones) in the same verse. See also
Stuhlmacher, *Romans*, 237.

85. "In his mission to the Gentiles Paul sees his function to be like that of a Jewish
priest dedicated to the service of God in his Temple" (Fitzmyer, *Romans*, 711). See also
Käsemann, *Romans*, 392; Stuhlmacher, *Romans*, 237.

236 PART 3 | PAUL AND THE MEANING OF SCRIPTURE

practices. Just as a priest would oversee the giving of sacrifices and offerings, so Paul understood his role to be similar with respect to the Gentiles. That he would refer to Gentile inclusion as an "offering" (προσφορὰ) is interesting in this regard, since the word evokes a cultic scene.[86] That this *offering* of the Gentiles is "sanctified (ἡγιασμένη) in (ἐν) the Holy Spirit" is also telling. Here ἐν should be taken instrumentally so as to read "by the Holy Spirit." According to Jewish law, being "holy" and being "sanctified" occurs by means of cultic rituals. This is seen clearly in a passage such as Lev 21, where being "holy" (ἅγιος) and being "sanctified" (ἁγιάζω) by God are both set within the context of cultic purity.[87] Interestingly, it is in this same passage where προσφέρω—which shares a common root (φέρ-) with προσφορά[88]—is routinely used to describe the act of *presenting* gifts (δῶρα) and sacrifices (θυσίας) to God.[89]

By describing his apostleship in the way that he has, Paul does not abstract his calling from the Jewish narrative. In his mind, he is continuing that narrative—albeit differently than his unbelieving Jewish contemporaries would anticipate, for his priestly work is christological and Gentile-oriented.[90] Paul's priesthood is characterized not by Jewish liturgical practice, but is instead situated around the Gospel of Jesus Christ.[91] Regarding his ministry, he can "boast in Christ Jesus" (v. 17).[92] It is Christ, after all, who has "worked through" Paul "to bring about the obedience of the Gentiles" (v. 18).[93] Moreover, Paul has come to believe that there is no

---

86. E.g., 3 Kgdms 7:34 (LXX). Various cognates are also used routinely in Leviticus LXX in the context of offering gifts and sacrifices (e.g., Lev 2:1, 4; 14:20; 21:6–8; 23:11–12; 27:9–11). See Weiss, "φέρω, κτλ," 56–57. See also 1 Esd 5:51–52.

87. See, e.g., Lev 21:6–8, 10–15, 23 (LXX).

88. Weiss, "φέρω, κτλ," 56–87, esp. 68.

89. See Lev 21:6–8, 17 (LXX).

90. Commenting on v. 16, Käsemann (*Romans*, 392) says Paul is "calling himself the priest of the Messiah Jesus to the whole of the Gentile world." It must be said again, though, that Paul's ministry to the Gentiles is not exclusively just that, for he also has in mind the salvation of the Jews *through* the Gentiles. This same thinking is no doubt still in mind for Paul in Rom 15, especially so in vv. 25–29.

91. Stuhlmacher, *Romans*, 237–38. He says: "Unlike the Levites and Priests who do service in the Jerusalem temple, Paul need no longer be concerned about the orderly offering of material sacrifices. . . . Instead, the liturgy which he must follow is prescribed for him by the gospel. The sacrificial offering with which he is charged consists of the offering of those Gentiles who have been converted to faith in Christ and sanctified through the sacrificial death of Christ and reception of the Holy Spirit, and are thus acceptable to God" (237–38).

92. Cf. Rom 3:27–31. On Paul's boasting, see Jewett, *Romans*, 908–9.

93. Cf. Rom 1:5. Wagner (*Heralds*, 331) makes an interesting point when he says, "It is apparent now that Paul has told the story of Jesus in Romans 15:7–13 in such a

more work left to do in his current region (vv. 19, 23).[94] In light of this, he seeks to move elsewhere and to preach the Gospel (εὐαγγελίζεσθαι) in those areas where no missionary has yet been present "in order not to build upon someone else's foundation" (v. 20).[95] He understands his mission to be ground-breaking, characterized by the act of "introducing Christ to persons and regions that had not yet heard of him."[96] In this respect, Paul endeavors to be a "pioneer."[97] Unsurprisingly, he bases his missionary calling on Scripture. Here he quotes a verse taken from a section of one of the Servant Songs of Isaiah: "But just as it is written, 'To those who have not been told (ἀνηγγέλη) about him shall see (ὄψονται), and those who have not heard (ἀκηκόασιν) [about him] shall understand" (v. 21, quoting Isa 52:15).[98]

It seems clear that Paul interprets this verse as speaking about Christ. First, he has just said in the verse immediately prior that his aim was "to preach the Gospel" (εὐαγγελίζεσθαι) in places where people have not yet heard of Christ. The quotation provides him with ἀνηγγέλη in order to link his own ministry with that of announcing the Servant in Isaiah.[99] Second, the quotation's original context speaks of Israel's rescue (52:9).[100] It also tells of the "revelation" of God's mighty act of "salvation," saying, "The Lord will reveal (ἀποκαλύψει) his holy arm before all the nations (πάντων τῶν ἐθνῶν), and the far reaches of the earth will see (ὄψονται) the salvation (σωτηρίαν) that is from God" (v. 10). Here ὄψονται connects to ὄψονται in

way that Jesus' life prefigures the shape Paul's mission has taken. By setting Christ forward as the archetypal missionary to Jew and Gentile—the one who not only became a servant to the circumcised but who also sings the praises of God in the midst of the Gentiles—Paul is able to claim that his apostolic ministry is nothing less than the continuation of Christ's own mission."

94. On this, see the discussion in Wagner, *Heralds*, 331–32.

95. Wagner rightly (*Heralds*, 332) thinks v. 20 clarifies v. 19 in that Paul has, indeed, completed his task *because* his aims were all along to preach to those who have yet to hear. Once the Gospel has come within earshot to people, he can move on to others. On Paul not wanting "to build upon someone else's foundation," see Jewett, *Romans*, 915–16.

96. Jewett, *Romans*, 915.

97. Jewett, *Romans*, 916.

98. Rom 15:21: ἀλλὰ καθὼς γέγραπται· οἷς οὐκ ἀνηγγέλη περὶ αὐτοῦ ὄψονται, καὶ οἳ οὐκ ἀκηκόασιν συνήσουσιν. Isa 52:15 (LXX): οὕτως θαυμάσονται ἔθνη πολλὰ ἐπ᾽ αὐτῷ, καὶ συνέξουσι βασιλεῖς τὸ στόμα αὐτῶν· ὅτι οἷς οὐκ ἀνηγγέλη περὶ αὐτοῦ, ὄψονται, καὶ οἳ οὐκ ἀκηκόασι, συνήσουσι. With respect to how Paul conceived of his own missionary activity, Wagner (*Heralds*, 332) is correct when he says "his strategy of pioneer church-planting is in accordance with what scripture prophesied would happen."

99. Wagner (*Heralds*, 333) is keen to observe that αὐτοῦ in the quoted portion of Isa 52:15 refers back to the servant (ὁ παῖς μου) in Isa 52:13. In the Pauline context of Rom 15:21, αὐτοῦ refers back to Christ in v. 20.

100. Cf. Rom 11:26.

238 PART 3 | PAUL AND THE MEANING OF SCRIPTURE

v. 15 (quoted in Rom 15:21), thus connecting the rest of v. 10 as well. Such a connection would be interesting given that Paul has already spoken how he is "not ashamed of the Gospel (εὐαγγέλιον)," since it is "the power of God" that brings "salvation" (σωτηρίαν) to both Jew and non-Jew (Ἰουδαίῳ τε πρῶτον καὶ Ἕλληνι) and how in the Gospel "the righteousness of God is revealed (ἀποκαλύπτεται)" (Rom 1:16–17). I have already shown how Rom 1:16–17 refers to the faithfulness of God through Christ, and we need not rehash that argument here.[101] Suffice it to say presently that it would be unreasonable to think Paul is not thinking along these same lines in Rom 15:21. That this is a reference to Christ is, once again, incontrovertible.

Why is this important? This observation confirms that the basis for Paul's missionary endeavors is the result of the fusion of the scriptural and christological horizons. He reads Scripture by means of his christological prejudgments. But, as I have said elsewhere, prejudgments (of the Gadamerian variety) do not operate by unilaterally imposing themselves upon the text. Instead, they are merely a way into the text. Paul's entire approach to missions, to church unity, and to ethics can be characterized in this way. His ministry is christological, but it is a christological ministry that has been informed by the Jewish narrative (hence why he can speak of his ministry in terms of the Jewish cult).

SUMMARY

We have seen that, because Paul believes Christ has called him to a christologically-oriented mission, the particular hortatory commands he gives necessarily follow. Paul's deliberations in this regard are shaped by the dialogue that occurs between his christology and the Jewish texts. Paul is thus able to craft a fresh vision for communal life within the Roman church, one not shaped by legal prescriptions or works of the law but rather by the fundamental convictions about what Christ has accomplished. These accomplishments, moreover, are not ahistorical abstractions. To the contrary, Paul situates them within the salvation-historical matrix of the story of Israel by means of various Old Testament quotations. And yet, Paul's interpretations of them proceed beyond the text's original horizon. In this vein, Paul also invites the Roman church to catch a glimpse of other horizons than just their own conflicted and fraught horizon of understanding. He beckons them to new horizons of understanding that emerge once the Jewish stories and the Christ event come into play. He invites them, in other words, to a new way to live.

101. See chapter 4.

Chapter 8

Paul's Use of Scripture as Dialogical Re-Authoring

The real meaning of a text, as it speaks to the interpreter, does not depend on the contingencies of the author and his original audience. It certainly is not identical with them, for it is always co-determined also by the historical situation of the interpreter and hence by the totality of the objective course of history.

HANS-GEORG GADAMER[1]

INTRODUCTION

In chapter 1, I introduced this study by presenting Paul's quotations from Hosea (Rom 9:25–26) as representative of the way Paul interpreted (and often revised) the meaning of Old Testament texts. I noted in subsequent chapters that Paul's interpretation of the Hosea oracle is quite consistent with his pattern of reading other scriptural texts in Romans. One interesting takeaway from the above study is that Paul's habit is to quote Old Testament texts almost in passing, seldom (if at all) offering explicit and detailed explanation for his interpretive decisions. And yet, as we have seen, Paul does

1. Gadamer, *TM*, 296.

drop strong hints along the way, seemingly in order to invite his readers to explore the structure of his horizon of understanding and to take note of his most important interpretive prejudgments.[2]

In what follows, I draw this study to a close by revisiting those same Hosea quotations. I offer them once more as representative of the other Old Testament texts Paul cites in Romans in order to highlight a Gadamerian perspective on Paul's understanding of them. Specifically, in keeping with a Gadamerian account of hermeneutics, I will offer a sketch as to how Paul found the *meaning* he did in his scriptural quotations. In the end, I think Gadamer's notion of *Horizontverschmelzung* (and its concomitant concepts) captures exactly what we see not only in Rom 9:25–26 but also in his other quotations in Romans. The conclusion that I draw is one that I have routinely mentioned throughout my study, namely, that Paul's use of Scripture is best described as dialogical re-authoring.

HERMENEUTICAL TENSION

Consistent with his ongoing re-appraisal of Jewish texts, stories, and motifs, Paul does nothing unique in 9:25–26. For example, that Paul allowed himself considerable freedom to invert the Hosea text, substituting καλέσω for ἐρῶ in 9:25, ought to be seen as an echo back to 4:17, where Abraham's justifying faith was described as a belief in the God who could "call [καλέω] the things that are not as though they are." It should be remembered, moreover, that this story took on applicability for Paul only from the standpoint of his christological horizon.[3] This observation needs to be given its due weight. With respect to christology specifically, the motif of God's "calling" remained significant for Paul throughout key parts of that narrative. This fact ought to be carried over to 9:25–26. For example, "faith" and "calling" were both depicted as opposed to "works" in the Abraham story (4:2–4, 16–17). Likewise, the motifs of "calling" and (covenant) "love," being contextually linked in Rom 9:12 and 13, were seen as opposed to "works" and covenant rejection, respectively. Tellingly, this is not unlike the Hosea quotation in 9:25, where the motifs of "calling" and "love"—situated, as well, within Paul's christological horizon—are likewise linked regarding the inclusion

---

2. In chapter 6, for example, I noted how in the narrative leading up to the Hosea quotations, important details, assumptions, and implied beliefs were already at work (hermeneutically). Cf. the argument given in Stanley, "Rhetoric," 42–62, esp. 56, 60–61, on Paul's lack of interpretive explanation.

3. See chapter 5.

of the New Covenant people of God, the Gentiles.[4] In v. 24, Paul says that the "vessels of mercy" are those who have been "called" (καλέω). Here it is not the Jews of Hosea's prophecy, but specifically the Gentiles, which the immediate quotation from Hosea reinforces:[5]

> I will call the Not My People, "My People," and the Not Loved, "Loved." And in the place in which it was said to them, "You are Not My People," they shall be called sons of the living God. (9:25–26)

And thus exists the hermeneutic tension: *Hosea's oracle originally pointed to Jewish re-inclusion while Paul used it as grounds for Gentile inclusion.* What does one do with the tension? Instead of interpreting Hosea and Paul in such a way that would lessen the tension, it is best to offer a hermeneutic that simply accounts for the tension.[6] I have already shown that Paul's christological prejudgments must be factored into the equation. But how can Paul's christology (as a prejudgment) solve the dilemma? This, in my estimation, is the benefit of Gadamer's hermeneutic. For him, prejudgments mean more than simply "assumptions." Moreover, the concept of prejudgment is not for Gadamer a ruse by which an interpreter like Paul can unilaterally impose his pre-commitments upon texts. Instead, it is a rich concept that allows for, indeed entails, the dialogical and performative nature of understanding. In this way, the "tension" I spoke about above can be accounted for such that the horizons of both Paul and Hosea are respected.

INTERPRETIVE HORIZONS

The clearing of distinction between Jew and Gentile was founded upon Paul's use of scriptural texts, stories, and quotations—all of which were christologically construed. Without christology, there is still "distinction" between Jew and Greek, for the law—which served to divide the two ethnic groups—would still be in place (3:20–31).[7] With the Jewish texts contributing to Paul's argument, Paul's christology dialogued with Scripture,

---

4. Juncker, "Children of Promise," 155.

5. Starling, *Not My People*, 116.

6. The goal of lessening the tension is something one arguably sees in some discussions on Paul's use of scripture—not least with respect to Rom 9:25–26, as we saw in chapter 1.

7. See esp. the way v. 29 functions significantly within the overall argument, as Wright, *Justification*, 211–12 (see also 52–53, 179), observes. See also Garlington, *Obedience of Faith*, 255.

functioning hermeneutically.[8] It was in the christological retelling of the Abraham story where this became evident. The story itself climaxed everything leading up to it by revealing how all who believe like Abraham are now his children (4:11–12). But Abraham's faith was never originally christological. Even though the Abrahamic covenant spoke of a future blessing upon the nations (e.g., Gen 12:3), and though Paul probably had this in mind in his retelling of the story,[9] it would be a mistake, as we have seen, to think that Paul's christological convictions contributed nothing to the Abraham story itself—and hence to the entire narrative which centered around the Jew-Gentile question.[10] This is apparent when one considers how the story was employed as a rhetorical event.[11] These christological convictions, being central to Paul's exposition, allow the story of Scripture to be *meaningful* to the Roman Christian community.[12] The place where the *Horizontverschmelzung* takes place (and only there) is where Paul's hermeneutic becomes intelligible.

Paul's hermeneutic can, at its core, be described as a dialogue with the text. As a partner in the dialogue, therefore, Paul is not engaged in a battle with Scripture. This is not the essence of his interpretive posture, for the Jewish text is important for him (Rom 1:2). However, as I have been at pains to show, one cannot clarify his interpretive activity without taking into account his prejudgments: His hermeneutics entailed more than merely repeating the original text and its original meaning. Paul's way of reading Scripture cannot be described as *interpretation-as-repetition*. Paul, after all, is reading the texts *as* a Christian. This is where Gadamer's hermeneutic is clarifying.[13] Interpretation cannot be limited to mere reproduction of the text, for every act of interpretation involves the interpreter's own prejudgments.[14] The text has its own horizon; the reader theirs. Understanding is

8. Cf. Starling, *Not My People*, 185, who observes the hermeneutical role christology played in Ephesians, saying, "For the writer of Ephesians, the death of Christ is thus not only a soteriological event (reconciling Jew and Gentile to God) and an ecclesiological event (reconciling Jew and Gentile to one another within the 'new humanity' of the church) but also a hermeneutical event, transforming the relationship of his readers to the scriptural promise, law and covenants."

9. See Holst, "Meaning of 'Abraham Believed God,'" 323–25.

10. Cf. the discussion about Gospel writing in Rae, "Theological Interpretation and Historical Criticism," 105–6.

11. In regard to the implicit role Paul's christological beliefs played in ch. 4, see Forman, "Politics of Promise," 316.

12. Cf. Holst, "Meaning of 'Abraham Believed God,'" 325, who argues that christology is subsumed under the broader category of "theology" and covenant.

13. See again chapter 3 above on Gadamer's idea of "tradition."

14. Gadamer, *TM*, 272–73.

accomplished when a fusion of horizons takes place.[15] It cannot be denied that Paul views the Jewish texts, motifs, and stories he cites from a christological horizon.

In this way, Paul's reading is not unidirectional but rather bi-directional. Both the horizons of the text and of Paul inform the other. It is, in other words, *dialogical.* For example, the text of the Abraham story demonstrated the historical fact of Abraham's reckoning of righteousness as being prior to Mosaic law observance—that is, prior to circumcision—and that is indeed what Paul concluded.[16] The text, as such, was a historically-distanced text. But texts must speak to the present, as Gadamer says: "In the course of our reflections we have come to see that understanding always involves something like applying the text to be understood to the interpreter's present situation."[17] In this same vein, it was in Rom 4:23–24 where Paul sought to apply the text to his contemporary situation (i.e., to the Christian community at Rome), establishing an "archetype of Christian belief in (relation to) Jesus."[18] The rhetorical force inherent to the Abraham story, therefore, served to validate his previous discussion about circumcision in 2:25–29, namely, that uncircumcised believers can share in the righteous status as well, which was exactly Paul's point with the Abraham story all along (4:16–17, 22–25). Moreover, underlying all this was a certain christological conviction—already in place for him, as well as, presumably, for his implied audience. Thus, the dialogical interplay between Paul's christological convictions (which were so integral to his use of the Abraham story) and the historical details of the story itself (which were also integral) must be given full consideration.

Though space does not permit a comparative analysis with the Qumran community, it is perhaps helpful to note that, just as the sect interpreted covenant inclusion from a decidedly sectarian sort of away, Paul's approach is similar.[19] For the pesherist, to be included in the covenant was to be *in the sect.* For Paul, it was to *be in Christ.*[20] With respect to the sectarian texts, DiMattei has argued that a "central characteristic" of the pesherist's reading of Scripture was its "contemporizing eschatological interpretation."[21] Inter-

---

15. Gadamer, *TM*, 305.

16. Dunn, *Romans 1–8*, 239.

17. Gadamer, *TM*, 306–7. See again chapter 4.

18. Dunn, *Romans 1–8*, 239. Recall Gadamer's idea of "contemporaneity," *Gleichzeitigkeit* (see chapter 4). See again DiMattei, "Narratives," 77–78.

19. See Halsted, "Intertextual Chaos?," 141–88.

20. See, e.g., 2 Cor 5:17.

21. DiMattei, "Narratives," 77–78.

estingly, and with an affirmative answer in mind, he asks, "Are these not the same hermeneutical principles that govern Paul's approach to biblical narrative . . . ?"[22] He also affirms, and gives recognition to the fact, that Paul's christology plays a role in the interpretive act, though he is quick to locate christology as something that "influences and shapes the content of [Paul's] hermeneutic" *in distinction to* "the underlying hermeneutical assumption that guides his interpretation," namely, a "contemporizing eschatological interpretation," an assumption shared between Paul and the pesherist.[23]

DiMattei's distinction is perhaps helpful, but I am hesitant to give it too much weight. Though he is correct to notice the similarity between the pesherist's and Paul's contemporizing hermeneutic, he falls short by not connecting it strongly to christology, seemingly pushing the latter to the background. The fact is that Paul's christology and his contemporizing interpretive assumptions go hand-in-hand: *Because Christ has come into the present time, old texts can be reconfigured.* For Gadamer, prejudgments are what they *are because of one's situatedness within their own time and place.* This is why, arguably, DiMattei's distinction is not that helpful. With Gadamer's hermeneutic in hand, Pauline christology can come to the fore as a key hermeneutical component, specifically as an integral prejudgment, one not shared by the pesherist.[24]

Thus, Joseph Fitzmyer, citing Rom 4:24–25, can say Paul "differed from his Essene contemporaries," not least regarding the fact that "Paul speaks of justification as an effect of the Christ-event. Christ Jesus has brought it about that sinners stand acquitted before God's tribunal. . . . That God's justifying grace comes to human beings through Jesus Christ obviously has no place in Essene thinking."[25] Thus, what makes possible Paul's re-appraisal of the Jewish tradition (i.e., the concepts and themes inherent to the Jewish nation—circumcision, Torah, etc.) is his christology.[26] Indeed, "Christ is the key to Pauline hermeneutics."[27] But as I mentioned above, christology (as a

22. DiMattei, "Narratives," 78. He does however see "one notable difference," namely, in the "form" between how a text is cited in Paul compared to the pesherist. I comment on this below.

23. DiMattei, "Narratives," 77. In DiMattei's view, the distinction is warranted because of a difference between "content and method," christology being placed in the former (77).

24. So Lim, *Holy Scripture*, 171.

25. Fitzmyer, "Paul and the Dead Sea Scrolls," 604–5.

26. Thus when Moyise ("Quotations," 20) asks whether or not there is "a 'christological' or 'messianic' dimension to Paul's hermeneutics that cannot be paralleled in the Qumran writings," demands—at least based upon the specific observations above—an affirmative answer in many respects.

27. Lim, *Holy Scripture*, 171. He says elsewhere that for Paul, "To understand the

prejudgment) is not for Paul a violent imposition onto the text. Rather, it is active in a dialogical sort of way (more will be said on this below). Again, on the one hand, the christological convictions allow stories such as that of Abraham to be meaningful for the community of Christians.[28] On the other hand, the story itself also informs these christological convictions.[29] The point, moreover, is that the Abraham story had the meaning it did because of its precise application to the Christ-believing community.[30] In this vein, Gadamer is clear: "Verstehen ist hier immer schon Anwenden."[31] Thus, Paul's christology and Abraham's story must be seen as engaged in a sort of dialogue.[32] Both inform the other, despite the fact that each distinct horizon remains exactly that: distinct, separate from the other.[33] Following Gadamer, Paul's christology was acting as a type of *Vorurteil*, a prejudgment by which

---

true meaning of scripture is to read the texts from Christological perspective" (171); "At the heart of Paul's hermeneutics is his own and fellow believers' experience of Christ" (172); "Paul's hermeneutics are anchored in the revelation of God through the belief that Jesus, the Messiah, was crucified, died, was buried, and resurrected. Through his own experience on the Damascus Road and subsequent, trance-like, ecstatic encounters with the visionary Christ, he has come to interpret scripture not according to the traditions of the fathers, but in the new light of this revelation" (172); "Central to Paul's hermeneutics is his own experience of Jesus and understanding of the significance of the cross. On this basis, all his exegetical techniques and scriptural interpretation depended" (175); "Whatever [Paul] may do exegetically, there is a theological agenda around which the biblical texts had to be conformed. . . . To be sure the authoritative writings of Israel constituted the framework in which he worked, but his hermeneutics and exegetical endeavors have their source beyond these boundaries" (176). The benefit of using Gadamer's hermeneutic is that it brings clarity to how Paul can do all that Lim has described above. For example, a hermeneutic that seeks to understand how Scripture contributes to Paul's arguments must coherently take into account Paul's assumption that his arguments *from* Scripture can only be what they are in light of what he brings *to* Scripture, namely, his christological prejudgments. Gadamer's theory provides such a hermeneutic.

28. As I have shown in chapter 5, the story holds very little rhetorical weight if christology is not already being assumed. Moreover, these observations are not without warrant; see, e.g., Käsemann, *Romans*, 129, who discusses this issue along the same lines when he mentions the circular relationship between christology and the doctrine of justification (see also 95–96). It is my contention that Gadamer's theory illuminates this fact.

29. Cf. Thiselton (*Hermeneutics*, 76–83), who discusses how the OT acts as a pre-understanding for NT writers (not least Paul). This study brings more attention to this idea.

30. See again Gadamer, *TM*, 306–8. Cf. Thiselton, *Hermeneutics*, 89. See also Gadamer, "Hermeneutics as a Theoretical and Practical Task," 263–65, specifically the comments about the "orator," "rhetoric," "application," and "questions." (See again Di-Mattei, "Narratives," 91, on his term the "Abraham-Christ story.")

31. Gadamer, *WM*, 314; Gadamer, *TM*, 308. See again chapter 3 above.

32. On dialogue, see again Gadamer, *TM*, 361–62.

33. See again Gadamer, *TM*, 271–72 (see also 302–6).

he was able to render his judgments.[34] This was a *pre*-understanding that enabled his *understanding* of the story of Scripture. Truly, "the being of the interpreter belongs intrinsically to the being of what is to be interpreted."[35] Paul's christological convictions served as the mediality between, and a means of entry into, the past stories of Israel (depicted in her texts) and his present situation—not least with respect to the various issues relevant to a mixed Jew-Gentile church (see again chapter 7 above).

For another example, let us consider once again Paul's argument in Rom 2. Paul's idea of covenant inclusion in vv. 12–16 and what counts as true circumcision in vv. 25–29 work only in light of his christological prejudgments (which were later revealed in Rom 3–4). What sustained his interpretation of "law" in 2:13? Though it was not told at the time (except for a subtle reference in 2:16), the decisive point for Paul was later seen to be christological (3:20–22; 4:23–24).[36] In Gadamerian terms, Paul's christological convictions permeated his historically-effected consciousness.[37] And so: "*Darum sind die Vorurteile des einzelnen weit mehr als seine Urteile die geschichtliche Wirklichkeit seines Seins.*"[38]

One should posit, then, that Paul's experience of the resurrected Christ on the Damascus road (see Acts 26:12–32; Gal 1:11–24) was an *experience* (in Gadamerian language) that helped give shape to his hermeneutic.[39] This thesis is not without warrant among some exegetes. For instance, Seyoon Kim grants special attention to Paul's account of his conversion on the Damascus road and offers a rather convincing exegetical case that Paul's gospel—not least his own mission to the Gentiles—found its beginning in his experience of the resurrected Christ.[40] Kim describes this event as having "brought about a revolution in Paul—both in his thought (i.e., theology) and life: he received his gospel and apostolic call to preach it among the gentiles."[41] My aim has

---

34. On the definition and role of prejudgments in Gadamer, see again chapter 3 above.

35. Gadamer, "Hermeneutics as a Theoretical and Practical Task," 263.

36. So Wright, *PFG*, 922 (see especially n412).

37. See again Gadamer, *TM*, 301–2.

38. Gadamer, *WM*, 281; Gadamer, *TM*, 278.

39. See Weinsheimer and Marshall, "Translator's Preface," xiii–xiv. Here, the translators observe the way Gadamer used the word Erfahrung ("experience"). See also Scott (*Paul's Way of Knowing*, 169–78), who, similarly, argues in the same vein and offers an excellent commentary on the relationship between Paul's narrative logic and Paul's experience in Galatians.

40. See Kim, *Origin*.

41. Kim, *Origin*, 274. In depth interaction with Kim's argument is not possible. However, his work demonstrates that my conclusions, which have been drawn from a distinctly philosophical-hermeneutical approach, are not without warrant among

been to elaborate more on this issue, namely, to propose *via Gadamer* that while christology indeed played a crucial part in shifting Paul's theology, it also served, arguably, to shift his hermeneutic.[42]

Though the entirety of Kim's exegetical work does not need to be affirmed, much of it lends to otherwise helpful conclusions.[43] Indeed, his insights serve to buttress the conclusions of the present study. Arguably, too, my study offers a philosophical, and hence hermeneutical, support for his own. For example, after spending a great deal of time working out the exegesis of the relevant texts, Kim concludes that Paul's gospel and apostleship (and all that these entailed) found its root in the Christophany itself.[44] But Kim rightly acknowledges along with this that Paul's Damascus road experience, while altering his theological disposition, does not imply "that up to that moment his mind was theologically a *tabula rasa*."[45] Kim acknowledges that Paul held to Jewish traditional thoughts and beliefs, e.g., "messianic beliefs," "conceptions of the law and Wisdom," as well as "other ideas and concepts in Judaism and the primitive Christian kerygma," and "Hellenistic ideas and concepts"—all things with which Paul would have been familiar.[46] That being said, Kim rightly asserts that "these *religionsgeschichtlichen* materials neither made Paul a Christian nor produced his theology."[47] The major turn, Kim says, was when Paul experience the resurrected Jesus, and at that point—that is, at that "catalyst of the living experience" of seeing Jesus— "were these materials precipitated into Paul's Christian theology."[48] He says,

---

standard scholarly exegesis.

42. Cf. Hays, *Echoes*, 182, who rightly says that one cannot separate Paul's gospel from his interpretive practices. Lim, *Holy Scripture*, 172, makes a remarkably similar observation: "Through his own experience on the Damascus Road and subsequent, trance-like, ecstatic encounters with the visionary Christ, he has come to interpret scripture not according to the traditions of the fathers, but in the new light of this revelation. The hermeneutical shift involved the reading of scripture around this basic belief that 'in Christ', a formula for the significance of the Christ-event, the intended will of God can be ascertained, and he used all the techniques known to him as [an] exegete to argue for its biblical indications."

43. E.g., his failure to see *telos* in Rom 10:4 as anything but "termination" (Kim, *Origin*, 307–8). This is not, arguably, a mistake with minor consequences.

44. See Kim, *Origin*, 330–35, esp. 332.

45. Kim, *Origin*, 334. Cf. Starling, *Not My People*, 121–22, who, although citing Kim's work positively (122n52), seems to suggest later that this would be untenable for passages like Rom 9:25–26 where OT texts are used as an argument. His fear is that this would amount to vicious circularity. Gadamer's theory, however, sets such fears aside.

46. Kim, *Origin*, 334.

47. Kim, *Origin*, 334.

48. Kim, *Origin*, 334.

To put it another way, the real experience of the Damascus revelation led Paul to use all those *religionsgeschichtlichen* materials as interpretive categories and concepts for his Christian theology. That is to say, those materials provided Paul only with certain categories and concepts with which he could interpret the Damascus experience and produce his theology. But without the real experience of the Damascus revelation Paul could not have had his gospel at all, not to mention his unshakable and lively conviction in it.[49]

Put in Gadamerian terms, one might say that Kim notices a certain Pauline dialectic where both the traditional "materials" come into a temporally-distanced (indeed, a tensioned) dialogue with his own experience of Christ. Thus, a fundamental dialogical interaction occurs in Paul's reading of Scripture—one informed by the horizon of the textual material (being imbedded with traditions inherent to the Jewish people) and with that which served to make up his own horizon, specifically his own christological convictions. Truly, *"the events of Jesus' death and resurrection . . . caused [Paul] to read old texts in new ways."*[50] Gadamer's hermeneutic gives language and philosophical depth to this dialogical tension in a way that does not lead to unintelligibility, but rather in a way that reveals, cogently, its essential role in the hermeneutic process.

Thus, Paul's use of key motifs like *righteousness* and *law keeping* were understood and interpreted in light of the Christ-event—and not least in light of his own experience of Christ on the Damascus road. Significantly, the question of Gentile inclusion was understood in light of his re-appraisal of these two motifs and thus in light of his christology.[51] In this way, Paul's christological horizon enveloped the entirety of his letter. Thus, Paul's christological convictions informed his readings of Jewish texts; conversely, the texts themselves, comprised of these motifs, served to give shape to this key conviction.[52] On this, let us consider in more detail Gadamer's idea of hermeneutical dialogue—a concept of which I have mentioned many times above.

---

49. Kim, *Origin*, 334.

50. Wright, *PFG*, 827. See the context of the discussion, esp. 825–28.

51. Cf. Garlington, *Faith*, 37.

52. Scott, *Paul's Way of Knowing*, 170–71, reaches similar conclusions, albeit via a different route. See also Garlington, *Obedience of Faith*, 247–48, who discusses how for Paul, in an act of "reversal of his heritage as a Jew" which would have made it "inconceivable" to understand the phrase ὑπακοὴ πίστεως "apart from Jewish identity," has allowed "the complex of eschatology and Christology" to be instrumental in "expand[ing] the horizons of 'the obedience of faith.'"

HORIZONS: TEXT AND READER IN DIALOGUE

Consider once more Paul's use of Hosea (Rom 9:25–26). This instance of intertextuality is clarified when one addresses it with Gadamer's notion of *horizons* (and from there, the *fusion of horizons*).[53] What comprised Hosea's interpretive horizon was Jewish unrighteousness and rebellion and the prophetic announcement that this would be reversed—with, to be sure, a Davidic King playing some role.[54] What made up Paul's horizon of understanding was the prophetic announcement of Christ, who, for Paul, was the means by which both reversal would be fulfilled and divine faithfulness be manifested for those who believe.[55] Paul read the oracle in light of this fundamental conviction, but his reading was not merely *his*.[56] Understanding as an interpretive event is not a one-sided process; it is dialogical.[57] Moreover, meaning is authored in this dialogical process. Paul's reading of Hosea, then, can be described as a *dialogical re-authoring* since it takes what is relevant from the original text (e.g., a new covenant reversal of unrighteousness) and applies it to the present question of Gentile inclusion.[58] But determining "what is relevant" (and consequently what is not relevant) in the original text is possible only in light of the specific questions Paul poses to the text and the specific answers Paul gives to the text's own questions. Texts must be able to speak;[59] the text's "otherness" must be respected, but this does not entail the preclusion of the interpreter's prejudgments.[60] Gadamer is clear that understanding is hindered if "the text remains mute."[61] But when the

---

53. See Gadamer, *TM*, 305.

54. See Hosea 3. See again chapter 1, n24 above.

55. See, e.g., Rom 3:22.

56. Cf. Moyise, "Hosea as a Test Case," 50, who says, "Paul *does* seem to be engaged in something more sophisticated than simply replacing the original meaning with his own" (see the discussion on 47–50).

57. See Gadamer, *PH*, 57; Gadamer, *TM*, 271–72, 361–62.

58. Cf. Moyise ("Dialogical Intertextuality"), whose essay is not, it seems, incompatible with the present thesis. Indeed, the idea of a "dialogical intertextuality" is helpful, for it gives space to multiple voices (see 13–14). It seems, though, that a better term might be *dialogical re-authoring*, as the reader does have a choice "to amplify one of the voices" involved in intertextuality (14). And when certain choices are made, new meaning is authored. This is, arguably, one of the benefits of utilizing Gadamer's theory. With his emphasis on dialogue, prejudgments, and, not least, application by the interpreter as being integral to interpretive activity, the notion of *re-authoring* must be given its due weight.

59. Gadamer, *PH*, 57.

60. Gadamer, *TM*, 271–72 (see also 272–85).

61. Gadamer, *PH*, 57.

text is unmuted and is speaking, its speaking is not "in lifeless rigidity," but rather "gives ever new answers to the person who questions it and poses ever new questions to him who answers it. To understand a text is to come to understand oneself in a kind of dialogue."[62] In this dialogue, Paul can understand the oracle afresh, letting what was irrelevant fall away (Jewish exclusivity) and what was situationally relevant emerge (covenant inclusion). This is the way one can account for the hermeneutical phenomenon—not in covering up the tension between Hosea's text and Paul's revisionist reading, but in letting it appear *so that what is relevant with respect to the dialogue between both horizons can emerge.*

Additionally, it was seen in one proposal for understanding Rom 9:25–26 that Paul was illuminated by a "new covenant awareness" which enabled him to read the oracle anew.[63] That hypothesis, however, lacked clarity for it could not account for the *entire* hermeneutical event: The citation was used rhetorically by Paul to argue for a so-called "new covenant awareness," not merely the other way around.[64] The quotations in 9:25–26 took on a specific function in the overall narrative. Thus:

> Inevitably, enquiries into Paul's hermeneutic and its relationship with other Second Temple readings of Scripture will be informed by assumptions, articulated or implicit, about the situations into which Paul understands his letters to be directed, the purposes which he intends them to accomplish, and the ways in which he expects his scriptural citations and allusions to serve those purposes.[65]

One sees this clearly in Rom 9:24, where Paul uses the word "calling" to refer to Gentiles who are now part of the covenant of God. The quotations from Hosea immediately follow this verse, and therefore serve to function in a way so as to reinforce that claim, namely, that Gentiles are included among the people of God. This reinforcement is done via scriptural citation, an argument *for* the fact of a new awareness of Gentile inclusion. The citation has a rhetorical function. The point in highlighting these features is to say that the otherness of each horizon—the text's and interpreter's—must be acknowledged without one overcoming the other. And it is the proposed *dialogical*

---

62. Gadamer, *PH* (see also 58).

63. See again chapter 1 and our analysis of this idea from Tanner, "New Covenant," 102–10; esp. 106.

64. See chapter 1. That said, I of course would affirm Tanner's thesis that something informed Paul's reading. My point presently is that Gadamer's hermeneutic can make sense of both realities. See below.

65. Starling, *Not My People*, 16.

re-authoring that can allow for Paul to read the text afresh in light of his horizon all the while allowing the text to speak rhetorically as part of an argument.[66] This observation is not insignificant. Thus, both text and reader contribute to the production of meaning (i.e., "author" it) together dialogically.

It is conceivable that one might object to the proposed term (dialogical re-authoring) on the grounds that it could lead to the charge of frenzied, interpretive relativism. If interpreters can re-author texts, after all, does this not do violence to the texts being read? A few responses are in order. First, dialogical re-authoring is a term in this study to describe Paul's reading of Scripture in light of the hermeneutic put forward by Gadamer. In this sense, the term is merely a description of Gadamer's theory. In light of this, Gadamer himself has already discussed the charge of this sort of relativism, dismissing the concern.[67] Second, the term "re-authoring" is deliberately qualified by the preceding term "dialogical," thus implying that re-authoring is always in light of, and not apart from, a dialogue with the text being read.[68] Third, with respect to the Pauline texts examined above, we have shown that Paul's re-authoring is not divorced from his christology.[69] Therefore, modern interpreters, if they are to follow Paul, are not free to re-author the biblical text apart from a thorough commitment to the limits set by christology.[70] On this note, let us revisit the hermeneutic role of christology.

Christology as Question and Answer

Being an answer to Paul's question, the Hosea text was read in light of his christological convictions. Paul's Christ illuminated the Hosea text. Tanner

66. This was the problem with Starling's thesis. Indeed, the idea of dialogical re-authoring alleviates some of the problems found in the scholars examined in chapter 1.

67. See again chapter 3, where I discuss the question of radical subjectivism in Gadamer's theory.

68. In light of Gadamer's discussion about "co-determined" interpretation (see Gadamer, *TM*, 296, and chapter 4 above), I often use the term "co-creation" as a description of his hermeneutic (see above and the discussion below; cf. Vanhoozer [*Is There a Meaning in This Text?*, 107], who also describes Gadamer's hermeneutic as a process of "co-creation."). Thus, for Gadamer, meaning is *determined* and *created* within a dialogical context and can therefore be described as dialogical re-authoring.

69. See again chapters 4–7 above.

70. Christology, of course, is inclusive of the teachings of Christ. Thus, to re-author the texts of Scripture, the interpreter reads the texts creatively and freshly *within* the boundaries of Christ's teachings (see below). In this vein, there is much to be commended about the way Luz (*Matthew in History*, 75–97, 103) directs and orients his enquiry into the questions of truth and interpretive relativity—though I am hesitant to embrace the entirety of his argument.

was correct to imply, then, that *something* informed his reading of Hosea.[71] Considering the exegetical investigations above, clarification is afforded when the Christ-event is seen as acting as the key prejudgment for Paul's reading of the oracle. It is only in light of this prejudgment that the text was able to take on new meaning. The relevance of Gadamer's hermeneutic is clear when Moyise's comments regarding intertextuality are considered:

> It is not that the meaning of Hos 1:10 and 2:23 can be "objectively" described as a reference to Gentile inclusion but rather that, when the text is read in the light of what Paul thinks God is doing in the present, his interpretation becomes understandable and perhaps even inevitable. . . . It should be noted that this does not imply that readers can make texts mean whatever they like. This is a common objection to 'reader-centered' approaches, but it is mistaken. We could not talk about interpretation at all if there were not a text to interpret. The point is that texts do not present themselves to readers as transparent packages of meaning; readers have to do something in order to interpret them. Intertextuality suggests that what they do is relate them to other intertexts, which might be actual texts or, more generally, events, cultural phenomena, or personal experiences and commitments.[72]

This is particularly clear when the interpretive differences between Paul and, say, the pesherist are once again considered. Moyise says the differences are what they are because of how each brings texts to bear upon "a different set of intertexts," and this includes their respective understandings about God's "particular purpose for their own community."[73] And yet for Paul, this "particular purpose" for the Christian "community" is decidedly christocentric. After all, Christ is the focus of the "obedience of faith" (Rom 1:5) for both Jew and Gentile, a truth that reaches its interpretive pinnacle in texts like Rom 9:25–26.

This is not a one-sided reading, as said above.[74] It is true that the oracle served to inform his apostolic horizon, for it is the subject of covenant inclusion spoken about in the original oracle that comes to bear upon the eschatological reality of Paul's Christ and what his work has accomplished, namely, covenant inclusion. It is, again, equally true that the Pauline

71. Tanner, "New Covenant," 106. Cf. Wright, *PFG*, 758–60; Moyise, *Paul and Scripture*, 84–85. Recall also the critique of Starling above.

72. Moyise, "Latency and Respect," 133–34. See also his thoughts on "theological outlook" and "rhetorical situation" (138).

73. Moyise, "Latency and Respect," 134.

74. See above.

Christ—and the profound effect that his coming occasioned on behalf of Gentiles—spoke afresh to the promised covenant inclusion of the "Not My People" in Hosea's text, for christology was itself not merely a question to which the text was an answer, but also an answer to which the text was a question. As Georgia Warnke says:

> We come to works of literature from the horizon of our lives; we bring to those works certain questions and issues, whether we have articulated them explicitly or not, and the answers we find in literature are answers to our questions, just as the questions literature asks of us are questions we apply to our lives. Gadamer thus sees the interpretation of works of literature as a dialogue in which both work and interpreter must raise and answer questions they address to one another.[75]

Thus, this intertextual event is neither (1) a mere repetition of the original meaning of the past into the present nor (2) a complete abrogation of the past in favor of the present. In other words, this interpretive event was not a monologue, an overbearing emphasis on either horizon. What characterizes Paul's reading of Hosea (and other scriptural texts such as the Abraham story, the Adam story, the Exodus story, etc.) is that it was *dialogical*. In this way, neither horizon is obscured.[76]

Horizontverschmelzung

At this point, the perceived problem of historical distance regarding Paul's use of Hosea is alleviated.[77] Gadamer's theory, after all, renders this not just as unproblematic, but rather "positive and productive."[78] For this distance, again, "is not a yawning abyss but is filled with the continuity of custom and tradition, in the light of which everything handed down presents itself to us."[79] The interpreter's consciousness of their "hermeneutical situation," that is, a "consciousness of being affected by history (wirkungsgeschichtliches

---

75. Warnke, "Literature," 91. Recall chapter 3 above.

76. In this way, the Gadamerian approach offers clarity into making sense of how Paul's use of the OT can be both "contextual in nature" yet all the while "fresh," as Beldman and Swales ("Biblical Theology and Theological Interpretation," 163) rightly observe in the general apostolic use of the same. The "issues are complex," as they say (163), but one must wonder if such complexity is not due to the meddling of certain enlightenment assumptions.

77. See again chapter 1 above.

78. Gadamer, *TM*, 297.

79. Gadamer, *TM*, 297.

Bewußtsein)," is what allows them to formulate and assert "the right questions to ask."[80] This emphasis on question and answer, as seen above, is
fundamental to the hermeneutical event. Paul's "hermeneutical situation,"
therefore, was "determined by the prejudices" he had.[81] And while these
made up his own "horizon of a particular present," they were not "fixed" or
existing in distinction to "the otherness of the past."[82] The place of meaning
was, therefore, in the act of application—in his "present situation."[83] Thus,
in ways perhaps foreign to hermeneutic approaches influenced by the Enlightenment, Paul is able to read the Hosea text with a considerable amount
of freedom. Interpretation is an act of co-creation. We can simply call this
dialogical re-authoring.

Paul's interpretive posture in this regard finds its genesis at his conversion, where he acquired a new conceptual language (though, again, not
one untethered from his Jewish past). And his new language—indeed, new
Welt—was the very thing from which he could read and understand and
find fresh meaning in the Hosea oracle. The oracle found "expression in
[Paul's] own language" by speaking not just about renewed Jewish people,
but Gentile people.[84] This was clear in my evaluation of Rom 2, where Paul
understood righteousness in terms of law-keeping.[85] But this was not the
type of law-keeping that meant being a Jew; it meant being in Christ. Faithfulness, righteousness, and covenant keeping culminates in Christ (Rom
2–4; 10:4). Thus, in what one could describe as nothing less than dialogue,
the Hosea oracle posed new answers and new questions to Paul, and he
to it. Hermeneutically speaking—as my analysis of the relevant passages
from Romans sought to elucidate—Paul's own apostolic questions (not least
about Christ and Gentiles)[86] came to be a conversation starter as he looked
backward to a text like Hosea. There, he found answers about covenant
inclusion. But, again, he also discovered this as a question itself, namely,
about divine promise and redemption for castaways, to which his Christ
was the answer. In an act of *Horizontverschmelzung*, Paul's reading can be
(and should be) understood as more than merely a repetition of the oracle.
Following Gadamer, rather than seeing (Paul's) interpretation as repetition,
one should understand interpretation as co-creation.

---

80. Gadamer, *TM*, 301.

81. Gadamer, *TM*, 304.

82. Gadamer, *TM*, 305.

83. Gadamer, *TM*, 307. See again chapter 3.

84. Gadamer, *PH*, 57.

85. See again chapter 4.

86. E.g., see Rom 1:5.

This act of question-and-answer between Hosea and Paul resulted in higher ground, indeed a higher horizon of understanding, such that the conclusion both (1) *affirmed* and (2) *moved beyond* Hosea's and Paul's respective horizons.[87] Paul found a basis for the claim of covenant inclusion and redemption in Hosea's oracle, thus affirming its promise. Yet, even so, Paul could move beyond the text's original horizon of understanding as his prejudgments allowed him to find the oracle meaningful to his own situation and apostolic calling to the Gentiles. On this, Paul's beliefs about covenant inclusion were likewise affirmed by the Hosea oracle in that it, too, promised so much. Yet, arguably, the Hosea oracle did more than merely affirm Paul's situation; it also expanded his horizon so as to move it beyond any false conception that the Christ event was an autonomous phenomenon, but rather one rooted and grounded in Jewish religion and tradition.[88]

Everything that I have said about Paul's use of Hosea can also be said about the way Paul understood Jewish concepts like *faith*, *righteousness*, and *law*. It can also be said about his rereading of the stories of Abraham, Adam, and the Exodus, as well as his recontextualization of election, ethics, and unity.

QUOTATION AS APPLICATION

In Gadamerian language, one would speak of the rhetorical use of the oracle as therefore being *applied* to an already working narrative. As Gadamer says, it is the understanding of "the text of Christian proclamation," that is, in the sermon, that "the understanding and interpretation of the text first receives its full reality."[89] Here understanding happens because the text speaks via the sermon and "begins to find expression" in the person's "own language."[90] Specifically, "one must take up into himself what is said to him in such a fashion that it speaks and finds an answer in the words of his own language."[91] Thus, the text is only understood if it speaks "directly" to the recipient in their situation, and the "completion of understanding" happens in the sermon's "reception as an appeal that is directed to each person who hears it."[92] Similarly, the rhetorical use of the Hosea quotations are an appeal

---

87. See again chapter 6.

88. See below.

89. Gadamer, *PH*, 57.

90. Gadamer, *PH*, 57.

91. Gadamer, *PH*, 57.

92. Gadamer, *PH*, 57–58.

for the claim of (Gentile) inclusion. This accords well with the notion of dialogical re-authoring.

Therefore, the use of the Hosea quotations is to be seen as an instantiation of Gadamer's idea of *Anwendung*.[93] The assumption behind the rhetorical use of these quotations is to bring the Hosea oracle into dialogue with Paul's present purposes, situation, and questions, namely, that of Gentile inclusion.[94] That narrative, we recall, was traced by calling attention to a substructure of motifs: faith, righteousness language, law-keeping. Along the way, these three have at times intertwined and intersected. As the claim for Gentile inclusion began to accelerate (particularly in Rom 2), that claim was later reinforced and anchored in a certain conviction—namely, Paul's christological convictions (Rom 3). These were especially fleshed out in the Abraham story (Rom 4). After placing the Hosea quotations in Rom 9:25–26 within their literary and thematic context (9:1—10:4), the use of the oracle itself can be said to be a pinnacle of that narrative. In other words, the oracle was the *applied* answer to the Gentile question itself—a question that began, we recall, in Rom 1–2. That is, as it was functioning rhetorically, it served to reinforce the claims made about Gentile inclusion earlier in his letter (e.g., Rom 2:12–16). The text of Hosea was applied to Paul's present situation, not least in regard to Gentiles and his apostolic Christian mission (Rom 1:1–5).[95] It was in this application that Paul found the meaning he did.[96] The text, if not applied, would have remained only a historical text concerning the New Covenant, but it found meaning when Paul assigned, or applied, to it the questions concerning him and the Roman church—not the least of which were issues surrounding what Gentile inclusion ought to look like (Rom 14:1—15:13).[97]

93. See chapter 3.

94. So Moyise, "Latency and Respect," 138.

95. Garlington, *Obedience of Faith*, 242, is right to connect Paul's train of thought in Rom 9:25 (with the citation of Hosea and use of ἠγαπημένην) back to the context of Rom 1:5, specifically 1:7 where Paul applies the "honorific title of Israel," ἀγαπητοὶ θεοῦ, to the Roman Christians.

96. See again Gadamer, *TM*, 306–8.

97. As Evans (*Reception History*, 234) has said, Gadamer has been criticized for not providing a means by which "valid" and "*responsible*" interpretation could be determined, citing Betti (*Die Hermeneutik als allgemeine Methodik*, 49) and Hirsch (*Validity*, 251); and Thiselton (in Lundin et al., *Responsibility of Hermeneutics*, 110), respectively. Evans states that what could "possibly" lend itself as a "constraint, a measure of 'adequacy', is [Gadamer's] emphasis on 'the rightness of the question'" (234). Evans then discusses how such "questions" find themselves in both the horizon of the text and the reader, such that the text and reader are both questions and answers to each other (234–35). In this dialogical process, "Understanding is neither merely the reconstruction of the author's view nor an assertion of the reader's. Understanding takes place

In terms of the *rhetorical* and *applicative* nature of the Hosea citation, Gadamer's insights remain key. In an important essay, Gadamer discusses the relationship between rhetoric and hermeneutics.[98] Importantly, he says, this relationship finds its link in that both require attention to *kairos*, "time." His thoughts are worth quoting at length:

> Only the individual is truly capable as a speaker who has ac-
> knowledged as good and right the thing about which he is trying
> to persuade people and is thereby able to stand up for it. This
> knowledge of the good and this capability in the art of speaking
> does not mean a universal knowledge of "the good"; rather, it
> means a knowledge about that to which one has to persuade peo-
> ple here and now, a knowledge of how one is to go about doing
> this, and a knowledge of those whom one has to persuade. Only
> when one sees the concretization required by the knowledge of
> the good does one understand why the art of writing speeches
> plays such a role in the broader argumentation. . . . In addition
> to all that goes into knowledge . . . , real knowledge also has to
> recognize the *kairos*. This means knowing when and how one is
> required to speak. But this cannot be acquired merely by learning
> rules or by rote. There are no rules governing the reasonable use
> of rules, as Kant stated so rightly in his *Critique of Judgment*.[99]

Linking rhetoric to application, Gadamer continues,

> In Plato this comes out in the *Phaedrus* (268ff.) by means of
> an amusing exaggeration: if anyone were to possess only all the
> physician's information and rules of thumb without knowing
> where and when to apply them, he would not be a physician.
> Were a tragedian or musician only to have learned the general
> rules and techniques of his art and yet produced no work using
> that knowledge, he would not be a poet or musician (280ff.). In
> the same way, the orator has to know all about where and when
> to speak (*hai eukairiai te kai akairiai*; 272a6).[100]

For Paul, *now that Christ has come in the present time*, the text of Hosea can speak afresh to the situation at hand, that is, be applied, in the most creative

---

in 'dialogue', in which to reach understanding (as a fusion of horizons) means 'being transformed into a communion in which we do not remain what we were' [citing Gadamer, *TM*, 371]. In this construction, 'truth', 'tradition' and 'prejudgment' are dialectically, not subjectively, conceived" (235).

98. Gadamer, "Hermeneutics as a Theoretical and Practical Task."

99. Gadamer, "Hermeneutics as a Theoretical and Practical Task," 253.

100. Gadamer, "Hermeneutics as a Theoretical and Practical Task," 253.

(indeed, artistic) of ways.[101] After all, Paul's arguments in the passages examined would not have worked had the Christ-event not yet happened.

As an example, let us return once more to the Abraham story (Rom 4). It is true that Paul's use of Abraham is rooted in Scripture. Scripture showed quite clearly that Abraham was deemed righteous before being circumcised (this was one of Paul's points in citing the story in the first place). And so, Paul's argument was exegetical: as a matter of textual and historical fact, that Abraham was justified prior to being circumcised was true, being clearly seen by a chronological reading of Scripture. But we recall that one conclusion Paul draws from the story is that Gentiles *qua* Gentiles are now, in the present time, to be included in the covenant. And so, as I have argued, it would be a mistake to think that Paul's argument rested entirely upon a historical/exegetical fact—namely, upon the fact that Abraham was deemed righteous prior to receiving circumcision. One cannot sustain Paul's conclusion that works of the law are unnecessary by simply asserting this fact. This is why I said in my analysis that Paul's argument should not be understood as resting simply upon exegesis. That historical/textual fact (that Abraham was justified prior to being circumcised) was true prior to the Christ event just as surely as it was after it. And yet no Jew in his right mind prior to the Christ event would therefore attempt to say that works of the law are no longer necessary. What mattered for Paul—and this is my entire point—is that he argues from the scriptural text by means of an already-assumed christological horizon of understanding. *Now* that Christ has come, the Jewish texts, stories, *and* oracles, as well as the small details in them (e.g., the historical fact that Abraham was declared righteous prior to being circumcised) are now, *in the present time and situation*, to be read quite differently. Recalling the two quotes from Gadamer above, the key to understanding Paul's use of the Abraham story (and, in fact, his use of the Old Testament generally) is to consider how *he* understood his *time* within salvation history.[102]

This philosophical-hermeneutical observation on application appears congruent with what some biblical scholars are saying.[103] For example, DiMattei notices a difference between the way the pesherist associated with Qumran and Paul employ Jewish texts. The former uses the paradigmatic

101. See my critique of DiMattei below. Additionally, it should go without saying at this point, but the term "Christ-event" as a hermeneutical prejudgment should be understood "to speak not only of Christ's life, death, and resurrection but also what followed, namely, the birth of the church and especially the inclusion of the Gentiles" (Moyise, "Does Paul Respect the Context?," 97n1)

102. See again my discussion on the Abraham story in chapter 5 above.

103. See again the discussion on "application" in chapter 3 above.

textual formula for introducing interpretations, namely, "this is interpreted," while such formulas remain largely absent in the latter.[104] "Usually," says DiMattei, "the scriptural passage is cited in its interpretive context; that is, the interpretive meaning of the base text is already assumed, and the text is simply presented in its *contemporized* context."[105] Interestingly, DiMattei observes this very feature in Paul's quotation of Hos 2:23 in Rom 9:25. He says:

> Unlike Pesher, Paul does not provide his readers with a hermeneutical key that bridges text and interpretation, translating Hosea's "my people" as "the Gentiles." He simply assumes the interpretive connection *by means of its application*: Hosea's "my people" are "the Gentiles." It has often been asserted that Paul cites this passage with no regard for its original context; *through its application*, the text assumes a new meaning and thus a new context. The hermeneutical assumption at work here, however, mirrors the principles of Qumran pesharim: for Paul, the prophetic text speaks of contemporary events and/or personages, here specifically the Gentiles. . . . Thus for Paul, the appropriate and perhaps the only context within which to read and understand the prophetic text is the contemporized eschatological context.[106]

DiMattei's findings largely confirm my own (though not forgetting my critique above): The essence of Paul's use of Hosea is its application to Paul's present situation. *Textually* speaking, DiMattei is right.[107] Indeed, in line with my investigations above, such was the case for many writers in the first century, not least Paul and the sectarians.[108] But I want to take things further

104. DiMattei, "Narratives," 78.

105. DiMattei, "Narratives," 78; emphasis added.

106. DiMattei, "Narratives," 78–79; emphasis added. I have waited until this point to highlight DiMattei's insights until after Gadamer's theory had been developed (and applied to Romans) so that the former's thesis might be given full weight and value.

107. My conclusion that the Hosea quotations should be understood most basically as being *applied* to Paul's *contemporary* situation was found independently of DiMattei, whose own conclusions were largely drawn from an awareness to the *textual* features of the passage. My own findings, however, have come via a distinct philosophical-hermeneutical analysis that offers its own unique approach (e.g., for Gadamer, the term "application" is a technical term, as we recall, loaded with philosophical meaning, being located within the context of his larger hermeneutical project). That said, DiMattei's textual work confirms exactly what I have been saying in terms of hermeneutic theory. For what further distinguishes my project from his ideas, see below.

108. See Moyise ("Does Paul Respect the Context?," 98), who observes how, in contrast to twenty-first century "conventions," these early writers would "fuse" the various steps of textual explanation and interpretation "in the form of a modified quotation." This is the very thing Paul does in Rom 9:25–26. It is worth comparing Moyise's

than DiMattei. Whereas he rightly shows *what* Paul is doing intertextually, I am attempting to go one step further to show *how* Paul is doing what he is doing, specifically in a way that is grounded upon a philosophical-hermeneutical approach.[109]

Interpretation as Performative and Situational

Recalling Gadamer's remark that "A drama really exists only when it is played, and ultimately music must resound," one quickly recognizes how his aesthetic critique can be applied presently.[110] That is to say, the Hosea text was a performative event, providing for Paul a picture, *ein Bild*, as to what covenant inclusion looks like in the present. As *Kunstwerk*, the original Hosea text existed for Paul in its presentation, a Gadamerian instance

---

observation here with Gadamer's hermeneutic which grants philosophical space for accounting for such fusion.

109. DiMattei's clarifying textual insight confirms my utilization of Gadamer's hermeneutic, and in many ways my study gives *hermeneutical* clarity to his *textual* observations. That said, there is still room for critique. My thesis has been that Paul's reading of Hosea is patterned after a larger project of reappraisal, one grounded largely on christology. Despite the otherwise helpful comments regarding the key role of application, DiMattei seems to minimize the hermeneutical role of christology. Commenting on another passage, DiMattei ("Narratives," 81) observes rightly how Paul does not "simply narrate the past" but rather that "he also reshapes it, retelling the story and often interjecting elements and themes drawn from the context of the contemporary situation to which the narrative is being applied." He is also keenly aware that "Past and present, the text and its re-presentation (not to mention its interpretation) seem to coalesce into a single narrative fabric," noting even how the "Qumran pesharim display this same tendency toward reshaping the historical story or narrative to suit the contemporized situation" (82). The problem, we recall (see above), is that DiMattei makes Paul's contemporizing of texts do too much hermeneutically. For Paul, this contemporizing is only possible in light of his christology and, in contrast, should therefore be seen as being part of Paul's hermeneutic posture; in other words, Paul's christology and contemporizing of texts must be seen as comprising one hermeneutical event. The problem, once again, is that DiMattei divorces the "content" from "method" (77). On "content," he says christology "influences and shapes the content of [Paul's] hermeneutic," for it is part of Paul's "specific historical circumstances" and is definitely central to Paul's "theological beliefs" (77). However, this "is not to be confused with the underlying hermeneutical assumption that guides his interpretation," what DiMattei calls Paul's "*approach*" and "method," namely, the idea that the text speaks to the reader's contemporary "situation" (77; see also 82–83). Such distinctions make his later comments about "Christ" being part of the interpretive context confusing (see 92). At any rate, as I have already said above, distinctions like these are hard to substantiate under a Gadamerian paradigm where situational application and the interpreter's prejudgments are closely intertwined. In this manner, Gadamer provides clarity.

110. Gadamer, *TM*, 115. See again chapter 3 above.

of *Darstellung*, bringing its latter reader into play; Paul's reading, then, was an act of *Spiel*, a deconstruction of autonomous subjectivity.[111] The Hosea text, as a reading, presented itself as a kind of play *for* Paul's aim of Gentile inclusion. Moreover, this intertextual reading is helpfully clarified if it is understood in light of the fact Paul "[brought] into play . . . certain ideational 'preconceptions.'"[112] After all: "There is no pure seeing and understanding of history without reference to the present. On the contrary, history is seen and understood only and always through a consciousness standing in the present."[113] Thus, the text itself is given the framework it is because of Paul's bringing into play his most basic present assumptions. Interpretation is thus performative and situational.

INTERPRETATION AS TRADITIONED AND AS A MOVEMENT WITHIN TRADITION

Yet, the beauty of Gadamer's theory is that it "affirms the operativeness of the past in the present: The present is seen and understood only through the intentions, ways of seeing, and preconceptions bequeathed from the past."[114] The past for Gadamer is not a "pile of facts . . . but rather is a stream in which we move and participate, in every act of understanding," as Palmer says.[115]

Considering all that has been said about Pauline prejudgments, it would be inaccurate to conclude that there is an inherent contradiction in Gadamer's theory. For example, if one's prejudice comes from tradition, then how can the interpreter's prejudice inform, critique, or modify the tradition from which it came? If such were the case, the problem this presents for my reading of Paul is obvious—I have, after all, been arguing that Paul's prejudices have allowed him to recontextualize and resituate his tradition in light of the revelation of Christ. Fortunately, however, such problems exist in appearance only. The truth is that Gadamer's "concept of tradition is not to be construed as something fixed or reified. Rather, it is a formal concept which exhibits no concrete content of its own and, perhaps, could be said to have more of a regulative than a constitutive function."[116] Camille Atkinson admits that "particular traditions" do carry with them content, but "truth or

111. See again chapter 3 above.

112. Palmer, *Hermeneutics*, 176. Here (and in the following quote) Palmer is commenting on Heidegger's thought, which was formative for Gadamer.

113. Palmer, *Hermeneutics*, 176.

114. Palmer, *Hermeneutics*, 176.

115. Palmer, *Hermeneutics*, 176–77.

116. Atkinson, "Gadamer's Hermeneutics," 289.

meaning" is found "by engaging in dialogue with it," that is, the questioning is what matters.[117] Thus, "Someone can embrace certain aspects of his traditions or he can reject those parts that he regards as degenerate, obsolete, or irrelevant. What finite human beings cannot do is transcend the effects of their history or traditions as a general rule."[118] The point is not so much that one cannot critique one's tradition as it is that one cannot critique that one has a tradition. Thus it is in this vein Gadamer says, "In fact history does not belong to us; we belong to it."[119]

It must not be forgotten, too, that "understanding always involves something like applying the text to be understood to the interpreter's present situation."[120] Thus, while each interpreter operates from within tradition, being historical persons, each nonetheless interpret from within their respective, even differing, present circumstances. Like a jurist who does not see the "law" as something "to be understood historically," but rather something "to be concretized," so also Paul sought to concretize the Old Testament text into his own situation.[121] Like a preacher who does not see the "gospel" as something "to be understood as a merely historical document, but to be taken in such a way that it exercises its saving effect," so also Paul sought to let the Old Testament text speak afresh *into his* present.[122] Therefore, "the text . . . if it is to be understood properly—i.e., according to the claim it makes—must be understood at every moment, in every concrete situation, in a new and different way. Understanding here is always application."[123]

This makes sense as to why Paul's reading might have been radically different from, say, that of his pre-Damascus Road experience. The differences lie in differing prejudgments, indeed in differing experiences, present situations, and horizons. Since, therefore, interpretation is both traditioned and also a movement within tradition, it makes sense, then, that Paul can at the same time both appeal to the Old Testament text (such as Hosea) as an argument from Scripture and also at the same time read it afresh. For, by virtue of how all interpretive activity happens, as Gadamer taught, "meaning" and "understanding" are not attained when the object of interpretation (the text) is dominated by the subject (the reader) or when the latter

117. Atkinson, "Gadamer's Hermeneutics," 289.

118. Atkinson, "Gadamer's Hermeneutics," 289 (and 290–93).

119. Gadamer, *TM*, 278. See chapter 3 above.

120. Gadamer, *TM*, 306–7. See chapter 3 above.

121. Gadamer, *TM*, 307.

122. Gadamer, *TM*, 307.

123. Gadamer, *TM*, 307–8. See Luz, *Matthew in History*, 19.

is dominated by the former.[124] If interpretation is dialogical,[125] the reader's own particular "situation" remains the place where the production of meaning happens.[126] That is to say, the text takes on meaning when the reader applies it in light of his or her own acquired tradition and historicality.

Thus, Gadamer described the process of understanding as being "neither subjective nor objective" but rather "as the interplay of the movement of tradition and the movement of the interpreter."[127] In this case, the traditionary text (the Old Testament) remains a dialogue partner with Paul. Gadamer states that the "anticipation of meaning that governs our understanding of a text is not an act of subjectivity, but proceeds from the commonality [Gemeinsamkeit] that binds us to the tradition."[128] To clarify the phenomenon of Paul's use of the Old Testament, one must enquire, therefore, into this "commonality" (Gemeinsamkeit). Gadamer is clear concerning the unstatic characteristic of this commonality, namely, that it is "constantly being formed in our relation to tradition."[129] It is important to remember again that tradition is itself unstatic. It is not "a permanent precondition," but something "we produce . . . ourselves inasmuch as we understand, participate in the evolution of tradition, and hence further determine it ourselves."[130]

This accords, then, with what is observed in Paul's reading of the text of Hosea, namely, its non-static characteristics. Paul's own "relation to tradition," as Gadamer might say, was in movement, for it is true that "ideological commitments are *integral* to the historical contingencies of both text and reader."[131] Moreover, given the original contexts of, say, Hosea and Rom 9:25–26 within the greater argument of Romans, it can surely be argued that Gadamer's "commonality" principle finds its instantiation in the New Covenant theme inherent to both biblical texts. The New Covenant motif itself, being a preoccupation for Paul (e.g., Rom 2:25–29), is what binds him

124. See again chapter 3.

125. See above and Gadamer, *TM*, 301, 356–71, especially 366–68.

126. Gadamer, *TM*, 306–7.

127. Gadamer, *TM*, 293. This effectively fills in gaps found in our analysis of several positions in chapter 1.

128. Gadamer, *TM*, 293; Gadamer, *WM*, 298.

129. Gadamer, *TM*, 293.

130. Gadamer, *TM*, 293.

131. Evans, *Reception History*, 254. Cf. 260–63, 272, where, in a different context and argument, Evans makes the point against critics who claim that "ideological" or "theological" claims are "*external*" in some way to the "process of understanding" (260). The context of these points are much different than my present one, though the point stands.

to the Hosea text. But this commonality is likewise not static; it, as Gadamer says, "is constantly being formed in [Paul's] relation to [Jewish] tradition."[132]

Moreover, as I have mentioned several times, tradition itself is not a "permanent precondition," for Paul himself is active in its own production and "evolution."[133] Because Paul's own horizon is itself in movement,[134] as the Christ-event dawned, his horizon was filled with the light of christology and therefore was able to find fresh meaning in the Hosea text, a meaning that spoke to the question of the place of Gentiles in the commonality of New Covenant. "The real meaning of a text, as it speaks to the interpreter," says Gadamer, "does not depend on the contingencies of the author and his original audience."[135] As we have already seen, meaning for Gadamer is a "co-determined" process "by the historical situation of the interpreter and hence by the totality of the objective course of history."[136] Hence, Gadamer's famed line: "It is enough to say that we understand in a *different* way, *if we understand at all*."[137] Such statements reveal the heart of Gadamer's theory. Joel Weinsheimer's comments are helpful in this regard:

> Sameness and difference are indivisible in Gadamer's herme-
> neutics, and neither can be suppressed if interpretation is to be
> made intelligible. An interpretation that is not the same as what
> it interprets is not an interpretation but a new creation; an in-
> terpretation that is not different from what it interprets is not an
> interpretation but a copy. What distinguishes Gadamer's herme-
> neutics in this regard is that for him interpretation involves this
> interminable interplay between sameness and difference, the
> irreducible *methexis* of the one and the many.[138]

INTERPRETATION AS PREJUDICED

The notion of prejudice, as seen above, was for Gadamer a subversive concept in light of the Enlightenment's project of neutrality.[139] I have shown,
moreover, that the concept of prejudice was for Gadamer more than the

132. Gadamer, *TM*, 293.

133. Gadamer, *TM*, 293.

134. Gadamer, *TM*, 303.

135. Gadamer, *TM*, 296.

136. Gadamer, *TM*, 296.

137. Gadamer, *TM*, 296.

138. Weinsheimer, "Meaningless Hermeneutics?," 165.

139. See chapter 3 above.

mere imposition of the interpreter upon texts; rather, prejudice was seen to exist within an horizon, which is capable of genuine fusion.[140]

Gadamer's concept of prejudgment, therefore, is helpful in regard to Paul's use of the Old Testament in Romans. Consider again Paul's use of Hosea. The concept of prejudgment is able to (1) deflect the charge of an interpretation of Hosea that merely imposes upon Hosea and (2) still provide an account for an active and creative role of Paul as reader. Because of its dialogical character, Gadamer's theory, while accounting for Paul's prejudgments, can also at the same time account for Paul's rhetorical use of the oracle. Though I have already mentioned this fact, it is worth saying again: With Gadamer's concept of prejudgment, one can make sense of how Paul can *both* argue from Scripture, saying, "As it is written," all the while account for his often-revisionary conclusions of Scripture. Hence, by reflecting on Gadamer's idea of *Vorurteile* (and all that it entails), Paul's reading of Hosea is afforded clarity.[141] Indeed, the same could be said for other texts he quotes and other motifs, concepts, and stories he interprets.

There is one final issue to consider. It is surely the case that any enquiry into the legitimacy of Paul's use of the Old Testament—that is, whether Paul's is a good reading, a good *judgment* of the texts—is to be placed squarely back upon Paul's christological *pre*judgments. One cannot evaluate the validity of Paul's judgments without eventually reckoning with what lies behind them. One might ask, then: Are Paul's christological convictions warranted?[142] In my estimation, that is the ultimate hermeneutical question.

---

140. See chapter 3 above.

141. See again Gadamer, *TM*, 278, where he discusses the prime position a person's *pre*judgments have in relation to their judgments. Cf. 1 Cor 15:14.

142. Cf. Gadamer, *TM*, 298–99, about the "question of critique." See again chapter 3. Cf. Rae, "Theological Interpretation and Historical Criticism," 105–6. This is not unlike Moyise's observations about the use of Hos 13:14 in 1 Cor 15:54. He discusses how, for those who argue for a christological interpretation, the question of what it means to "respect" a text is to be placed squarely back upon the veracity of the christological assumptions that make them possible in the first place (Moyise, "Hosea as a Test Case," 43; see also his evaluation of this on 44). I think Gadamer's hermeneutic is congruent with this idea.

Bibliography

Achtemeier, Paul J. *Romans*. IBC. Louisville: John Knox, 1985.

Aland, Barbara, et al., eds. *Novum Testamentum Graece*. 28th ed. Stuttgart: Deutsche Bibelgesellschaft, 2012.

Allen, Graham. *Intertextuality*. 2nd ed. TNCI. New York: Routledge, 2011.

Atkinson, Camille E. "Is Gadamer's Hermeneutics Inherently Conservative?" *FPIJP* 14.2 (2009) 285–306.

Baker, Murray. "Paul and the Salvation of Israel: Paul's Ministry, the Motif of Jealousy, and Israel's Yes." *CBQ* 67.3 (2005) 469–84.

Baron, Lori, and B. J. Oropeza. "Midrash." In *Exploring Intertextuality: Diverse Strategies for New Testament Interpretation of Texts*, edited by B. J. Oropeza and Steve Moyise, 63–80. Eugene, OR: Cascade, 2016.

Barrett, C. K. *The Epistle to the Romans*. 2nd ed. BNTC. London: A. & C. Black, 1991.

Bartholomew, Craig G. *Introducing Biblical Hermeneutics: A Comprehensive Framework for Hearing God in Scripture*. Grand Rapids: Baker Academic, 2015.

Bates, Matthew W. "Beyond Hays's Echoes of Scripture in the Letters of Paul: A Proposed Diachronic Intertextuality with Romans 10:16 as a Test Case." In *Paul and Scripture: Extending the Conversation*, edited by Christopher D. Stanley, 263–91. Atlanta: SBL, 2012.

———. *The Hermeneutics of the Apostolic Proclamation: The Center of Paul's Method of Scriptural Interpretation*. Waco, TX: Baylor University Press, 2012.

———. *Salvation by Allegiance Alone: Rethinking Faith, Works, and the Gospel of King Jesus*. Grand Rapids: Baker Academic, 2017.

Beentjes, Pancratius C. *The Book of Ben Sira in Hebrew: A Text Edition of All Extant Hebrew Manuscripts and a Synopsis of All Parallel Hebrew Ben Sira Texts*. VTSup 68. Atlanta: SBL, 2006.

Beldman, David J. H., and Jonathan Swales. "Biblical Theology and Theological Interpretation." In *A Manifesto for Theological Interpretation*, edited by Craig G. Bartholomew and Heath A. Thomas, 149–70. Grand Rapids: Baker Academic, 2016.

Betti, Emilio. *Die Hermeneutik als allgemeine Methodik der Geisteswissenschaften*. Tübingen: Mohr, 1962.

Bird, Michael F. *An Anomalous Jew: Paul among Jews, Greeks, and Romans*. Grand Rapids: Eerdmans, 2016.

————. *The Saving Righteousness of God: Studies on Paul, Justification, and the New Perspective*. PBM. Eugene, OR: Wipf & Stock, 2007.

Bockmuehl, Markus. *Seeing the Word: Refocusing New Testament Study*. STI. Grand Rapids: Baker Academic, 2006.

Boyd, Gregory A. *Crucifixion of the Warrior God: Interpreting the Old Testament's Violent Portraits of God in Light of the Cross*. 2 vols. Minneapolis: Fortress, 2017.

Calvin, John. *Epistle to the Romans*. Grand Rapids: Baker, 1979.

Campbell, Constantine R. *Paul and the Hope of Glory: An Exegetical and Theological Study*. Grand Rapids: Zondervan, 2020.

Campbell, Douglas A. "The Faithfulness of Jesus Christ in Romans 3:22." In *The Faith of Jesus Christ: Exegetical, Biblical, and Theological Studies*, edited by Michael F. Bird and Preston M. Sprinkle, 57–71. Colorado Springs, CO: Paternoster, 2009.

Cho, Jae Hyung. "The Christology of Romans in Light of Πιστις Ιησου Χριστου (Rom 3:22–26)." *RQ* 56.1 (2014) 41–51.

Ciampa, Roy E., and Brian S. Rosner. *The First Letter to the Corinthians*. PNTC. Grand Rapids: Eerdmans, 2010.

Cranfield, C. E. B. *Romans*. 2 vols. ICC. Edinburgh: T. & T. Clark, 1979.

Crenshaw, James L. *The Book of Sirach*. NIB. Nashville, TN: Abingdon, 1997.

Crowell, Steven Galt. "The Early Decades: Positivism, Neo-Kantianism, Dilthey." In *Columbia History of Western Philosophy*, edited by Richard H. Popkin, 667–75. New York: Columbia University Press, 1999.

DeSilva, David A. *Introducing the Apocrypha: Message, Context, and Significance*. Grand Rapids: Baker Academic, 2002.

Dilthey, Wilhelm. *Gesammelte Schriften*. Vol. VII. Stuttgart: Teubner, 1958.

DiMattei, Steven. "Biblical Narratives." In *As It Is Written: Studying Paul's Use of Scripture*, edited by Stanley E. Porter and Christopher D. Stanley, 59–93. Atlanta: SBL, 2008.

Dodd, C. H. *The Epistle of Paul to the Romans*. London: Fontana, 1959.

Donaldson, Terence L. *Paul and the Gentiles: Remapping the Apostle's Convictional World*. Minneapolis: Fortress, 1997.

Dostal, Robert J. "Hans-Georg Gadamer." In *EP* 258–61.

Dunn, James D. G. "Biblical Hermeneutics and Historical Responsibility." In *The Future of Biblical Interpretation: Responsible Plurality in Biblical Interpretation*, edited by Stanley E. Porter and Matthew R. Malcolm, 85–100. Downers Grove, IL: IVP Academic, 2013.

————. *Romans 1–8*. WBC 38a. Dallas: Word, 1988.

————. *Romans 9–16*. WBC 38b. Dallas: Word, 1988.

————. *The Theology of the Apostle Paul*. Grand Rapids: Eerdmans, 1998.

Eberhard, Philippe. *The Middle Voice in Gadamer's Hermeneutics: A Basic Interpretation with Some Theological Implications*. HUT 45. Chicago: Mohr Siebeck, 2004.

Elliger, K. and W. Rudolph, eds. *Biblia Hebraica Stuttgartensia*. 5th ed. Stuttgart: Deutsche Bibelgesellschaft, 1997.

Ellis, Teresa Ann. "Is Eve the 'Woman' in Sirach 25:24?" *CBQ* 73.4 (2011) 723–42.

Evans, Robert. *Reception History, Tradition, and Biblical Interpretation: Gadamer and Jauss in Current Practice*. New York: Bloomsbury T. & T. Clark, 2016.

Fehér, István M. "Religion, Theology, and Philosophy on the Way to Being and Time: Heidegger, the Hermeneutical, the Factical, and the Historical with Respect to Dilthey and Early Christianity." *RP* 39.1 (2009) 99–131.

Fitzmyer, Joseph A. "Paul and the Dead Sea Scrolls." In *The Dead Sea Scrolls after Fifty Years: A Comprehensive Assessment*, edited by Peter W. Flint and James C. VanderKam, 599–621. Boston: Brill, 1999.

———. *Romans: A New Translation with Introduction and Commentary*. AB 33. New York: Doubleday, 1993.

Forman, Mark. "The Politics of Promise: Echoes of Isaiah 54 in Romans 4.19–21." *JSNT* 31.3 (2009) 301–24.

Fowl, Stephen. "The Use of Scripture in Philippians." In *Paul and Scripture: Extending the Conversation*, edited by Christopher D. Stanley, 163–84. Atlanta: SBL, 2012.

Frank, Manfred. "The Text and Its Style: Schleiermacher's Hermeneutic Theory of Language." *Boundary 2* 11.3 (1983) 11–28.

Fuß, Barbara. *"Dies ist die Zeit, von der geschrieben ist . . .": Die expliziten Zitate aus dem Buch Hosea in den Handschriften von Qumran und im Neuen Testament*. NTA n.F. 37. Münster: Aschendorff, 2000.

Gadamer, Hans-Georg. "Classical and Philosophical Hermeneutics." In *The Gadamer Reader: A Bouquet of the Later Writings*, edited and translated by Richard E. Palmer, 41–71. THP. Evanston, IL: Northwestern University Press, 2007.

———. "Die Universalität des hermeneutischen Problems." In *Kleine Schriften: Philosophie Hermeneutik*, 1:101–12. Tübingen: Mohr Siebeck, 1976.

———. *The Gadamer Reader: A Bouquet of the Later Writings*. Edited by Richard E. Palmer. THP. Evanston, IL: Northwestern University Press, 2007.

———. *Heidegger's Ways*. Translated by John W. Stanley. Albany: State University of New York, 1994.

———. *Heideggers Wege: Studien zum Spätwerk*. Tübingen: Mohr, 1983.

———. "Hermeneutics as a Theoretical and Practical Task." In *The Gadamer Reader: A Bouquet of the Later Writings*, edited by Richard E. Palmer, 246–65. Evanston, IL: Northwestern University Press, 2007.

———. *Philosophical Hermeneutics*. Edited and translated by David E. Linge. Berkeley: University of California Press, 2004.

———. *The Relevance of the Beautiful and Other Essays*. Edited by Robert Benaconi. Translated by Nicholas Walker. Cambridge: Cambridge University Press, 1986.

———. "Rhetorik, Hermeneutik und Ideologiekritik." In *Kleine Schriften: Philosophie Hermeneutik*, 1:113–30. Tübingen: Mohr Siebeck, 1976.

———. *Truth and Method*. Translated by Joel Weinsheimer and Donald G. Marshall. 2nd rev. ed. New York: Continuum, 2004.

———. "Über die Festlichkeit des Theaters." In *Kleine Schriften: Interpretationen*, 2:170–77. Tübingen: Mohr Siebeck, 1979.

———. *Wahrheit und Methode: Grundzüge einer philosophischen Hermeneutik*. 7th ed. GW 1. Tübingen: Mohr Siebeck, 2010.

Garland, David E. *1 Corinthians*. BECNT. Grand Rapids: Baker Academic, 2003.

Garlington, Don. *Faith, Obedience, and Perseverance: Aspects of Paul's Letter to the Romans*. Eugene, OR: Wipf & Stock, 2009.

———. *The Obedience of Faith: A Pauline Phrase in Historical Context*. Eugene, OR: Wipf & Stock, 2009.

Gjesdal, Kristin. "Hermeneutics and Philology: A Reconsideration of Gadamer's Critique of Schleiermacher." *BJHP* 14.1 (2006) 133–56.

Gorman, Michael J. *Apostle of the Crucified Lord: A Theological Introduction to Paul and His Letters*. Grand Rapids: Eerdmans, 2004.

Grondin, Jean. *Hans-Georg Gadamer: A Biography*. Translated by Joel Weinsheimer. New Haven: Yale University Press, 2003.

——. "Gadamer's Basic Understanding of Understanding." In *The Cambridge Companion to Gadamer*, edited by Robert J. Dostal, 36–51. Cambridge: Cambridge University Press, 2002.

——. *Introduction to Philosophical Hermeneutics*. New Haven: Yale University Press, 1994.

Halsted, Matthew. "Intertextual Chaos? Investigating Paul's Use of Hosea in Romans 9:25–26 in Light of Hans-Georg Gadamer's Philosophical Hermeneutics." PhD diss., Middlesex University/London School of Theology, 2018.

Hays, Richard B. *Echoes of Scripture in the Letters of Paul*. New Haven: Yale University Press, 1989.

——. *Reading Backwards: Figural Christology and the Fourfold Gospel Witness*. London: SPCK, 2015.

Heath, Stephen. "Intertextuality." In *DCCT* 348–49.

Heidegger, Martin. *Being and Time*. Translated by John Macquarrie and Edward Robinson. New York: Harper & Row, 1962.

——. *Sein und Zeit, Gesamtausgabe, 1. Abteilung: Veröffentlichte Schriften 1914–1970*. Band 2. Frankfurt: Vittorio Klostermann, 1977.

Heil, John Paul. "Christ, the Termination of the Law (Romans 9:30—10:8)." *CBQ* 63.3 (2001) 484–98.

Heiser, Michael S. *The Unseen Realm: Recovering the Supernatural Worldview of the Bible*. Bellingham, WA: Lexham, 2015.

Hirsch, E. D., Jr. *Validity in Interpretation*. New Haven: Yale University Press, 1967.

Holst, Richard. "The Meaning of 'Abraham Believed God' in Romans 4:3." *WTJ* 59.2 (1997) 319–26.

Holt, Robby, and Aubrey Spears. "The Ecclesia as Primary Context for the Reception of the Bible." In *A Manifesto for Theological Interpretation*, edited by Craig G. Bartholomew and Heath A. Thomas, 72–93. Grand Rapids: Baker Academic, 2016.

Hoy, David Couzens. *The Critical Circle: Literature, History, and Philosophical Hermeneutics*. Berkeley: University of California Press, 1978.

Irwin, William. "Against Intertextuality." *PL* 28.2 (2004) 227–42.

Jewett, Robert. *Romans: A Commentary*. Edited by Eldon Jay Epp. Hermeneia. Minneapolis: Fortress, 2007.

Jipp, Joshua W. "Rereading the Story of Abraham, Isaac, and 'Us' in Romans 4." *JSNT* 32.2 (2009) 217–42.

Johnson, Patricia Altenbernd. *On Gadamer*. WPS. Belmont, CA: Wadsworth Thompson Learning, 2000.

Juncker, Günther H. "'Children of Promise': Spiritual Paternity and Patriarch Typology in Galatians and Romans." *BBR* 17.1 (2007) 131–60.

Kant, Immanuel. *The Critique of Judgment*. Translated by J. H. Bernard. Amherst, NY: Prometheus, 2000.

Käsemann, Ernst. *An Die Römer*. Edited by Günther Bornkamm. HZNT 8a. Tübingen: Mohr, 1973.

——. *Commentary on Romans*. Translated by Geoffrey W. Bromiley. Grand Rapids: Eerdmans, 1980.

Keesmaat, Sylvia C. *Paul and His Story: (Re)Interpreting the Exodus Tradition*. JSNTSup. Sheffield: Sheffield Academic, 1999.

———. "Paul's Use of the Exodus Tradition in Romans and Galatians." DPhil diss., Oxford: Oxford University, 1994.

Kim, Mitchell. "Respect for Context and Authorial Intention: Setting the Epistemological Bar." In *Paul and Scripture: Extending the Conversation*, edited by Christopher D. Stanley, 115–29. Atlanta: SBL, 2012.

Kim, Seyoon. *The Origin of Paul's Gospel*. Grand Rapids: Eerdmans, 1982.

Kittel, Gerhard. "Ἀκούω, κτλ." In *TDNT* 1:216–25.

Koch, Dietrich-Alex. "Der Text von Hab 2 4b in der Septuaginta und im Neuen Testament." *ZNW* 76.1–2 (1985) 68–85.

———. *Die Schrift als Zeuge des Evangeliums: Untersuchungen zur Verwendung und zum Verständnis der Schrift bei Paulus*. BHT. Tübingen: Mohr Siebeck, 1986.

Kögler, Hans-Herbert. "Horizon." In *OCP* 400.

Kolarcik, Michael. *The Book of Wisdom: Introduction, Commentary, and Reflections*. NIB. Nashville: Abingdon, 1997.

Kristeva, Julia. *Desire in Language: A Semiotic Approach to Language and Art*. Edited by Leon S. Roudiez. Translated by Thomas Gora et al. New York: Columbia University Press, 1980.

———. *Revolution in Poetic Language*. Translated by Margaret Waller. New York: Columbia University Press, 1984.

Kujanpää, Katja. "From Eloquence to Evading Responsibility: The Rhetorical Functions of Quotations in Paul's Argumentation." *JBL* 136.1 (2017) 185–202.

Lapointe, Roger. "Hermeneutics Today." *BTB* 2 (1972) 107–54.

Lawn, Chris, and Niall Keane. *The Gadamer Dictionary*. New York: Continuum, 2011.

Lebech, Flemming. "The Concept of the Subject in the Philosophical Hermeneutics of Hans-Georg Gadamer." *IJPS* 14.2 (2006) 221–36.

Lim, Timothy H. *Holy Scripture in the Qumran Commentaries and Pauline Letters*. Oxford: Clarendon, 1997.

Linge, David E. "Editor's Introduction." In *Philosophical Hermeneutics*, by Hans-Georg Gadamer, edited and translated by David E. Linge, xi–lviii. Berkeley: University of California Press, 2004.

Longenecker, Richard N. *The Epistle to the Romans*. NIGTC. Grand Rapids: Eerdmans, 2016.

Lundin, Roger, et al. *The Responsibility of Hermeneutics*. Grand Rapids: Eerdmans, 1985.

Luz, Ulrich. *Matthew 1–7: A Commentary*. Edited by Helmut Koester. Translated by James E. Crouch. Hermeneia. Minneapolis: Fortress, 2007.

———. *Matthew in History: Interpretation, Influence, and Effects*. Minneapolis: Fortress, 1994.

Malpas, Jeff, and Santiago Zabala. "Introduction." In *Consequences of Hermeneutics: Fifty Years after Gadamer's "Truth and Method"*, edited by Jeff Malpas and Santiago Zabala, xi–xviii. Evanston, IL: Northwestern University Press, 2010.

Matlock, R. Barry. "Saving Faith: The Rhetoric and Semantics of πίστις in Paul." In *The Faith of Jesus Christ: Exegetical, Biblical, and Theological Studies*, edited by Michael F. Bird and Preston M. Sprinkle, 73–90. Peabody: Hendrickson, 2009.

McComiskey, Thomas Edward. "Hosea." In *The Minor Prophets: An Exegetical and Expository Commentary*, edited by Thomas Edward McComiskey, 1:1–237. Grand Rapids: Baker, 1992.

McLean, B. H. *Biblical Interpretation and Philosophical Hermeneutics*. New York: Cambridge University Press, 2012.

Meek, Russell. "Hans-Georg Gadamer: His Philosophical Hermeneutics and Its Importance for Evangelical Biblical Hermeneutics." *Eleutheria* 1.2 (2011) 97–106.

Mohanty, J. N. "Dasein." In *DCCT* 177.

Moo, Douglas J. *The Epistle to the Romans*. 1st ed. NICNT. Grand Rapids: Eerdmans, 1996.

———. *The Letter to the Romans*. 2nd ed. NICNT. Grand Rapids: Eerdmans, 2018.

Morris, Leon. *The Epistle to the Romans*. PNTC. Grand Rapids: Eerdmans, 1988.

Mounce, Robert H. *Romans*. NAC. Nashville: Broadman & Holman, 1995.

Moyise, Steve. "Dialogical Intertextuality." In *Exploring Intertextuality: Diverse Strategies for New Testament Interpretation of Texts*, edited by B. J. Oropeza and Steve Moyise, 3–15. Eugene, OR: Cascade, 2016.

———. "Does Paul Respect the Context of His Quotations?" In *Paul and Scripture: Extending the Conversation*, edited by Christopher D. Stanley, 97–114. Atlanta: SBL, 2012.

———. "Does Paul Respect the Context of His Quotations? Hosea as a Test Case." In *"What Does the Scripture Say?" Studies in the Function of Scripture in Early Judaism and Christianity: The Letters and Liturgical Traditions*, edited by Craig A. Evans and H. Daniel Zacharias, 2:39–50. New York: Bloomsbury, 2014.

———. *Evoking Scripture: Seeing the Old Testament in the New*. New York: T. & T. Clark, 2008.

———. "Latency and Respect for Context: A Response to Mitchell Kim." In *Paul and Scripture: Extending the Conversation*, edited by Christopher D. Stanley, 131–39. Atlanta: SBL, 2012.

———. *Paul and Scripture: Studying the New Testament Use of the Old Testament*. Grand Rapids: Baker Academic, 2010.

———. "Quotations." In *As It Is Written: Studying Paul's Use of Scripture*, edited by Stanley E. Porter and Christopher D. Stanley, 15–28. Atlanta: SBL, 2008.

Nelson, Eric S. "Impure Phenomenology: Dilthey, Epistemology, and Interpretive Psychology." *SP* 10 (2010) 19–44.

Novenson, Matthew V. "The Jewish Messiahs, the Pauline Christ, and the Gentile Question." *JBL* 128.2 (2009) 357–73.

Olhausen, William P. "The Role of Hermeneutics and Philosophy in Theological Interpretation." In *A Manifesto for Theological Interpretation*, edited by Craig G. Bartholomew and Heath A. Thomas, 110–30. Grand Rapids: Baker Academic, 2016.

Oropeza, B. J., and Steve Moyise, eds. *Exploring Intertextuality: Diverse Strategies for New Testament Interpretation of Texts*. Eugene, OR: Cascade, 2016.

Ortlund, Dane C. "'Zeal without Knowledge': For What Did Paul Criticize His Fellow Jews in Romans 10:2–3?" *WTJ* 73.1 (2011) 23–37.

Owen, Ian Rory. "Learning from Twentieth Century Hermeneutic Phenomenology for Human Sciences and Practical Disciplines." *IPJP* 8.1 (2008) 1–12.

Palmer, Richard E. *Hermeneutics: Interpretation Theory in Schleiermacher, Dilthey, Heidegger, and Gadamer*. NUSPEP. Evanston, IL: Northwestern University Press, 1969.

———. "Two Contrasting Heideggerian Elements in Gadamer's Philosophical Hermeneutics." In *Consequences of Hermeneutics: Fifty Years after Gadamer's "Truth and Method"*, edited by Jeff Malpas and Santiago Zabala, 121–31. Evanston, IL: Northwestern University Press, 2010.

Piper, John. *The Justification of God: An Exegetical & Theological Study of Romans 9:1–23.* 2nd ed. Grand Rapids: Baker Academic, 1993.

Plantinga, Theodore. "Commitment and Historical Understanding: A Critique of Dilthey." *FH* 14.2 (1982) 29–36.

Porter, Stanley E. "Biblical Hermeneutics and Theological Responsibility." In *The Future of Biblical Interpretation: Responsible Plurality in Biblical Interpretation*, edited by Stanley E. Porter and Matthew R. Malcolm, 29–50. Downers Grove, IL: IVP Academic, 2013.

Porter, Stanley E., and Christopher D. Stanley, eds. *As It Is Written: Studying Paul's Use of Scripture.* Atlanta: SBL, 2008.

Rae, Murray. "Theological Interpretation and Historical Criticism." In *A Manifesto for Theological Interpretation*, edited by Craig G. Bartholomew and Heath A. Thomas, 94–109. Grand Rapids: Baker Academic, 2016.

Rahlfs, Alfred, ed. *Psalmi cum Odis.* Vol. X. Vetus Testamentum Graecum. Auctoritate Academiae Scientiarum Gottingensis Editum. Göttingen: Vandenhoeck & Ruprecht, 1979.

Rahlfs, Alfred, and Robert Hanhart. *Septuaginta: Id est Vetus Testamentum graece iuxta LXX interpretes.* Stuttgart: Deutsche Bibelgesellschaft, 2006.

Risser, James. "Gadamer's Hidden Doctrine: The Simplicity and Humility of Philosophy." In *Consequences of Hermeneutics: Fifty Years after Gadamer's "Truth and Method,"* edited by Santiago Zabala and Jeff Malpas, 5–24. Evanston, IL: Northwestern University Press, 2010.

Rosner, Brian S. *Paul and the Law: Keeping the Commandments of God.* NSBT. Downers Grove, IL: InterVarsity, 2013.

Sanders, E. P. *Paul and Palestinian Judaism: A Comparison of Patterns of Religion.* 40th Anniversary Edition. Minneapolis: Fortress, 2017.

Sarna, Nahum M. *Exodus שמות.* JPSTC. New York: Jewish Publication Society, 1991.

Schleiermacher, F. D. E. *Hermeneutics: The Handwritten Manuscripts.* Edited by Heinz Kimmerle. Translated by James Duke and Jack Forstman. AARTTS 1. Atlanta: Scholars, 1977.

———. *Hermeneutik.* Edited by Heinz Kimmerle. Heidelberg: Winter, 1959.

Schreiner, Thomas R. *Romans.* 1st ed. BECNT. Grand Rapids: Baker Academic, 1998.

———. *Romans.* 2nd ed. BECNT. Grand Rapids: Baker Academic, 2018.

Scott, Ian W. *Paul's Way of Knowing: Story, Experience, and the Spirit.* Grand Rapids: Baker Academic, 2009.

Seifrid, Mark A. "Romans." In *Commentary on the New Testament Use of the Old Testament*, edited by G. K. Beale and D. A. Carson, 607–94. Grand Rapids: Baker Academic, 2007.

Skehan, Patrick W., and Alexander A. Di Lella. *The Wisdom of Ben Sira: A New Translation with Notes.* AB 39. New York: Doubleday, 1987.

Smiles, Vincent M. "The Concept of 'Zeal' in Second-Temple Judaism and Paul's Critique of It in Romans 10:2." *CBQ* 64.2 (2002) 282–99.

Smith, John H. "Living Religion as Vanishing Mediator: Schleiermacher, Early Romanticism, and Idealism." *GQ* 84.2 (2011) 137–58.

Stanley, Christopher D. *Arguing with Scripture: The Rhetoric of Quotations in the Letters of Paul.* New York: T. & T. Clark, 2004.

———. *Paul and the Language of Scripture: Citation Technique in the Pauline Epistles and Contemporary Literature.* SNTSMS 69. Cambridge: Cambridge University Press, 1992.

———. "Rhetoric of Quotations." In *Exploring Intertextuality: Diverse Strategies for New Testament Interpretation of Texts*, edited by B. J. Oropeza and Steve Moyise, 42–62. Eugene, OR: Cascade, 2016.

Starling, David I. *Hermeneutics as Apprenticeship: How the Bible Shapes Our Interpretive Practices.* Grand Rapids: Baker Academic, 2016.

———. *Not My People: Gentiles as Exiles in Pauline Hermeneutics.* BZNW 184. Berlin: de Gruyter, 2011.

Strawn, Brent A. "Pharaoh." In *DOTP* 631–36.

Stuhlmacher, Peter. *Paul's Letter to the Romans: A Commentary.* Translated by Scott J. Hafemann. Louisville: Westminster/John Knox, 1994.

Tanner, J. Paul. "The New Covenant and Paul's Quotations from Hosea in Romans 9:25–26." *BSac* 162 (2005) 95–110.

Teigas, Demetrius. "Gadamer, Hans-Georg." In *DCCT* 292–96.

Thielman, Frank. "The Story of Israel and the Theology of Romans 5–8." In *Pauline Theology*, edited by David M. Hay and E. Elizabeth Johnson, 3:169–95. Minneapolis: Fortress, 1995.

Thiselton, Anthony C. *The First Epistle to the Corinthians: A Commentary on the Greek Text.* NIGTC. Grand Rapids: Eerdmans, 2000.

———. *Hermeneutics: An Introduction.* Grand Rapids: Eerdmans, 2009.

———. *New Horizons in Hermeneutics: The Theory and Practice of Transforming Biblical Reading.* Grand Rapids: Zondervan, 2012.

———. *The Two Horizons: New Testament Hermeneutics and Philosophical Description with Special Reference to Heidegger, Bultmann, Gadamer, and Wittgenstein.* Grand Rapids: Eerdmans, 1980.

Thomas, Matthew J. *Paul's "Works of the Law" in the Perspective of Second-Century Reception.* Downers Grove, IL: IVP Academic, 2020.

Ticciati, Susannah. "The Nondivisive Difference of Election: A Reading of Romans 9–11." *JTI* 6.2 (2012) 257–78.

Tobin, Thomas H. *Paul's Rhetoric in Its Context: The Argument of Romans.* Peabody, MA: Hendrickson, 2004.

Torrance, J. B. "Foreword." In *The Two Horizons: New Testament Hermeneutics and Philosophical Description with Special Reference to Heidegger, Bultmann, Gadamer, and Wittgenstein*, by Anthony C. Thiselton, xi–xiv. Grand Rapids: Eerdmans, 1980.

Valgenti, Robert T. "The Tradition of Tradition in Philosophical Hermeneutics." In *Consequences of Hermeneutics: Fifty Years after Gadamer's "Truth and Method"*, edited by Jeff Malpas and Santiago Zabala, 66–80. Evanston, IL: Northwestern University Press, 2010.

Vanhoozer, Kevin J. *Is There a Meaning in This Text? The Bible, the Reader, and the Morality of Literary Knowledge.* Grand Rapids: Zondervan, 1998.

Vedder, Ben. "The Provisionality of Thinking in Heidegger." *SJP* 43.4 (2005) 643–60.

Venema, Dennis R., and Scot McKnight. *Adam and the Genome: Reading Scripture after Genetic Science.* Grand Rapids: Brazos, 2017.

Vessey, David. "Gadamer and the Fusion of Horizons." *IJPS* 17.4 (2009) 525–36.

Volpi, Franco. "Phenomenology as Possibility: The 'Phenomenological' Appropriation of the History of Philosophy in the Young Heidegger." *RP* 30 (2000) 120–45.

Wagner, J. Ross. *Heralds of the Good News: Isaiah and Paul "In Concert" in the Letter to the Romans*. NovTSup. Boston: Brill, 2002.

Walters, J. Edward. "How Beautiful Are My Feet: The Structure and Function of Second Isaiah References in Paul's Letter to the Romans." *RQ* 52.1 (2010) 29–39.

Walton, John H. *The Lost World of Adam and Eve: Genesis 2–3 and the Human Origins Debate*. Downers Grove, IL: IVP Academic, 2015.

Warnke, Georgia. "Literature, Law, and Morality." In *Gadamer's Repercussions: Reconsidering Philosophical Hermeneutics*, edited by Bruce Krajewskie, 82–102. Berkeley: University of California Press, 2004.

Watson, Francis. *Paul and the Hermeneutics of Faith*. 2nd ed. New York: T. & T. Clark, 2016.

Wedderburn, A. J. M. *The Reasons for Romans*. Minneapolis: Fortress, 1991.

Weinsheimer, Joel. "Gadamer and Aesthetics." In *EA* 264–67.

———. *Gadamer's Hermeneutics: A Reading of Truth and Method*. New Haven: Yale University Press, 1985.

———. "Meaningless Hermeneutics?" In *Gadamer's Repercussions: Reconsidering Philosophical Hermeneutics*, edited by Bruce Krajewski, 158–66. Berkeley: University of California Press, 2004.

Weinsheimer, Joel, and Donald G. Marshall. "Translator's Preface." In *Truth and Method*, by Hans-Georg Gadamer, translated by Joel Weinsheimer and Donald G. Marshall, xi–xix. 2nd rev. ed. New York: Continuum, 2004.

Weiss, Konrad. "φέρω, κτλ." In *TDNT* 9:56–87.

Westphal, Merold. *Whose Community? Which Interpretation? Philosophical Hermeneutics for the Church*. TCPC. Grand Rapids: Baker Academic, 2009.

Wevers, John William, ed. *Deuteronomium*. Vol. III, 2. Vetus Testamentum Graecum. Auctoritate Academiae Scientiarum Gottingensis Editum. Göttingen: Vandenhoeck & Ruprecht, 2006.

———, ed. *Exodus*. Vol. II, 1. Vetus Testamentum Graecum. Auctoritate Academiae Scientiarum Gottingensis Editum. Göttingen: Vandenhoeck & Ruprecht, 1991.

———, ed. *Genesis*. Vol. I. Vetus Testamentum Graecum. Auctoritate Academiae Scientiarum Gottingensis Editum. Göttingen: Vandenhoeck & Ruprecht, 1974.

———, ed. *Leviticus*. Vol. II, 2. Vetus Testamentum Graecum. Auctoritate Academiae Scientiarum Gottingensis Editum. Göttingen: Vandenhoeck & Ruprecht, 1986.

———, ed. *Numeri*. Vol. III, 1. Vetus Testamentum Graecum. Auctoritate Academiae Scientiarum Gottingensis Editum. Göttingen: Vandenhoeck & Ruprecht, 1982.

Winston, David. *The Wisdom of Solomon: A New Translation with Introduction and Commentary*. AB 43. Garden City, NY: Doubleday, 1979.

Wright, Kathleen. "Gadamer, Hans-Georg: Survey of Thought." In *EA* 261–64.

Wright, N. T. "Justification: The Biblical Basis and Its Relevance for Contemporary Evangelicalism (1980)." In *Pauline Perspectives: Essays on Paul, 1978–2013*, 21–41. Minneapolis: Fortress, 2013.

———. *Justification: God's Plan & Paul's Vision*. Downers Grove, IL: InterVarsity, 2009.

———. "Justification: Yesterday, Today and For Ever (2010)." In *Pauline Perspectives: Essays on Paul, 1978–2013*, 422–38. Minneapolis: Fortress, 2013.

———. "The Law in Romans 2 (1996)." In *Pauline Perspectives: Essays on Paul, 1978–2013*, 134–51. Minneapolis: Fortress, 2013.

———. *The Letter to the Romans*. NIB. Nashville: Abingdon, 2002.

———. "New Exodus, New Inheritance: The Narrative Substructure of Romans 3–8 (1998)." In *Pauline Perspectives: Essays on Paul, 1978–2013*, 160–68. Minneapolis: Fortress, 2013.

———. *The New Testament and the People of God*. COQG 1. Minneapolis: Fortress, 1992.

———. "A New Tübingen School? Ernst Käsemann and His Commentary on Romans (1982)." In *Pauline Perspectives: Essays on Paul, 1978–2013*, 52–67. Minneapolis: Fortress, 2013.

———. *Paul and His Recent Interpreters: Some Contemporary Debates*. Minneapolis: Fortress, 2015.

———. *Paul and the Faithfulness of God*. COQG 4. Minneapolis: Fortress, 2013.

———. "Romans 2.17—3.9: A Hidden Clue to the Meaning of Romans? (2012)." In *Pauline Perspectives: Essays on Paul, 1978–2013*, 489–509. Minneapolis: Fortress, 2013.

Young, Stephen L. "Romans 1.1–5 and Paul's Christological Use of Hab 2.4 in Rom. 1.17: An Underutilized Consideration in the Debate." *JSNT* 34.3 (2012) 277–85.

Ziegler, Joseph, ed. *Duodecim Prophetae*. Vol. XIII. Vetus Testamentum Graecum. Auctoritate Academiae Scientiarum Gottingensis Editum. Göttingen: Vandenhoeck & Ruprecht, 1984.

———, ed. *Iob*. Vol. XI, 4. Vetus Testamentum Graecum. Auctoritate Academiae Scientiarum Gottingensis Editum. Göttingen: Vandenhoeck & Ruprecht, 1982.

———, ed. *Isaias*. Vol. XIV. Vetus Testamentum Graecum. Auctoritate Academiae Scientiarum Gottingensis Editum. Göttingen: Vandenhoeck & Ruprecht, 1983.

———, ed. *Sapientia Iesu Filii Sirach*. Vol. XII, 2. Vetus Testamentum Graecum. Auctoritate Academiae Scientiarum Gottingensis Editum. Göttingen: Vandenhoeck & Ruprecht, 1980.

Subject Index

Scripture Index

Leviticus (continued)

14:20 LXX	236
18:5 MT LXX	183–85
19:18 LXX	220–22, 228
21:6–8 LXX	236
21:10–15 LXX	236
21:17 LXX	236
21:23 LXX	236
23:11–12 LXX	236
27:9–11 LXX	236

Numbers

9:15 LXX	159
11:4–5	146
14:3–4	146
14:14	158–59
20:7–11	144
33:1–4	164

Deuteronomy

5:6 LXX	160
5:17–19 LXX	220
5:21 LXX	141, 154, 220
6:4	119–20
6:4b LXX	118
6:12 LXX	160
7:8 LXX	160
8:7 LXX	158
8:14 LXX	160
8:14b–15a LXX	158
9:4 LXX	183
10:16	104, 141
13:10 LXX	160
23:14 LXX	159
23:18 LXX	159
29:4 LXX	203
29:5 LXX	158
30:6	104, 141
30:12–13 LXX	183, 186–87
30:12 LXX	183, 186
30:13 LXX	187
30:14 LXX	183–84, 186, 188, 190
30:19	137
32	194–95, 219, 233
32:12 LXX	159
32:21 LXX	192–94, 198
32:27–33	193

32:34–42	193
32:34 LXX	231
32:35–43 LXX	219
32:35 MT	219
32:35 LXX	218–19

1 Kingdoms

12:22	199

2 Kingdoms

22:50	231

3 Kingdoms

3:2	159
7:34	236
8:10	159
12:27	159
19:1–3	199
19:4–9	200
19:9	200
19:10	200
19:11–13a	200
19:13b	200
19:14	200
19:18	200

Job

41:3 MT LXX	210

Psalms

13:1 LXX	115–18
13:1c LXX	116
17:44 LXX	232
17:48 LXX	233
17:49 LXX	233
17:50 LXX	231–33
18:1–5 LXX	190
18:5 LXX	190
18:5a LXX	190
19:1–6	190
31:1–2 LXX	123–24
31:1 LXX	124
31:2a LXX	123–24
31:2b LXX	124
31:5 LXX	123
43:23 LXX	141, 163
50 LXX	114

APOCRYPHA

The Wisdom of Solomon

Romans (continued)

1 Corinthians

2 Corinthians

Galatians

Philippians

1 Timothy

Hebrews

1 Peter

RABBINIC WRITINGS

t. Sukkah

www.ingramcontent.com/pod-product-compliance
Lightning Source LLC
Chambersburg PA
CBHW071337280326
41949CB00038B/20